the cultur

e of pain

DAVID B. MORRIS

UNIVERSITY OF
CALIFORNIA PRESS
BERKELEY
LOS ANGELES
LONDON

University of California Press
Berkeley and Los Angeles, California

University of California Press
London, England

First Paperback Printing 1993

Library of Congress
Cataloging-in-Publication Data

Morris, David B.
    The culture of pain / David B. Morris.
      p.   cm
    Includes bibliographical references.
    Includes index.
    ISBN 0-520-08276-1
    1. Pain—Social aspects.   2. Pain—
    Psychological aspects.
    I. Title.
    [DNLM: 1. Medicine in Art.
    2. Medicine in Literature.   3. Pain—
    psychology.   4. Social Environment.
    WL 704 M875f]
    RB127.M67   1991
    306.4'61—dc20
    DNLM/DLC
    for Library of Congress   90-11305
                                              CIP

Printed in the United States of America

    1   2   3   4   5   6   7   8   9

TO EMILY B. MORRIS & ALLSTON J. MORRIS, M.D.

He has seen but half the universe who has not been shown the house of pain.
—RALPH WALDO EMERSON

CONTENTS

FIGURES

ACKNOWLEDGMENTS

Writing, like most other extended activities in our culture, requires money and support. I am grateful for generous fellowship aid from the National Science Foundation and from the National Endowment for the Humanities. Stanley Holwitz, assistant director of the University of California Press, early on extended a trust that helped me keep working and for which I am most deeply appreciative.

No less important is the help of friends, acquaintances, and even perfect strangers. The individual doctors and scholars who helped me along the way can hardly be repaid by appearing here in a mere list. I hope that they know how much I appreciate their help. The many patients who shared their experience with me unfortunately cannot be named, and I have altered details to keep their identities unknown. But they are at the heart of this book.

Several debts cannot go unnamed. My father, Allston J. Morris, who holds the unofficial Delaware record as the doctor most often selected as personal physician by his fellow doctors, has shown me by example that medicine, literature, and the arts need not belong to separate worlds. My mother, Emily, tireless, supportive, courageous, and unfailingly generous, has likewise been an example of someone for whom books, music, painting, and drama are inseparable from life.

Richard M. Caplan—whose gifts as physician, pianist, author, teacher, and administrator overflow a single vocation—first offered me the challenge of team-teaching a course about medicine and literature. Our collaborations, formal and informal, remain among my happiest memories.

I would especially like to thank Diether H. Haenicke, president of Western Michigan University, who granted me faculty privileges at Waldo Library, and such thanks extend as well to Heidi Rawson-Ketchum and her colleagues in the Interlibrary Loan Office who kept me in business. I feel great sadness that I cannot thank in person my talented friend Bill Burian, late dean of the College of Health and Human Services at Western Michigan University, whose vision stretched from China to Oakland Drive and well into the future.

Gerald L. Bruns invited me to deliver the annual series of Ward-Phillips Lectures at the University of Notre Dame, where I first began to work out the structure for this book. Other parts have developed on various occasions. I would thus also like to thank G. S. Rousseau, who invited me to give one of the annual lectures at the William Andrews Clark Memorial Library (UCLA). My thanks for similarly productive invitations go to Ralph Berry at Florida State University; to David Wright and Tess Tavormina at Michigan State University; and to David Barnard and Mary Simmonds, M. D., at The Milton S. Hershey Medical Center. Their many kindnesses mean a great deal to me.

The ultimate measure of thanks, however, belongs to my wife, Ruth. I can say with certainty that she alone puts the pleasure in my life. She is not only a friend and partner, loving, free-spirited, wise, and full of wonders, but also at the most crucial times an invaluable collaborator: her thoughts, doubts, protests, and deft surgical interventions have helped bring this book to its final shape. I could not have written it without her.

D. B. M.

INTRODUCTION

At the end of the mind, the body. But at the end of the body, the mind.

PAUL VALÉRY[1]

*P*AIN IS AS elemental as fire or ice. Like love, it belongs to the most basic human experiences that make us who we are. Perhaps pain is most like love in that it comes and goes of its own accord, as if obeying laws from whose knowledge we remain almost totally shut out. Yet our lack of knowledge continues to recede. Every year—now sometimes every month—researchers uncover new details about the secret life pain leads within us. It is thus easy to believe, as science has argued for the last hundred years, that pain is no more than a particularly complex signal broadcast over nerves leading from the site of injury to the brain. The injury in effect creates the pain, and it goes on creating more pain until the injury heals.

This book tells a related but very different story. It describes how the experience of pain is decisively shaped or modified by individual human minds and by specific human cultures. It explores what we might call the historical, cultural, and psychosocial construction of pain.

This story, which cannot be disentangled from our growing knowledge of the human nervous system, must be gathered together from episodes scattered throughout human history, across cultures and across time.[2] We need to begin in the present, however, with a fact so fundamental that (like the purloined letter hidden in a place too conspicuous for notice) it seems pointlessly obvious. Our culture—the modern, Western, industrial, technocratic world—has succeeded in persuading us that pain is simply and entirely a medical problem. When we think about pain, we almost instantly conjure up a scene that includes doctors, drugs, ointments, surgery, hospitals, laboratories, and insurance forms.

Doctors, of course, who can serve here as shorthand for the entire system of modern health care, play a large role in the cultural construction of pain because the scientific worldview of medicine so thoroughly dominates our society. Yet the story of pain cannot be reduced to a neat parable about biomedical progress. Pain, I want to argue, is always more than a matter of nerves and neurotransmitters.

Certainly we can take comfort in assuming that pain obeys the general laws of human anatomy and physiology that govern our bodies. The fact is, however, that the culture we live in and our deepest personal beliefs subtly or massively recast our experience of pain. Normally the shaping force of culture and belief passes almost unobserved. Like upright posture, our everyday experience of the world seems so natural—so "given"—that we take it for granted. It is less our pain than our culture, however, that draws us irresistibly toward the medicine cabinet, as if pills and tablets held a kind of magnetic, eternal attraction for the unseen torments of a bad back. The story of how our minds and cultures continuously reconstruct the experience of pain demands that we look beyond the medicine cabinet. Medicine, in fact, because of its dominant position in our culture, tends automatically to suppress or to overpower all the other voices that offer us a different understanding of pain, including voices of dissent within medicine.

It is my premise in this book that we need to achieve a new understanding of pain that allows us to recover the voices that mainstream medicine has rendered more or less unheard. This new understanding must not perpetuate in reverse the errors of the immediate past and foolishly suppress everything that recent biomedical research has taught us. What we need is a dialogue among disciplines that normally do not speak to one another. Clearly, one of the major voices in this dialogue must belong to doctors, nurses, researchers, clinicians, and everyone connected with the medical understanding and treatment of pain. These medical voices, however, will need to enter into conversation with a wider, more scattered, neglected community of voices speaking (with less authority but no less insight) about pain.

The voices most often neglected belong of course to patients. Yet theirs is most often an evanescent, oral testimony difficult to recover except, as

I have tried here, through interviews. We also need to recover the voices that speak most effectively for patients in the essays, poems, novels, plays, and other genres we call literature. I will thus speak of writers as a convenient shorthand term referring to the numberless nonmedical voices normally shut out from contemporary discussions of pain. Writers in fact express a range of knowledge and experience for which the person struggling with pain quite often cannot find the words. Most important, they tell a story about pain that differs significantly from the traditional medical account and helps to reveal its limitations. Such voices suggest that pain is never the sole creation of our anatomy and physiology. It emerges only at the intersection of bodies, minds, and cultures.

The writers who give voice to an otherwise often inarticulate discourse about pain also create a body of error and misrepresentation along with their knowledge. Pain passes much of its time in utter inhuman silence, and writers who describe something so inherently resistant to language must inevitably shape and possibly falsify the experience they describe. There is no completely pure or innocent account of pain untouched by the constraints of writing—including scientific writing. Yet writers also offer a unique resource because they use language in ways that, paradoxically, acknowledge (without necessarily falsifying) the silences and inarticulate struggles we most often completely overlook. But they do more. They also allow us to examine various moments—specific historical junctures—when pain thrusts above the plane of silent, blind, unquestioned suffering in which it ordinarily lies concealed.

The specific subjects I treat here cannot hope to constitute a full history of pain. No one could bear to read or write such an impossible study.[3] Because pain leads its existence mostly in secret, in silence, without leaving written records or eloquent testimony, our main evidence in documenting the historical life of pain lies in fragmentary episodes and in scattered moments. Such fragments nonetheless prove fully adequate to support the claim that what surgeon René Leriche in 1937 aptly called "living pain"—pain experienced outside the laboratory and not reduced to a universal code of neural impulses—always contains at its heart the human encounter with meaning.[4]

It is the neglected encounter between pain and meaning that lies at the center of this book and that the voices captured and created in writing from Homer to Beckett so powerfully help us to recover. The story they tell—unfolded here through a series of fragments and vignettes—cannot follow a straightforward sequence from beginning to end. Pain holds too many byways and secret passages. The end is not yet in sight, the beginning lost in untraceable prehistoric origins. Still, as we look around us, exploring the back alleys and listening to neglected voices, it is possible to detect the outlines of a general movement or plot. The unique pain we feel today has its basis, in effect, in a cultural shift so immense that we can grasp its implications only by stepping back from the present—only by questioning our normal assumptions and exposing their roots in the recent past.

The vast cultural shift that gives the story of pain its hidden plot centers on the eradication of meaning by late nineteenth-century science. The great breakthroughs in anatomy and physiology by Bell, Magendie, Müller, Weber, Von Frey, Shiff, and other nineteenth-century researchers created the scientific basis for believing that pain was owing simply to the stimulation of specific nerve pathways. We are the heirs of the transformation in medical thought whereby we think of pain as no more than an electrical impulse speeding along the nerves. In fact, this powerful medical myth has influenced our lives almost as crucially as the great political and social revolutions that have changed our government, education, and sexual habits.

What we feel today when we are in pain, I want to claim, *cannot* be the same changeless sensations that have tormented humankind ever since our ancestors crawled out of their caves. Our pain, now officially emptied of meaning and merely buzzing mindlessly along the nerves, is the product of its own specific modern history. The story of the modern reconstruction of pain, however, does not end with the recognition of our unique position within time. We are not doomed to wait passively for the latest wonder drug concocted to interrupt the transmission of pain impulses. Pain, after all, exists only as we perceive it. Shut down the mind and pain too stops. Change the mind (powerfully enough) and it may well be that pain too changes. When we recognize that the experience of pain is not timeless but changing, the product of specific periods and particular cultures, we may also recognize we can *act* to change or influence our own futures.

"Man is an apprentice, pain is his master": so wrote nineteenth-century French poet Alfred de Musset.[5] Let us assume, at least for the immediate future, that we cannot forswear our biological relationship to pain. The concept of masters and apprentices, nonetheless, belongs to an earlier stage of human social history. Can we never abandon a cultural training in pain that now proves erroneous, outdated, and misguided? Can we never free ourselves from the myths and errors of nineteenth-century science? I want to emphasize that I am *not* suggesting we reject our hard-won biomedical knowledge about pain: that way lies folly. What we need, instead, is to supplement and to enrich it with a knowledge gained from the neglected voices—within the history of literature and within the newest laboratories and clinics—that we have trained ourselves, like mere apprentices, not to hear. With the help of this additional knowledge, I am convinced, we can begin to recover some of the individual control over pain that as a culture we once possessed and too hastily gave up.

This is not meant to be an argumentative book, but an argument should nonetheless emerge from its deliberately indirect style. Let me thus try to summarize here in the strongest terms several of the crucial claims that will reappear more like musical themes than like propositions in a chain of logic. First: that chronic pain constitutes an immense, invisible crisis at the center of contemporary life. Second: that traditional Western medicine—by which I mean not so much individual doctors and researchers as an entire scientific-medical worldview that permeates our culture—has consistently led us to misinterpret pain as no more than a sensation, a symptom, a problem in biochemistry. Third: that our present crisis is in large part a dilemma created and sustained by the failures of this traditional medical reading of pain. Fourth: that by taking back responsibility for how we understand pain we can recover the power to alleviate it.

My aims follow directly from these basic propositions. I want to show that the traditional misreading of pain as no more than a problem in biochemistry is now under direct challenge by a revolution in contemporary medical thought symbolized most vividly by the emergence of the pain clinic. I also want to show how a dialogue between doctors and writers (between medical and nonmedical voices) can help to support and to extend the important changes beginning to alter our current thinking about pain. Pain in such a rethinking will emerge as far more than a matter of electrical impulses speeding along the nerves. We will recognize that our biochemistry is inextricably bound up with the personal and cultural meanings that we carve out of pain.

The future of pain will reveal its shape distinctly only if we recover and understand the past. It is the past that helps us understand how we got where we are now. It is where the future begins. The past not only contains many of the raw materials from which we will construct the future, much as medieval builders created new structures by recycling the stones cut by their vanished precursors. Like an antique photograph, the past also allows us to recognize the crucial differences that set us apart from our ancestors. We see ourselves a little differently by comparison. It is only a knowledge of past pain that will allow us to understand the future *as* future, not just the present in disguise.

Pain, we know, is such an immense, almost oceanic subject that even a large book cannot avoid leaving much undone. Thus my argument that pain is always historical—always reshaped by a particular time, place, culture, and individual psyche—cannot finally be historical enough. I simply cannot work out all the differences distinguishing, say, Victorian hysterical pain from Nazi Holocaust pain, or pagan Stoic pain from medieval Christian pain. To do so would require descending fully into the thick texture of everyday life in numerous diverse communities from the pre-Socratics to the postmodern era with their complex economic and social contradictions. The result would be a phantom history of the world. My exploration is above all an effort at synthesis: a selective, strategic engagement with the key moments of the past as a means for helping us understand our experience today, when millions of people—despite all our research—find themselves alone, disabled, and dispossessed by pain.

A synthetic, integrative work such as mine, I should add, aims at virtues that complement the more analytic procedures of various historians, theorists, and medical researchers. For example, undoubtedly the boldest recent analytical and theoretical work is Elaine Scarry's *The Body in Pain: The Making and Unmaking of the World* (New York: Oxford University Press, 1985). Scarry views pain as the unseen basis for every act of cultural creation, from a wool overcoat to Keats's "Ode to Autumn." A theory so inclusive—developed with learning and argued with skill—requires careful consideration, but what it does not require here is a full counter-theory concerning the origin and development of human culture.[6] Scarry in fact has very little to say about recent medical research into pain, about the crucial medical distinction between acute and chronic pain, or about the vast literature that falls outside her focus on torture, war, Marx, the Old Testament, and human creativity. The virtues of her admirable book need to be supplemented by other approaches and by other bodies of knowledge about pain. Indeed, people in pain today owe no small amount of their torment to the lack of a cultural understanding that combines the insights of numerous fields now separated by specialized vocabularies and divergent theories.

My exploration of the conflict between medical and nonmedical understandings of pain is in one sense a study in cultural change. As an emblem of change we might think of Immanuel Kant sitting up late at night in Königsberg, at the end of the eighteenth century, with his toes glowing red from an excruciating attack of gout. Kant's method for dealing with his affliction was to concentrate with all his might on one object, no matter what. He would think, for example, of the Roman orator Cicero and of everything that could be thought in connection with the name of Cicero. Through this method he was so successful in banishing his pain that in the morning he sometimes wondered whether he had simply imagined it.[7] True, Kant as a philosopher no doubt possessed unusual powers of concentration. The crucial point, however, is that he did not merely distract himself, as if watching a sitcom. Nor did he sit fretting about his health. He employed the full force of his mind. In effect, he employed a resource for opposing pain that we have almost completely forgotten how to use.

There is much to learn by revisiting persons such as Kant who do not share our own cultural assumptions about pain. I hope my shifting focus, with a fluid movement across periods and topics, will finally create a richer dialogue of voices than an exact chronology or narrowly restricted focus. My aim is a book that deliberately crosses boundaries and mixes categories, because such risks are necessary to help move us toward a new understanding of human pain. This process of change is already at work both inside and outside medicine. It promises to put each of us on different ground as we encounter the old antagonist lurking within us. Pain on this new ground will not be understood solely as a medical problem involving the transmission of nerve impulses but rather as an experience that also engages the deepest and most personal levels of the complex cultural and biological process we call living.

I

LIVING PAIN: MYSTERY OR PUZZLE?

I want to know whether any one of us would consent to live, having wisdom
and mind and knowledge and memory of all things, but having no sense of
pleasure or pain, either more or less, and wholly unaffected by these and the
like feelings?

PLATO, *PHILEBUS*[1]

HIS IS A book about the meanings we make out
of pain. The greatest surprise I encountered in
discussing this topic over the past ten years was
the consistency with which I was asked a single unvarying question: Are
you writing about physical pain or mental pain? The overwhelming consistency of this response convinces me that modern culture rests upon an
underlying belief so strong that it grips us with the force of a founding
myth. Call it the Myth of Two Pains. We live in an era when many people
believe—as a basic, unexamined foundation of thought—that pain comes
divided into separate types: physical and mental. These two types of pain,
so the myth goes, are as different as land and sea. You feel physical pain
if your arm breaks, and you feel mental pain if your heart breaks. Between these two different events we seem to imagine a gulf so wide and
deep that it might as well be filled by a sea that is impossible to navigate.

The force of this myth—like all myths—no doubt depends on the ser-
viceable truth it brings into a murky world. I don't mean to claim that
there is no difference at all between a heartache and a toothache. The pain
of a stubbed toe obviously has a different immediate source than the pain
of a no-holds-barred divorce. Yet, in the long run, different sources do not
necessarily imply different pains. In fact, one main purpose of this book
is to begin to collapse the artificial division we create in accepting a belief
that human pain is split by a chasm into uncommunicating categories
called physical and mental. Not all societies and languages recognize such

a division, as we shall see. In our culture, chronic pain (like stress) offers a particularly good example of the interdependence of mind and body, although our commitment to the Myth of Two Pains usually prevents us from recognizing the power of the example. (One important social function of myth—in preserving a portion of truth—is to blind us to what it cannot explain.) Still, a formidable task lies ahead in any effort to demythologize our widespread cultural assumption that body and mind produce two utterly different kinds of pain.

Two brief illustrations at the start—one verbal, one visual—may help to clarify the unworkable dualism we tend to cling to. Suppose a loving but very traditional father loses his only son to AIDS. We would not find it strange to speak about his shock and loss as painful, especially when his grief persists for many months, long past the period of normal mourning. Perhaps he wakes up doubled over with inexplicable stomach cramps. Clearly, grief and pain are not exactly identical. The father's pain, however, is far more than an empty metaphor, as if we meant merely that his grief is "like" pain. Instead, his grief and pain eventually proceed together, intertwined, in such a way that it becomes almost impossible to experience them apart. Further, the pain may be immensely complicated by the oppressive social myths and meanings attached to AIDS. We cannot neatly seal off the father's affliction in a sanitary class labeled "mental" pain, even as it would be foolish to insist that AIDS—in opening the individual to all manner of opportunistic infections—involves merely "physical" pain. Severe emotional trauma, like illness or injury, is no less something felt along the pulses.

Or consider the painting "Anguish" (fig. 1) included in a recent exhibition of Headache Art. Is such anguish—suffering so vividly embodied—really best understood as "mental" pain? Does it make sense to say that the physical pain of headache remains completely separate from the mental pain of anguish? It is always possible, of course, to argue that the painter, George Dergalis, trapped like all of us in the inadequacies of language, has given his work a misleading title. Perhaps he should have called it "Physical Pain." My approach, however, is to assume that we can learn much by exploring, at least provisionally, the insights that artists and writers bring to the experience of pain. The painting by George Dergalis encourages us, I think, to question the adequacy of an understanding of pain that separates mind from body.

FIGURE 1. George Dergalis (b. 1928). *Anguish*. Headache Art Exhibition (1989).

Two illustrations obviously cannot prove a point. My aim in citing them, however, is not to prove an argument, but rather to raise or reopen a basic question as to whether we can legitimately continue to divide pain into separate compartments labeled body and mind. True, faced with the need to offer medication, doctors may find it convenient, even indispensable, to prescribe one drug for physical pain and a second drug for mental suffering. If the Myth of Two Pains (no matter how erroneous) helps physicians provide better relief to patients struggling with chronic illness, it is worth preserving for that reason alone. Yet today—in the era of the twofold Myth—patients often go without adequate care for pain. The habit of dividing pain into separate categories of mind and body may ultimately create or sustain more torment than it relieves. Pain, unfortunately, is not a subject we can master through a knowledge of drugs alone. The question of how we should think about pain needs to be raised—and held open—so that we may examine the assumptions we now take for granted.

We need to challenge our unthinking culture-wide assumptions about pain because our own health is at stake. Even to think about pain—instead of automatically ignoring or denying it—represents a large step forward. Such thinking, I believe, while still far from complete, will lead to an inevitable conclusion. As current research both inside and outside medicine now suggests, the rigid split between mental and physical pain is beginning to look like a gigantic cultural mistake, perhaps similar to the belief that the world was flat. Mistakes, we know, can prove very difficult to abandon or correct when we have invested centuries of belief in them. Certainly, the accumulating evidence against the Myth of Two Pains has not yet been absorbed in such a way as to change how we act and think and feel. Something very strange will occur when the coming change takes hold. It may then turn out that the pain we come to feel—and no one, I trust, is so cruel as to wish us a *completely* pain-free life—will differ not only from the pain our ancestors felt. It will also be different from any pain we have ever experienced before.

✝

What would it be like never to feel pain? Is the total absence of pain—obviously the result of a rare neurological deficit—in some sense a cultural as well as a biomedical event? We can explore one possible response to these questions through the experience of a shadowy figure, born in Prague, who during the 1920s spent almost two years on the American vaudeville stage billed as Edward H. Gibson, The Human Pincushion.[2] Twice each day, clad only in shorts, Gibson would walk on stage and ask a man in the audience to stick pins in him anywhere except the abdomen and groin. Some fifty or sixty pins—carefully sterilized—would be inserted up to their heads. Then, still in the presence of the audience, Gibson would methodically pull them out, one by one. This forgotten spectacle in the history of American entertainment lasted for some nineteen months.

It is not true that Gibson never, ever, felt pain. Once, when he was seven, he was struck in the skull with a lathing-hatchet. It stuck in so deeply that he ran home, about fifty yards, where his father removed it. He felt no discomfort at the time, he said, except for a headache lasting several days. Mostly, however, he lived a life immune from the normal electrochemical penalties that flesh is heir to. Once in a fit of anger Gibson broke his nose by banging it on a piano—but felt no pain. It is hard to imagine being unable to vent your anger except by inconveniencing yourself, like deliberately running out of gas or purposely missing the bus.

Audiences responded to Gibson in ways that tell us something about our acquired habits of thought. A person who cannot feel pain seems a kind of freak or outsider: a sideshow wonder. Indeed, it is clear that Gibson's audience, no doubt reflecting a general human response, found themselves incapable of imagining a truly pain-free existence. They instinctively supplied the pain he did not feel. For example, as a special stunt Gibson planned a reenactment of the Crucifixion. He prepared a rough cross and four gold-plated spikes with sharp points. On the appointed day, the Human Pincushion spread his arms against the wooden cross. A man with a sledgehammer drove the first spike through the palm of Gibson's hand—at which point a woman in the audience fainted dead away.

Gibson wisely canceled the event. Even on the vaudeville circuit, his un-Christlike imitation of Christ was not likely to win him many admirers. Our half-conscious assumptions about pain also made the escalation from pins to spikes intolerable. The audience had no room for retreat into comforting suspicions that they were watching an illusionist trick. According to the physician who examined him several years later, the path of the single spike through Gibson's hand had left an unmistakable scar.

A pain-free life for Edward Gibson proved to be a meaningless benefit that left him more or less indifferent. He could never really know what he was spared and could never figure out how to turn his strange gift into something more than a spectacle. Thus after leaving the vaudeville stage, Gibson employed his "power" in amusing friends or in idle distraction.

As his physician wrote: "Anytime, most casually, with no adequate incentive at all, he will, for example, push a large hypo-needle through his cheek or arm or leg; or a long hat-pin through both cheeks above the tongue."[3] This is the act of man whose freedom from pain leads to a dead end.

The medical literature describing the rare cases of people born unable to feel pain suggests that painlessness is not a gift but a disguised curse. These pain-free children tend to die early. We constantly employ the sensation of pain, even at very mild levels, to adjust our posture or shift position, and without such continual minor adjustments we would suffer from inflammations and infections developed when our bones grind down their protective connecting tissue. Parents of pain-free children must mount around-the-clock guard duty since menace is lurking everywhere. The playground holds a dozen potential deathtraps for the child who falls twenty feet without pain. At times it is easy to wish that affliction had no claims on us, but probably we should train ourselves to think the peculiar thought that the real gift is not painlessness but pain.

Edward Gibson's painlessness can also help us grasp some of the unnoticed ways in which its reverse state, pain, is also a cultural and psychosocial event. For example, his painlessness obviously influenced Gibson's choice of occupation and shaped the ways in which other people regarded him. It trapped him in a role resembling that of the bearded lady in a carnival. Less obviously, pain, too, places us within a social world where what we feel cannot be easily disentangled from what we learn from our culture and from how other people respond to us. Pain may keep us from working, push us into the role of invalid, drive away friends, and wall us up in a personal prison of isolation. Gibson's random parlor games suggest that painlessness had in some sense unmoored him, but they serve as a reminder that pain can achieve such dislocations too, even as it fixes us within a particular place and time.

Pain is certainly the result of a biochemical process. But nerve pathways and bodily reflexes do not tell the whole story. Pain is also a subjective experience, perhaps an archetype of subjectivity, felt only within the solitude of our individual minds. It is, in addition, always saturated with the visible or invisible imprint of specific human cultures. We learn how to feel pain and learn what it means. Indeed, the aimless life of Edward Gibson suggests strongly that what matters most about pain—at least outside the laboratory—may well be the personal and social meanings with which we and our surrounding culture endow it.

†

Interpreting pain today is, if anything, even more difficult than in ancient times when the entire process could be referred to the gods. We thus might as well stop right now if in order to talk about the meaning of pain we must first provide clear, distinct, and universally accepted definitions. "Our language can be seen as an ancient city," wrote the philosopher Ludwig Wittgenstein—"a maze of little streets and squares, of old and new houses, and of houses with additions from various periods; and this surrounded by a multitude of new boroughs with straight regular streets and uniform houses."[4] Scientists and philosophers seek to make pain into an orderly citizen of the new suburbs of knowledge, but at some point it invariably darts back into the maze of ancient city streets where maps prove almost useless and where you know your way around, if at all, by feel.

Different languages handle the native elusiveness of pain with different strategies. French, like other Romance tongues, normally employs a term built on the Latin root *dolor*. Significantly, the French *douleur* and Latin *dolor* do not separate so-called physical from mental pain. Depending on context, they might as easily be translated "anguish" or "ache," like the less common French term *peine*, which ranges in its connotations from penalty and punishment to affliction and sorrow.[5] Some Asian languages tend to define pain less by a single noun than by the various modifying adjectives that always accompany it. History offers no firmer ground. Aristotle, for example, considered pain an emotion, like joy, whereas Descartes saw it as a sensation, like heat or cold. As it turns out, meaning may be even harder to define than pain. It should surprise no one that scholars have established a prosperous light industry devoted to analyzing the multiple meanings of meaning.[6] Anyone who insists at the beginning on an absolutely unambiguous definition of terms will end up settling for bogus clarity.

The problems of definition proliferate if we assume—as we usually do—that pain is one thing: single, coherent, unified. The truth is that pain comes in more spins and flavors than quarks. Some researchers, for example, find it useful to base their studies on third molar pain.[7] Third molar pain, however, differs greatly from the forest fire of agony ignited—often by nothing more than the slightest touch or sound—in the strange condition known as causalgia. The pain of causalgia, in turn, differs from the nauseous, dizzying pain of migraine. Muscular pain is not identical with visceral pain, and both differ from the central pain associated with lesions of the thalamus or spinothalamic tracts. Some pain—known as "referred"—is felt at bodily sites far distant from its organic source. Other types originate or survive in the complete absence of an identifiable organic cause. In fact, anyone rushing in at the start with an all-embracing perfect definition of pain should probably be dismissed as a harmless crank.

The International Association for the Study of Pain (IASP)—founded in 1973—responded to this general disarray by appointing a Subcommittee on Taxonomy charged with creating a definition suitable for scientific discourse. This subcommittee consisted of fourteen of the most distinguished pain specialists in the world, and they did far better than the famous blind men defining an elephant. Pain, they reported, is "an unpleasant sensory and emotional experience associated with actual or potential tissue damage, or described in terms of such damage."[8] We should notice that they define pain not as a sensation but as an "experience." Notice also that they do not require actual organic damage but only experience described "in terms of" organic damage. These small but radical changes (to which we will return later) slip by almost silently—so silently, in fact, that traditionalists are free to ignore them, which is one mark of an effective subcommittee and a standard ploy in the history of scientific change.[9] Still, a thousand nineteenth-century physicians must have groaned in their sleep.

There are good reasons for suspending the quest for absolute clarity and instead accepting the virtues of ordinary language, common usage, and everyday experience. A French woman crippled in a 1960 automobile accident, whose comments I take seriously, responded to inquiries about her pain this way: "It is impossible to define physical pain, one cannot describe it, and it is only a matter of experience. One cannot speak of pain with a capital P . . . it is a succession of seconds, a succession of minutes, and this is what makes it so hard to withstand."[10] Pain clinics, seeking to make sense of something so elusive and indescribable, sometimes employ the McGill-Melzack Pain Questionnaire, which confronts the patient with a grid of preselected adjectives organized into groups describing sen-

McGill - Melzack Pain Questionnaire

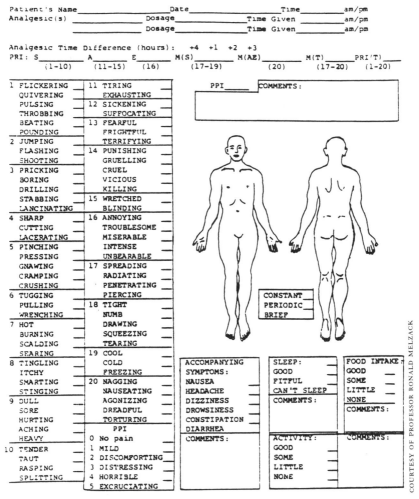

FIGURE 2. *McGill-Melzack Pain Questionnaire.*

sory, affective, or evaluative responses. Is your pain stabbing, taut, grinding, piercing, burning, hateful, sore? (fig. 2).[11] The value of such ordinary language, even if regimented for diagnostic purposes and keyed to the vocabulary of a white, middle-class culture, lies in an intrinsic slipperiness that corresponds to our experience of a slippery world. The words *pain* and *meaning* serve an indispensable social function precisely because they cannot be easily pinned down.

The fact is that writers on medicine—without recourse to grids or blinders—have begun to talk sensibly about the meanings of illness.[12] It is clear, for example, that the pain of a chronic, degenerative condition such as rheumatoid arthritis comes wrapped in a web of personal and social implications. What will a crippling disability mean to an older man's self-esteem or to his career? A young woman struggles with her belief that arthritis is a condition of old people. She worries whether her pain will prevent her from living a full life as wife and mother. A working-class woman already supporting her disabled husband fears that her family will fall apart when they discover that even turning on the water tap is too painful for her to manage. "A condition such as rheumatoid arthritis cannot be viewed in terms of physical functioning alone," writes Michael Bury. "Patients must also live with what the illness means; with its consequences for daily life and an altered future."[13]

The way to begin learning about pain, then, is not to start by defining it—as if by sheer will we could forge it into something very clear and simple—but rather to explore the ways in which it tends to get away from us. We need not remove all possible uncertainties in order to think clearly. What we end up thinking clearly about, with all its uncertainties removed, will certainly not be pain. We can learn much by seeing where our ordinary language, with its inherent slipperiness, will take us. In this way, we will at least begin with the knowledge that meaning and pain do not belong to the class of clear and distinct ideas cherished by empiricist philosophers but rather constitute a summons to look further, to resist prefabricated definitions, to examine the terrain for ourselves, and, most important, to proceed in a spirit of openness.

†

An understanding of pain requires many kinds of knowledge, but the knowledge we most consistently ignore or dismiss, as I have claimed, concerns the bond that links pain with meaning.[14] The point I want to emphasize is that humankind—across cultures and across time—has persistently understood pain as an event that demands interpretation. Pain not only hurts but more often than not frustrates, baffles, and resists us. It seems we cannot simply suffer pain but almost always are compelled to make sense of it. This process of making sense goes on at several levels. Individual sufferers seek and often supply a personally satisfying explanation for what is happening to them, yet the process of interpreting pain goes on also at the level of general cultures or subcultures. When we fall into pain, we also fall into a net of already constructed meanings.

Today our culture has willingly, almost gratefully, handed over to medicine the job of explaining pain. This development, accelerating with the prestige of science over the last several centuries, has brought with it consequences that remain almost completely unanalyzed. We are in fact standing at the dawn of an entirely new but not so brave world. Although almost all eras and cultures have employed doctors, never before in human history has the explanation of pain fallen so completely to medicine.

This new age also confronts us with a distinctive paradox. Although biomedical research has enormously expanded our knowledge of the anatomy, physiology, and pharmacology of pain, never before has pain—particularly chronic pain—reached its present epidemic proportions.[15] We possess more knowledge and better remedies than ever before. Like the sorcerer's apprentice, however, medicine even in its most heroic efforts cannot seem to push back the ever-increasing waves of fresh pain.

Consider a few figures. Although we now boast a cornucopia of new wonder drugs, chronic pain ranks as an economic and social problem of enormous magnitude. Five million Americans suffer from back ailments alone. Another two million Americans are so disabled by back pain that they cannot work.[16] One family in three contains someone suffering from persistent pain. Authoritative figures prepared for the year 1983 estimated that 90 million Americans suffered from chronic pain, that 60 million Americans were either partially or totally disabled, and that their disabilities resulted in the loss of 750 million workdays. The same sources claimed that in 1983 the cost of chronic pain in America ran between 60 and 90 billion dollars annually.[17] Medical costs, needless to say, have not been going down.

The most important and least accessible costs of chronic pain are of course not monetary. Arthritis, migraine, cancer, and depression (to name just a few contemporary maladies) each identifies a vast body of illness where pain has been absorbed into the routine conditions of modern life. Stress turns even well-paying occupations into the breeding grounds of disease, while marginal groups such as migrant workers or the homeless know pain as an everyday fact of life. Professional athletes and dancers face injury as an almost foregone conclusion, but jogger's-knee, tennis-elbow, and aerobic-shins have also turned the health and fitness boom into an unofficial pain factory. Old age meanwhile is almost synonymous with bodily ills. ("I knew it would be hard," my grandmother whispered from her bed in the nursing home, "but I never thought it would be *this* hard.") We may well ask whether anyone can think clearly about such a borderless sea of affliction. Small wonder that we prefer to leave such a crushing burden of thought to a small caste of scientists and doctors.

The problem of chronic pain has grown so large and the resources of medicine so strained (especially in a culture battling poverty, cancer, AIDS, and drug addiction) that this may be the right moment to consider recovering a knowledge perhaps too hastily set aside in favor of drugs, surgery, and nerve blocks. Medicine for centuries has supplied powerful, if changing, systems for explaining pain, yet these medical explanations often supplemented, rather than openly opposed, the explanations offered by, say, philosophy or religion or folklore or literature. No one would seriously propose that we revive the vanished world of the ancient Greeks who sought relief from pain by sleeping all night at the temple of Asklepios (the god of medicine). Nevertheless, the current epidemic of chronic pain takes place largely within a system of explanation based solely upon the mechanistic assumptions of traditional modern medicine. Pain is understood something like the wheeze and cough from a broken motor.

Pain, as I have proposed, is far more than simply or exclusively a medical problem. It cannot be reduced to a mere transaction of the nervous system. The experience of pain is also shaped by such powerful cultural forces as gender, religion, and social class. It is reinforced—and sometimes created—by psychological and emotional states such as guilt, fear, anger, grief, and depression. Further, pain is not always an unmitigated disaster. We willingly, if grudgingly, accept pain that accompanies growth or achievement. Some people have experienced the bizarre paradox that it is in moments of extreme pain that they have never felt more alive. Even when it just grinds on aimlessly, pain, like love, belongs among the basic human experiences that make us who we are. If tomorrow someone invented a foolproof, cost-free pill, with no side effects, guaranteeing lifetime immunity from pain, we would at once have to set about reinventing what it means to be human.

It is writers who have proved especially interested in understanding the place of pain in human life. Writers in fact have been directly involved in creating—not just observing—the social and personal meanings that we make out of pain. The gulf separating doctors and writers is fortunately beginning to narrow. A dialogue between medicine and literature is already under way in conferences, specialized periodicals, university courses, and even in a few medical schools.[18] It now needs to spill over into the wider culture where millions of people spend their days and nights in solitary chronic suffering. It will take much more than new pills and drugs if we hope to confront pain using all our available resources. One crucial place to begin is with the acknowledgment that, despite our high-tech laboratories and surgical innovations, pain remains one of the most perplexing mysteries of our time. There is no authority today who can tell us exactly what pain is and how it works. Pain thus plunges us instantly into the midst of controversy and the unknown.

✝

It is important to emphasize the mysteriousness of pain—its link with the unknown (to which I will soon return)—because few of us suspect how little the medical profession knows about pain, especially about chronic pain. Information, of course, is piling up monthly. There are now numerous thick, expensive, medical-scientific journals that specialize in research on or related to pain.[19] Yet, in 1974, in the preface to a volume of studies from the first international symposium on pain, Dr. John J. Bonica (first president of the International Association for the Study of Pain) cautioned his medical audience about "the great void in our knowledge of the mechanisms and physiopathology of pain."[20] Today the void is not quite so vast, but it is still there.

The uncomfortable and unwelcome truth is that doctors know far less about pain than most patients assume. As one specialist put it: "There is no medical understanding of pain—in the sense that physicians agree about what pain is and how to treat it, as they agree about (say) the tuberculosis bacillus. There is a medical understanding of tuberculosis, but there is no basis of agreement, in modern medicine, about pain." Until the last few years, medical education and training, despite its legendary rigors, seemed almost purposely designed to keep doctors in the dark about pain. It is a long-standing tradition. The eighteenth century provides little writing about pain beyond a few Latin dissertations. Although the nineteenth century witnessed a vast explosion of medical research and writing, pain continued to occupy a place at the periphery of medical education and knowledge.[21] Far into the twentieth century, medical students still cannot find departments or courses dedicated to the study of pain. As John Bonica put it bluntly in a 1989 interview: "No medical school has a pain curriculum."[22]

Bonica's remarks about the absence of a pain curriculum are likely to strike modern patients as surprising. There are more surprises to come as we turn to specific examples. Most surgical and medical oncologists, Bonica continues, "don't know anything about cancer pain. They don't know how to treat it because they haven't been taught how to treat it." Certainly Bonica does not mean to single out oncologists as somehow uniquely untaught. The nature and treatment of pain may surface in no more than an isolated lecture or fragment of a lecture in the long months and years of medical education. Is it surprising, then, that pain is a problem to which many doctors still have not assigned a high priority? One time-tested medical response to pain, of course, is simply to dismiss it. Once pain has served its (limited) use in the process of diagnosis, the doctor can safely turn to more pressing matters. Patients, after all, don't die from pain. In fact, hospital research shows that doctors habitually prescribe inadequate doses for effective pain relief.[23]

Why would ordinarily compassionate doctors fail to provide adequate relief from pain? Some doubtless fear that hospitalized patients will grow addicted to narcotic painkillers. There is strong evidence, however, that morphine and other narcotics are not addictive among the vast majority of patients. (The odds of hospital addiction are less than 1 percent.) In some instances the patient's pain may serve a clinical need, however dimly understood. On a hospital burn unit, for example, where massive, disfiguring injuries over the entire body and agonizing procedures such as "debridement" threaten to sap the patient's will to live, doctors seemed to interpret pain as a reassurance that life had not simply faded away into defeat and nothingness.[24] It served as a vital sign. Nevertheless, the Japanese shiatsu therapist Eizo Ninomiya stated explicitly what many doctors outside the burn unit no doubt silently assume. As he insisted: "It's not my pain, it's yours." "If there's no pain," he adds cheerfully, "I go home."[25]

†

The long medical tradition of ignoring or denying pain has begun to assimilate, slowly and unevenly, a related tradition. In recent years it has become possible, even fashionable, to talk about the imminent conquest of pain. This rhetoric of conquest feeds on the impressive progress of modern research in overcoming such previously deadly or crippling illnesses as smallpox, cholera, polio, and tuberculosis. Indeed, metaphors of triumph borrowed from earlier victories over disease have come to dominate recent biomedical writing, as in H. B. Gibson's *Pain and Its Conquest* (1982)—dedicated, as befits its title, to Gibson's colleagues in the International Association for the Study of Pain. Almost as if their vocation required it, researchers and journalists seem particularly drawn to the language of conquest.[26] It is significant that clinicians who experience the daily frustrations of trying to help patients in chronic pain often reveal far less taste for triumphal images and predictions of victory.

What prevents an immediate, full-scale conquest of pain, from a biomedical point of view, is simply the lack of a few key pieces of information. Thus another wave of titles in the voluminous scientific literature describes pain as a problem or riddle: something to be solved or unraveled.[27] Ronald Melzack and Patrick D. Wall gave to the first edition of their classic text *The Challenge of Pain* (1982) a slightly different title: *The Puzzle of Pain* (1973). Their revised edition adds the results of nearly a decade's immensely productive research, but the change in title does not reflect a change in underlying philosophy or approach. The point of view remains consistent; pain in effect challenges biomedical science to solve a puzzle or, more accurately, a series of interlocking puzzles. The puzzles have simply turned out to be tougher than anyone expected.

We are so accustomed to hyperboles of conquest and breakthrough that we tend not to notice how they influence our thinking. Is pain really the sort of thing (like a mountain or an army) that we can expect to conquer? Is it truly like a jigsaw puzzle with merely one or two key pieces still missing? It is understandable that biomedical researchers would want to answer yes. Certainly our knowledge about pain has grown immensely in recent years. Yet patients struggling with chronic pain may be seriously deceived if led to think that relief is just around the corner. The promise of an imminent cure, continually deferred, in some ways makes a difficult struggle even more difficult. Thus I would like to introduce a distinction that offers an alternative to the language of conquest, challenge, and puzzles. Suppose—temporarily putting aside the promise of an impending breakthrough—we consider in what sense pain might be regarded not as a puzzle but as a mystery.

Mysteries—if we reinvest the concept with something of its ancient prestige—designate a truth *necessarily* closed off from full understanding. They remain always partly veiled in silence. Such mysteries differ fundamentally from puzzles, challenges, and riddles. A riddle, for example, gives up all of its secrets as soon as we know the right answer. Good riddles often generate more than one correct answer—there are potentially endless witty replies to the question of why the chicken crossed the road—but in the absence of a satisfying answer the riddle remains incomplete. We continue to feel, well, puzzled. When a correct answer finally appears, suddenly everything feels right and a kind of closure occurs. One crucial piece of information in effect finally completes the puzzle. A mystery operates on very different principles.[28]

"Mortals," wrote the philosopher Martin Heidegger in 1950, "have not yet come into the ownership of their own nature. Death withdraws into the enigmatic. The mystery of pain remains veiled."[29] For Heidegger, the veils that surround pain do not describe merely a few missing facts that obscure an otherwise clear and complete scientific understanding. A true mystery, as opposed to a puzzle or riddle, cannot be known *apart from* the veil that separates us from a full understanding. The veil in a sense is what makes the mystery visible; it gives a presence or appearance to the unknown, much as a shroud emphasizes rather than merely conceals the strangeness of death. A mystery, then, is not something that exists principally to be solved. In fact, it transcends or eludes every normal technique of solution. Mysteries, in resisting closure and in retaining an essential openness, refuse to yield up every quantum of their darkness to research or to bright ideas. Instead, they introduce us to unusual states of being which, for a time, we enter into and dwell within.

The idea of dwelling within a mystery may provide a useful, even necessary, complement to the scientific rhetoric of conquest. As patients, we dwell within mysteries like pain not because we lack a crucial piece of information—although crucial information is always lacking—but because we have no choice. A mystery is an experience that life thrusts upon us. We cannot evade it. Willingly or unwillingly, we enter into a realm that is somehow set apart, where our familiar modes of thought and experience simply do not suffice. Puzzles and riddles belong to our comfortable world of competitive striving: they attract us and draw out our powers and reward us with prizes. In the presence of mystery, however, nothing looks quite the same. Mysteries disturb the world we take for granted.

I would propose that while the doctor typically approaches pain as a puzzle or challenge, the patient typically experiences it as a mystery. Pain takes us out of our normal modes of dealing with the world. It introduces us to a landscape where nothing looks entirely familiar and where even the familiar takes on an uncanny strangeness. What complicates this picture immeasurably, however, is the paradox that we now live in a culture saturated with scientific explanations and assumptions, including the assumption that cures and conquests are daily events. Thus even when we experience pain as a mystery, we continue to *think* of it—to our infinite perplexity—simply as an unsolved puzzle. We hastily schedule an appointment with a doctor who as a matter of training looks upon our condition as a challenge to current biomedical knowledge.

We might say that it is the most earnest wish of almost every patient, ancient or modern, to be released not just from pain but from the requirement of dwelling within its mysteries.

The mystery of pain, however, will not soon go away, no matter how earnestly we wish it. One day, of course, biomedical research may discover a hidden switch in the brain that turns off pain, once and for all. If that millennial event occurs, pain would instantly stand revealed as no more than a centuries-old puzzle to which science has at last supplied the correct answer. Yet even a hidden switch will not somehow stop the cultural process by which we construct meanings and uses for pain. The power to eradicate pain at will also supposes the power to create it (or at least the power to refuse to relieve it). How will politicians, judges, generals, and police chiefs think about this new tool? What limbo would you enter— the reverse of Edward Gibson's world—if the switch suddenly and inexplicably malfunctions? Pain is always personal and always cultural. It is thus always open to the variable influx of meaning.

We must also consider the possibility that pain has not yet yielded up all its secrets because it is not entirely or strictly a puzzle. Suppose that everything biomedical research eventually tells us about pain still amounts to far less than an answer that finally reveals a hidden switch. Suppose that there is no magic bullet. Will there then come a time when it will not seem unscientific to claim that pain always embraces an element of ineradicable mystery? It seems likely that mystery can never be entirely eliminated from pain as long as pain remains a subjective experience. It also seems likely that doctors—without necessarily abandoning the hope of conquest and cure—will one day find it important, even crucial, to understand what it means for their patients to dwell for long periods within a realm of mystery and the unknown.

The future of pain, in fact, is beginning to arrive. It is becoming clear that doctors who ignore what pain means to an individual patient cut themselves off from relevant knowledge as surely as if they practiced medicine from an eighteenth-century textbook and still thought of nerves as hollow tubes filled with speedy little organisms called animal spirits. The cultural and psychosocial construction of pain is not something I have recently dreamed up: some very strong thinkers both inside and outside medicine have already begun to explore it.[30] Nor does such exploration promise a quick fix or panacea. Because I do not regard pain as a puzzle, I certainly do not propose to supply the long-sought answer or missing piece. Pain—especially chronic pain—is too complex for one-track approaches.

There is no inherent reason, however, why we cannot helpfully begin to think of pain as embracing elements of *both* puzzle and mystery. Unquestionably, the neurobiology of pain has recently yielded up fascinating facts and clues, such as the analgesic properties of opiatelike neuropeptides produced by the brain. We need all the facts and clues we can get. My aim, however, is not to review new biomedical research but rather to explore an area too often ignored and dismissed as irrelevant. There is persuasive evidence, as I will show, that the human experience of pain also inescapably involves our encounter with meaning. The network of nerves and neurotransmitters crucial to pain may well prove nearly universal: the same for everyone. Meaning, however, is something that exists only within the shifting processes of human culture and of individual minds. It therefore can never successfully shut itself off from change. The meaning of pain, like the meaning of any complex text, always remains open to impermanent personal and social interpretations. It contains areas of darkness or mystery where firm answers may be simply unavailable. Its meanings thus must leave room not only for what we know and will come to know but also for what may remain forever unknown.

†

Literature provides an especially rich field for examining the different meanings that humankind over the centuries has discovered within pain. Indeed, from Homer to Beckett, literary texts engage in a vastly neglected process of representing and elucidating our encounters with pain.[31] An adequate explanation for this neglect would require a long detour through the blind alleys of recent scholarship and criticism. One reason seems clear, however, and we have met it before. Many readers suspect that literature does not deal with *real* pain, and by real pain they mean physical pain. A broken arm or leg is real pain. Literature, so the common suspicion goes, occupies itself entirely with various thin, intellectualized, etiolated subspecies of affliction such as angst, anguish, or existential dread.

It is no doubt tempting to emphasize the intellectual seriousness or spiritual value of literature by turning away from its treatment of something so base and unedifying as the body. The feeling that literature does not deal with real pain, however, also depends upon the relentless modern dualism that divides pain into separate categories called mental and physical. American newspapers and advertisements almost every day contain vivid examples in which pain is attributed to serious, if common, afflictions from heartache to depression. The familiar German noun *Schmertz* lends itself even to such exotic concepts as a deep spirit-crushing ennui or world pain (*Weltschmertz*). Yet somehow, when it comes time to analyze, we reject such unscientific usage and assume that nothing counts as pain short of demonstrable tissue damage. This absolute dualism of mental and physical pain is a comparatively recent idea whose time, as I contend, has long passed. A truly effective dialogue between medicine and literature may just succeed in driving a stake through its heart.

It is probably quixotic to think that we will ever completely remove the terms "mental pain" and "physical pain" from our language. They perform a certain commonsensical work in identifying very different afflictions, which may thus make them almost ineradicable elements of our thought. We may in fact need to preserve the terms simply to protest and to undermine the rigorous division they set up. Mental pain and physical pain—given a subversive reformulation—would need to be understood not as rigidly divided but rather (in all except the most extreme cases) as inextricably bound up with each other. Authors of medical textbooks or philosophers or English teachers may try to keep them apart, artificially, for the purpose of maintaining order, but there is good reason for believing that pain—as it abides with us through the long days and nights of conscious human suffering—always involves the mutal interaction of body and mind.

René Leriche was professor of clinical surgery at the University of

Strasbourg, and in his pioneering medical text *The Surgery of Pain* (1937) he insisted that pain studied in the laboratory—pain circumscribed and sanitized and dwindled to a clear-cut science of nerve pathways—bore little resemblance to "living pain": pain as it was experienced by individual patients and encountered by practicing doctors. The mystery of pain has surely found few better descriptions than Leriche's account of what it is like as a physician to try to understand something so elusive:

In the suffering patient, the pain is like a storm, which hardly admits of assessment once it is over. While it is present, the patient is beside himself, quite beyond all capability of analysing it, unless, on the contrary, he fixes his attention altogether on his suffering. And there you are, powerless to understand, distressed in the face of this abyss into which you cannot descend, which you try unsuccessfully to picture to yourself, impressed by something of great severity that you would like to be able to alleviate, touching lightly with your hand the region of pain, surprised that you can feel nothing, and yet at times, by your touch, even exciting dreadful recurrent spasms of pain.[32]

Leriche left no doubt that he was concerned with pain registered in the body with its intersecting systems of nerves and muscles. Yet in addressing his medical audience, employing all the resources of technical precision, Leriche also articulated the principle that literary texts, in numerous different ways, illustrate so powerfully. "Let us understand each other," he asserts boldly: "Pain is always a cerebral phenomenon."[33]

It would be possible to construe Leriche's powerful challenge to traditional thought in ways consistent with my own approach. Leriche insists that "it is always along the sensory pathways in the spinal cord that the impressions pass which will be recognised in the brain as pain." Yet he also regards what he calls "the conception of the physiologists" as "too mechanical, too purely artificial, to be capable of reconciliation with what we doctors see in the human patient."[34] Pain, as I want to argue in a similar spirit, is not simply an automatic and unchanging response somehow hard wired in the body. The impressions communicated by the sensory pathways and spinal cord must be construed or interpreted in the brain that receives them. Brains, of course, do not operate alone in vats (except in the speculation of modern philosophers and in old-time horror films). They belong to individuals who in turn exist only within human history and within specific cultures. Gertrude Stein could not say truthfully of pain what she said of roses. It is not true that a pain is a pain is a pain: everywhere and eternally the same. Pain can be described as always a cerebral phenomenon in the sense that it is never simply a sensation but rather something that the time-bound brain interprets and that the time-bound mind constructs: a specific human artifact bearing the marks of its specific human history.

Here is perhaps the most difficult thought to accept about pain. We experience pain only and entirely as we interpret it. It seizes us as if with an unseen hand, sometimes stopping us in mid-sentence or mid-motion, but we too capture and reshape it. Our individual and cultural struggles to refashion pain remove it from the realm of the unthinking distress we share with the rest of the animal kingdom. It is in struggling to understand our pain that we saturate it in human history. The pain we feel thus always belongs to a particular place and time and person. It may be trivial or negligible (if we choose to interpret it so) but it is never simply an impersonal code of neural impulses, like changeless, computer-generated messages sent over an internal telephone line. Human pain is never timeless, just as it is never merely an affair of bodies.

We need to recover the premodern belief that bodies and minds proceed through life together in ways that directly influence our experience of health and illness. William Blake, in a sentence that bears long pondering, wrote that "a Tear is an Intellectual Thing."[35] Clearly, weeping depends not only on our anatomy and physiology but also, crucially, on our minds and emotions. Our thoughts always interpenetrate our emotional life—we fall in love knowing a thousand disorganized things about what it means to fall in love—even as our emotions and our bodily feelings influence our thoughts. When King Lear weeps for his murdered daughter Cordelia, he weeps not just with his anatomy but with his entire intellectual and emotional and spiritual being.

Human pain similarly lives within us only as we have brains and minds to perceive it, only as we possess intellect and emotions to register its depth, source, and implications. In perceiving our pain, we transform it from a simple sensation into the complex mental-emotional events that psychologists and philosophers call perception.[36] The conceptual shift that occurs when we consider pain a perception rather than a sensation is so radical that many doctors and researchers, understandably, remain wedded to the older view. A major change in our thinking is nevertheless under way. Allan I. Basbaum, professor of anatomy and physiology at the

University of California (San Francisco), reflects this new thinking when he writes:

Pain is not just a stimulus that is transmitted over specific pathways but rather a complex perception, the nature of which depends not only on the intensity of the stimulus but on the situation in which it is experienced and, most importantly, on the affective or emotional state of the individual. Pain is to somatic stimulation as beauty is to a visual stimulus. It is a very subjective experience.[37]

He adds—in a complete reversal of older ways of thought—that severe pain can occur without any somatic stimulation at all.

The revolution that Basbaum announces, however quietly, opens a truly new era in the understanding and treatment of pain. The body, we might say, still gives pain its local residence, its *modus operandi*, but pain is no longer simply a technical malfunction (or function) of the arm or back or tooth. William Blake could add, as current medical research increasingly tends to confirm, that pain, like weeping, is also an intellectual thing. It has a human history no less complex, though no less hard to decipher, than the histories of fire or ice. It is the historical meanings of pain—created in the mysterious process that binds human sensation to emotion, perception, language, time, and place—that we must now begin to explore.

2

THE MEANINGS OF PAIN

The human body is the best picture of the human soul.
LUDWIG WITTGENSTEIN[1]

NYONE WHO HAS endured a period of intense pain has probably asked, silently or openly, the following incessant questions: Why me? Why is this happening? Why won't it stop? Suddenly we simply do not possess the knowledge we need. The combination of doubt and fear can loosen an avalanche of related questions. How will I earn a living if I can't go back to work? Will my sex drive ever return? Am I doomed to spend the rest of my life in pain? To be in pain is often to be in a state of crisis. It is a state in which we experience far more than physical discomfort. Pain has not simply interrupted our normal feeling of health. It has opened a huge fault or fissure in our world. We need answers. We want to know what all this torment in our bones—the disarrangement of our personal cosmos—adds up to. What does it mean?

Today, of course, we seek the meaning of pain at the doctor's office. Sometimes, mercifully, the answer is straightforward. The pain you feel is caused by a ruptured disk or an infected ear. An operation or a course of antibiotics will set you right and eliminate your questions. But suppose that a successful operation still leaves you with constant pain. Suppose x-rays and lab tests reveal no hidden organic cause. Suddenly the questions multiply and seem more urgent. Your doctor refers you to a specialist, who finds nothing and refers you to another specialist, who also finds nothing wrong, but still the pain continues. The meaning of pain seems a nonissue as long as medicine can provide its reassuring explanations and magical cures. When cures repeatedly fail, however, or when the explanations patently fall flat, we must confront once again—with renewed seriousness, even desperation—the ever-implicit question of meaning.

✝

Ivan Ilych was an ordinary man: intelligent, cheerful, capable, sociable, good-natured. After his graduation from law school, he became a successful magistrate, performing his duties with honesty and exactness. He made a good salary, married an attractive young woman, and settled down to a life of domestic comfort. In due course, several children arrived. Soon he was promoted to Assistant Public Prosecutor and—after experiencing a slight but unpleasant friction in his marriage—thereafter redoubled his application to the law. His greatest pleasure was playing bridge. A life so pleasant and so industrious brought further rewards. Before long he and his wife, who now got along better, moved into the house of their dreams.

It was in climbing a ladder (the metaphor is almost too common) while decorating the new house that Ivan Ilych slipped and fell, bruising his side. The bruise was painful but the pain quickly passed. Soon, however, he noticed a queer taste that lingered in his mouth and an uncomfortable pressure where the bruise had subsided. He grew worried, uncharacteristically irritable, and at times quarreled openly with his wife. Eventually he developed in his side a dull, gnawing ache that never left him. He saw a doctor, got a prescription, consulted new doctors, got new prescriptions. There was no improvement. The pain in his side was like a slow poison relentlessly destroying his sense of satisfaction with life. He felt changed, alone, as if on the edge of a precipice.

The physical change in his appearance shocked him. At length even his family recognized that something was terribly wrong. It occurred to Ivan Ilych that he was dying, but the thought was impossible to grasp or understand. All the ordinary events at home and at work now seemed a sham or falsehood. He could not concentrate on them. His pain alone occupied his mind. His pain alone seemed real. It grew worse—and worse still because his family (wishing to encourage him) steadfastly maintained the pretense that he was not dying. As his pain increased, Ivan Ilych began to wonder whether his entire life had been a lie: a carefully maintained structure of fraud and self-deception. When the crisis finally came, he began to scream, and he screamed continuously for three days.

It is said that one could not hear the screaming through two closed doors without feeling horror.

Tolstoy's spare, parablelike story *The Death of Ivan Ilych* (1886) provides a useful beginning, because it introduces us so clearly to what specialists might want to call the hermeneutics of pain. Borrowing its name from Hermes, the Greek messenger-god who presided over dreams and rites of divination, hermeneutics concerns the art or science of interpretation. The Greeks and Romans seldom took important actions—an invasion, say, or a long journey—without the support of a favorable omen, but dreams and sacrificial rites were often full of ambiguous images (snakes killing eagles, discolored intestines, strange patterns in the rising smoke). Someone in a position of authority, usually a priest, was needed to interpret the omen. Pain, while perhaps less eloquent than a discolored intestine, is something that almost intrinsically calls for interpretation.

Interpretation came naturally to ancient medicine because for countless centuries our ancestors lived with the belief that all disease and healing came from the gods: Isis, Ishtar, Dhanvantari, Asklepios, Apollo.[2] Doctors were thus also often priests, and priests doctors. The modern Asiatic and American Indian shaman (from a word meaning literally "he who knows") still openly performs this double role, since in these cultures the power to heal the sick flows directly from the power to communicate with the world of spirits.[3] Like the shaman, ancient doctor-priests mediated between the physical and spiritual worlds as specialists in the art of interpretation. Pain thus took its place among the signs of hidden meaning.

The crucial shift in ancient medicine came with the writings attributed to Hippocrates.[4] The Hippocratic writings mark a clear break from the primitive medicine of gods and spirits. Illness now finds its explanation in the natural world of biological process. The Hippocratic impulse of budding scientific inquiry, however, never wholly eliminated the spirit-based medicine (with its dreams, prayers, and magical drugs) which continued to exist alongside. The ancient Greeks regarded the natural world as divine, and thus pain could be read in a double sense as implying, simultaneously, both unseen biological processes within the body and a visitation (usually a punishment) from the gods.[5] This ambivalent reading of disease still survives in pious claims that AIDS patients deserve to suffer. While modern science has mostly abandoned an interest in human spiritual life, doctors regularly encounter patients who attribute their pain to divine punishment and who interpret illness as God's will. The changes that separate us from the ancient world are sometimes less immense than we imagine: no matter whether the culture is ancient or modern, pain and illness cannot be disentangled from complex social and personal systems of explanation.

✝

Pain, whatever else philosophy or biomedical science can tell us about it, is almost always the occasion for an encounter with meaning. It not only invites interpretation: like an insult or an outrageous act, it seems to *require* an explanation. As David Bakan writes:

> To attempt to understand the nature of pain, to seek to find its meaning, is already to respond to an imperative of pain itself. No experience demands and insists upon interpretation in the same way. Pain forces the question of its meaning, and especially of its cause, insofar as cause is an important part of its meaning. In those instances in which pain is intense and intractable and in which its causes are obscure, its demand for interpretation is most naked, manifested in the sufferer asking, "Why?"[6]

Generally, of course, the explanations we expect today center on questions of medicine, and Bakan is especially useful in reminding us that such medical diagnoses constitute an interpretation. They implicitly help us to make sense of pain: to give it a meaning.

The interpretation of pain, however, has not always centered so exclusively on questions of medicine. The impulse to phone our local physician, which seems now almost instinctive and certainly belongs to the domain of absolute common sense, has required over the centuries significant learning and unlearning. Consider the biblical patriarch Job as he sits on his dunghill, covered with boils, struggling to figure out why God has punished him. What from a medical perspective appears to be simply a problem in dermatology lies at the distant horizon, not the center, of his experience with pain.

Like the Book of Job, Tolstoy's *Death of Ivan Ilych* illustrates quite powerfully how pain inescapably engages us in struggles of interpretation. But it does more. With an almost geometrical precision, it also shows us how the experience of pain falls within a continuum bounded by opposite states so extreme that we seldom recognize their existence. At one limit, we might imagine pain as filled with a total, conclusive, unambiguous meaning, much as Job understood his boils as unquestionably a punishment sent by God. At the opposite limit, instead of a meaning that wholly fills up pain, we should imagine a condition of complete and often desolate meaninglessness. Pain in effect spends its existence moving in-between the extremes of absolute meaninglessness and full meaning.

Tolstoy's story gives us especially clear insight into this bipolar pattern. Thus for Ivan Ilych pain enters his life—at the pole of meaninglessness—as an almost unnoticed intrusion into the ordinary texture of his days. In a sense, we come to depend upon viewing pain as nothing more than an insignificant sensation swallowed up within the momentous events that absorb us, from launching careers to playing bridge. Such pain, we might say, passes through a life. Its power to vanish stands as the symbol of its insignificance, as if (by vanishing) pain testified to its inherent lack of meaning. Indeed, bumps and bruises remain our everyday figure of speech describing whatever we regard as automatically *not* serious. They affirm simply that we continue to hold our place in an obstinately material world where, like eternal adolescents, we are forever running into things.

The normal meaninglessness of pain, however, serves a more important function than we might at first suspect. Running into things is never wholly insignificant. That is, when we describe life's passing bumps and bruises as insignificant, we have simultaneously, if unknowingly, assigned them a meaning. It is of course an extremely minimal meaning. In effect, we imply that they signify nothing. Yet to signify nothing, like the figure zero in mathematics, is very different from not signifying at all. Suppose, for example, that you suffer from a mysterious symptom. Perhaps a lump has appeared where lumps do not normally belong, or a patch of skin has grown swollen and sensitive. Perhaps the ankle you injured jogging three months ago still bothers you. Even a very minor pain, if it persists, can set us to thinking.

Now suppose that your doctor runs a battery of conclusive tests, calls you into the office, and announces with full authority, "It's nothing." The most welcome meaning your pain can possess at that moment is, paradoxically, its meaninglessness. Like Ivan Ilych, we absolutely depend on our normal assumption that pain most often does not deserve a second thought. In the absence of this assumption we would turn into textbook hypochondriacs obsessively monitoring the body for signs of illness.

The pole of meaninglessness, then, is not itself meaningless. In fact, it establishes a kind of foundation. The meaninglessness of pain is what allows us to recognize the very different occasions when pain begins to take on crucial and complicated significance. Pain in this sense points or gestures toward something else. Thus for the great eighteenth-century moralist and lexicographer Samuel Johnson, kicking a stone—an ordinary encounter between solid flesh and solid rock—served as equivalent to a demonstration in logic: a "refutation" of the idealist philosophy of Bishop Berkeley.[7] The warm shaft of pain that no doubt mounted briefly through Johnson's massive leg carried, at least to his way of thinking, the full weight and dignity of British empiricism. We need to treat with respect the prosaic fact that pain is often wholly meaningless, if only because pain, in its mobility, tends not to rest in one state very long.

The Death of Ivan Ilych offers a vivid illustration of the mobility of pain. The accident that Ivan Ilych first dismissed as insignificant, a trivial event in the course of an ordinary life, becomes over time subject to reinterpretation. Understood with hindsight, his pain sheds its original air of meaninglessness and at last exposes the origin of an unseen chain of events. An insignificant pain finally turns scandalous and terrifying. Like the devil impersonating a country salesman, its insignificance turns out to be merely a clever disguise that death has employed in forcing an entry into Ivan Ilych's otherwise well-insulated life.

"Pain," writes Emily Dickinson, "has but one Acquaintance / And that is Death."[8] The dimly sensed kinship with death is what no doubt helps to account for our sometimes terrified responses to pain. Pain brings us as close as we will ever come to knowing our own annihilation. Here, for example, is a portrait offered in the eighteenth century by Johnson's friend Edmund Burke: "I say a man in great pain has his teeth set, his eye-brows are violently contracted, his forehead is wrinkled, his eyes are dragged inwards, and rolled with great vehemence, his hair stands on end, the voice is forced out in short shrieks and groans, and the whole fabric totters."[9] The conventions for depicting pain have changed somewhat in our time, but not the underlying association with bodily ruin. Burke's tottering human fabric suggests imminent, total destruction. For Ivan Ilych, too, pain quickly enters into this unstated but implicit embrace with death.

The meaning of pain, as Tolstoy develops the story of Ivan Ilych, expands beyond a symbolic union with death. Tolstoy shows us with remarkable clarity how pain continues to change over time. In fact, the specific changes he describes also reveal the larger sense in which pain—far from constituting a single, simple, unified entity—is inherently changeable. *The Death of Ivan Ilych* suggests that pain does not possess an unchanging essence but rather continues to move between the poles of meaninglessness and meaning, even as its meanings continue to change. It is as if pain were never fixed but perpetually in motion across the plane of a human life.

The variable meanings of pain in *The Death of Ivan Ilych* do not stop with the terrifying revelation of its link with death. All at once, after three days spent in screaming and struggle, Ivan Ilych suddenly experiences a deep calm, and his relation to pain changes once again. In effect, he passes through pain to a state of spiritual awakening. After this awakening, he is still aware of his pain—the pain has not diminished or disappeared—but now it somehow no longer matters, no longer torments him. He can address it as one might address an old enemy, long forgiven:

> "And the pain?" he asked himself, "What has become of it. Where are you, pain."
> He turned his attention to it.
> "Yes, here it is. Well, what of it? Let the pain be."[10]

The pain of Ivan Ilych now stands stripped of its terrors. His pain is, once again, simply pain.

Tolstoy's narrative describes a kind of circular motion. For Ivan Ilych, the pain which began in meaninglessness and later revealed its symbolic link with death finally came to rest once more in meaninglessness. Yet the two types of insignificance are profoundly different. Ivan Ilych's final disregard of pain marks the attainment of a spiritual, almost otherworldly vision in which human life looks vastly different than it did in his period of career-building and social-climbing. At the very end of his life, Ivan Ilych unexpectedly scales a religious height from which he views his pain—even agonizing, excruciating, terminal pain—as truly insignificant. His final *understanding* of his pain (his acceptance of its place and meaning in his life) is Ivan Ilych's profoundest act. It is, needless to say, an act of interpretation.

The peculiarly changeable nature of pain—its power to take on new meaning or abruptly to lose, to regain, or to transform the meaning it temporarily possesses—requires that we understand this most ancient and personal of human experiences as indelibly stamped by a specific place and time. Pain seems the quintessential solitary experience. We are probably never more alone than when severe pain invades us. Others appear to go about their business mostly unchanged, thinking that the world is just the same, but we know differently. The isolation of pain is undeniable. Yet it is thus especially important to recognize that pain is also always deeply social. The pain we feel has in large part been constructed or shaped by the culture from which we now feel excluded or cut off.

The Death of Ivan Ilych shows how pain inescapably absorbs the scent and feel of its social life. The screams that accompany Ivan Ilych's descent toward death also reflect, in another register, his struggle to retain a belief in the value of his secular, self-centered, commonplace, bourgeois existence. Further, Tolstoy encourages us to interpret Ivan Ilych's final painful struggle as a process of spiritual awakening. So again we encounter pain not simply as a biological fact but as suffused with social and religious meaning. Tolstoy portrays Ivan Ilych ultimately at peace with his pain in a detachment that suggests the attainment of a theological position almost outside of time. Yet this vision of a timeless, spiritualized pain, we must remember, is also the creation of a nineteenth-century Russian writer whose motives in portraying pain as timeless are unavoidably personal, social, and historical, rooted in the specific populist, utopian Christianity from which Tolstoy drew his strength.

The crucial point to emphasize is that pain—this most ancient of afflictions—never proves entirely timeless or solitary. The pain of Ivan Ilych occurs within the life of a bourgeois civil servant in late nineteenth-century Russia. It is in a sense quintessential bourgeois pain. Further, as readers of Tolstoy, we too are situated in a place and time that deeply influence how we interpret pain. Readers in a culture or period unconcerned with religious awakening—perhaps contemptuous of human spiritual life—will surely find Tolstoy's conclusion empty or almost incomprehensible. The only feature that proves truly consistent across cultures and periods is the process we watch unfolding with such clarity in *The Death of Ivan Ilych*, which draws pain inside a structure of changing interpretations.

†

History can offer us almost unlimited examples to illustrate the idea that pain is not just a biological fact but an experience in search of an interpretation. Most often, indeed, pain comes already interpreted for us by our social and cultural background. Consider for a moment the institution of slavery. The ancient world had a saying that a man loses half his soul the day he becomes a slave. In America, where black slaves were regarded as merely, and by law, a form of property, the white, racist mentality that made a slave system possible included, as a crucial provision, the belief that slaves were incapable of human feelings and desires. It thus became a paradoxical article of faith among slaveholders that slaves did not feel pain.

The faith was paradoxical because painful punishments served as a common means of discipline and control. Yet slaves might be beaten in the same spirit that horses were broken to the saddle or dogs trained. The slave felt enough pain to permit obedience but not enough pain to expose such methods (to the slaveholders who employed them) as inhuman. The belief thus persisted among white slaveowners and their apologists that blacks and whites lived in a very different relationship to pain. The pain of slaves was considered either wholly trivial or—however inconsistent the logic—richly deserved. Black pain, in the eyes of the white-run Southern culture, had in effect a minimal social existence. White pain, by contrast, cried out for relief.

We are dealing in this spoken and unspoken discourse on slavery not simply with ignorant prejudice or uneducated opinion. The prevailing Enlightenment thinkers on primitivism celebrated the pain-free state of the natural savage, who supposedly did not suffer the debilitating illnesses and nervous disorders of the "hypersensitive" European races. Thus the widely published observations of sophisticated travelers and amateur anthropologists lent credence to the white man's belief that his own pain was somehow special. "In our process of being civilized," wrote S. Weir Mitchell, the famous nineteenth-century American neurologist, "we have won, I suspect, intensified capacity to suffer. The savage does not feel pain as we do."[11]

Such familiar racist assumptions about black and white pain quickly surfaced to justify the white man's treatment of the American Indians. Like slaves, Indians, it was claimed, were inherently insensitive to pain. Pain thus helped to support the practice of suppression and genocide, since pain-free enemies made an especially terrifying prospect to settlers and soldiers, while in part excusing the cruelties apparently required to rid the world of such vicious, unfeeling foes. Nor was such thinking, turned back upon the community of black slaves, mere speculative philosophy disengaged from practice or simply a crude rationale for the brutality of plantation life. Dr. J. Marion Sims, America's most distinguished gynecological surgeon, performed excruciating experimental operations on slave women, which he justified by explaining that white women could not bear the pain. "Negresses . . . will bear cutting with nearly, if not quite, as much impunity as dogs and rabbits": so said the British *Medical and Chirurgical Review* in 1817.[12]

The distant past is not only a source of examples demonstrating beliefs that the pain of some particular group—blacks, Indians, women, madmen, children—either does not exist or (much the same thing) does not matter. The barbarous medical experiments carried out by Nazi doctors assumed that the pain felt by their victims simply did not count. In wartime, torture is justified on various pragmatic or tactical grounds, but ultimately it reflects a belief that the pain of an enemy has no status in law or in ethics. The enemy is the Other, and the Other does not feel pain as we do. My point here is not to replay familiar modern atrocities but simply to insist that such pain is deeply historical. A black slave woman in 1850 lives in a different relation to pain than does a white Russian magistrate in 1880. A Jew imprisoned in a Nazi death camp in 1943 lives a different relation to pain than does an American cancer patient in 1990.

Perhaps the best way to emphasize the historicality of pain is to choose an extreme example. The *Gentleman's Magazine* in 1751 reported an episode in which a butcher who was driving a flock of sheep punished one of the animals by cutting out its eyes. When objections were raised, he replied that he could do what he liked with his property. The pain of a piece of property seemed—at least to this eighteenth-century English butcher—completely irrelevant. If we cringe at such a report, our response may owe less to innate revulsion than to the effectiveness of Victorian crusades against cruelty to animals.[13] The slaveholder Simon Legree threatens the noble slave Tom in Harriet Beecher Stowe's American classic *Uncle Tom's Cabin* (1852) in words that suggest how easy it is to disregard the pain of anything or anyone we regard as insignificant: "An't I yer master? Didn't I pay down twelve hundred dollars cash, for all there is inside yer old cussed black shell? An't yer mine, now, body and soul?" The next time we see Tom he lies "groaning and bleeding" in an abandoned storeroom full of broken and damaged goods.[14]

†

The meanings of pain are sometimes so deeply bound up with the historical culture within which they occur that an outsider may find them utterly incomprehensible. In *The Iliad*, for example, Greeks and Trojans suffer terrifying injuries described in anatomical precision. Here (from book twenty) is the Greek hero Achilleus cutting a typical swath through the Trojans:

Now he hit Echeklos the son of Agenor/ with the hilted sword, hewing against his head in the middle/ so all the sword was smoking with blood, and over both eyes/ closed the red death and the strong destiny. Now Deukalion/ was struck in the arm, at a place in the elbow where the tendons/ come together. There through the arm Achilleus transfixed him/ with the bronze spearhead, and he, arm hanging heavy, waited/ and looked death in the face. Achilleus struck with the sword's edge/ at his neck, and swept the helmed head far away, and the marrow/ gushed from the neckbone, and he went down to the ground at full length.[15]

Such moments typify the bloody panorama of Homeric battle. Homer—or the ancient oral bards who bear his name—dismembered the human body with loving inventiveness. What such moments rarely contain, however, is an extended description of anguish or agony. Homeric warriors normally expire all at once in a black mist or in a bone-crunching clatter of armor; they groan, gasp, and vomit blood; but, in an epic where we have little access to the interior life of the characters, they seldom die in pain.

The strange painlessness of Homeric combat might well leave a modern reader with the sense that something crucial in the depiction is missing: as if the sound were suddenly switched off during a lavish Hollywood battlefield scene. Yet two crucial scenes in book five depart from the formula of painless combat. They concern a moment when the deities Aphrodite and Ares appear at Troy and are wounded in separate encounters. Their unrestrained shrieks and bellows—truly Olympian pain—give us a standard for measuring the almost inaudible wounds of the human warriors. Here is Ares—god of war—stabbed in the belly with a spear: "Then Ares the brazen bellowed/ with a sound as great as nine thousand men make, or ten thousand,/ when they cry as they carry into the fighting the fury of the war god./ And a shivering seized hold alike on Achaians and Trojans/ in their fear at the bellowing of battle-insatiate Ares."[16] Suddenly the volume is turned up full blast.

The pain of Ares and Aphrodite is especially significant because Homer normally characterizes the gods as living at ease and as strangers to death. Man lives in a completely different dimension. "Among all creatures that breathe on earth and crawl on it," Zeus intones, "there is not anywhere a thing more dismal than man is."[17] Perhaps, like Ares in his pain, only the immortal gods are permitted to be fully human. At any rate, *The Iliad* contains only a few scenes of human conflict where Homer explicitly mentions pain or dwells on the experience of injury.[18] In fact, pain concerns Homer far less than death, and death too seems to exist in detachment from the agonies of dying. The most common descriptions of wounding seem entirely external, almost impersonal, as if the poet had no knowledge of pain. At other times pain is mentioned simply to emphasize its immediate disappearance in scenes of medical treatment or divine assistance, often both together. Typical is the prayer to Apollo by Glaukos ("a man in pain"). As Homer tells us, Apollo "at once made the pains to stop."[19]

The absence of pain in *The Iliad* no doubt owes much to the conventions of ancient narrative, whereby we have only oblique or indirect access to the consciousness of the characters. No doubt it also served a specific social purpose by persuading its male audience that they had nothing to fear from pain, at least when they suffered in a great cause. The epic world shows us how warriors accept their fate with heroic equanimity. Yet there is an uncannily accurate, if unintentional, realism in the Homeric account. In 1946 Lieutenant Colonel Henry K. Beecher published a classic study entitled "The Pain in Men Wounded in Battle." He drew his data from prolonged action on the Venafro and Cassino fronts and later at the Anzio beachhead in World War II. "There is a common belief," he writes, "that wounds are inevitably associated with pain and, further, that the more extensive the wound, the worse the pain. Observation of men who had just been wounded in combat showed this generalization to be misleading."[20]

To his astonishment, Beecher found that among seriously wounded soldiers who were questioned within twelve hours of receiving their wounds, 25 percent reported only slight pain and 32 percent reported no pain at all. This unexpected data demanded an explanation. Beecher found that he could not explain the strange absence of battlefield pain by assuming that badly wounded men have a general decrease in sensitivity. On the contrary, they protested vigorously at an ineptly punctured vein, for example. Yet 75 percent also felt so little pain in the hours immediately following their wound that they did not want medication. Beecher postulated that a civilian similarly injured in an automobile crash will not show the same disinterest. Emotions surrounding the events may have made all the difference:

Strong emotion can block pain. That is common experience. In this connection it is important to consider the position of the soldier: his wound suddenly releases him from an exceedingly dangerous environment, one filled with fatigue, discomfort, anxiety, fear, and real danger of death, and gives him a ticket to the safety of the hospital. His troubles are about over, or he thinks they are. He overcompensates and becomes euphoric. Whether this actually reduces the pain remains unproved. On the other hand, the civilian's accident marks the beginning of disaster for him.[21]

The central point is that here again, at Anzio as at ancient Troy, we encounter pain not as a timeless or universal phenomenon but rather as something anchored in a specific time and place: in combat or leisure, in soldier or civilian, in butcher, suburbanite, or slave.

Beecher's explanation surely contains a useful measure of truth. We now know that under conditions of stress and shock the body produces opiatelike analgesic peptides that may well account for much of the strange painlessness among recently wounded soldiers. Yet it is now also well established that the mind and emotions can powerfully exaggerate or diminish the perception of pain.[22] Thus the painlessness immediately following injury may yield later to a pain made all the worse by a sudden flood of grief and fear. Beecher offers a compelling description of the mental and emotional experience of the soldiers he examined. He reviews the extreme and unique daily strain faced by troops under fire, including anxiety, stress, and sorrow over the loss of friends; the sights and sounds of prolonged combat; exposure to harsh weather, inadequate food and drink, loss of sleep, exhaustion. "On top of all this," he continues, "the newly wounded man suddenly has to face the consequences of his wound. His arm is injured—will he lose it? There is blood around his genitals—will he be impotent? That wound in his chest—is he going to die?"[23] The pain cannot be separated from the personal questions and social meanings it inescapably evokes.

†

When we begin to explore the multiple meanings that humankind has discovered in pain or that pain almost always discloses and conveys, we unfold a story in which the meanings we create (or accept or intuit) can prove at least as important as the medicines we consume. Nowhere is the relation between pain and meaning more important than in the history of religion. Here, for example, is the famous seventeenth-century philosopher and mathematician Blaise Pascal in his *Prayer to Ask God for the Good Use of Sickness*:

Make me fully understand that the ills of the body are nothing else than the punishment and the encompassing symbol for the ills of the soul. O Lord, let them be the remedy, by making me aware, through the pain that I feel, of the pain that I did not feel in my soul, deeply sick though it was and covered with sores. Because, Lord, the greatest sickness is insensibility. . . . Let me feel this pain sharply, so that I can make whatever is left of my life a continual penance to wash away the offenses I have committed.[24]

For Pascal, pain is not just a sensation he feels or endures but something he interprets, something he enfolds within a system or circle of thought that endows it with meaning.

The religious meanings that sickness enfolds for Pascal prove both traditional and personal. It is highly traditional that he should interpret his pain both as a divine punishment and as a continuous act of penance or expiation. Indeed, the Christian view of pain as penance or contrition flows directly from the parallel that links bodily pain to Christ's suffering on the Cross. Pascal also adds, however, a more personal, almost mathematical interpretation that regards bodily pain as a sign that refers, as if by a law of opposites, to the absence of pain in his soul. His affliction thus makes sense for Pascal only within the Christian schema that divides humankind between a perishable sinful body and an immortal soul. His pain is thus filtered through his understanding of an entire universe. In an age of science, we too tend to read our pain in ways that confirm or support or illuminate a general understanding of the cosmos.

Pascal's experience should remind us that Christianity, at least in its Augustinian versions, has consistently explained pain as the effect of original sin.[25] Such pain becomes a personal and internal sign of man's disobedience to God. It may not seem especially comforting to interpret pain as a divine punishment, but such an interpretation at least defines a world very different from one in which God is absent, unconcerned, or, as

Nietzsche would have it, dead. Further, a theological (as opposed to, say, medical) interpretation of pain allowed the development of numerous subreadings which understood suffering as, for example, a test or trial of faith or means of redemption.

The main thought to emphasize is this: pain is not just blindly felt or unreflectively endured as a series of biochemical impulses. It changes with its place in human history. Like Pascal, we experience our pain as it is interpreted, enfolded within formal or informal systems of thought that endow it with a time-bound meaning—whether theological, economic, scientific, or psychological. We make sense of pain in much the same way that we make sense of the world. Sometimes pain can even reveal to us beliefs and values we did not know we held. When we are in pain, the most commonplace actions and events, such as going to the movies, taking a walk, or driving a car, suddenly seem like invaluable privileges that have been cruelly taken away. Pain can reorder priorities in a hurry. It can show us what truly matters.

It is worth remembering that our pain—however modern and personal—also links us with a primitive world that has now almost completely vanished. Human bones exhumed from early burial sites sometimes reveal small round holes bored through the skull (fig. 3). These holes are the result of a prehistoric surgery called trepanation, which is still practiced in primitive areas.[26] Trepanation involves removal of a piece of the skull (called the calvarium) without damage to the underlying membranes and tissue. The medicine man or witch doctor had various purposes for drilling or, alternately, scraping, rasping, cutting, and sawing these ominous holes. Ancient skulls in Peru, for example, show that the Incas employed trepanation as a standard treatment for head wounds received in battle. Apparently, if we may judge from the evidence of healed bone, most patients survived the operation.

One common purpose for trepanation was to relieve the pain caused— as everyone believed—by evil spirits. Almost any affliction from headaches to insanity might be attributed to an influx of demons sent by an enemy (through black magic) or arrived in punishment for the violation of a tribal taboo. In such cultures, people understand their pain as supernatural, and the witch doctor thus bored holes in the skull so that the evil spirits had a way out. Added to the burden of pain, then, was the

FIGURE 3. Ancient skulls showing circular incisions of trepanation.

knowledge that you were under attack—invaded and inhabited—by demonic powers. Such beliefs, of course, are not restricted to prehistoric times. Trepanation is still practiced in parts of Africa. Nineteenth-century artists from Cruickshank and Gillray to Daumier found images of the demonic a half-serious language for describing colic, gout, headache, and various painful afflictions that science could do little to relieve (figs. 4–6). Today the Jackson Memorial Hospital in Miami retains several voodoo doctors on call in order to treat Haitian patients who believe themselves bewitched.

Demons, however, were sometimes merely an indirect cause of this prehistoric pain. The real source of trouble might lie in the *absence* of a protecting spirit or power. For example, a belief developed in the second millennium B.C. that a personal god—something like a guardian angel in later theology—could offer protection from demons. Thus one of the more poignant fragments of ancient Babylonian writing describes the condition of a person unprotected against the strategies of the demonic world:

> One who has no god, as he walks along the street,
> Headache envelops him like a garment.[27]

THE MEANINGS OF PAIN

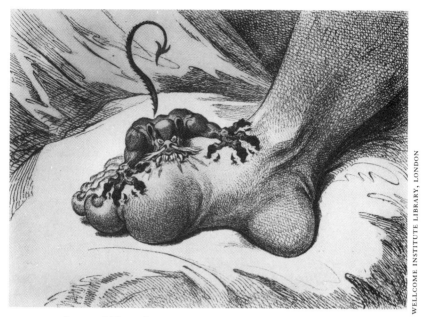

FIGURE 4. James Gillray (1756–1815). *The Gout* (1799).

The godless man is wrapped up in pain. Pain here becomes the sign of his bereft and godless state. It is no doubt vastly different from the headache experienced by a Wall Street executive as the bond market mysteriously plummets, yet we are less far removed from the world of evil spirits than we sometimes think.

Pain in the ancient world had almost the character of a cash transaction. In its meaning it resembled a currency passed back and forth between gods and men. The bloody rites of the Mayan civilization in southern Mexico and central America, for example, involved ceremonial beheadings and human sacrifices in which priests ripped the heart from a living victim in order to placate the gods. Such brutal acts seem to repel analysis, yet they clearly made sense within Mayan culture. Imagine living in a world where violent and unpredictable gods at any moment might decide to crush an entire people by destroying crops or favoring their enemies. In a world terrorized by cruel deities, the ritualized pain of human sacrifice served to buy peace. It offered to the gods a measured, symbolic quantity of pain in order to limit the truly immeasurable suffering that the gods in their anger or whimsy might decide to pour down.

THE MEANINGS OF PAIN

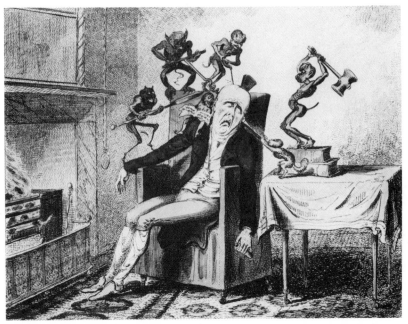

FIGURE 5. George Cruickshank (1792–1878). *The Head Ache* (1835).

†

What Pascal and ancient Babylonian wisdom literature help us understand, indirectly but inescapably, is how far we in our culture have built our own historical relation to pain upon denial. The modern denial of pain—through pills, narcotics, alcohol, pornography, televised violence, social isolation, and the endless pursuit of youth and pleasure—will soon concern us directly. Its sources and consequences are in some ways the indirect subject of this book. At the moment, however, it is useful to reflect on why and how earlier, preanesthetic cultures responded to pain not with denial but with curious forms of affirmation. One brief example must suffice.

Pain for medieval Christians served as a sign and means of contact with the divine, as we have seen. Had they denied pain, the medieval Christian community would have erased its spiritual value. A meaningless pain would threaten to cast them back upon an utterly meaningless world. They had good reason, then, to transform pain from a private sensation into a public spectacle, in the manner of the flagellants who during times of plague paraded through the streets lashing themselves in guilt, pen-

FIGURE 6. Honoré Daumier (1808–1879). *La Colique* (1833).

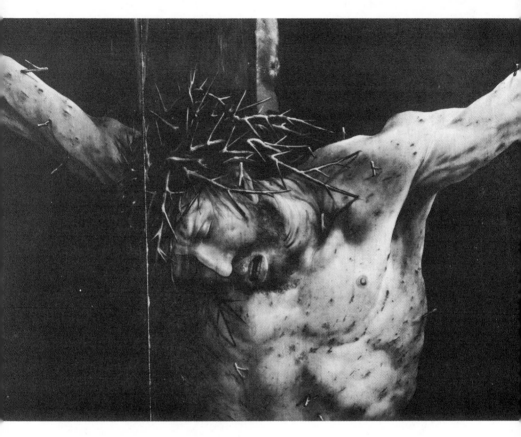

FIGURE 7. Matthias Grünewald (d. 1528). Detail of Crucifixion
(*c.* 1505–1515). GIRAUDON/ART RESOURCE, NEW YORK

ance, and hope of mercy.[28] Such spectacles drew their meaning from the
central reality of medieval life: the human pain of the Crucifixion.

No painter has captured the mystery of this central Christian rite—
the suffering god—more vividly than the late fifteenth-century German
court painter Matthias Grünewald (fig. 7). It is a painting that uses pain
to emphasize the "human-ness" of Jesus and that gives point to the troubled prayer he makes in Gethsemane: "My Father, if it be possible, let this
cup pass from me." Martin Scorsese's film *The Last Temptation of Christ*
(1988) also seeks to restore the human pain of the Crucifixion by an opening scene that depicts the execution of a prisoner nailed to a cross in an
act so bloody and shocking (the thick, heavy spikes pounded through
bone and flesh) that the decorative crosses worn today like jewelry sud-

denly resemble nothing so much as little icons of forgetting and denial. Pain in the Middle Ages was a kind of internal crucifix.

Our own strong need to deny and to desanctify pain, whatever it says about our scientific, drug-taking culture, may also have much to do with the bloody course of our own century. In Europe and Russia between 1914 and 1945 some seventy million people died in warfare, concentration camps, massacres, and famine. Film archives show us emaciated bodies tossed like garbage into corpse-filled pits. We no doubt find it impossible to understand or to grasp what so much pain entails. There is perhaps some consolation in the claim by C. S. Lewis that no one can experience pain as a collective sum.[29] No matter how much pain we witness or imagine, according to Lewis, we can *feel* only our own singular pain, much as a single glass can hold only one glassful.

This claim may be technically true, but it also ignores what happens to our minds and emotions when the scale of disaster escalates. The suffering of a community or the brutalization of an entire race has consequences that Lewis underestimates. Even if we cannot absorb in our own bones each gram of human pain, as surely we cannot, the genocidal program of mass murder carried out under Hitler or Pol Pot inevitably affects how we think, how we act, how we feel. Pain on such an immeasurable order of magnitude will very likely defeat or cancel thought. The mind simply blocks what it cannot comprehend, casting us back as a culture on doomed escapes into amnesia, repression, and denial. Quite literally, we can make nothing of it.

The failure of interpretation in cases of unthinkable suffering and massive disaster helps indirectly to emphasize how important it is that we ordinarily, if tacitly, understand a meaning for our pain. The importance grows particularly clear in times of unusual conflict and rapid change. Within a homogeneous culture, that is, certain well-established meanings (such as the penitential and redemptive quality of pain for medieval Christians) remain stable for long periods. For example, few people in the Middle Ages openly disputed the belief that sinners would face an eternity of torment in Hell. Pain thus gave Christians a taste of what it meant—theologically speaking—to be damned. It brought theology down to earth. It put the fear of God inside one's own flesh and bones (fig. 8). When the uniformity of belief breaks down, however, differences about pain expose and often exacerbate the veiled conflicts that now erupt into open disagreements or warfare. Such differences offer vivid evidence that individuals and cultures tend to construct—rather than simply feel—their pain.

Mark Zborowski in 1969 published a fascinating (but now seldom cited) book entitled *People in Pain*.[30] He held the unusual position of staff anthropologist at the Mount Zion Hospital and Medical Center in San Francisco, and what makes his work so valuable is that Zborowski studied attitudes toward pain among male veterans at the Mount Zion Hospital between 1951 and 1954. Thanks to his work we possess a unique snapshot of American life during the aftermath of World War II. We might expect that Zborowski would find a general agreement in the attitudes toward pain among men who had fought together and survived the same disaster. We would be half right.

The men Zborowski interviewed fell into four groups, which he classified by ethnic origin as Irish, Jewish, Italian, and Old American. (The latter group referred not to senior citizens but to white, Anglo-Saxon, usually Protestant families established in America for more than three generations: in short, WASPS.) What Zborowski discovered was that Jews and Italians tended to be uninhibited and expressive in their response to pain, while Irish and Old American patients tended to hide their pain, to avoid company, to engage in strategies of silence and denial.

The strikingly homogeneous behavior within each group was matched at times by other similarities that cut across ethnic lines. For example, regardless of ethnic origin, many patients from lower social classes similarly interpreted pain as a threat of unemployment and financial ruin. ("When my back goes," said one veteran, "everything goes. You are out of business.") In responding to this threat, the Irish and Old American patients searched for interpretations of their pain that would minimize the danger. They gave every pain a safe or nonfatal explanation: it was only a cramp, a backache, a sore muscle. In effect, their responses to pain included overlapping attitudes based on social class as well as on ethnic origin. The main point is that pain extracted more than simply an individual response. As Zborowski concluded, "People responded to their pain not only as individuals, but also as Italians, Jews, Negroes, or Nordics."[31]

The wards of Mount Zion Hospital offered Zborowski strong evidence

FIGURE 8. Clerics in Hell: fifteenth-century French illustration to
Augustine's *City of God*.

THE MEANINGS OF PAIN

that pain tends to take on the meanings that various social groups assign it. He found that among Irish patients, for example, pain often became an occasion or source of pride. He asked the Irish patients what they did to relieve their pain. The following laconic answers from three Irish patients are typical:

—Well, what can you do? Have to take it.
—Just have to take it, that's all.
—I don't mind taking it. I can take it if I had to.[32]

These responses convey more meaning than their bluntness and brevity at first suggest. The Irish patients in effect interpret their pain as something to be "taken" much as a fighter might pride himself on being able to take a punch. In this interpretation, taking pain is an action, not passive suffering, and the ability to absorb punishment becomes a semiheroic sign of courage and endurance. Taking pain means refusing to surrender. In their silence, the Irish patients win a moral victory by showing that pain cannot crush them. It can batter them, but they can take it. They can make it mean something beyond defeat.

The Irish interpretation of pain finds almost its polar opposite in the attitudes of the Jewish patients whom Zborowski interviewed in the same San Francisco hospital. Like Augustinian Christianity, Jewish scripture and Jewish teaching regard pain as a punishment for sin, as a test of faith, and, most important, as a possible means of redemption. Yet another prominent tradition within Judaism views pain as simply and completely evil. Nothing good can come of pain. One Jewish patient in the mid-1950s described his experience this way:

Well, I tell you what I think was pain—and to me I think it's a lot of pain. Do you know what a gall bladder attack is? Well, for eight months I took it. I rolled on the floor from this wall to that wall—chewing the carpet. For eight months! Now do you think that's pain?

Although the reference to "taking" pain suggests similarities with the Irish patients, this is a very different style of absorbing punishment. It is a style galvanized by the desire to get rid of the pain at any cost, as if pain were a demon or ferocious animal. The speaker continues:

I bang my head against the wall, I've shoved my face into boiling water, I've taken heat lamps and gotten so close to it as to where I've seared the skin. I have rolled around where one minute I'm lying prone and the next minute I'm up with my head buried between my legs; the next minute I'm walking around, lying down again, trying all sorts of things that might give me relief.[33]

For the hyperactive, hyperverbal Jew, taking pain is not a source of pride or a sign of courage. It is an unavoidable evil that sets off a desperate struggle to escape. The wild contortions seem to guarantee that his pain cannot be ignored or denied. His pain means merely that he is a man under assault.

Zborowski openly confronts the criticism that his research conceals or promotes a racist agenda. The responses to pain that he discovered no doubt fit ethnic or racist stereotypes that now seem very dated. Yet, stereotypes will inevitably emerge if our response to pain is always a sociocultural artifact. The risk that stereotypes will prove offensive belongs to the facts of life when research moves outside the laboratory. "The physiology of pain," Zborowski writes, "acquires cultural and social attributes, and its analysis calls for investigation not only in laboratories and clinics but also in the complex maze of society."[34] Although a few medical books now include brief comments on the ways in which culture influences our experience of pain, doctors have not yet widely pondered the implications of Zborowski's basic insight.[35] Medicine itself constitutes a powerful culture or subculture that promotes its own stereotypes, such as the picture of the human body as machine (which may explain a lot about the medical mistreatment of pain). Zborowski reveals what contemporary research increasingly confirms. In addition to their status as biological events, pain and illness are always cultural artifacts.

The day is still distant, however, when most doctors will treat patients as if pain belongs as fully to human social structures as to the structure of the nervous system. Science prefers to work with airtight, repeatable experiments, and pain measured outside the laboratory supplies very messy data (as cultural variants keep breaking in). Yet skeptics who complain that they cannot duplicate Zborowski's research miss the point completely. Social responses to pain will not remain unchanging because society rarely stands still. The world of the early 1950s that Zborowski studied now survives mainly in old films, old magazines, and television reruns. We cannot reproduce Zborowski's results because they apply to a cultural world that has undergone, like the old neighborhoods, an almost total transformation.

The surest way to invalidate Zborowski's research would be to duplicate it today. In a new sociocultural world of MTV, nuclear warheads, cocaine, yuppies, medicare, and international late consumer capitalism, the assimilated offspring of Zborowski's Jewish and Irish immigrants will not respond to pain exactly as their grandfathers did. Zborowski's laconic Irishman and galvanic Jew may well seem like characters from a late-night movie, because that is among the few places where we can still find them today. Yet their grandchildren, who experience pain within the context of a new mass culture that most often repudiates earlier styles of behavior, are no less thoroughly caught up in a process that imbues our pain with meanings of which we are, in most cases, completely unaware.

What makes this new culture so puzzling and so frightening is that the pain we experience today seems somehow separated from its past. We have denial without pride, suffering without notice. The colorful ethnic diversity that Zborowski discovered now seems almost comfortingly human compared with the gray tide of affliction now sweeping across the land. Indeed, chronic pain has begun to spread with the speed of suburban shopping malls. This apparent explosion of pain proves even more demoralizing because it is almost invisible. We simply don't see the damage all around us. It is thus crucial that we learn more about the crisis in chronic pain—the product of a quite recent, unique sociocultural order—and ask how we seem to be holding up, or not holding up, under its high-speed, high-stress, high-tech changes. It may be the most damaging change of all that the new world of chronic pain, which finds its most prominent symbol in the proliferating offices of freshly opened pain centers and clinics, is a world in which pain has become almost utterly without meaning.

3

AN INVISIBLE EPIDEMIC

Pain—has an Element of Blank—
It cannot recollect
When it begun—or if there were
A time when it was not.

EMILY DICKINSON[1]

HE WHITENED BONES dug up from prehistoric sites reveal abscessed teeth and unhealed fractures that provide unmistakable evidence of suffering among our ancestors. One fragment from a human skeleton still contains an ancient stone arrowhead embedded in the sternum (fig. 9). A shot striking the sternum so directly in the front may not be fatal, since it would penetrate no vital organs, but it would make the victim easy prey, and it is certain that this New World casualty did not survive to extract the arrow.[2] We could not speak the language of such ancient ancestors or perhaps even recognize it as human speech. Yet we probably believe that we can understand the pain they felt when an arrow suddenly tore through the skin and bone, as if the entire chest were on fire. Still further back in time, however, our remotest ancestors perhaps lived in a world where consciousness operated in ways we cannot imagine, like madness. Perhaps they understood no more (and no less) about their own individual pain than a lion or tiger understands.

The awareness that I trust will emerge from the evidence gathered in this book is that the pain we feel today differs from the pain our ancestors felt. It is not even the same pain that Freud's cultivated and well-heeled European patients experienced less than a century ago. Too much has changed. Today we experience pain within a cultural field as unique and original as the skylines of our major cities. We take for granted a way of understanding pain that would have seemed very odd not merely to Plato

FIGURE 9. Ancient fragment of human sternum with flint arrowhead still embedded.

and Aristotle or to Shakespeare and Cervantes or to Jeremy Bentham and Cardinal Newman but also to our own grandparents and great-grandparents. The social forces responsible for this momentous change are so powerful that wholly escaping them is almost as difficult as evading the earth's gravitational field.

Differences, then, are our subject: differences between ancient and modern pain, between visible and invisible pain, between acute and chronic pain. The reason for exploring such differences is quite simple.

They help to explain how we got where we are now—how the present constitutes an enormous break with the past—and what the future may bring. For a modern patient struggling with torments no less debilitating (and often far more mysterious) than an arrow shot directly into the chest, the differences we will examine all converge on the curious new social and medical institution known as the pain clinic. It is a door that anyone who wishes to understand pain today must open.

†

The white coat I was assigned after long, formal negotiations with three or four layers of administrative bureaucracy gave me an immediate stab of self-doubt. But as I walked from the Department of Anesthesiology to the distant location of the pain clinic, I felt growing within me the dangerous exhilaration that no doubt inspires the world's greatest impostors. My years as a professor had never conferred such a mantle of power. A handful of the more obsequious, confused, or respectful students invariably addressed me as doctor—technically correct in view of my doctoral degree—but among my colleagues in the humanities only the terminally insecure encouraged such Germanic formality. My main problem, as I struggled to imitate a confident stride through the long, indistinguishable corridors of the hospital, was trying not to appear lost.

I will not deny that I enjoyed the sense of power that came with my white coat. The desire never seized me to dash off a prescription or to suture up a wound, but I made a point of not switching back to civilian dress for my return across the river to the main campus. (Consider the genius required to place the medical school and English department on opposite sides of a river.) Inside the hospital I blended into the surroundings like an average, slightly overage resident. I smiled a reassuring professional smile to patients who seemed particularly anxious. My white coat, of course, told a monstrous lie, but only about me. Patients expect a doctor to radiate competence, and I did not want to disappoint them by looking nervous or wandering aimlessly through the halls.

A cold panic, however, stopped me in mid-sentence as I finally asked directions at a nurses' station. Our bookshelves at home as I was growing up contained several slim collections of humor among my father's ponderous medical textbooks and journals. One anecdote described an especially unpleasant three-star general who was a patient at a military hospital. In revenge, the long-suffering staff left him lying face down for twenty minutes with a daffodil instead of a thermometer sticking out of his rectum. Medical humor, I had noticed, tends to be a little rough and anal. As I walked away clutching a diagram of the quickest path to the pain clinic, I secretly glanced back to see whether the nurses were slumped against the filing cabinets in laughter.

On the neat, red-inked nametag of my cherished white coat I had just read, horrified, the name "Dr. O. Bastard."

Several weeks later—when I trusted the pain clinic staff well enough to ask about my shameful nametag—I received assurance that Dr. Oliver Bastard had been a visiting resident, from overseas, who on returning home simply left his coat in the departmental closet. (Sure, I thought, a story I can't verify: perfect.) Eventually I came to believe this explanation, but it was too late. I could not help secretly thinking of my nametag as an allegorical statement. It asserted something beyond my illegitimate claims to a white coat. It reminded me that doctors and patients belong to fundamentally different worlds and that the experience of pain in our culture always looks very different depending on which world you belong to. Yet whenever I entered the freshly painted doors of the pain clinic, the distance between these two worlds began to shrink a little. Here doctors and patients seemed to be working out a new understanding.

†

A new understanding seems absolutely necessary if we hope to deal with the unprecedented crisis in chronic pain. Indeed, the most distinctive, insidious feature of this contemporary epidemic, as it has been rightly called, is that we cannot recognize it as an epidemic. Disasters such as AIDS or drug addiction leave a visible wreckage behind. They also openly change our behavior and our culture: they alter our sex lives, infiltrate our homes and schools, dominate our films, books, and newscasts. Chronic pain, by contrast, generally escapes notice, even though one in ten Americans suffers from its often crippling assault. Thus, as a way of bringing the problem of chronic pain into sharper focus, it will be useful before we enter the clinic to shift our gaze in space and time. The world we have recently left behind was a place where no one would call pain invisible.

The medicalization of pain is indeed so characteristic of our own time that historians seeking a date to mark the advent of modernism might do far worse than select 1899, when salicylic acid was first commercially developed into acetylsalicylic acid, popularly known as aspirin. It is hard to imagine either medicine or the modern world without aspirin. Aspirin achieved such instant fame in the early twentieth century that it even figured prominently in World War I.[3] The (German) Bayer Chemical Company held manufacturing secrets and world patent rights. Britain therefore offered a large cash prize for anyone able to "reformulate" aspirin and to discover a workable manufacturing process. At the German surrender, the British Custodian of Enemy Property sequestered the Bayer trade name "aspirin," which thereafter became simply the generic term for acetylsalicylic acid. It was a rich prize. Today the annual world output of aspirin runs well over thirty thousand tons: a figure of course that represents merely a fraction of the total consumption of legal and illegal substances for relieving pain.[4]

Probably no other drug—not even such modern favorites as Valium or cocaine—has established itself so firmly in our culture as aspirin. Yet aspirin is far more than our most common over-the-counter analgesic. It is an emblem of our immense faith in chemical assaults on pain. Americans spend more than four billion dollars annually for various painkilling medications.[5] This mountain of pills, if it could be measured, might stand as a monument to our belief in a medical solution to the problem of pain, like the weird statue (still standing in the Boston Public Garden) that commemorates the first surgical use of ether. Dedicated in the mid-nineteenth century, this four-sided pillar topped by a stone healer ministering to his stone patient bears on its pedestal the brief, unfulfilled prophecy from Revelation: "And there shall be no more pain."

Our nineteenth-century predecessors had good reason for erecting a statue to commemorate the surgical use of ether. The year 1846 effectively divided human history into periods so different that we really cannot recapture what life was like before that date. Before 1846 surgical procedures—from pulling teeth to amputations—took place without any form of effective modern anesthesia (figs. 10 and 11). Early dentists set up makeshift wooden platforms in the center of town and pulled teeth with hideous elongated pincers the size of fireplace tongs. In England before 1743 surgeons still belonged to the guild of barbers. The best educated and most highly skilled surgeons operated in the patient's home. On the appointed day, one can easily imagine the mounting sense of dread as the

FIGURE 10. Anonymous. *Acute Pain* (1810).

FIGURE 11. Thomas Rowlandson (1756–1827). *Amputation* (1785).

AN INVISIBLE EPIDEMIC

carriage stops in the street, as the surgeon knocks at the door, as he slowly climbs the stairs with perhaps three or four burly assistants to hold you down.

The novelist Fanny Burney—perhaps best remembered for her friendship with Samuel Johnson—has left us a detailed account of the mastectomy she underwent in Paris on September 30, 1811. No woman would forget such a date, just as Samuel Pepys each year celebrated the anniversary of his successful operation for removal of an agonizing kidney stone the size of a tennis ball. Her only preparation was a wine cordial, possibly containing laudanum. When the surgeon and his assistants arrive—"7 Men in black"—she is at first startled and upset. ("Why so many? & without leave?") Fear grips her with such force that she cannot utter a syllable in protest. She regains a measure of dignity and composure in the presence of these overbearing black-robed figures by somehow getting to the bed under her own power and refusing to let them hold her down. Over her face they drape a transparent cambric handkerchief through which she watches the chief surgeon trace on her breast the path his knife will take.

With a passion for exactness, Burney records every detail of this brutal operation. She describes the knife plunged into her breast, "cutting through veins—arteries—flesh—nerves." She describes the air rushing into the wound like a mass of "sharp & forked poniards"—the surgeon "cutting against the grain" as he repeatedly scrapes at her breast bone. Who would not be impressed by her enormous courage? It was not, however, a courage of silence and denial. Modern readers will find it hard to forget the scream that she says lasted uninterruptedly during the entire time of the incision. "I almost marvel that it rings not in my Ears still!" she wrote afterward: "so excruciating was the agony."[6]

This preanesthetic world of pain is now enormously difficult, if not impossible, to reenter. Like Burney, thousands of less eloquent patients somehow endured their surgery without more than a stiff drink in preparation. Yet it is not just modern patients who find this ordeal almost unthinkable. Courage was required on both sides of the knife. For example, one admiring modern physician—who had studied with the earlier nineteenth-century surgeons steeled to the demands of cutting into the bodies of fully conscious patients—described his predecessors as if recalling a race of vanished demigods: "They were indeed giants in the surgical profession in those pre-anesthetic days, men of iron nerve and indomitable will, who could bring themselves to inflict such untold anguish upon their fellow-men, even in the hope of ultimate relief."[7] It is a tribute offered as if from a different universe.

The tribute was offered in 1914 by John M. T. Finney, professor of clinical surgery at Johns Hopkins, in an address delivered at the Massachusetts General Hospital. There, sixty-eight years earlier on October 16, 1846, a group of skeptical doctors and medical students witnessed the first public demonstration of the surgical uses of ether. To their astonishment, a Boston dentist named William Morton with an ether-soaked sponge and a hastily contrived inhaling apparatus (delivered only a few hours earlier) succeeded in putting the patient into a deep sleep. Then the distinguished senior surgeon John Collins Warren—as surprised as anyone—effortlessly removed a large tumor from the patient's jaw in what was otherwise fated to be an operation of unimaginable pain.

Warren knew that few spectators in the room were prepared to believe the almost miraculous event they had just witnessed. The scene required such a complete reversal of previous modes of thought that even eyewitnesses suspected it was a carnival trick. New England in the mid-nineteenth century sheltered a host of itinerant snake-oil salesmen, mesmerists, and assorted amateur chemists all professing to rid the world of pain. Even as late as 1890, to the accompaniment of a loud brass band, an American Indian named Sequah drew large crowds in London with his offer to extract teeth free and painlessly.[8] Warren knew how to rise to an occasion. He faced his audience with the full authority of a Victorian sage. "Gentlemen," he announced to the disbelieving students and colleagues assembled in the operating theater, "this is no humbug."[9]

The events of October 16, 1846 changed more than the art of surgery. (No longer was the best surgeon necessarily the fastest.) They also forever transformed our cultural assumptions about pain. The anniversary came to be known as Ether Day, and each October 16, for well over half a century, the Massachusetts General Hospital celebrated the event with ceremonies and distinguished lecturers. The renowned Oliver Wendell Holmes delivered one of the first celebratory addresses. It was the equally famous nineteenth-century American neurologist and popular novelist S. Weir Mitchell, however, who best captured the sense of irreversible change. In 1896—speaking at the Massachusetts General Hospital on the fiftieth anniversary of Ether Day—he recited a long poem he had composed for the occasion, including these dramatic couplets:

Whatever triumphs still shall hold the mind,
Whatever gift shall yet enrich mankind,
Ah! here no hour shall strike through all the years,
No hour as sweet as when hope, doubt, and fears,
'Mid deepening stillness, watched one eager brain,
With Godlike will, decree the Death of Pain.[10]

After 1846 it was not just medicine but human life that would never be quite the same again.

†

Pain, of course, did not die. We still inhabit a planet filled with more pain—from war, poverty, disease, injury, and neglect—than an entire mountain range of pills could erase. In fact, we now face an unprecedented dilemma. Although we possess not only ether and its subsequent generations of chemical painkillers but also innumerable over-the-counter remedies, the epidemic of chronic pain seems to be gaining ground. The pills in a sense just make things worse. Treatment at pain centers and pain clinics often begins with a period of detoxification in which patients gradually withdraw from the host of ineffectual and even harmful medications that they consume, fruitlessly, in hopes of relief.

Weir Mitchell would probably be surprised at the most recent evidence that he was somewhat premature in announcing the death of pain. One report—from the distinguished Institute of Medicine—describes the situation in sober but forceful prose. "Chronic pain, especially musculoskeletal pain," the authors write, "is a common health problem afflicting a substantial proportion of the adult population and interfering with every aspect of their lives."[11] The new pain clinics and pain centers that have sprung up in most major hospitals since 1960 are packed with patients whose lives have been disrupted. Pain is so far from dead that it has become a booming business.

Chronic pain, indeed, though far less visible than cancer or AIDS, certainly belongs among the characteristic maladies of our time. It seems clear that specific historical periods possess not only their characteristic crimes (treason for the Elizabethans, robbery for the Georgians, drug-dealing and stock manipulation in the postmodern era) but also their defining or representative illnesses.[12] Thus leprosy and plague haunted the medieval world with their aura of demonic terror much as madness obsessed the Renaissance. Gout (considered the disease of luxury and high living) aptly reflected the more secular, hedonistic spirit of the eighteenth century, while the Romantic era spun a vast mythology of spiritualizing illness around tuberculosis. Recently, as Susan Sontag has argued, cancer and now AIDS have accrued around them the mystery, fear, and morbid fascination that make them far more than mere diseases.[13] Chronic pain, mysterious, dull, and nonfatal, might be called the defining illness of our low-profile, private, safe-sexed, self-absorbed era.

Its relative invisibility gives chronic pain a feature that makes it both insidious and almost unique. What AIDS, cancer, tuberculosis, leprosy, madness, and other representative illnesses share is a graphic power to seize the imagination. They not only threaten personal and public health but also, equally important, fill the world with disturbing new images of our vulnerability to disaster. Chronic pain, by contrast, proves especially treacherous because it works almost totally in secret. Its presence is completely undramatic, like white collar crime or a terrorist in a business suit. It does not inspire telethons and rock concerts. There is simply nothing photogenic about an aching back that will not let you sleep, sit, travel, or make love and never stops hurting.

Chronic pain keeps its low profile by doggedly failing to convey the macabre glamor of deformity, contagion, and imminent death. Former U.S. Surgeon General C. Everett Koop contrasted the current publicity surrounding AIDS with our relative unconcern about the vastly more common affliction of migraine. "You almost have to die of something in order to get the attention that the disease process deserves in the American health system," he said. "That's why AIDS, which is 100 percent fatal, attracted so much attention. People could understand that. Migraine is 100 percent nonfatal."[14] Koop is correct, I think, that the problem is not simply lack of publicity about pain but lack of understanding. The damage is all around us. The typical patient at Seattle's Multidisciplinary Pain Center has low back pain, has had 2.6 operations, and has been off work for 3.6 years.[15] Still, we find it hard to grasp or comprehend a condition that attacks millions of people without leaving outward signs of damage.

Chronic pain is invisible in large part, then, because it is commonplace and nonfatal. Almost every serious illness seems more important. Only within the past several decades have specialists appeared ("algologists": from the Greek *algos* or pain) who devote themselves full-time to the study and treatment of chronic pain. A doctor who has no special training in chronic pain often finds such patients deeply frustrating. Understandably, many physicians prefer the postpenicillin model of swift and total cure. Patients with chronic pain, however, too often just do not seem to get well. They may undergo multiple surgeries—between ten and twenty are not uncommon. They often take vast, exotic, and harmful combinations of prescription drugs, mixed with home remedies and drugstore staples, as if concocting a desperate smorgasbord of analgesia. Medical staffs sometimes refer to such people as "thick-folder" patients. They shuttle from specialist to specialist, in a revolving door of referrals, seen so often by so many different doctors that finally no one really sees them.

Like shadowy Homeric spirits of the dead, chronic pain patients tend to move in an in-between realm: they clearly are not well, but their malady will not let us see them as absolutely sick. An affliction that operates in-between and in secret, of course, generates endless paradoxes. How can we combat an epidemic so clandestine that no one (except its victims) really notices it? We hardly know how to mobilize public opinon when denied access to the lurid rhetoric of crisis. A dilemma so quiet, we are tempted to assume, cannot be a serious problem. It is easy to entertain this thought until one day chronic pain hits you with its invisible fist, like a knife in the back that the doctors cannot find. Suddenly nothing looks the same. It is as if the world has abruptly and completely changed, turned sinister, even evil, but no one knows except you.

†

What surprised me most when I began my research at the pain clinic of a large university hospital was the apparently normal faces of the patients. I had steeled myself to expect agonized expressions and frightful cries. The clinic, I anticipated, would probably look and sound something like an antiseptic Nazi torture chamber. It amazed me that patients arriving for appointments talked with the receptionist in calm, hushed voices. They thumbed through out-of-date magazines or sat quietly on the hard, vinyl chairs with the resignation of people who know exactly how hospitals suspend the everyday flow of time. The waiting room— more like a wide, blind tunnel—had the air of a place in which your name is never called.

The patients looked far more cheerful than their surroundings. The pain clinic consisted of three small rooms: the so-called waiting room, a treatment room, and a minuscule staff room. That was it—a sure sign in medical circles of a young program with shaky funding. The treatment room held in the center a standard examining table with its swatch of stiff white paper running down the middle like a blank scroll. Against the walls stood various low cabinets and tables containing surgical gowns, sterilized instruments sheathed in plastic, and standardized legal consent forms. I was impressed at how carefully the Director explained to patients each new procedure, describing in great detail the risks, possible benefits, and inevitable uncertainties. Pain seemed capable of dissolving otherwise rock-hard resistances. I never saw anyone refuse to sign the consent form. Patients did not flinch at hypodermic needles so long and thick that (even from across the room) they resembled hollow barbecue skewers.

The stories that the patients shared with me when I explained my research belied their normal faces. One young woman (I'll call her Laura) rolled up her loose jeans, exposing along the length of the calf a fiery mass of twisted scar tissue. Modern farming depends upon machines more dangerous than many weapons. An augur, for example, is a vast enclosed funnel used for processing grain. At the center, where the sides slope downward toward a narrow opening, a rounded screwlike blade turns slowly to move the grain. Occasionally the augur needs cleaning, and then a farmhand climbs inside to sweep down the sides. If at that moment someone by mistake turned on the machine, the effect would be like falling into a giant, vertical meat grinder.

Luckily they turned off the augur before it had mangled more than half of Laura's lower leg. A helicopter flew her several hundred miles to the university hospital, where a team of surgeons worked for hours to repair the shattered bones and to rebuild the shredded muscles. Almost miraculously, they managed to avoid an amputation. With a cane and heavy metal brace she now walked to her appointments at the pain clinic, stiffly, awkwardly. But no one who saw her during those first terrible hours following the accident believed that she would ever walk again.

It is not a pleasant trait, but we sometimes feel suspicious of people who say they are in pain but who do not groan or writhe or pound the floor. Pain patients know what it means to face daily suspicion. Laura's leg, however, contained a pain no one could doubt. Its sources lay deep within the flesh, beneath thick layers of scar tissue, but doctors were unable to locate its exact source. Where the damage was so extensive, pain might issue from a hundred different hiding places, like the smoke from a smoldering ruin. Very likely, explained the Director, there were multiple sources, layer upon layer of pain. Unmask one pain and the next simply took its place. Even if the process of medical unmasking might finally discover the last pain hidden beneath overlapping and intervening strata, doctors might be unable to repair the damage or to relieve the suffering.

For Laura, what proved finally worse than the awful moment when the augur mangled her leg was a constant, irreparable pain that lingered long after the process of healing should have run its course. The leg in its healing had sealed in a tormenting and never-ending ache that gave her no freedom. She was in effect a prisoner shackled to her pain. She told me in a cold, emotionless tone that she wished the surgeons had simply cut off her leg at the knee. An artificial leg was something she could learn to live with: she could still cook, dance, work, take care of the kids. Chronic pain, however, had made the rest of her life a permanent daily torment. Bitterly, she warned me never to accept treatment at a university hospital, because the surgeons use you for practice or research. They don't care what pain does to you later on, she added.

Laura's experience—which includes her lingering bitterness—offers a particularly clear picture of the difference between chronic and acute pain.[16] Almost everything in the modern medical treatment of pain can be said to follow from this fundamental distinction. Thus, although a fully adequate definition of pain continues to elude us, we nonetheless need to distinguish carefully between two essentially different *kinds* or classes of pain. What Laura felt when the augur tore into her leg belongs, like the minor daily injuries or short-term illnesses that befall us, to the class of pain that doctors call acute. Acute pain descends in a sudden storm. The misery that lingers months and years later belongs to the class of pain that doctors call chronic. On this simple but absolutely basic distinction rests an entire revolution in medical understanding.

Chronic pain is the medical term for a pain that, perversely, refuses to disappear or that reappears over extended periods, in episodes. Sometimes, as in the pain from inoperable tumors or in degenerative diseases such as rheumatoid arthritis, the cause is clear but cure impossible. Sometimes the pain persists long after healing is complete or, as with migraine headaches, it may recur at frequent intervals. Sometimes there is no identifiable organic cause. Despite the variations, one feature remains constant: unlike acute pain, chronic pain simply will not go away and stay away.

Chronic pain in addition possesses no biological purpose. Acute pain, by contrast, serves a recognizable function in protecting us from further harm. It warns us to remove a hand from a hot stove, it accompanies the process of healing, and it leads to growth and accomplishment. Acute pain is what weight-lifters celebrate when they say "no pain, no gain." Doctors sometimes speak of chronic pain as bringing with it a "secondary gain," by which they usually refer to some dimly perceived psychological benefit that the patient receives from the pain, such as increased attention or even the unconscious gratification of a guilty need for punishment. But secondary gain comes only at the cost of an unending conscious misery that the patient desperately wants to shed. Chronic pain solves nothing. It is sheer hell.

The refusal to disappear, which characterizes chronic pain, creates a condition that often baffles and defeats medical judgment. Doctors know pretty well how to deal with acute pain. They understand many of its basic mechanisms, and the local pharmacy stocks dozens of tested remedies. In chronic pain, by contrast, the usual remedies simply do not work, or they do not work for long. (Some operations once commonly used for chronic pain actually left 15 percent of the patients with *worse* pain.) Over the months or years of persistent pain, the patient's behavior changes. One typical change in behavior is a reliance on large numbers of prescribed or unprescribed drugs. (Laura was up to fifteen aspirins a day, but there are patients who use many more.) Although much remains unknown about this frustrating malady, on one point we can be absolutely clear. Chronic pain may *begin* as acute pain, but is not merely acute pain that persists. Over time the pain seems to change its nature. Chronic pain and acute pain are as different as cancer and the common cold.[17]

Like most classifications, of course, the contrast between acute pain and chronic pain contains ambiguous, twilight areas. Inevitably, specialists propose technical adjustments designed to wipe out twilight, with the result that new categories suddenly spring to life: subacute, ongoing acute, chronic benign neoplastic, and so on. Our categories for thinking about pain still remain less flexible than pain itself. It is merely an arbitrary convention that sets six months as the period when ongoing acute pain gets reclassified as chronic. Why not seven months or five and a half? Such questions, however, miss the crucial point. We enter into a very different state of being when our pain passes, at whatever arbitrary point, from acute to chronic.

Acute pain keeps us within a daylight world that remains fundamentally familiar. We know what to expect, and the gradual lessening of our pain assures us that our expectations are valid. Chronic pain destroys our normal assumptions about the world. It never releases us from its grip and continually frustrates our hopes for gradual improvement. Ultimately it introduces us to an unsettling counterworld where, as Emily Dickinson described it, time has stopped. (The time before pain is almost inconceivable, or else recedes in memory like a faded dream.) It is a place where, gradually, almost without noticing, you find yourself at last all alone. Chronic pain penetrates so completely that it leaves no escape. It lives within us like an unimaginably dull nightmare.

Nightmare is not simply a figure of speech when applied to chronic pain. Lawrence LeShan, from the Institute of Applied Biology, described the universe perceived by the patient in chronic pain as structurally identical with the universe of the nightmare. Nightmares, according to LeShan, possess three unvarying features: (1) terrible things are being done and worse are threatened; (2) we are helplessly under the control of outside forces; and (3) we cannot predict when the ordeal will end. LeShan concludes: "The person in pain is in the same formal situation: terrible things are being done to him and he does not know if worse will happen; he has no control and is helpless to take effective action; no time-limit is given."[18] Only one feature should be added to LeShan's description. Chronic pain is a nightmare from which we may never truly awaken—or a waking state in which the nightmare never ends. One pain patient expressed the uninterrupted dislocation he felt as follows: "It's always three o'clock in the morning."[19]

†

We can better grasp the dilemma facing people with chronic pain—especially their sense of dislocation—if we consider the ways in which our culture teaches us to confront pain with silence and denial. Americans today probably belong to the first generation on earth that looks at a pain-free life as something like a constitutional right. Pain is a scandal. Leonardo da Vinci in his notebooks wrote that "the chief evil is bodily pain."[20] Leonardo and his age, however, also knew something about how to live in a world where evil cannot be routinely exorcised with a bottle of pills.

We are not well equipped for what happens when our pills fail. Suppose the pain simply will not go away. Suppose it follows us and takes up residence in our bones so that nothing we buy or swallow or rub on our skin will make it vanish. What then?

Silence is among the most frequent responses to chronic pain. We tend to think, with good reason, that pain almost instantly finds a voice. All newborn infants cry, and their cries (as all parents know) come in distinctively different tones. Yet this apparently natural response to pain—although not itself learned—is swiftly *un*learned and *re*learned. We very soon replace our earliest natural responses to pain with carefully calibrated understandings about how much crying is permitted, about when and where you can cry, about who can cry and for what reasons. The truth is that we learn almost everything we know about pain, including the need to deny it and to smother it in silence.

Ronald Melzack, one of the major figures in modern pain research, early in his career designed an experiment in which he raised dogs from birth in the laboratory equivalent of padded cells. They were isolated from other dogs and completely sheltered from painful stimuli. When full grown, these dogs proved deficient in the ability to perceive and respond to pain. Melzack reports that one dog, observed in a room with low-lying water pipes, knocked its head on the pipes more than thirty times in an hour without showing any evidence of pain behavior.[21] Such experiments strongly suggest that an understanding of pain is something we learn in the course of our normal growth. ("People were taught to bear necessary pain in my day," says a sixty-year-old man in an 1899 play by Shaw.)[22] As soon as we are born, we are educated day and night in the school of pain. But it is mostly acute pain that we learn about. No one teaches us what to do with a pain that never stops.

Nevertheless we learn. Patients with chronic pain soon discover that their complaints (potentially endless, like their pain) often exhaust, frustrate, and finally alienate family and friends and physicians. Many patients thus learn to retreat into a defensive isolation. They keep to themselves. They experience firsthand the failure of words in the face of suffering. Virginia Woolf wrote: "The merest schoolgirl, when she falls in love, has Shakespeare or Keats to speak her mind for her; but let a sufferer try to describe a pain in his head to a doctor and language at once runs dry."[23] The normal failure of language under the assault of acute pain, which Woolf describes, is a common but not devastating experience. A pain that lasts for months or years, however, begins to wear out everyone's patience and goodwill; it constitutes a radical assault on language and on human communication. There is simply nothing that can be said.

It is not entirely clear why language should run dry or crumble under the influence of pain. Love is no less mysterious, yet it fills thousands of songs, poems, and novels with its apparently inexhaustible speech. Even the inventive McGill-Melzack Pain Questionnaire reduces the patient's experience of pain to a mere seventy-eight words. Love, of course, draws people together, creating an intimacy that bypasses and transcends normal communication. The understanding between lovers is deep, instant, and unspoken. Chronic pain, in contrast, most often seems to build up walls of separation. It breaks down understanding. It places people in utterly different worlds of feeling. It surrounds them with silence. In many ways, the person in chronic pain might as well be standing on the moon.

"Pain," wrote Aristotle, "upsets and destroys the nature of the person who feels it."[24] Notice how even a minor irritant—a passing headache, say, or stiffness in the neck—tends to change your mood. Pain makes most of us irritable and cranky. The composed face with which we greet the world begins to look slightly pinched or haggard. A stronger pain can succeed in driving out every erotic impulse. ("Not tonight, dear.") It can turn a normally imperturbable man suddenly mean and hostile, as if replacing him with his savage twin. A scream, which we might think of as speech unraveled, seems to be the natural language of intense acute pain. Yet all these instances are somehow familiar. Even a scream manages to communicate something, if only the presence of a nameless terror. The shift from acute to chronic pain, however, initiates a difference of kind, not degree. Prolonged chronic pain threatens to unravel the self.

There is much to be said for the view that silence is the natural language of chronic pain. Everyone responds to acute pain with more or less distinctive but related cries: in English, *ow*! in French, *aie*! in German, *ach*! in Yiddish, *oy*! These hollow monosyllables, however, are eminently social. Like a scream, they communicate instantly and quite often constitute an implicit request for help. Chronic pain opens on an unsocial, wordless terrain where all communication threatens to come to a halt. Cries for help prove mostly useless. Indeed, at its most intense or most protracted, chronic pain may push us toward an area of human life we know almost nothing about. Its inarticulate silences serve as the expression of an otherness so alien that we have no words and no language with which to comprehend it.

†

Chronic pain is usually an unrelieved disaster to the person who suffers it, but the challenge it poses to traditional medicine seems to be moving us into a new era of understanding and treatment. Any future history of pain will need to meditate on the particular moment in which Western culture now uncomfortably finds itself fixed. Medicine—like the culture surrounding and interpenetrating it—is entering a period of profound transformation. The invention of the multidisciplinary pain clinic beginning about 1960 promises in fact to overturn centuries of medical thinking about pain.[25] This quiet medical revolution is far from complete. Too many doctors still know little about it. What is happening goes far beyond the development of miscellaneous new treatments. The pain clinic stands as an innovative, revolutionary way of thinking about our oldest and most implacable foe.

This new medical understanding of pain can be best summarized by contrast. From the time of the ancient Hippocratic writings, pain has held the clear and secure status of a symptom. In effect, Western medicine has understood pain as a more or less readable inscription that the skilled physician might interpret for its revelations about processes hidden deep within the flesh. Pain on this view is a message composed, sent, and delivered by illness. The medical revolution now under way does not seek to overthrow the ancient—and surely sound—wisdom that interprets pain as a symptom. Rather, alongside this familiar view it introduces a basic change in perspective from which we see that pain is sometimes completely illegible. This more or less unreadable pain no longer resembles a message that passes, by means of a common code or language, in-between the physician and the illness. Now the message *is* the illness.

The pain clinic serves as a convenient symbol of this new paradigm in medical thought. "We treat pain as a diagnosis, not a symptom," explains anesthesiologist Michael Kilbride, founder of the new Pain Management Center at the Muskegon (MI) General Hospital.[26] This view of pain as diagnosis rather than symptom—an approach typical of the pain clinic movement—requires an enormous shift in perspective. It is not just a new thought but the basis for an entirely new way of thinking. Chronic pain, in this rethinking, no longer always points beyond itself to a hidden disease or illness that constitutes the real object of medical attention. Now pain itself has emerged as the malady under treatment. We might think of the transformation of pain from symptom to diagnosis—from the sign of illness to the illness itself—as representing a kind of Copernican revolution within medicine. No longer a satellite circling around disease, pain has begun to move toward the center. Increasingly, illness now circles around pain.

A shift so fundamental will take years to accomplish, of course, and will encounter steady resistance, both open and covert. Some doctors remain skeptical, even suspicious, about the activities of pain clinics. It surprised me to find specialists sometimes deeply hostile as (off the record) they discussed how their colleagues in other disciplines treated pain. One oncologist I interviewed flatly refused to send his patients to the anesthesiologists running the local pain clinic, claiming that anesthesiologists know next to nothing about cancer pain. Many clinics never entirely break free from the institutional politics of medicine. If the Department of Psychiatry runs the pain clinic, for example, orthopedists may want nothing to do with it. Treatment can differ greatly depending on whether the director is, say, a neurologist or a behavioral psychologist. Some clinics emphasize managing pain; some aim for rehabilitation; some promise cure. The best, in my view, have staffs drawn from multiple disciplines and departments. Despite political wrangling and philosophical conflict, however, the trend is clear. There are now close to one thousand private and public pain treatment centers in the United States alone.[27] In 1960 there were no more than a handful.

The shift from symptom to diagnosis finds a parallel in another momentous change. Many of the best pain clinics, reflecting new directions in research, accept the bold thinking that redefines pain not as a sensation but a perception. This shift represents an absolute repudiation of the dominant thinking about pain that has characterized nineteenth- and twentieth-century medicine—a mode of thought that the general public has accepted on faith, to our lasting confusion. Sensations, like heat and cold, require little more than a rudimentary, functioning nervous system. A salamander or a june bug can experience sensation. Perceptions, by contrast, require minds and emotions as well as nerves. When we understand pain as a perception, we are implicitly challenging the deeply entrenched mechanistic tradition in medicine that treats us as divided into separate and uncommunicating blocks called body and mind.[28]

The new clinics that regard chronic pain as a perception rather than a sensation (and not all clinics accept this view) necessarily acknowledge the importance of understanding body and mind as inseparably linked. Further, because people experience pain only within specific cultures or subcultures, the link between bodies and minds extends also to the surrounding field of social life. Families, lovers, ethnic groups, advertising campaigns, wars, scientific discoveries—all directly or (most often) indirectly influence our perception of pain. A medicine willing to take account of cultural and psychosocial influences on the perception of pain needs to consider resources not generally explored or even acknowledged by medical schools. Eventually, modern doctors and writers may find—to their mutual surprise—they no longer gaze at humankind from opposite sides of an abyss.

The benefits that flow from viewing the mind as absolutely intrinsic to the experience of chronic pain do not require us to abandon decades of progress in medical research. We are not turning back the clock to a time before aspirin and ether, but rather moving forward in an advance that also finds a purpose for what Plato and Aristotle and Cervantes have to teach us about pain. Change comes slowly, however, when ideas entrenched in medical education and in the general culture—ideas such as the absolutely rigid division between mental pain and physical pain—must be challenged. It is likely that many doctors will not change their thinking about pain until patients begin to demand it. Luckily, however, modern medicine is a consumer-driven enterprise. Doctors will decide that change is a good thing when patients demand a change. If in the manner of the best new pain clinics we insist on understanding and treating our pain as a perception rather than a sensation, we will find, I think, that the medical profession suddenly believes we are right.

†

A revolution in medical thinking about pain—like a political revolution—falls far short of creating an instant utopia. We need to recognize that, despite the avalanche of new research and publications, despite promising work at the new clinics and centers, the mysteries of pain remain veiled. The person in pain belongs to a world that no one else can entirely share or comprehend. Perhaps there is something finally incomprehensible in pain that supplies, as Emily Dickinson saw so clearly, its peculiar quality of blankness. "It was the whiteness of the whale that above all things appalled me," writes Melville's narrator, Ishmael, in *Moby Dick*. This mysterious, unresponsive absence of color—"a dumb blankness," as Ishmael calls it—seems to him somehow infinitely terrible. "There yet lurks an elusive something in the innermost idea of this hue," he writes, "which strikes more of panic to the soul than that redness which affrights in blood."[29] Pain partakes of this eerie and sometimes appalling power to drain off everything that gives the world vividness, color, coherence, and value. The blankness of pain may be its most terrifying attribute. It casts us back upon a featureless landscape.

The meanings that over the centuries we have carved out of pain—the features we have imposed upon its oppressive blankness—constitute an achievement of the human spirit. A hard look at pain, however, will force us to acknowledge that these personal and cultural achievements are not uniformly fine. The uses and meanings of pain, from Nazi death camps and the torture of the Inquisition to the latest death squad or political tyranny, also reflect our worst abilities to rationalize and to accept the unspeakable. The same progressive Enlightenment culture that built Monticello, with slave labor, also decreed that slaves were subhuman creatures who did not truly feel affliction. In the achievements it has called forth, pain ranks with the soaring cathedrals and hideous dungeons of medieval Europe as a testament to the contrary powers of the human spirit.

It is the final thrust of my argument to contend that the history of pain has brought us to a moment of profoundest change. The human spirit must again choose directions. It is not just we who have changed as the invisible tide of chronic pain rises around us. Pain too has changed. Isolated from the various cultural and personal systems of explanation that formerly gave it meaning, pain today still presents itself most often as entirely and solely a medical problem. The medical problem most often presents itself as a matter of hidden tissue damage that constitutes an occasion for drugs, surgeries, and referrals. We have entered a time, in short, that confronts us with a radically new threat. It is a time when, outside and inside the specialized language of medicine, pain threatens to become entirely meaningless.

Certainly the cultural resources available in previous ages now generally lie forgotten or ineffectual, largely because they cannot compete with our faith in medical cures. Chronic pain, as one of its most troubling features, eventually robs us of our ordinary belief in medical solutions. When denial too fails to work (and it fails with absolute regularity), we are left more or less without resources. Such inexplicable pain is not simply too complex or too severe to be contained within language. As one medical treatment after another fails, chronic pain becomes an experience about which there is increasingly nothing to say, nothing to hope, nothing to do. It is pure blank suffering.

This new chronic affliction—the creation of our own scientific, demystifying era—may rapidly and closely approach the inhuman: a pain to which we can assign no meaning at all. Yet there is also reason to resist despair. The pain clinic movement offers a sign of significant change. Groups inside and outside medicine have initiated programs to educate physicians in the rights of patients and in new methods of pain relief. Ancient, concealed wrongs that fill the world with pain, such as wife-beating and child abuse, are beginning to emerge into the light of discussion and reform. We still have a long way to go. Nevertheless, as glib or heartless as it may seem, it is altogether possible that in the struggle against the blankness and meaninglessness of modern pain we may find occasion to recover an indispensable but disdained and neglected resource whose therapeutic value we have vastly misunderstood: laughter.

4

THE PAIN OF COMEDY

The most suffering animal on earth invented for itself—laughter.
FRIEDRICH NIETZSCHE[1]

HE 1986 FRANK OZ film *The Little Shop of Horrors* contains a moment that raises serious questions about the relation between comedy and its ancient antagonist, pain. It is a pain linked, of course, to the ridiculous, since *The Little Shop of Horrors* features a gigantic, singing, space-traveling, man-eating plant named Audrey II. In its spoof of various mutant genres of musical comedy, horror films, and low-budget science fiction, *The Little Shop of Horrors* turns inside out Northrop Frye's famous theory about the benign "green world" of comedy: a protective, maternal, nurturing enclave, identified with the healing spirit of pure nature, where conflicts and contradictions from the world beyond are magically resolved.[2] Audrey, the self-described "Mean Green Mother From Outer Space," eliminates contradictions by eating them.

The scene that best typifies the unlikely link between comedy and pain occurs in the brief cameo appearance where Steve Martin plays the sadistic dentist Orin Scrivello. As we watch him beginning his day, Martin roars off to work on his motorcycle in a black leather jacket and Elvis Presley haircut. He sweeps into his office, twists the head from a child's doll, slugs the nurse, and slams his knee into the groin of a seated, male patient, all the while (as if possessed by the spirit of a dead rock star) singing a catchy song that repeats his mother's advice to her bullying offspring: "Son, be a dentist." A taste for inflicting pain, so the song advises, can lead to a profitable career in the oral health industry.

79

Steve Martin's comic sketch offers something more, however, than a portrait of the dentist as a young sadist. The effectiveness of the scene—unlike, say, comedy that centers on politicians or piano teachers—depends upon tapping into our deep fears of the dentist's office as a space given over to pain. Plato concisely defined fear as the anticipation of pain, and no doubt our fears begin to mount as Scrivello swings his enormous drill toward the patient's soft, defenseless, wide-open mouth.[3] The fear-based black comedy only accelerates when comedian Bill Murray—playing Martin's masochistic patient—eagerly requests a "long, slow root-canal." Dentistry, it seems, has become something of a modern comic metaphor for pain, and dentists a favorite target. Audiences in the Middle Ages must have experienced similarly mixed feelings of fear and glee when in the liturgical drama performed on carts or makeshift stages outside the cathedral they saw the arch-tormentor Satan and his minor devils routed with firecrackers.

It would be easiest to decide that *The Little Shop of Horrors* is simply an aberration. I would contend, however, that the film is atypical only in the openness with which it grounds its comedy in pain. Except for the crude lambastings of slapstick, comedies usually establish much more subtle and more indirect relationships with affliction. Yet *The Little Shop of Horrors* enormously exaggerates and therefore makes visible something at work—almost beneath the level of normal observation—in almost all comedies. It shows us how far comedy is committed not simply to pleasure but to the mixture of pleasure and pain. Pain, however indirectly, usually finds a way to infiltrate the scene of comedy. Johnny Carson, king of American nighttime television, well expressed the paradox we need to explore: "Comedy," he observes, "is a cruel business."[4]

†

Pain certainly offers an odd, even perverse, entry into the comic world. In a terrain crisscrossed by disagreements, it seems almost everyone should agree with the proposition that pain, whatever else it is, is not funny. This proposition is true enough that the underground link between pain and comedy surely cannot be without significance. If one accepts Elaine Scarry's sweeping argument that every artifact of human culture, from wool overcoats to Keats's "Ode to Autumn," takes its shape by addressing (directly or, most often, indirectly) the body's vulnerability to pain, it is hard to see why comedy should provide the single exception.

Yet comedy in fact offers a very special case of the relation between artifice and affliction. Comedy, we might say, finds its implicit subject, technique, and purpose in the unremitting human encounter with pain.

The neglected link between comedy and pain will seem clearer if we begin by exploring the unique status of the comic body. Indeed, its reliance on the body is one reason why comedy tends to make critics and scholars a little uneasy. Comic art, that is, often prefers to appear vulgar, clumsy, demented, frivolous, and unedifying, deficient in such satisfying Arnoldian virtues as philosophical depth and intellectual dignity. Thus Matthew Arnold could dismiss Chaucer from the rank of classic poets because, in Arnold's view, the great medieval comic poet of the body lacks "high seriousness."[5] Woody Allen seems to consider his superb (sex-based) comedies as somehow unworthy of the solemn Franco-Scandinavian masterpieces to which he aspires. Comedy holds an ambivalent position within the world of art precisely because comic writers, like doctors, insist upon viewing humankind from almost the same demystified point of view: as creatures whose fundamental attribute is the possession of a body.

Comedy and pain both share the body as their common ground. In fact, bodies—from a comic point of view—are almost inherently funny. As medicine will attest, the possession of a body absolutely guarantees the comic prerequisite that sooner or later something will go wrong, often painfully wrong. If we speak with exactness, perhaps nothing is comic *inherently*. The sources of comedy do not lie outside us but only within. In fact, everyone who laughs—from New Guinea tribesmen to the high table at Oxford—laughs by means of a vastly complex, coordinated bodily response involving the brain, facial muscles, larynx, diaphragm, and the entire respiratory system, bringing into play the muscles of the chest, abdomen, neck, and back.[6] It is not simply that humankind seem to be the only creatures biologically equipped with a sense of humor. A person who is utterly humorless—who cannot under any circumstances see the comedy of our lives—will strike most observers as not just flawed but deeply inhuman.

The neuroanatomy and physiology of laughter, as one researcher put it mildly, still remain poorly understood, even as they are subjects studiously ignored by most scholars of comedy. Several specialists have postulated a "laughing center" somewhere within the brain: the hypothalamus, thalamus, and limbic systems have all been nominated as candidates.

Comedy of course is not identical with laughter, and laughter is no more exclusively characteristic of the body than are tears. Further, understandings of the body, like attitudes toward bodily life, change over time and across cultures: an audience of seventeenth-century Puritans (assuming we could trick them into a theater) will not react to a comic scene in the same manner as an audience of twentieth-century hedonists (open to every pleasure).[7] Modern feminists may well take offense at the same patriarchal, sexual humor that pleased an audience of Restoration wits. Still, despite such important allowances, comedy could not exist without somewhere conspicuous in its social history the full-bodied presence of human laughter. Laughing is not simply anchored in the body, like the power to dunk a basketball. Our bodies also provide a fundamental source and object of human laughter.

The single figure who best represents the body-centered view of comedy that I am recommending is Shakespeare's Falstaff, "this bed-presser, this horseback-breaker, this huge hill of flesh."[8] What Falstaff confronts us with—above all else—is the irrepressible life of the body. That is largely why his companion Prince Hal (the future King Henry V of England) must renounce him in the name of higher values. The kingly world of honor, virtue, and realpolitik simply cannot carry on its business (or carry on its business with a straight face) in the presence of a figure dedicated to bodily pleasure. Like Falstaff, the body has a subversive habit of interrupting us with its clamor just when we think we have a grip on truly serious matters. At precisely the worst moment we discover that we are hungry or sleepy or inflamed by an attractive stranger. Thus Prince Hal's banishment of Falstaff is a cold-blooded political choice that we can trace back ultimately to Plato's Republic, which banished poets because they stir up unruly emotions and tell disreputable stories about the all-too-fleshly Olympian gods.

Comedy needs the body in the same way that the sonnet needs fourteen lines and unrequited love. The life of the body—which most philosophers can afford to ignore or dismiss as trivial—is almost a formal requirement of comic practice. Falstaff, we might recall, is not only witty but (as he observes) the cause of wit. His wit—with its endless jokes about food and fat and sex—seems continuously to return us to the life of the body. Even his speech is not simply a series of statements but, like singing or dancing, something produced by the body—an earthy, sensuous flow of breath and sound. Of course, the body for Shakespeare is not exclusively centered on pleasure. We hear too much about age, obesity, and illness to ignore the Renaissance belief that a life of luxury and pleasure led directly to disease and pain. (Images of disease follow Falstaff like a bad dream.) Nonetheless, for better or for worse, Falstaff on stage stands before us as the opposite of an abstraction: bawdy, profane, corporeal. He is the embodiment of body—the embodiment of what it means to be embodied.

†

What can the body tell us about comedy that theorists and definers—in their doomed quest for an essence—always seem to miss? It might remind us, first, that comic laughter seems among our most ineradicable bodily endowments. Clinicians report that patients suffering from severe aphasias—crippling or destroying normal speech—still retain the ability to laugh. No matter what culture they grow up in, all normal infants smile and (a little later) laugh at roughly the same age: during the third and fourth months of life. Laughter, we may assume, must be genetically coded in the body, and laughing perhaps served purposes that permitted our protohuman ancestors to survive when their unsmiling cave-fellows perished. Joseph Addison, in the eighteenth century, reports skeptically on the views of a Capuchin monk who argued that in paradise Adam and Eve did not laugh. Laughter, according to this monkish theory, entered the world with original sin, and we know how quickly sin makes us intimately acquainted with the fun-loving, pain-filled life of the body.[9]

The body, with its ancient aura of the profane and the unclean, can also remind us that comedy often depends on the threat of painful transgressions. Freud argued that jokes are no less meaningful than dreams in their indirect disclosures about our innermost (secret and unacceptable) desires. Moreover, recent anthropologists have shown that jokes constitute a highly ritualized mode of defusing conflict among primitive tribes whose world is booby-trapped by dangerous taboos.[10] Comedy from Aristophanes to Mel Brooks seems propelled into action whenever it encounters a sign that says *Off Limits*. It thus takes a special pleasure in that indispensable expression of human bodily life: sex.

Sexuality doubtless constitutes the single topic—traditionally off limits or at least hedged round with restrictions—without which comedy as we know it would cease to exist. To the extent that comedy depends for its lifeblood on the curious rituals of human sexual behavior, it necessarily draws its strength from the body. Significantly, when scholars trace the historical origins of comedy they lead us back to the *komos*, or revel, associated in ancient Greek rites with Dionysus, a bacchanalian fertility god who also serves as the god of wine, with its attendant intoxication, song, music, and carnal excess.[11] The classic boy-meets-girl sequence identifies a primal structure of comic plots, and, even when we see this sexualized pursuit overlaid with the refined elegance of Fred Astaire and Ginger Rogers, it is still the life of the body—singing, dancing, falling in and out of love—that provides the pulse of comic art. Elizabethan comedies concluded traditionally with a marriage and a dance that celebrate (like Astaire's inspired footwork) an ideal union of social form and the life-affirming powers of the body, but it is probably the unruly phallus, in its limitless incarnations, that stands as the omnipresent symbol of the comic body.

The phallus may ultimately convey more than the male bias of traditional Western comedy. (A history of comic practice would rightly associate most traditional comedies with the direct or indirect maintenance of male power, as in Shakespeare's *The Taming of the Shrew*.[12]) Modern theory, however, has taught us to interpret the phallus not only as a direct image of power or desire but also as the indirect sign of a lack. Comedy in effect calls attention to what is missing or absent from everyday life. What is missing, of course, is the rich, pleasurable life of the body that comedy (however briefly and imperfectly) restores to us. It is not *entirely* missing, not nonexistent, but rather wholly lacking in significance, thoroughly reduced to the status of a banality, shunted off to the sunny corner of bourgeois life labeled vacation. No one today seems satisfied with Aristotle's brief remark that comedy specializes in the ugly or deformed. Yet Aristotelian deformity and ugliness also serve—like Falstaff's corpulence—as a medium for bringing the absent body into prominence. Whatever makes us laugh restores to us momentarily a part of our own bodily existence that work and reason and seriousness always seem to deny.

Comedy, then, as distinct from other literary genres, belongs fundamentally and uniquely to the body. Clearly, not all comedies operate on the premise of a Dionysian revel. It is nonetheless significant that comedy maintains its power even when stripped of every redeeming social value and reduced to its lowest level of intellectual life. King Lear rises to a rare moment of tragic awareness when—during the storm on the heath—he examines, as if seeing him for the first time, a ragged, drenched, half-naked beggar. "Unaccommodated man," Lear observes, "is no more but such a poor, bare, fork'd animal as thou art."[13] Comedy, we might say, knows this truth from the outset and finds it more or less hilarious.

†

Comic pain, then, finds its precondition in the unique relationship between comedies and bodies. Their relationship, however, is deeper and more curious than we have yet seen. Comedy needs to be understood as an ancient human mode of dealing with pain. Indeed, I should like to propose that there are really two major traditions that bear on our understanding of comic pain. These opposed traditions descend from the two great philosophical antagonists of antiquity, Plato and Aristotle. From Aristotle, we derive the dominant tradition that associates comedy with pure pleasure. From Plato we derive the competing and normally unacknowledged tradition that associates comedy with the mixture of pleasure and pain.

This genealogy is overlooked not only because scholars and critics rarely mention comic pain but also because they usually omit Plato and Aristotle from discussions of comedy, while less powerful thinkers such as Bergson and Meredith are quoted like oracles. The omission makes some sense. Aristotle's treatise on comedy disappeared in antiquity—a loss that has sparked numerous attempts to reconstitute the missing text, most recently in Umberto Eco's best-selling novel *The Name of the Rose*.[14] Plato, moreover, never wrote directly on comedy, so postclassical theorists have been thrown back on their own resources, generally with inadequate results. We have been far too hasty, however, in assuming that Aristotle and Plato are unimportant or marginal figures in the history of comic thought.

Aristotle actually discusses comedy in some detail during the first five chapters of his great treatise on tragedy, the *Poetics*. It is from this discussion that we can derive the dominant tradition in comedy that implicitly or explicitly associates comedy with pure pleasure. Here is the crucial passage from the *Poetics*:

> As we have said, comedy is an imitation of baser men. These are characterized not by every kind of vice but specifically by "the ridiculous," which is a subdivision of the category of "deformity." What we mean by "the ridiculous" is some error or ugliness *that is painless* and has no harmful effects. The example that comes immediately to mind is the comic mask, which is ugly and distorted but *causes no pain*.[15]

The (smiling) mask of comedy offers a convenient emblem to summarize the Aristotelian emphasis upon pleasure. Comedy for Aristotle depends upon an absolute opposition between pleasure and pain.

It would seem obvious that Aristotle is correct in claiming that comedy takes pleasure rather than pain for its subject and goal. A comedy that fails to give pleasure comes dangerously close to renouncing its status as comedy. If tradition has one truism to pass on about comedy it is that comedy always deals in pleasure.[16] Plato does not deny this traditional view so much as complicate it, fatally. He offers us, through his portraits of Socrates, an implicitly anti-Aristotelian theory in which the comic always consists in the impure mixture of pleasure with pain.

Socrates in fact is something of a comedian among philosophers. This description will not immediately ring true for readers who have struggled with long, humorless stretches of Platonic dialogue. His arguments, however, with their breathtaking naiveté, gave him an air of comic foolishness that he was too wise not to cultivate. As his great admirer Alcibiades reported, anyone listening to Socrates for the first time would find his arguments simply laughable. In addition, Socrates' philosophical style— based upon his famous pose of naive or innocent unknowingness—borrows directly from a stock character of Greek comedy, the *eiron*, who, like Socrates, preferred to play dumb and to speak in practiced understatement. As Alcibiades (rather drunk but frank) observes of Socrates: "He spends his whole life playing his little game of irony, and laughing up his sleeve at all the world."[17]

Plato and Socrates, then, are not altogether unskilled guides to comic theory and practice, despite the absence of a Platonic dialogue on comedy. We get a glimmering of Platonic comedy in the final scene of *The Symposium*, when Socrates out-drinks Aristophanes (the comic poet) and Agathon (the tragic poet) while soberly lecturing them on the true nature of comedy and tragedy. Unfortunately, Plato in *The Symposium* does not record this lecture. It reappears, however, at least in part, in the *Philebus*. For our purposes, we can skip the argument and take a shortcut directly to the "general principle" that—according to Socrates—lies behind his thoughts on comedy. As he puts it: "Whether the body be affected apart from the soul, or the soul apart from the body, or both of them together, we constantly come upon the mixture of pleasure with pain."[18]

This Socratic theory offers an utterly fundamental challenge to Aristotle. For Socrates, pleasure rarely comes pure or unmixed. Comedy, in fact, serves for Socrates as a crowning example of the mixed nature of human life. In life as in comedy, he argues, pleasure always mingles with pain. The difference could not be clearer: while Aristotle consistently places comedy and tragedy in sharp opposition, Plato sees comedy as shot through with traces of the pain we usually tend to think it excludes, ignores, or opposes. For Plato, comedy depends for its pleasures in large part on its intimate connection to the surrounding, interpenetrating world of pain.

†

The Platonic theory of comedy as necessarily mixing pleasure with pain is not an aberration. We have simply been so dazzled by the dominant Aristotelian emphasis on pure pleasure that we have lost sight of a tradition that earlier comic writers understood quite vividly. In fact, it is necessary chiefly that modern comic theory should catch up with an enduring comic practice. Against Aristotle's pleasure-centered theory summarized in the image of the painless comic mask, we might oppose the drawing that Leonardo da Vinci entitled "Allegory of Pleasure and Pain" (fig. 12). Here is how Leonardo in his notebooks described the two interconnected allegorical figures:

Pleasure and Pain are represented as twins, as though they were joined together, for there is never the one without the other. . . . They are made with their backs turned to each other because they are contrary the one to the other. They are made growing out of the same trunk because they have one and the same foundation, for the foundation of pleasure is labour with pain, and the foundations of pain are vain and lascivious pleasures.[19]

Falstaff's pursuit of vain and lascivious pleasures would clearly suggest to Leonardo an almost visible future of pain, just as Leonardo implies that the painful labor of the marketplace occurs in the same space given over to the pleasures of carnival. Pleasure and pain are contrary and antithetical figures but nonetheless inextricably joined.

Plato and Leonardo can help us recognize that we seriously underestimate the slipperiness of comic pleasure if we forget what it works so hard to cover up. Comic pain in effect is the normally invisible counterpart—the shadowy double—that comic pleasure almost desperately contrives that we should not see. Pain is the deformed and unacknowledged twin. Yet it is not always invisible. It stands out plainly in comedies such as *The Little Shop of Horrors*. Writers who are not theorists of comedy

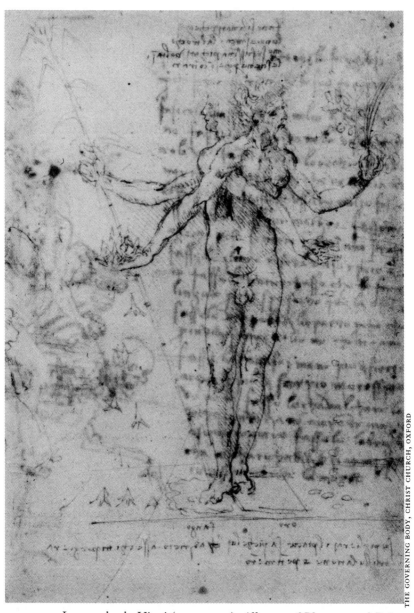

FIGURE 12. Leonardo da Vinci (1452–1519). *Allegory of Pleasure and Pain* (*c.* 1483–1485).

sometimes see it quite distinctly. In fact, no one has captured so eloquently as Freud the relation of comedy to the noncomic contexts within which it always makes its appearances.

Freud's vision of civilized life grows dark enough at times to approach the tragic, so that jokes, humor, and the comic assume an unappreciated importance in his thought. They are especially important for Freud because he views them not simply as instruments of civilized aggression but also as techniques for creating or recapturing the pleasures of a childlike consciousness. "For the euphoria which we endeavour to reach by these means," he writes in the plangent final sentence of *Jokes and Their Relation to the Unconscious* (1905), "is nothing other than the mood of a period of life in which we were accustomed to deal with our psychical work in general with a small expenditure of energy—the mood of our childhood, when we were ignorant of the comic, when we were incapable of jokes and when we had no need of humour to make us feel happy in our life."[20] The comic, for Freud, is in some sense a compensation for our inescapable unhappiness and pain.

Freud can help remind us that the link between comedy and pain is not an isolated Platonic whim. We tend to emphasize Freud's well-known theory that laughter expresses sublimated aggression, where the relation between comedy and pain is quite explicit. It is useful to recall, however, that Freud also sees a much more subtle and disguised relation linking comedy and pain. In a late essay, for example, he describes humor as a crucial means for *evading* the compulsion to suffer that he elsewhere finds endemic to human mental life.[21] The evasion of suffering nevertheless still requires suffering as its precondition. It thus remains true that in a Freudian universe where the pleasure principle—so fundamental to comedy—meets at every point with resistances, obstacles, and crushing defeats, the pleasure of comedy comes always accompanied by the ghostly or palpable imprint of pain. As for Plato and Leonardo, pain colors the spectrum of comic tone which stretches from the gross exuberance of the Greek satyr plays to the deep melancholy of Chekhov. It is this normally invisible trace of comic pain that now demands our direct attention as we turn to one of the world's great examples of comic practice.

The Platonic argument that comedy regularly mixes pain with pleasure finds probably its most influential European embodiment in Don

Quixote: the knight of the dolorous countenance. *Dolorous*, of course, derives from the Latin word for pain, and there is good reason why Dostoevski described *Don Quixote* (1605–1615) as the world's "grandest and saddest book."[22] We are now rather distant from the emotional and literary traditions underlying what might be called the comedy of affliction. Yet affliction is central to the plays of Ben Jonson, for example, and reappears whenever comedy joins ranks with satire, in which the voodoolike capacity to inflict pain through language underlies the ancient origins of satiric art. We will understand only an incomplete arc of comic practice if we fail to explore the ways in which comedy at any moment may turn dark and menacing.

Bodies hold a prominent place in *Don Quixote*, as throughout the comedy of affliction. The hero's extreme gauntness, like the Falstaffian corpulence of his sidekick Sancho Panza, helps to make the body almost an unnamed actor in the novel. Don Quixote's scrawny frame no doubt reflects his insubstantial diet of chivalric romance. He lives immersed in an unreal, bookish, idealized realm set apart from the banal demands of everyday life—and the penalty that Don Quixote pays for his neglect of flesh-and-blood actuality is that he rides through the novel like a comic punching bag. Consider the entirely typical episode of his battle with the wineskins.

Two details of the battle help to illuminate the crucial place occupied by bodies in the comedy of affliction. The knight, after retiring at an inn, awakens to mistake a large wineskin above the bed for the head of a giant. Hearing the commotion, Sancho Panza and his helpers rush in:

They found Don Quixote in the strangest outfit in the world. He was in his shirt, which was not long enough in front to cover his thighs completely, and was six inches shorter behind. His legs were very long and thin, covered with hair, and not over-clean. On his head he wore a little greasy red cap which belonged to the innkeeper, and round his left arm he had wound the blanket of the bed. . . . In his right hand was his naked sword, with which he was lamming out in all directions, shouting all the time as if he were really fighting with a giant.[23]

Modern illustrations that depict Don Quixote as a melancholy, introspective, almost tragic figure of inwardness tend to make us forget how thoroughly Cervantes describes a creature of flesh, bone, and body. The knight's misdirected courage (like his passion for justice) certainly expresses an indomitable spirit, but the spirit for Cervantes necessarily inhabits the world of matter and body, where it makes its appearances in league with a greasy red cap and a bare backside. Pain is never far off.

The adventures of Don Quixote depict a protracted and deeply physical comedy of the body in which pain plays an indispensable role. The second detail illuminates this role. The bedroom is now flooded with wine. Cervantes continues:

> At the sight of this the innkeeper flew into such a fury that he fell on Don Quixote, and began punching him repeatedly with his clenched fists. Indeed if Cardenio [the barber] and the priest had not pulled him off he would soon have put an end to the war with the giant. But, despite all this, the wretched knight did not wake up until the barber brought a large pitcher of cold water from the well and threw it with a jerk all over his body. This awakened Don Quixote, but not sufficiently for him to realize the state he was in.[24]

Such pummelings—as if administered not so much by individuals as by the invisible hand of the universe—prove a regular feature of Cervantes's novel. In fact, Don Quixote observes that this is the second drubbing he has received in the same house. ("The last time, right in this very spot where I'm standing, I got a regular punching and beating; yet I never knew who gave it me and never saw anybody at all.")[25] In *Don Quixote* the body repeatedly calls attention to its distance from the immaterial world of romance (fig. 13). For Cervantes, the repeated beatings, drubbings, and bone-crunching punishments serve finally an almost cumulative philosophical purpose: they represent the inescapable material condition of our being.

Cervantes introduces us to the central paradox of comic pleasure. Comedy must implicitly include pain in order somehow to overcome it. When Sancho Panza notices that Don Quixote is riding "lop-sided," he attributes the odd posture to bruises obtained in the fight against the windmills. (Don Quixote's shoulders were, Cervantes tells us, "half dislocated.") " 'That is the truth,' replied Don Quixote. 'And if I do not complain of the pain [del dolor], it is because a knight errant is not allowed to complain of any wounds, even though his entrails may be dropping through them.' "[26] Sancho Panza's response ("I must say, for my part, that I have to cry out at the slightest twinge") reveals the truth of the body that Don Quixote, immersed in the otherworldly values of romance, so comically and heroically disregards. His dignity no doubt resides in his power to absorb and to brush off the indignities of the flesh in pursuit of

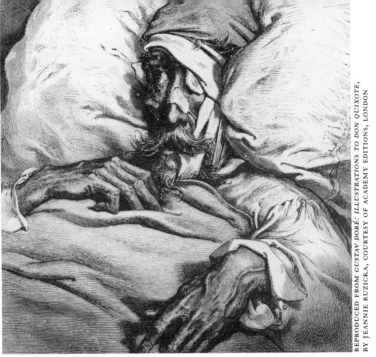

FIGURE 13. Gustav Doré (1832–1883). Wood-engraved illustration appearing in J. W. Clark's English version of *Don Quixote* (1880).

a vision, however crazy, that gives his life meaning. He may not openly complain, yet the groans and aches of Cervantes's hero leave no doubt about the presence of comic affliction.

How comedy manages to triumph over such pain is difficult to say with certainty. Aristotle seems to understand comedy as evoking in the audience a sense of fearlessness, as if we remain for a time wholly superior to pain.[27] Comic laughter certainly achieved a victory over fear in such moments as the burning of a stage set called "*Hell*" at the zenith of medieval carnivals.[28] It is quite possible that the punishing misfortunes in *Don Quixote*, like sexuality in Rabelais and excrement in Swift, celebrate a perverse energy in bodily life that manages to overcome every effort to deny or subdue it: an energy particularly characteristic of burlesque.[29] These explanations, however, should not explain away the pain. Plato, Leonardo, and Freud would tell us that comedy cannot avoid mixing pain with pleasure. Comedy functions so often as a defense against pain—as numerous comic writers attest—that the absence of pain would deprive comedy of its chief villain and underlying purpose. The pleasure of comedy undoubtedly depends in large part on the presence of the pain it overcomes.

THE PAIN OF COMEDY

The presence of pain in comedy may not always reflect kindly on human motives. Although comedy allows us to construct a defense against pain, Freud and Hobbes also suggest a darker truth: that comedy and laughter sometimes depend on a sense of power we feel when *someone else* suffers, especially when we feel that they deserve to suffer. Comedy, therefore, deals not only in benign confusion but also in malign transgressions that require punishment, and pain holds a long association with reprisal. In this sense, pain, like comedy, is an agent of instruction and control. Generations of parents disciplined their children through corporal punishment, even as Prospero in *The Tempest* controls Caliban through threats of physical affliction. (As Prospero warns: "If thou neglect'st, or dost unwillingly / What I command, I'll rack thee with old cramps, / Fill all thy bones with aches, make thee roar / That beasts shall tremble at thy din.")[30] Comedy depends on the presence of pain in part to keep the comic universe from spinning totally out of orbit.

Yet there is a final twist to the paradox of comic pain. Comedy seems to mirror the structure of acute pain in its movement from affliction to disappearance. (There is nothing funny about chronic pain, and its failure to disappear would wreck the structure of comic plots.) Comedy in effect confronts us with situations where pain, somewhat like the Cheshire cat, makes its appearances simply to stage a (smiling) withdrawal. The situations call for pain, but pain mysteriously turns up missing. Such comedies offer us a vision in which—despite beatings, collisions, and man-eating plants—there is no cost to pay and nothing really hurts. This strange absence of pain in situations that everyone recognizes as painful constitutes an important sign that we have entered the comic world. It is a semiotic principle of comic action. Such comedies, we might say, invoke pain not simply to overcome it but to imagine a world in which pain no longer counts. In contrast to the comedies of affliction, where pain is an almost palpable presence, we could describe this strange absence or disappearance of pain as creating comedies of pure wish fulfillment.

†

Comic pain does not belong simply to the film or novel or play that contains it. Comedy also relies upon a pain that belongs to the reader or spectator. No large audience ever contains people who are all one hundred percent pain-free. The aches and pains that fill an average auditorium also find a ghostly trace in our personal memories of pain and in our fears of pain to come. This hidden presence of affliction within the comic audience may seem simply coincidental, since we can assume that noncomic works also draw readers and spectators invisibly burdened with pain. Comedy, however, can play upon this hidden presence of pain in a special way.

The Bible tells us that "a merry heart doeth good like a medicine" (Proverbs 17:22), and historians can point to several periods that revive and revamp the argument that imaginative writing—and comedy in particular—holds a therapeutic power to relieve our pain, to heal and to restore us. In the postclassical world, the therapeutic power of comedy first attracted notice during the Middle Ages. At a time when pious authorities attacked all secular entertainment as the devil's work, apologists for literature found a useful defense in the belief that hard spiritual struggle demanded brief periods of rest and recuperation.[31] Comedy, according to this view, helped to strengthen Christian readers for resuming their combat against the world, the flesh, and the devil. Some apologists, however, went much further in proposing that comic literature could strengthen the body as well as the spirit.

Boccaccio's *Decameron* provides a good illustration of the potentially therapeutic powers of comedy. The narrative describes a group of townspeople who escape from the plague devastating Florence in 1348 by retiring to a country villa. The bawdy, comic stories they told not only helped pass the time as they waited out the plague; various medieval authorities took quite literally the biblical argument that laughter creates and preserves good health. One typical medieval physician wrote: "The patient should avoid all sadness and worry: bring joy and happiness to him by means of all those things he finds delightful." The numerous plague-tracts repeat a similar message: "Whoever wishes to keep himself healthy and fight against death from pestilence should flee anger and sadness, leave the place where the sickness exists, and associate with cheerful companions."[32] Comedy—like other sources of mirth—might be viewed as a medical prescription for opposing the black death.

Several hundred years later another great epidemic produced a second wave of arguments that comedy holds therapeutic powers. The retreat of bubonic plague left the population prey to a more insidious and equally devastating malady, alternately called spleen or vapors or melancholy. This affliction (thought to be caused by particles released when black bile overheated in the spleen) proved so common in postmedieval England

FIGURE 14. Albrecht Dürer (1471–1528). *Melancolia I* (1514).

that it came to be called "the English malady." Today we would probably call it clinical depression. As pictured in Dürer's famous engraving, melancholy reduced both mind and body to a leaden inertia that at times approximated madness (fig. 14). Robert Burton in his encyclopedic *Anatomy of Melancholy* (1621) wrote that the "torture" and "insufferable pains" of this melancholic state were sometimes so oppressive that they drove the sufferer to suicide.[33] People were desperate for a cure.

It should not surprise us that one of the most important medical prescriptions for opposing melancholy was laughter. Burton, while exploring a range of palliatives from exercise to writing books, is quite explicit in arguing for the benefits of mirth or humor. Physicians generally prescribe mirth, he wrote, as a "principal engine to batter the walls of melancholy, a chief antidote, and a sufficient cure of itself."[34] The medical conviction that laughter is not just therapeutic but entirely "sufficient" to banish pain and to transform illness stands behind numerous Renaissance comic works. Indeed, Don Antonio Moreno in *Don Quixote* (II.lxv) regrets that the knight should ever come to his senses because his antics can turn melancholy itself (*la misma melancolía*) into mirth.

A faith in the curative powers of laughter lasted well into the eighteenth century. In fact, later writers created a small library of therapeutic literature, including popular jestbooks with titles such as *Laugh and Be Fat: or, an Antidote against Melancholy* (12th ed., 1741); *The Cure for the Spleen: Or, Kill Care and Laugh* (1769); and, most succinct in linking medicine with laughter, *Splenetick Pills* (1750).[35] This tradition culminates in Laurence Sterne's great comic novel *Tristram Shandy* (1760–1767). As Tristram tells the reader about the book that bears his name:

If 'tis wrote against any thing,—'tis wrote, an' please your worships, against the spleen; in order, by a more frequent and more convulsive elevation and depression of the diaphragm, and the succussations of the intercostal and abdominal muscles in laughter, to drive the *gall* and other *bitter juices* from the gall-bladder, liver, and sweet-bread of his majesty's subjects, with all the inimicitious passions which belong to them, down into their duodenums.[36]

Sterne's deliberately overwritten and over-explicit passage exposes a weakness of the theory he recommends. The idea that laughter held therapeutic powers soon came to seem antiquated and irrational in the approaching era when medicine, with its new germ theory of illness and its new clinical gaze, allied itself as closely as possible to science. We are the direct heirs of this nineteenth-century scorn for the medicinal properties of mirth, which quickly vanished into the museum of prescientific cures, like cupping and leeches.

The theory of therapeutic laughter, however, did not utterly die with the passing of *Tristram Shandy*. We can be quite exact about the date of its revival. In 1976 Norman Cousins—respected editor of the monthly magazine *Saturday Review*—created something of an international furor when the vastly influential *New England Journal of Medicine*, opening its pages to a layman for one of the few times in its history, published his autobiographical essay entitled "Anatomy of an Illness (As Perceived by the Patient)."[37] Suddenly therapeutic laughter was back.

Cousins in his essay and in the popular book (with an almost identical title) that swiftly followed it in effect rediscovered for a scientific era the ancient theory that laughter holds restorative powers. His book also adds an entire chapter devoted specifically to pain, with which Cousins had firsthand experience. A mysterious illness later diagnosed as "ankylosing spondylitis"—a disease involving degeneration of the connective tissue in the spine—struck him down without warning. As he wrote: "The bones in my spine and practically every joint in my body felt as though I had been run over by a truck."

This personal acquaintance with pain led Cousins to more general reflections on American culture. "Americans," he observed, "are probably the most pain-conscious people on the face of the earth." He sees us as simultaneously obsessed and ignorant, a combination that actually increases our distress. He concludes: "We know very little about pain, and what we don't know makes it hurt all the more. Indeed, no form of illiteracy in the United States is so widespread or costly as ignorance about pain—what it is, what causes it, how to deal with it without panic."[38] Cousins decided to deal with his pain, much as comedy would teach us, through laughter.

The unorthodox program of self-healing that Cousins devised with the help of his physician sparked instant controversy in the medical world. (He received over three thousand letters from doctors around the globe.) The program emphasized his active role in his own treatment and supplemented his doctor's efforts with a regimen of personal therapy. This therapy included large doses of ascorbic acid (vitamin C) and exercises designed to strengthen an already strong will to live. Also central to his program was a third and most controversial technique of self-healing. Here is how Cousins describes it:

Nothing is less funny than being flat on your back with all the bones in your spine and joints hurting. A systematic program was indicated. A good place to begin, I thought, was with amusing movies. Allen Funt, producer of the spoofing television program "Candid Camera," sent films of some of his CC classics, along with a motion-picture projector. The nurse was instructed in its use. We were even able to get our hands on some old Marx Brothers films. We pulled down the blinds and turned on the machine. It worked. I made the joyous discovery that ten minutes of genuine belly laughter had an anesthetic effect and would give me at least two hours of pain-free sleep. When the pain-killing effect of the laughter wore off, we would switch on the motion-picture projector again, and, not infrequently, it would lead to another pain-free sleep interval.[39]

On the basis of such claims, traditional medicine for years has openly or privately regarded Cousins as something of a self-deceived and possibly dangerous screwball. It is easy to imagine why many doctors remained skeptical. Yet Cousins may well get the last laugh. Recent scientific studies now strongly support the belief that laughter alters our psychology and biochemistry in ways that can indeed relieve pain.

The revived medical interest in laughter, humor, and comedy might be said to take its origin from Cousins's bold experiment in active self-healing. He sensibly refrained from claiming to have invented a new medicine. "It is quite possible," Cousins wrote, "that this treatment—like everything else I did—was a demonstration of the placebo effect."[40] Placebos refer most commonly to medically inert substances, such as sugar pills, which a patient takes in the belief that they possess medicinal properties. In addition, various practices and paraphernalia associated with medicine (say, white coats or housecalls) may also serve as the equivalent of sugar pills, which is why researchers sometimes prefer to speak of a placebo *effect*. The most significant point is that placebos work only when the patient believes in them. When such belief exists, placebos prove as effective as morphine at relieving pain in an astonishingly consistent 35 percent of patients.[41]

Medicine does not know quite what to make of placebos. Normally the placebo effect gets dismissed as merely an annoying variable in pharmaceutical research. Any new drug will have to prove more than 35 percent effective to receive approval from the Food and Drug Administration. Yet the lowly placebo attests to the mind's forgotten power over illness. Current studies on stress show conclusively that we can make ourselves sick. Why should comedy prove less powerful than sugar pills or white coats in evoking a short-term placebo effect, especially if (like Cousins) we believed in its power to help us? In fact, current research indicates that what psychologists call "positive emotional states" (such as comedy traditionally inspires) serve to enhance the body's immune system and thus to protect against illness.[42] Further, researchers are beginning to discover the psychological and physiological importance of humor to such pain-prone populations as the aged and the terminally ill.[43] The placebo response, it begins to appear, might be celebrated as among our most effective and inexpensive defenses against the maladies of everyday life.

The physiological basis of the placebo response remains a topic of controversy. In 1978 Jon Levine, Newton Gordon, and Howard Fields published an influential study arguing that the basis of the placebo response lay in the activity of endorphins.[44] Endorphins, of course, as every weekend athlete now knows, are among the class of friendly neuropeptides produced by the brain that provide a home-grown, internal (endogenous) system of analgesia. Stimulation of various kinds—from electrodes inserted in the midbrain to long-distance running—in effect triggers the release of endorphins and of the related neuropeptides called enkephalins and dynorphins. These three chemicals bind to opiate-receptors in the nerve cells or neurons blocking the transmission of pain impulses across synapses located at various points in the nervous system, from the dorsal horn of the spinal column up to the midbrain and even to the cerebral cortex. The story of the nearly simultaneous discoveries of this family of endogenous painkillers, which arrived on the scene with great suddenness between 1975 and 1983, requires—and has received—a separate volume.[45] Few breakthroughs in recent medical history have so profoundly altered our knowledge of how our own biochemistry allows us, unknowingly, to handle pain.

Does comedy set in motion the stimulation-produced analgesia (SPA) that cancels pain? Reliable answers should be forthcoming, since the pain-killing action of endorphins and SPA is always reversed or undone by a compound called naloxone. If comedy makes you feel better because it releases endorphins, naloxone will make you feel worse. The reversal of analgesia by naloxone provides a clear sign that the endorphin system is at work. It seems wisest to wait for conclusive studies on the physiology of comic laughter. At the moment, however, we can assert with confidence that laughter is almost inherently social and thus at the very least helps to break the pyschological isolation of pain. Notice how odd it feels on a cross-country flight to watch a film comedy, wearing headphones, and to find yourself laughing alone. Comic laughter puts us back into connection with the social world that pain almost always sets at a distance.

There is growing and reliable, if still inconclusive, evidence to support the biblical adage that laughter doeth good like a medicine. In his latest book, Norman Cousins reproduces the list of humorous materials provided for patients by the Duke University Comprehensive Cancer Center.[46] The widely respected Michigan Head-Pain and Neurological Institute (Ann Arbor) deliberately integrates laughter and humor into the style of daily staff-patient relations, as well as providing one formal class in laughter to patients under hospitalization. Research from a health-care center in Sweden reports a statistically significant link between humor and symptom reduction.[47] Neurologist and psychiatrist Viktor Frankl, a prisoner of the Nazis, emphasized the importance of humor at Auschwitz and Dachau as among "the soul's weapons in the fight for self-preservation."[48] Comic laughter in such cases is not merely a form of distraction, although distraction is a recognized therapy for pain. It is not simply opposed to pain, as we might say tall is opposed to short. Comedy appears to contain the power—if only for a few hours—to allay or even to eradicate pain.

†

A number of distinguished writers—Byron, Nietzsche, Beckett, and Brecht, for example—would encourage us to reflect upon the hidden biomedical connections between comedy and pain. Skeptics, mesmerized by the tradition linking comedy with pure pleasure, may argue that Romantic and post-Romantic writers such as Byron or Brecht simply express a peculiar, eccentric swerve of the modern spirit. This argument has some merit. Undoubtedly, the pain-centered vision of various darkly comic modern writers assumes its significance in part because it openly departs from the traditional emphasis upon comic pleasure. Surely, too, the changed conditions of twentieth-century life stand behind a film such as *Dr. Strangelove* (1963), with its gleeful, concluding vision of nuclear apocalypse. The visible presence of pain in contemporary comedies and in theories of comedy, however, is not unprecedented but (as I have tried to show) the recovery and renewal of something ancient and apparently permanent within comedy.

We do not need Plato or Socrates to affirm the antiquity of comic pain. The orgies, carnival feasts, and primitive rites that gave rise to comedy overflowed with the blood of animal and human sacrifices. The Greeks laughed at misfortune, deformity, or ugliness. The Roman poet Horace tells us in his *Ars Poetica* that Greek Old Comedy maintained a "ius no-cendi" (a right of injury) that Middle Comedy gave up; but in fact comedy never truly gave up its link with pain—only refined and disguised it. We see it again in the wife-beatings of the aptly named Punchinello—ances-tor of the famous Punch and Judy puppets, which reached England from Italy in the late seventeenth century. Even the lighthearted world of Shakespearean romantic comedy contains a latent pain in the abundant threats of loss, injury, banishment, revenge, and death.[49] From a historical perspective, the genial, joyous, compassionate spirit of pure pleasure we now associate with comedy is a relative newcomer.

"In tragedy," writes the modern English playwright Christopher Fry, "we suffer pain; in comedy pain is a fool, suffered gladly."[50] As Fry's sum-marizing comparison suggests, comedy shrinks and detoxifies pain. Comic pain no longer frightens, but rather provides a source of amuse-ment and healing. Thus what we regularly encounter in comedy is vio-lence without violent consequences. The situation calls for pain but pain does not answer. It remains conspicuous by its absence. This is the familiar landscape of the Saturday morning cartoon character who stands holding the round, black bomb as the fuse relentlessly burns down. Comedy, as we have seen, includes such threats of violence as a precondition for over-coming them. A comic world in which pain must be overcome, however, differs greatly from a world in which pain is wholly excluded or un-imaginable. Pain comically deprived of its power to hurt is not exactly pain, but it reminds us—even in allowing us almost to forget—how much we know about the real thing.

Perhaps as the archetype of this curiously erased pain we should con-sider the lowly pratfall. The pratfall—meaning a fall on one's buttocks or (slang) "pratt"—became an early staple of modern film comedy. Mack Sennett, whose films set the world record for pratfalls, found in such as-saults upon authority and pretension the central action or meaning of comic art. "The whacking of Fat Lady's backside," as he declared in a revealing mixture of metaphor, sexism, and literal-mindedness, "is the ba-sis of all true comedy."[51] Sennett's Fat Lady, even if she embodies male fantasies and rites of dominance, belongs also to a long tradition that stretches from Falstaff and Sancho Panza back through the medieval Lenten contest between the Fat Man and the Thin Man to the priapic, big-bellied satyrs of the Greek stage. It matters to comedy that the backside in question is a large and inviting target. Slapstick at its most basic is an affirmation of the comic body. The resounding whack assures us that the cosmos contains something ultimately solid and resilient. It demonstrates that the body, which is such a troublesome source and site of affliction, also serves through its link with comedy and laughter as a potent (if imperfect) compensation for our pain.

5

HYSTERIA, PAIN, AND GENDER

Of all chronic diseases hysteria—unless I err—is the commonest.
THOMAS SYDENHAM[1]

HE ABSENCE OF pain does not always bring magical relief and comic pleasure. Laughter, for example, in extreme cases is not only *not* therapeutic but also pathological. Consider the following curious case recorded in recent medical literature on rare diseases and lesions. In 1962 an epidemic of contagious laughter broke out at a mission-run girls middle school in the village of Kashasha, East Africa. Forty-five days later the school had to be closed and the laughing girls were sent home, but they simply spread the epidemic laughter to neighboring villages. Another girls school and two boys schools within a fifty mile radius were forced to close. For some six months, the authors report, the normal life of the community was disrupted, with serious implications for public health.[2] Laboratory investigations showed no infectious or toxic origin for the attacks. This well-documented episode, which no organic process can explain, offers useful evidence that the once potent malady known as hysteria (surviving now mainly in the cliché "hysterical laughter") has not completely vanished from the earth.

It is a puzzling fact that in the twentieth century hysteria has declined precipitously as a medical diagnosis.[3] The near disappearance of hysteria represents a social and medical change on the same order of magnitude as the almost total annihilation of tuberculosis. The comparison is especially pertinent because, like tuberculosis, hysteria was far more than merely another illness. It too collected around it an aura of myth that meant patients unavoidably found themselves entangled in the social meanings and values that accrue to certain illnesses. Yet one crucial difference separates tuberculosis from hysteria as dominating, mythic nineteenth-century illnesses. Tuberculosis struck men and women alike. Hysteria, in myth although not always in fact, was understood as entirely an affliction of women.

The affliction was everywhere. Invalids—most of them women, many of them hysterics—filled the homes of nineteenth-century America and Europe. Freud based the new practice of psychoanalysis on his early studies of hysterical women, who seemed in inexhaustible supply. Women who were not themselves hysterics faced a strong possibility that they would end up as nurses for hysterical mothers, sisters, or daughters. Yet the disappearance of the hysteric is less complete than we may imagine. Today doctors refer to hysteria (an unpopular diagnosis) through such impenetrable euphemisms as Briquet's Syndrome, while doubtless few people suspect that the ubiquitous Minnesota Multiphasic Personality Inventory (MMPI) tests them for hysterical tendencies.[4] The *Diagnostic and Statistical Manual of Mental Disorders*—the bible of the psychiatric profession—contains a long entry entitled "Conversion Disorder (or Hysterical Neurosis, Conversion Type)."[5] We may begin to wonder whether hysteria has not so much disappeared as simply changed its name and gone underground.

There is good reason for returning to the subject of hysteria. Hysteria, both ancient and modern, provides important evidence that pain is constructed as much by social conditions as by the structure of the nervous system. It allows us to understand how women and men may face illness in cultural contexts so different as to create what can only be called male pain and female pain. Male pain tends to play itself out today in openly public places: football fields, street fights, combat. Female pain is more elusive and harder to see. Further, the invisible bond that hysteria allows us to detect—the bond linking women to a peculiarly gender-marked pain—encourages the suggestion that Western culture is not yet entirely free from the perils that threatened our great-grandmothers. Hysteria cannot be dismissed as merely a relic of the distant past. As we will see, it may even have found new uses and new shapes within the changed sexual politics of twentieth-century life.

†

Silas Weir Mitchell (1829–1914) was undoubtedly the most famous nineteenth-century American physician specializing in the diseases of women (fig. 15). His talents and interests spread as well to other fields. His name is still revered in medical schools, where he is regarded as the father of modern neurology. His celebrated work on nerve injuries drew upon his experience during and after the Civil War when as a young doctor—even then a commanding figure—he treated wounded Union soldiers at the Philadelphia Stump Hospital. Later, with his medical career flourishing, he began to publish stories and novels that won him wide popular acclaim. Even several of his medical texts became best-sellers, and he was thus a distinguished choice as speaker for the fiftieth annual Ether Day celebration at the Massachusetts General Hospital, where we earlier encountered him delivering the poem he had written for the occasion, entitled "The Birth and Death of Pain."

Mitchell's unusual background as physician and writer lends particular interest to a scene he described in his medical text entitled *Doctor and Patient* (1887):

As I look from my window, on the lawn below are girls at play—gay, vigorous, wholesome; they laugh, they run, and are never weary. How far from them and their abounding health seem the possibilities of such torment as nature somewhere in life reserves for most of us. As women, their lives are likely, nay certain, to bring them a variety of physical discomforts, and perhaps pain in its gravest forms. For man, pain is accidental, and depends much on the chances of life. Certainly, many men go through existence here with but little pain. With women it is incidental, and a far more probable possibility.[6]

As Mitchell continued to meditate on the idyllic scene beneath his window, his curious language of calculation led him to firmer statements on the nature of sexual difference. "We may be sure," he concluded, "that our daughters will be more likely to have to face at some time the grim question of pain than the lads who grow up beside them."[7]

Mitchell in this passage from *Doctor and Patient* does not invoke hysteria by name, but the context makes it unmistakable that he is writing not about pregnancy or childbirth but about hysteria. His meaning is quite clear: an alarming number of the girls playing beneath his window will sooner or later require a physician's care as incapacitated hysterics. Hysteria in Mitchell's day was not *exclusively* a disease of women. Before 1618, hysteria had been held to occur in women only—its male counter-

FIGURE 15. Silas Weir Mitchell, M.D. (1829–1914). Photograph (1859).

part being hypochondria. But Sydenham in the late seventeenth century writes about hysterical symptoms in men; one of Freud's early papers concerns male hysteria; and various maverick physicians—early and late—have resisted the dominant tradition that regards hysteria as feminine.[8] Both language and social practice have, however, established a firm association between women and hysteria. Derived from the Greek root *hyster* or womb, hysteria automatically posits a biological connection between female sexuality and illness.

Mitchell's readers knew instantly what specific illness it was that gave the grim question of pain a different answer for women than for men. A woman living in the last half of the nineteenth century ran a very good chance of finding herself under the care of Dr. Mitchell or Dr. Freud or their contemporaries. Indeed, the period from 1870 to 1910, when Mitchell's career was at its zenith and when Freud's studies of hysterics were just beginning to build the foundations of psychoanalysis, is sometimes described as the "golden age" of hysteria. An understanding of hysteria, however, requires a sense that it was in some ways the most ancient and the most modern of female illnesses.

The womb, often pictured as the source of female irrationalism, far outdistances any other organ in its power to spark the irrationality of male writers. Plato uncritically transmits the ancient belief that the female womb was not an organ at all but rather—incredibly—an animal.[9] According to ancient thought, this strange animal called the womb lived independently within the female body. Like other animals, it was thought to roam around, moving restlessly from place to place, often straying from its customary post near the genitals. This "wandering womb" is what the ancients regarded as the source of numerous female maladies, and treatment often consisted of attempts to lure the womb back toward its normal location, by the use of sweet-smelling salves or fumes. Some doctors, following this logic in reverse, would try to drive the womb down with foul medicines taken by mouth.

The ancient world considered this unstable animal, the womb, as the source not only of specific female maladies but also of woman's very nature, especially her shifting emotions, her changeability, her carnal appetites (in contrast to the calm reasonableness that classical male writers considered typical of well-born males). We are surely correct to understand the womb—in this prescientific medical discourse—as an image for everything about women that troubled and terrified men. Hysteria thus tells us as much about male doctors as about female patients. Doctors regarded hysteria as especially prominent among virgins and widows, who recovered from their symptoms (so popular wisdom believed) with the acquisition of a husband. If this belief has any basis in fact, no doubt the social conditions that oppressed women in ways both obvious and subtle help to explain why widows or unmarried women might experience their isolation as a kind of emotional disorder. It is also easy to understand why a male-centered culture, which prided itself on rational control, would brand such emotion in women as illness.

The speculations of Plato about the womb as a wandering animal seem almost innocent when compared with the assaults against women conducted during the nineteenth century in the name of science. Neurologist Nikolaus Friedrich (1825–1882), for example, treated hysteria by cauterizing the clitoris of hysterical patients whose sexual appetites he deemed immoderate. Gynecologist Alfred Hegar (1830–1924) performed ovariectomies.[10] These overt, if possibly well-meaning, medical assaults upon the female body must be understood as reflecting wider cultural threats associated ultimately with women's sexuality. Nor should it surprise us that surgical efforts to cure women of a disease rooted in their social oppression and in male fears did not restore order. Throughout the nineteenth century hysteria remained what Thomas Sydenham (the "English Hippocrates") had called it two hundred years earlier, "a farrago of disorderly and irregular phenomena."[11]

The disorder and confusion that Sydenham recognized in hysteria referred to its symptoms, not to its cause. (There was only one cause, of course: the womb.) Like the mythological old man of the sea, Proteus, who when captured would escape by changing his shape, hysteria was less a single disease than the name for a hodgepodge of changing symptoms. At least from the time of Galen in the second century, such symptoms included dysfunctions ranging from coughs and hiccups to tremors, tics, fainting, convulsions, and innumerable deficits of vision, hearing, taste, sight, and speech. According to Sydenham, in fact, hysteria could imitate the symptoms of almost every known disease. "The frequency of hysteria," he wrote in 1681, "is no less remarkable than the multiformity of the shapes which it puts on. Few of the maladies of miserable mortality are not imitated by it."[12]

Its power to imitate other diseases made hysteria unique among maladies. For example, the index to Freud's collected works lists one hundred and one symptoms of hysteria, from abasia to zoöpsia. (Abasia is the inability to walk, zoöpsia the hallucination of insects or animals.) An illness equipped with more than one hundred disguises clearly confronted physicians with an insoluble diagnostic puzzle. Yet, because of its gender-marked bias, hysteria was not simply another puzzling illness. Any woman whose symptoms did not respond to conventional treatment—especially if her doctor judged her too emotional, too theatrical, too self-centered, too moody, or oversexed—might soon find herself classified and implicitly condemned as hysterical. Hysteria provided a convenient diagnostic box for imprisoning women whom male doctors were unable to cure.

The kaleidoscope of hysterical symptoms nonetheless failed to stop scientific research from probing for an underlying pattern. Thus it became normal practice in nineteenth-century treatises on hysteria to describe the disease through certain characteristic dysfunctions called *stigmata*. "Since the beginning of the scientific study of hysteria," wrote the eminent French psychologist and neurologist Pierre Janet, "all the attention of clinicians of any merit has been directed to the study and search of the stigma."[13] Janet's own influential study entitled *The Major Symptoms of Hysteria* (1907) reminds readers that in the previous century hysteria had taken as its "essential stigma" the convulsive attack or well-known "hysterical fit." Other familiar *stigmata* that Janet discusses include paralysis, sleepwalking, and amnesia, which he had studied in an earlier work entitled *The Mental State of Hystericals* (1901). For over a hundred years physicians trained in scientific method and statistical analysis had been searching fruitlessly, with the best modern tools, for a way to pin down hysteria.

Paul Briquet's *Traité clinique et thérapeutique de l'hystérie* (1859) probably deserves credit for beginning the scientific study of hysteria. Although soon overshadowed by his more famous French colleague Jean-Martin Charcot (1825–1893), Briquet provided the first important clinical and epidemiological analysis of hysteria—based on a study of 430 cases seen over a ten-year period in his unit at the Hôpital de la Charité in Paris. For our purposes, his account is notable chiefly for the precision and compassion with which he surveyed the wasted lives of his female patients. "No illness is more difficult to cure than hysteria," he observed sadly:

Half of hysterical women recover only when advancing age dulls their sensitivities. One quarter never recover or have the illness their entire lives. Some young girls who become hysteric before the age of 12 or 13 years are condemned to a lifetime of suffering, malaise, and sometimes serious illness. They may spend a year or more in bed, completely incapacitated. They are always sick, abort easily, or if they go to term, give birth to more hysterics. Some remain ill until an advanced age, become cachectic, thin and irritable, and old before their time, leading but a wretched life for themselves and those around them.[14]

Charcot—something of an artist—was among the first physicians to bring the new technique of photography to the service of clinical medicine, and the grainy photographs from his hysteria ward provide haunting images of the devastation endured by nineteenth-century women, whose available roles outside of marriage sometimes extended no further (as Charcot's pictures suggest) than the quick slide from spinster to whore (fig. 16). Such, indeed, was the grim vision that Weir Mitchell, with his novelist's eye, saw superimposed upon the scene of carefree, energetic girls running and playing beneath his window.

†

Pain ranks prominently among the most familiar symptoms of hysteria. Briquet wrote: "Pain in the muscles is so common that there is not a single woman with this neurosis who does not have some muscle pain during the course of the illness."[15] But muscle pain was only one type of hyperesthesia from which the typical hysteric suffered. The hysterical woman seemed a labyrinth of curious and largely unresponsive pains. In describing Frau Emmy von N. in his *Studies on Hysteria* (1895), Freud observes the following combination of symptoms: "She has had distressingly severe pains in her face, in her hand on the thumb side and in her leg. She gets stiff and has pains in her face if she sits without moving or stares at some fixed point for any considerable time. If she lifts anything heavy it bring on pains in her arm."[16] The hysterical patient lived in a world where pain flowed continuously through her body and settled in the most unexpected places. It provided the solid, changeless background against which hysteria played out its more florid and transient symptoms.

Doctors did not need to wait for a full theory of psychoanalysis before suspecting that the often diffuse, confusing, multiple symptoms of hys-

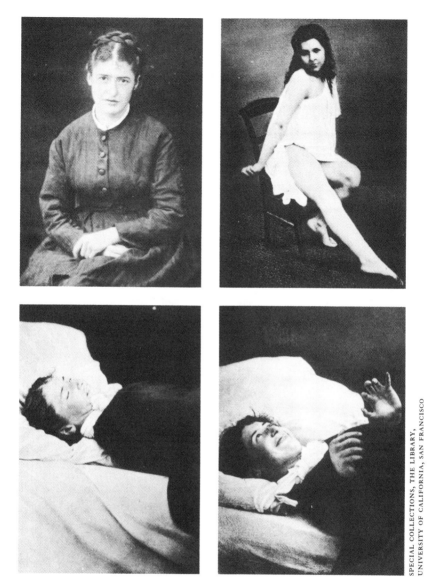

FIGURE 16. Jean-Martin Charcot (1825–1893). Four photographs of hysteria (1878).

teria originated mainly in the patient's mind. Women were regularly suspected of faking illness. Thus, writing in the *British Medical Journal* for
1858, the Liverpool physician Thomas Inman reported that doctors commonly tested the female hysteric with a secret ploy. While steadily increasing the pressure of his hand on the sensitive area, the doctor deliberately distracted the patient in order to see whether she complained
about the steadily increasing pressure. If the woman failed to complain,
the doctor concluded that her pain was unreal, that is, *"only hysterical."*[17]
Hysteria quickly became medical code for made-up, factitious, or imaginary illness.

Hysteria from the perspective of this century looks increasingly like a
form of sexual theater acted out between male doctors and female patients.[18] At issue was the question of whether a woman's pain was real.
This question owed much to the specific changes in nineteenth-century
medicine. Sydenham in the seventeenth century had followed ancient tradition (which we can trace back to Aristotle) that classified pain as an
emotion. He would no more question the reality of women's pain than
the reality of their grief or anger. It simply made no sense, within this
older Aristotelian tradition, to say that a woman *imagined* she was angry
or in pain. The positivist medicine that emerged in the nineteenth century, however, rejected the traditional view that pain was an emotion.
Doctors increasingly identified pain with organic lesions of the nervous
system. A nineteenth-century woman who complained of pains incompatible with current medical knowledge about the nervous system thus
ran the serious risk of finding her illness dismissed as imaginary.

The hysteric in effect became the victim of a double affliction. She suffered not only from multiple pains but also from the suspicion of male
doctors that her pain was merely the gossamer product of an overheated,
labile, sexually deranged, morally corrupt female imagination. Further, it
was commonly thought that women did not so much imagine their pain
as deliberately fake it, and such suspicions have proved hard to dislodge.
The guidelines for physicians published by the American Pain Society in
1989 thus begin with the unequivocal direction: "Tell patients you believe
their pain is real."[19] In *An Essay on Hysteria* published in 1840 the American surgeon Thomas Laycock summed up the stated or unstated assumption of much nineteenth-century medicine when he claimed: "Of
all animals, an artful woman is the most artful, and when we consider
how this faculty may be exalted by the influence of the generative organs,

there is not much real ground for surprise at the grotesque forms which it sometimes assumes in the hysterical female."[20]

$$\dagger$$

The nineteenth-century struggle over the status of female pain finds oblique expression in a now acclaimed work by Charlotte Perkins Gilman entitled *The Yellow Wallpaper* (1892). Gilman possessed such talents, energy, and conviction that it sometimes seems she single-handedly launched the feminist movement in America, but not without great personal cost. At one point while she suffered the added pressures of an unhappy marriage that led to her scandalous decision to seek divorce, a nervous breakdown put her under the care of Weir Mitchell, who prescribed his famous "rest cure." She reports his diagnosis in words that suggest how close the hysteric lived to fears of madness: "There was no dementia, he said, only hysteria."[21]

The rest cure offered an enormous advance over cauterization of the clitoris, but the patriarchal attitudes behind it simply took a less brutal form. Mitchell's female patients were confined to bed, completely isolated from friends and family, fed a high fat diet round the clock, forbidden any form of activity, even reading or sewing, and regularly subjected to edifying lectures on women's household duties and moral obligations.[22] An often-repeated anecdote, perhaps apocryphal, captures the spirit of Mitchell's authoritarian and patriarchal regime. When one woman patient refused his order to get up, he frightened her out of bed by unbuttoning his trousers as if to join her. After four to six weeks of such treatment, some women emerged plump and eager (understandably) to resume the less stultifying routine of nineteenth-century bourgeois marriage.

There is no question that Mitchell's rest cure reinforced the values of a male-centered world in which the roles permitted to women focused mainly on the household. At the end of her treatment, Gilman received from Mitchell the following strict instructions: "Live as domestic a life as possible. Have your child with you all the time. . . . Lie down an hour after each meal. Have but two hours' intellectual life a day. And never touch pen, brush or pencil as long as you live." Gilman, a dynamo among writers, reports that in attempting for a short time to follow Mitchell's instructions she came "perilously near" to losing her mind.[23]

The Yellow Wallpaper is Gilman's meditation on the psychosocial bond that links domestic confinement, male domination, and the distinctive, elusive pain of women's illness. The story concerns a young wife who suffers a mild nervous collapse. Her doctor-husband describes it as "temporary nervous depression—a slight hysterical tendency."[24] Weir Mitchell had written that doctors make the best husbands because they understand so well (as he put it) the special weaknesses of women. The doctor-husband in Gilman's story treats his wife with tyrannical solicitude, including the threat that if she fails to follow his instructions exactly he will send her to Mitchell for a rest cure. ("I am a doctor, dear," her husband tells her, "and I know.")[25] The story follows the stages of her gradual collapse into madness. The wife whom her husband treats like a child ultimately ends up locked in the attic-nursery where she imagines that she sees a crouched woman imprisoned behind the barlike stripes of the yellow wallpaper. In effect, she hallucinates the truth of her own social confinement. Gilman sent a copy of the story to Mitchell in order to show him, she said, the "error of his ways."[26] She received no response.

The Yellow Wallpaper might be said to invite exactly the same misunderstanding that it exposes. There are no explicit descriptions of pain, no clear indications of organic illness. On the basis of such evidence the young woman's physician-husband continues to insist that nothing is wrong. "You see," the woman explains, "he does not believe I am sick!" A little later she emphasizes how far her husband fails to recognize pain that has no obvious organic source. "John does not know how much I really suffer. He knows there is no *reason* to suffer, and that satisfies him." As her hysteria turns to madness, the woman spends her nights crawling the perimeter of her sickroom, tearing off the wallpaper, wearing a channel into the wall with her shoulder. She lifts and pushes at her immovable bed until she is "lame"; enraged, she bites off a corner until her "teeth hurt." The wallpaper, she says, "slaps me in the face, knocks me down, and tramples upon me."[27] Still, despite this language of violence, Gilman does not make any direct use of the word "pain," and unwary readers may simply repeat the error of her doctor-husband. Like the nineteenth-century medical world, he refuses to take seriously an illness that does not explicitly announce itself through the scientifically acceptable symptoms of tissue damage.

Her husband's refusal to recognize suffering that he (literally) cannot put his finger on was not willful blindness. But it was blindness nonetheless, and such well-meaning ignorance today is especially dangerous because it perpetuates a habit of mind now centuries old. Gilman shows us how female pain is regularly disregarded, discounted, and dismissed, largely because it does not always conform to the clear organic model of appendicitis or a broken arm. Anything else is regarded as simply not pain. Gilman—in many ways still half-confined by the thinking that she attacks—once distinguished sharply in describing her own illness between what she called "physical pain" and "mental torment."[28] Certainly, as we have seen, it is possible to suffer emotional torment such as grief, at least for a short period, without necessarily feeling pain.

Yet *The Yellow Wallpaper* also shows how, over time, the line between these two states quickly begins to blur. The ascending central pain pathways include projections to the thalamus, hypothalamus, and limbic system, which make emotional distress absolutely intrinsic to the perception of pain. The isolated young wife in Gilman's story, lamed and gnawing on the corner of her bed until her teeth hurt, acts out a suffering that the male medical world cannot acknowledge until her distress at last grows openly deranged and subject to incarceration. Gilman allows us to understand that the image of Weir Mitchell gazing down from his window on the playful young girls reveals more than the prophetic compassion of an eminent doctor-writer. Unknowingly, as the authoritarian representative of a male-centered culture that confined women within rigidly constricted roles, as the spokesman for a medical science that acknowledged pain only in cases of explicit tissue damage, he was also an indirect cause of the suffering he sought to relieve.

†

The gender-marked pain of hysteria—pain denied its status as pain—gives rise to another mysterious affliction suffered by the countless women who filled the sickbeds of nineteenth-century Europe and America. We normally think of pain as defined in part by its relation to opposite or contrary states, much as we define heat in part through its opposing relation to cold. The opposite of pain—at least in everyday speech—is pleasure. Yet if we consider only the relation between pleasure and pain we may miss a far less obvious and more troubling alliance. This is the peculiar kinship, which emerges fully in the literature on hysteria, between pain and numbness.[29]

Numbness is in effect the photographic negative of pain. It is pain reversed, turned inside out. Almost everyone has experienced the ambiguous moment when—in grasping, say, a block of ice—we find it hard to know exactly whether what we feel is pain. Prolonged numbness, however, is not an ambiguous, intermediate state. Intense pain often represents or stands for feeling itself, and prolonged numbness represents feeling drawn back toward a zero degree where pain and sensation vanish together. More precisely, prolonged numbness is not so much the absence of pain as the paradoxical state in which we feel that we have lost the power of feeling. Like pain, numbness has long ranked among the most common symptoms of hysteria.

The importance of numbness among the stigmata or symptoms of hysteria is clear from Pierre Janet's description of the great nineteenth-century French neurologist Charcot. "You are aware," Janet wrote to his medical audience in *The Major Symptoms of Hysteria*, "that, especially under the influence of the school of Charcot, one symptom has become the preëminent stigma; namely, *anesthesia*."[30] Janet shrewdly—but without grasping its full significance—associates the clinician's search for numbness with the witch-hunting procedures of the Inquisition. When the authorities suspected a woman of being a witch, they employed a female assistant to prick her with sharp needles in order to locate the so-called *devil's claw* (an insensitive patch of skin) once considered infallible evidence of witchcraft. "In our clinics," Janet continues, "we are somewhat like the woman who sought for witches. We blindfold the subject, we turn his head away, rub his skin with our nail, prick it suddenly with a hidden pin, watch his answers or starts of pain; the picture has not changed."[31] The pronouns, of course, are misleading. Hysteria, like witchcraft, was a woman's province.

Numbness, then, quickly took its place along with pain as a characteristic mark or sign of hysterical women. "Almost all the hystericals who, at present, show a serious phenomenon," reported Janet, "have had in the past one of those accidents that leave behind them, as a trace, some persisting anesthesia."[32] Although it may appear that hysteria has gone the way of Weir Mitchell and his rest cure, traces of hysterical anesthesia undoubtedly penetrate deep into the modern world. We do not call the condition hysteria, and it is unaccompanied by the repertoire of florid symptoms catalogued by nineteenth-century doctors, but we must not be deceived by a change in style and vocabulary. The gender-linked pain and numbness of hysteria have direct, if cunning, counterparts in the twentieth century.

The historical changes that separate us from our nineteenth-century ancestors mean that the pain and numbness suffered by women today are not exactly identical with the afflictions of the past. Women now have unprecedented access to jobs, education, and personal development. Yet Riane Eisler in *The Chalice and the Blade* (1987) is surely correct that in one sense we still inhabit a landscape defined by a dominator/dominated model of social relations. Eisler also seems to me correct in arguing that our hierarchical system of dominator/dominated social relations takes its origin—and maintains its present-day power—in the inequalities of male and female roles. True, the pain and numbness of nineteenth-century hysteria cannot be *exactly* identical with the afflictions women continue to suffer today, but differences in this case prove far less revealing than major similarities. There is probably no better place to explore the linked traces of hysterical pain and anesthesia persisting in the modern world than in a French novel now hailed as something of a classic: Marguerite Duras's *The Ravishing of Lol Stein* (1964).

The plot, as in all of Duras's works, is so spare and hauntingly simple that a summary misses almost everything that gives the book its power. Duras examines the consequences of a lost love and begins when Lol Stein as a young woman suffers a devastating shock: her fiancé deserts her at the public town ball and vanishes with a beautiful stranger. This melodramatic event, however, interests Duras far less than its lingering traces, years later, in the everyday life of her enigmatic heroine Lol Stein. Indeed, this minimalist plot is typical of the slender threads by which Marguerite Duras constructs what we might best describe as narratives of desire or, more precisely, narratives in which desire is blocked, attenuated, or unfulfilled.

The bond that links desire to pain and numbness will grow clearer if we briefly trace Lol's experience following the town ball.[33] She eventually recovers from the breakdown and marries a dull but devoted husband. Her loveless marriage, however, and her life of middle-class tedium seem finally less like health than like a waking coma. She revives from this vacant, passive, sleepwalking state only after many years when she meets an old school friend, Tatiana Karl, who had stood beside her on the night when Lol's fiancé vanished. Tatiana too has settled for a loveless, middle-class marriage, but she has taken as her lover a young doctor named Jacques Hold. The remainder of the novel describes the powerful attraction between Lol Stein and Jacques Hold, which never fully succeeds in breaking through the peculiar vacancy in which Lol lives, as if in an abstracted state of posttraumatic shock.

Lol is typical of Duras's obsessive and inward-turned heroines, who (even when their passion finds an object) experience feeling with an ardor that ultimately drains them of the power to feel. Intensity and detachment—pain and numbness—prove almost inseparable.[34] We can gain insight into Lol's state through lines that Emily Dickinson wrote one hundred years earlier, out of her own isolation and crisis of spirit, at a time when across Europe and America hysteria was producing thousands of female invalids who were simultaneously hypersensitive and anesthetized:

> There is a pain—so utter—
> It swallows substance up—
> Then covers the Abyss with Trance—
> So Memory can step
> Around—across—upon it.[35]

Certainly Lol, after her trauma at the town ball, seems to live on a surface so fragile that any abrupt movement or feeling might plunge her into the abyss. Desire has brought with it a trancelike indifference, as if pain and obsession always end in emptying out the self. It is not women alone who exhibit the strange anesthesia of desire. A young woman tells the obsessive male protagonist of Duras's *The Malady of Death* that, until meeting him, she did not know death could be lived.[36] Duras's women, however, far more often than her men find themselves following desire into this banal and frightening limbo of death-in-life.

The medical term "malady" in Duras's title is not a metaphorical flourish. Like Lol Stein, her women frequently live on the edge of breakdown. Their unofficial illness is perhaps most deathlike in its almost complete emptiness of feeling. Thus Jacques Hold reports that Lol's desertion at the town ball was marked by "the strange absence of pain."[37] Her later response proves equally strange: Lol, we are told, is "feigning death." Her husband finds an appropriate image for her state of numb, protracted trance when he compares Lol to Sleeping Beauty. Duras gives no technical name to the anesthesia that grips her women. Its causes, she suggests, lie less in a painful trauma than in various failures to experience it fully. In an interview, she says simply of Lol that "the pain wasn't lived out."[38]

Duras in interviews tends to talk about her characters not as fictional creations—beings she has invented and fully understood—but as complex people whose motives and actions she cannot entirely grasp. Duras sees Lol's denial of pain—her refusal to live it out—as linked to a larger refusal to feel. Yet we risk distorting Duras's novel if we understand Lol's delirium and numbness, her strange absence of feeling, as merely the specific response to her trauma at the town ball. Duras's larger point seems to be that female illness cannot be traced back to a single point of origin, in the manner of psychoanalysis. Thus Lol's final return with Jacques Hold to the scene of the town ball changes nothing. Her illness, it seems, has more to do with her gender than with the unique details of her experience.

For women in Duras's work, trauma somehow always seems to *precede* events. Events, such as Lol's desertion at the town ball, serve mainly to precipitate a trauma already, if secretly, present. For Lol, the female trauma that precedes events is visible—in retrospect—even in childhood. Tatiana describes Lol's school years this way: "She never seemed to suffer or be hurt, had never been known to shed a sentimental, schoolgirl's tear."[39] In this anesthesia, Lol seems initially different from other girls, but she simply anticipates the experience that many of them later, in various ways, will come to share. We might say that Duras's women inhabit a world that seems to require an almost prenatal immersion in an unnameable grief, sadness, and pain which leaves them desiring but finally numb. "I cry for no reason that I can explain," says another Duras heroine. "It's as though I were shot through with grief. Someone has to weep, and I seem to be the one."[40]

Pain is without question a central subject and preoccupation in Duras's work. The 1985 book describing her years in occupied Paris during World War II—her first work to receive widespread acclaim in France—bears as its title the resonant French word for pain, *La Douleur*. In this collection of short pieces we find the same relationship between suffering and numbness that permeates her other books. Yet even the most personal writing in *La Douleur* requires us to understand that the pain Duras treats is not simply personal but crucially linked with gender. "These books are painful, to write and to read," she said in an interview. "What I mean is that they're painful, painful because they're works that move toward an area that's not hollowed out yet, maybe. . . . I mean something about what is feminine. . . . Maybe that's what causes the pain."[41]

These somewhat cryptic and halting comments, typical of Duras's interviews, at least suggest clearly enough that she thinks of pain and numbness as intimately connected with the experience of women. About the woman who said someone has to weep and she seemed to be the one, Duras made this comment: "It flows in her, you see, like a river that's traveled through her; it's as if she's tunneled by this river of pain."[42] Duras frequently returns to the image of female pain as something that excavates or hollows out. Even when they experience trauma, most of the men in Duras's fiction live a less internal existence. They are less porous, less open to the extremes of numbness and pain. Pain does not seem to flow through them in subsurface spaces that for Duras represent something unique to women's experience.

†

Feminist historians and critics rightly emphasize that hysteria was in part a response to social conditions that particularly oppressed and constricted women. The logical question is, why should hysteria wait until the nineteenth century to explode in such epidemic proportions? After all, the oppression of women had continued for centuries; in ancient Greece as in eighteenth-century England, women had the legal status of property transferred between fathers and husbands. Indeed, the nineteenth-century explosion of hysteria is in part merely a sudden prominence given to a medical problem that had persisted on a less public level for centuries. Thus Thomas Sydenham in the seventeenth century describes hysteria as the most common of chronic illnesses.

The new prominence that hysteria attained in the nineteenth century also reflects important and unprecedented social changes. Medicine was energetically transforming itself into a modern profession, and young doctors with families to feed and careers to launch found a ready source of income—and a rich field of study—in the unending supply of bizarre hysterical symptoms. Of equal importance, age-old custom, prejudice, and injustice seemed suddenly a little less inevitable, less preordained in a God-given social order that traced the favored position of males back to the garden of Eden. In the nineteenth century, during the aftermath of the American and French revolutions, with the emergence of strong voices such as Mary Wollstonecraft and Charlotte Perkins Gilman arguing for the rights of women, society no longer seemed fixed in an unquestioned, unchanging order that required the absolute, eternal subordination of women.

The pain and numbness of hysteria during the nineteenth century in effect expressed the conflicts of a society in rapid change, where women now glimpsed a freedom that their male-centered culture was nevertheless still mostly unwilling to grant. Hysterical pain and numbness served as ballots cast secretly in an election from which women were still legally excluded. Such symptoms, as Dianne Hunter has proposed, are a form of thwarted or inarticulate speech, "a discourse of femininity addressed to patriarchal thought."[43] We can sense the power of Hunter's argument in the tone with which Weir Mitchell describes a successful product of his rest cure. "Her change in tint, flesh, and expression was so remarkable that the process of repair might well have been called a renewal of life. She went home," he concludes, "changed no less morally than physically, and resumed her place in the family circle and in social life, a healthy and well-cured woman."[44]

✝

Marguerite Duras would say that among the most important gifts that well-cured women have resigned in accepting a place within an oppressive, male-centered social order (that has persisted, despite improvements, throughout the twentieth century) is a knowledge of their own speech. She is fond of citing a story that she found in a book on witchcraft by the great nineteenth-century French historian Jules Michelet. In Duras's retelling, it was during one of the interminable medieval crusades or feudal wars that women, left alone on their farms, began out of boredom to talk with the foxes and birds and trees. No one objected to this behavior, Duras adds, except that the men eventually returned and found their women out speaking to trees. It was then that men—finding this discourse of women intolerable—invented witchcraft.[45]

Duras treats this speculative history of witchcraft as a myth expressing the masculine suppression of female discourse. "They burned them," Duras says of the male response to the women they branded as witches: "To stop it, block up the madness, block up feminine speech."[46] Michelet's account gives Duras a way to suggest how the writing of contemporary women represents the imperfect recovery of a speech that the male social order and male reason have long suppressed and driven underground, forced into such outlawed spaces as witchcraft, madness, and sexual transgression. The writing of women, she believes, when it is not simply the imitation of male writing, makes contact with a dimly understood level of experience that men have tried to burn out of human consciousness, to bury beneath a desperate masculine monologue of reason and control.[47] This specifically feminine writing—for which we can find ready examples in the lyrical, mysterious, disruptive later novels of Duras—often takes the fractured logic and syntax of the hysteric as its aggressive symbol.

In fact, hysteria has become among feminist circles almost a symbol of women's writing. "Can women's writing ever be anything other than hysterical?" asks Mary Jacobus.[48] "The woman novelist must be an hysteric," writes Juliet Mitchell: "Hysteria . . . is simultaneously what a woman can do both to be feminine and to refuse femininity, within patriarchal discourse."[49] Feminists divide over whether to commend the hysteric as a protofeminist, a woman valiantly resisting oppression without the resources of feminism, or to criticize the hysteric as the passive victim of a repressive social order. The salient point for our purposes is that feminist criticism recognizes and even celebrates the link between Duras and hysteria. Critic Patricia Fedikew thus finds in Duras's novels a recurrent drama in which the woman—forced to live in a world of male law and male desire—plays out the hysteric's role as the mad, indecent, transgressive Other.[50] Indeed, Lol Stein runs a good risk of becoming the most overanalyzed female character in contemporary fiction.[51]

What has not been sufficiently understood is how Duras connects the chronic pain and numbness of women's experience with a new mode of writing that finds its symbol in hysterical discourse. The connection may be clearer if we think of chronic-pain patients—disproportionately female—as the subdued modern successors to the flamboyant nineteenth-century hysteric. We have encountered before the isolation and silence typical of chronic pain. Duras finds these conditions still characteristic of women's lives today, despite progress—vastly uneven—toward eradicating the almost immemorial injustice, oppression, and misogyny that women have suffered. As she writes:

Neurosis in women is so ancient, thousands of years old. Of course women express this neurosis differently in our day. They no longer talk to animals or trees, because, apparently, they aren't alone. In fact, however, they are completely alone in their millions, in their poverty, in their comfort, and in their slums, in all their completely functional marriages—whether rich or poor. They are alone as before. And everywhere. Madness has found other expressions, but it is still there. It is still the same madness.[52]

The question for Duras is how to give voice to a pain that is now not only silent—that is, unexpressed—but almost inexpressible: completely bereft of language and voice.

Duras provides a strong example of the contribution that writers can make toward understanding maladies still resistant to the analytical lenses of medicine. Somehow in her work she finds the means to express or describe experiences that normally retreat from language. In her later novels she chooses to write in a fluid style of ellipsis, understatement, and poetic compression that fills her own texts with enigmatic gaps and absences. It is a style that gives female silence if not exactly a clear voice (which is of course impossible) then at least a language in which to make its presence known. She describes the almost elemental pain of women's experience (with its steady, inarticulate flow) in a way that simultaneously invites and resists what she sees as the masculine impulse to rush in and fill it up with reason and meaning. It is in expressing the numbness of a female pain beyond language that Duras makes us aware of the persisting trace of hysteria (changed but still tenacious) in modern life.

One of the stories in *La Douleur* describes a woman member of the French Resistance, exhausted, resigned, and almost numb beyond feeling, who directs the interrogation of a Nazi informant while he is slowly beaten into a bloody, terrified stupor. She recognizes that the interrogation is useless, since everyone knows the man is an informant. She hates such violence. Still, a confession is necessary, and she wearily goes ahead with the brutal questioning until what is left of the man scarcely seems human. Duras in an autobiographical note, alluding to her own role in occupied Paris, tells us that she was the woman directing the torture. In the same note, she adds: "*I give you the torturer along with the rest of the texts. Learn to read them properly: they are sacred.*"[53]

What Duras has given us in her writing and films—at an incalculable cost in self-knowledge—cannot be called, in the traditional modern sense, confessional literature. They might better be described as sacred texts of pain. A "proper" reading of sacred texts assumes that they are never simply texts. Sacred texts such as the Bible or the Koran are a special kind of writing that makes a continuing claim on us, much like laws or marriage vows or political constitutions. How we understand them is not just a matter of pure thought, as if understanding resembled the process of solving a problem in mathematics. How we understand a sacred text bears directly on how we live our lives.

Duras's sacred texts of pain suggest two very specific directions for thinking about how we live. First, she encourages the idea that hysteria has not totally disappeared but rather changed its style and expression. According to this line of thought, today the socially acceptable symptoms of chronic pain and numbness have simply replaced the outmoded theatrical style of nineteenth-century fits, fainting spells, and back-room invalids. Women, it is certain, constitute the substantial majority of chronic-pain patients. Privately, doctors still talk of "hysterical" tendencies in patients who seem to transform anxiety and emotion into bodily symptoms. Yet Duras's work not only supports the suggestion that hysteria in the modern world has shifted its social location from the darkened bedroom of Victorian women to the pain clinic. It suggests that this shift has robbed women of the voice that once gave their pain a distinctive, if inarticulate and self-defeating, presence.

Second, Duras encourages the thought that numbness, like pain, has found a new place in modern life that is not exclusively the enclave of women. Hysteria, as Sydenham and Freud recognized, has spread across the lines of gender. It is as if the numbness associated in the nineteenth century with hysterical women has become simply a normal condition in a world where everyone lives on intimate terms with holocaust, genocide, the greenhouse effect, and prospects of nuclear winter. Perhaps man-made disaster on such a massive, unprecedented scale simply resists thinking. Its pain, as Duras said of Lol Stein, cannot be lived out. The only way to acknowledge such disaster at the deepest level of the emotions would be through repression and denial: not by feeling but by a self-induced, self-protective, trancelike inability to feel: a culture-wide anesthesia. Hysteria, as we know, formerly possessed the mysterious power to imitate almost any illness. Now it may have discovered its ultimate disguise and learned how to simulate the invisible omnipresent malady that passes these days for health.

6

VISIONARY PAIN AND THE POLITICS
OF SUFFERING

History is what hurts.
FREDRIC JAMESON[1]

*T*HE SECULAR, SCIENTIFIC spirit of modern medicine has so eclipsed other systems of thought as almost to erase the memory that pain—far from registering its presence mostly in meaningless neural circuits or in the sterile, living-death of hysterical numbness—once possessed redemptive and visionary powers. We need to recover this understanding partly because it shows so clearly how pain inhabits a social realm that sprawls well outside the domain of medicine. Nor are the redemptive, visionary implications of pain merely a thing of the past. Many people today experience pain within systems of belief that Western doctors have long dismissed or forgotten. The religious and prophetic uses of pain are at odds not with medicine alone, however. They stand in conflict with almost all ordinary ways of seeing. In effect, visionary experience tends to demand a full-scale reinterpretation of the everyday world. Further, in its call to reinterpret the world, it is also implicitly political. As we shall see, this political and visionary pain, no matter how alien to the dominant system of medical thought, is still actively at work in the modern world, like a neglected but potent sacred text.

Pain has long served as a bridge not only between health and illness but also between entirely different realms of value. While we remain in normal health, we often tend (like Tolstoy's Ivan Ilych) to fix our gaze on the horizon of worldly goods, as if the world ended at the horizon. Illness and pain, by contrast, tend to disrupt the daily routines that arrest our attention and bind us to things of this world. Suddenly the miser would give up half his wealth for a pain-free stroll or a good night's sleep. Our priorities change. We see things with different eyes. Some such experience of changed priorities is common to many people who suffer from chronic pain. There is a much stronger sense, however, in which pain serves as a bridge between worlds. It has sometimes provided access to vision so alien from our normal consciousness that it can only be called prophetic, utopian, or revolutionary.

†

Saint Sebastian lived during the third century at a time when the persecution of Christians had become established as something like a national pastime in Rome. Legend tells that he journeyed to Rome from his birthplace in Gaul—now modern France—and joined the Roman army under the emperor Carinus. (Saint Ambrose calls Sebastian a native of Milan—where Sebastian's parents lived and where he was raised—but then Ambrose was also bishop of Milan and perhaps not impartial.) By the reign of Diocletian he had risen to the rank of captain. Although Diocletian was a superb administrative reformer, he saw nothing to reform in the practice of persecuting Christians. When it was discovered that Sebastian spent his time comforting Christian prisoners and converting Roman soldiers to Christianity, Diocletian ordered him shot to death with arrows. As the medieval encyclopedia of saints' lives called *The Golden Legend* tells us, a detachment of archers kept shooting at him until he was "covered with barbs like a hedgehog."[2]

The story of Saint Sebastian does not end with a corpse full of arrows. The events described in *The Golden Legend* include Sebastian's miraculous recovery when a Christian widow nursed him back to health. Once recovered, he presented himself before the surprised emperor Diocletian, who, as befits a man of thoroughgoing administrative genius, ordered him put to death again. Sebastian did not recover from this second execution. He was beaten to death and his body thrown into a sewer. But even his corpse achieved a kind of prolonged afterlife when another pious Christian woman discovered it and (as instructed by Sebastian in a dream) buried his remains near the catacombs. A popular cult developed around his tomb in the fourth century; Pope Damasus, as one of his first acts, built a basilica over the spot in 367; and Sebastian's relics continued to attract numerous pilgrims throughout the Middle Ages.[3] His martyrdom became a favorite subject of painters, and you can find him today in almost any major art museum: half-naked, arms bound behind him, his legs and torso stuck with arrows.

The depictions of Saint Sebastian vary more than the claims about his birthplace. Early versions show him as an old, bearded soldier; later he is a clean-shaven, handsome young man.[4] Clearly, without good factual evidence, painters and sculptors created a figure who soon conformed to a mythic stereotype. Thus, with some exceptions, most portraits of Saint Sebastian build up their composition out of three main features: a handsome male body, arrows buried in the flesh, and up-raised eyes. Each feature is important, but the eyes prove especially telling. From the altarpiece by Antonio Pollaiuolo in the fourteenth century to later Renaissance and Baroque paintings by Caravaggio and Guido Reni, the number of arrows differs greatly and the emphasis on his beauty changes, but Sebastian suffers with his gaze consistently lifted upward.

The painting by Antonio Pollaiuolo offers us a good introduction to visionary pain (fig. 17). In contrast to Saint Sebastian, the executioners keep their eyes glued to their earthly task, raised only to sight their target or lowered to reload. In either case, the material world strictly limits their vision. They neither see nor suspect the existence of a higher realm. The painting thus depicts two utterly different orders of being eerily brought into contact by the moment of execution. Sebastian exists suspended between the world of the body, which he has not yet entirely abandoned, and the world of the spirit, which he has not yet entirely attained. His elevated gaze in effect represents his power to see a truth beyond the horizon of earth and matter. It suggests that he is already entering into the spiritual state of direct, intuitive knowledge of God known as beatific vision.

Pollaiuolo's rigorously symmetrical treatment—with its framing arch and bluff, its carefully matched trio of paired executioners, its clear division into foreground, middle ground, and background—deliberately places Sebastian in the upper half of the canvas, where he seems to occupy a space precisely in-between earth and heaven. The pain of martyrdom is thus represented as a crucial moment of transition. On one hand, we see a richly detailed, visual, earthly, temporal, finite landscape (with the shattered arch—suggesting impermanence—framing the lush Tuscan plains in the distance). It is the everyday world of suffering that W. H. Auden recognized in paintings of the old masters: "Where the dogs go

FIGURE 17. Antonio Pollaiuolo (1431–1498). *The Martyrdom of Saint Sebastian* (1475).

on with their doggy life and the torturer's horse / Scratches its innocent behind on a tree."[5] On the other hand, Sebastian's martyrdom directs our thoughts toward an abstract, eternal, invisible otherworld toward which he raises his eyes. Visionary pain almost requires a sense of conflict or tension between two radically opposed worlds brought together (but not fused) at the moment of martyrdom.

The crucial feature of this painterly tradition, for our purposes, is that Saint Sebastian's moment of otherworldly vision proves inseparable from the experience of pain. More precisely, we automatically understand his experience as painful, because we have no other way of thinking about what it means to be shot full of arrows. Yet the paintings require us to question our experience and assumptions. Unlike the anguished sinners represented by medieval and Renaissance painters as roasting in hellfire or spitted by devils, Sebastian's uplifted eyes assert a vision that seems not so much to dramatize suffering as to accept and transcend it. Sebastian suffers with a composure that confirms him as already beyond our normal experience.

Understanding pain as a medium of visionary experience can help account for the almost loving recitation of gruesome martyrdoms so familiar from the lives of the Christian saints. Some martyrs passed through far more barbarous suffering than Sebastian. Such suffering, of course, holds an almost sanctified place in the process of sainthood as a test or trial of faith. The fires through which various saints passed to their heavenly reward were also understood as an imitation of Christ's suffering on the Cross. The stoning of Saint Stephen or the burning of Saint Dorothy reënact—on a less elevated plane—the central Christian mystery of a being who suffers pain in order to redeem others. Bodily torment thus assumes specific meaning as a sign that points to a realm of eternal truth beyond the perishable body. Yet we still have not yet explained why Sebastian—instead of Saint Stephen, say, or Saint Dorothy—seems to have held such a peculiar fascination for medieval and Renaissance painters.

One reason for this appeal probably has less to do with visionary experience than with the link between pain and beauty, which we will later examine in detail. A famous painting by Guido Reni shows Sebastian enduring martyrdom with the sensuousness of a languid Greek god (fig. 18). Neoplatonic traditions might here encourage some viewers to understand physical beauty as the outward expression of a beautiful soul. Yet surely more is involved. The body-obsessed Japanese writer Yokio

FIGURE 18. Guido Reni (1575–1642). *Saint Sebastian* (1615).

Mishima in his autobiographical novel *Confessions of a Mask* (1949) describes a young man whose encounter with the Guido Reni portrait of Saint Sebastian results in his first ejaculation. It is not religious meaning but rather the eroticism of a godlike male warrior in pain that heats his imagination:

His white and matchless nudity gleams against a background of dusk. . . . The arrows have eaten into the tense, fragrant, youthful flesh and are about to consume his body from within with flames of supreme agony and ecstasy. But there is no flowing blood, nor yet the host of arrows seen in other pictures of Sebastian's martyrdom. Instead, two lone arrows cast their tranquil and graceful shadows upon the smoothness of his skin, like the shadows of a bough falling upon a marble stairway.[6]

The final simile reads like a haiku. Indeed, in the year of his self-inflicted, ritualized death by *seppuku*, Mishima posed for a remarkable photograph modeled on the painting by Guido Reni, complete with arrows realistically penetrating his naked torso and, of course, upturned eyes. (The photograph is reprinted in John Nathan's *Mishima: A Biography* [1974].) Once again pain has changed its meaning, as Guido Reni's Renaissance Christian martyrdom enters into contact with the ancient Japanese tradition of *shudo* (the Way of Boy Love) and with Mishima's own contemporary, militarized homoerotic vision, mingling in a combination we may never entirely understand.

✝

Visionary pain, as Mishima recognized, sometimes contains a powerful element of sensuality, and an eroticism latent in the paintings of Saint Sebastian finds more open expression in the spiritual experience of female mystics. Arrows, of course, might come from Eros as easily as from Diocletian's archers. In fact, Guido Reni's Sebastian conveys the same mingled erotic and spiritual power that infuses Bernini's famous sculpture of another visionary figure in whom rapture and pain seem strangely united: Saint Teresa of Avila. Her experience will help us understand more fully the opposite worlds evoked and even reconciled by pain.

Teresa (1515–1582) described her best-known visionary experience when she wrote of the angel who appeared before her:

I saw in his hands a large golden dart and at the end of the iron tip there appeared to be a little fire. It seemed to me this angel plunged the dart several times into my heart and that it reached deep within me. When he drew it out, I thought he was carrying off with him the deepest part of me; and he left me all on fire with great love of God. The pain was so great that it made me moan, and the sweetness this greatest pain caused me was so superabundant that there is no desire capable of taking it away. . . .[7]

Pain is a vital element in Teresa's devotional life. Indeed, we might consider her a female counterpart of Sebastian: arrows, pain, beauty, eroticism, and otherworldly vision again prove inseparable. Teresa's erotic spirituality, in fact, seems to grow in importance at the very moment when Sebastian's influence begins to wane. The famous seventeenth-century English religious poet Richard Crashaw wrote intense devotional verse about Teresa's visionary union with God that, typically, emphasizes her "delicious Wounds," "intolerable *Joyes*," and "sweet & subtle *Pain*."[8]

Undoubtedly, however, the supreme expression of this blended, eroticized, mystical pain is Bernini's flowing, floating, white-marble, Baroque masterpiece *The Ecstasy of Saint Teresa* (1645–1652)—from the Cornaro Chapel in Santa Maria della Vittoria, at Rome (fig. 19). The visual details all tell of mystical insight: the unseeing, heavily lidded eyes (absorbed in visions), the mouth half open in painful rapture, and the almost postcoital loosening of the limbs. "I should so much like to explain this deep pain," Teresa writes, describing it hesitantly (unable to pin it down) as a mingled pain of body and soul.[9] All the details in Bernini's sculptural embodiment of this state suggest that the arrow of divine love has just pierced Teresa's heart. It is impossible to say where pain leaves off and ecstasy or vision begins.

The eroticized pain of mystical vision that we encounter in Saint Teresa also finds powerful expression in Saint Catherine of Siena. Catherine and Teresa, in fact, are the only two women whom the Catholic Church has granted the title of doctor. Like Saint Teresa, Catherine was an ascetic for whom the humiliation of the flesh provided an indispensable avenue for a direct approach to God. God in fact does most of the talking in her daring book of conversations with the deity, entitled *The Dialogue* (1377–1378). There she describes the reversal of values on which she based her personal cultivation of pain. She sees the material world with its vain pleasures as a place of "venomous thorns" and therefore recommends that the godly—in spurning the thorns of pleasure—should actively seek out suffering through humiliations of the flesh. Such spiritualized suffering, paradoxically, fills them with joy. "When they are suffering they are happy," she writes of the godly, "when they are not suffering they are in pain."[10] In effect, pain experienced for religious motives gets redefined as joyful suffering.

Catherine's paradoxical redefinition offers a mystical version of the Myth of Two Pains. She argues that the godly soul finds happiness in a physical pain that is transitory and undertaken or accepted in God's name, whereas the absence of such physical pain creates an unendurable spiritual pain. Certainly Christians in the Middle Ages saw the spirit and the

FIGURE 19a. Gian Lorenzo Bernini (1598–1680). *The Ecstasy of Saint Teresa* (1645–1652).

flesh locked in more than mortal combat. The medieval dualism of spirit and body long predated Descartes. Indeed, the greatest pain imaginable by medieval doctors of the Church was the agony of the soul shut out from God. Catherine, in seeking a nearness to God that would exempt her from unending spiritual torment, maintained a discipline of painful self-starvation so extreme that it ultimately killed her. When her confessor

VISIONARY PAIN AND THE POLITICS OF SUFFERING

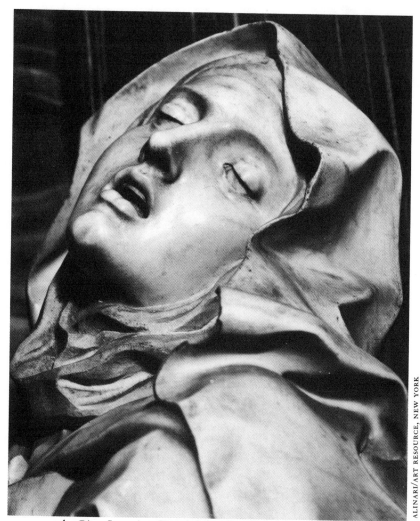

FIGURE 19b. Gian Lorenzo Bernini (1598–1680). *The Ecstasy of Saint Teresa* (1645–1652), detail.

urged her to stop forcibly vomiting her food, she replied that such pain was penance for her sins and that she preferred to receive her punishment in this world rather than in the next.[11] Her penitential sufferings allowed her to experience a personal internalization of the Passion.[12] She thus understood her everyday bodily pain as almost a means of grace.

It is the dualism implicit in Catherine's references to the spiritual torment of a soul shut out from God that underlies her emphasis on bodily pain as means and symbol of her union with God. Yet she recognized dangers implicit in this formula. Thus she insisted that an active (egotistical) quest for suffering can prove profitless or harmful. Nothing matters except the intention to do God's will. "The value is not in the suffering," she wrote, "but in the soul's desire."[13] Her biblical model for such ego-less suffering was Lazarus, tormented by leprosy, who through uniting his will with God found "refreshment and consolation in his pain."[14] She imagines God recommending such ego-less pain as the only possible path to beatific vision:

There is no other way to know the truth. In so knowing me the soul catches fire with unspeakable love, which in turn brings continual pain. Indeed, because she has known my truth as well as her own sin and her neighbor's ingratitude and blindness, the soul suffers intolerably. Still, this is not a pain that shrivels up the soul. On the contrary, it makes her grow fat. For she suffers because she loves me. . . .[15]

Pain of the body inspires a pain of the soul that expands rather than contracts the soul's power of vision. This medieval version of sacred or sacramental suffering is ultimately far less like the modern Myth of Two Pains (rigorously secular) than like the innumerable varieties of mystical Oneness. Thus Plato described Socrates standing for hours on guard duty barefoot in the snow, presumably lost in the contemplation of ideal forms. Through pain Catherine grasps a vision beyond pain— where nothing matters except bringing the soul closer to an otherworldly truth.

Modern pain, of course, normally chains us down to the material world. It keeps us centered in the flesh. It places us within the secular circle of medical science. The visionary pain of Catherine, Teresa, and Sebastian, by contrast, contains the power to transcend the world and the flesh. In providing release into a pure communion with the divine, it becomes not something to be cured or even endured but rather a means of knowledge, offering access to an otherwise inaccessible understanding. Visionary pain employs the body in order to free us from the body. It initiates or accompanies an experience that escapes the time-bound world of human suffering. The visionary, as Saint Catherine cautioned, does not court pain but rather welcomes it when it inevitably arrives, unsought, as a sign that always points beyond itself. It gestures toward an ecstatic union with God in which suffering is finally indistinguishable from love.

Visionary pain no doubt drew much of its significance and appeal from an implicit contrast with the extremely harsh conditions under which most medieval Christians scratched out a living. The "venomous thorns" of the material world included an unremitting sequence of cold, injury, malnutrition, overwork, and disease. Men and women laboring within this everyday world of pain believed that Sebastian, like other saints, could intervene in their behalf by supplying divine help and solace. There was a special reason, however, why Sebastian proved such a popular figure in medieval Europe. He was known as the intercessor who offered protection against the most devastating and unpredictable malady that terrified the medieval mind: plague.

Sebastian's association with plague dates at least from the summer of 680 A.D. According to legend, a plague that was ravaging the area around Rome completely vanished when the city of Pavia raised an altar to Sebastian. At first it is not clear why the citizens should ask Sebastian for help. The incident may be merely legend, yet Sebastian's association with plague has a plausible history. The Latin word *plaga* means wound, blow, stripe, or stroke. Since remote antiquity, arrows had been emblematic of plague, perhaps because plagues seemed to shoot out of nowhere with their painful and deadly assault. Sebastian's identifying emblem being an arrow, which some painters represent him as holding in his hands, it is easy to see why he became (however macabre) the patron saint of archers. The Romans probably invoked his aid in 680 in part because they associated arrows with an end to bad luck. Further, Apollo, the Greek archer god, also served among his many offices as the god of healing. Thus when the Christian world appropriated fragments of pagan mythology, Saint Sebastian easily absorbed some of the healing attributes of Apollo. The saintly healer, with his vividly afflicted body and his gift for lifting plagues, had far more aid to offer than doctors did in the era of the Black Death.

People of the Middle Ages and the Renaissance lived with the anxiety of knowing that genocidal plagues might break out at any time. This was not a theoretical or abstract knowledge. Death by plague was a recurrent fact that regularly sent city dwellers fleeing toward the countryside and filled the streets with half-crazed flagellants. Its sheer painfulness made death by plague a terror that Sebastian—with his torso pierced by arrows—might seem well placed to understand.[16] Anyone fallen into the last stages of plague would experience several days of unrelieved agony from the knotlike swellings that no medicine could relieve. Here is a typical passage from Daniel Defoe's *Journal of the Plague Year* (1722), in which the narrator describes scenes from the great plague that terrorized London in 1665:

The swellings which were generally in the Neck, or Groin, when they grew hard, and would not break, grew so painful, that it was equal to the most exquisite Torture; and some not able to bear the Torment, threw themselves out at Windows, or shot themselves, or otherwise made themselves away, and I saw several dismal Objects of that Kind: Others, unable to contain themselves, vented their Pain by incessant Roarings, and such loud and lamentable Cries . . . that would Pierce the very Heart to think of.[17]

Defoe was born five years before the great plague. Yet, while he did not personally see the suffering he describes, he certainly knew from eyewitnesses the terrifying consequences of falling prey to the plague.

Defoe perpetuates the medieval view that describes plague as a punishment sent by God. (The English word *pain* derives directly from the Latin *poena*, meaning punishment.) His explicitly religious language consistently describes the outbreak as a divine "visitation" and regards any temporary abatement a godly "deliverance." Thus his quite modern, secular description of London in its gritty, realistic details—which inspires some scholars to pronounce him the first British novelist—coincides with an account of illness that belongs to an ancient theological framework. Yet the framework in 1722 is beginning to seem a little worn. Defoe continues to employ the older vocabulary of divine visitation and punishment, but the pain brings with it no compensating vision and no saintly intercessor. In Defoe, disease has come close to assuming its customary place in the modern world.

Defoe's secular description inside a worn theological frame helps to illustrate the limitations of traditional voices that describe plague and pain as a divine punishment. This explanation held something like official status, since it was endorsed regularly from the pulpit and press, but an authorized explanation does not necessarily drive out unofficial points of view. For example, the gossipy and amorous seventeenth-century diarist Samuel Pepys, who lived through the same plague that Defoe describes so vividly, managed to dispense altogether with the framework of theology. A religious but not devout man, Pepys fixed his eyes resolutely on the horizon of secular life. His typical entry for July 26, 1665 can remind us how far we have left behind the mystical pain of Sebastian and Teresa:

"Sad news of the death of so many in the parish of the plague, 40 last night—the bell always going—I back to the Exchange, where I went up and sat talking with my beauty, Mrs. Batelier, a great while, who is indeed one of the finest women I ever saw in my life."[18]

✝

Visionary pain in its contact with a realm beyond the secular, material world where Pepys toyed with Mrs. Batelier may seem entirely removed from the world of political power. Yet its otherworldliness serves as an implicit critique of worldly power. It exposes the secular *as* secular. Indeed, the exposure is not always indirect but sometimes sets the two worlds in direct and violent conflict. Sebastian, we should remember, died at the hands of the Roman empire. Moreover, the political implications of Sebastian's pain continued to radiate years later when (canonized as a saint) he became, so to speak, the property of the very political and militant medieval Catholic Church. The essential point is this: visionary pain rarely exists in a purely apolitical, religious context but regularly takes up a position that sets it in conflict with competing systems of power. The political dimensions of pain will be clearer if we examine another text that might be called an archetype of visionary experience: the Book of Job.

The Old Testament story of Job—reputedly the richest man in the East—is among the most compelling narratives in the long human struggle to make sense out of human suffering.[19] Its familiar frame story tells of a wager between God and Satan. (The name Satan here means simply Accusing Angel, not the devil of later Christian theology.) Satan argues that Job's legendary uprightness and faithfulness to God are merely the result of prosperity. God then gives Satan permission to test Job's faith. The subsequent assaults create something like a ritual of dispossession as Satan relentlessly strips away all of Job's worldly comforts. It is a stark parable of human vulnerability. Once treated like a king, Job is spat upon in the marketplace (30:10). The richest man in the East successively loses his wealth, goods, family, friends, and health. He ends up a pain-wracked beggar sitting in misery on a dunghill.

The Book of Job, despite Job's reputation for patience, is not the story of a patient man. Job is the story of an innocent, upright, godly man who loses everything, suffers terribly, and demands to know why. Pain, of course, is certainly not Job's only problem. Yet Satan shrewdly saves for

FIGURE 20. William Blake (1757–1827). "Satan Smites Job with Boils" (1825).

last the plague of boils, which William Blake in his *Illustrations of the Book of Job* (1825) depicts as a complete shutting down of the body (fig. 20). The sun sets; the four senses of sight, smell, hearing, and taste all retract; the fifth sense, touch, is transformed into nothing but a conduit of torment.[20] People can accept the loss of external goods, Satan reasons, but intense pain suffered within our own bodies is finally unacceptable and unendurable. He taunts God for keeping Job's losses external and for

VISIONARY PAIN AND THE POLITICS OF SUFFERING

not testing him in the fire of pain. (As Satan says: "All that a man has he will give for his life. But put forth thy hand now, and touch his bone and his flesh, and he will curse thee to thy face" [2:4–5].) Pain is Satan's last, best weapon for turning Job against God.

The plague of boils is important because it reminds us that Job's anguish does not consist solely in spiritual torment. His distress of spirit coincides with an excruciating and complex suffering that has multiple sources. He endures not just the agonizing boils but also the violence of the entire community toward the fallen leader who now serves as scapegoat or Other.[21] Indeed, separation from the community is represented as a powerful source of pain by the biblical writers. "Days of affliction have taken hold of me," Job says. "The night racks my bones,/and the pain that gnaws me takes no rest" (30:16–17). His accusations against the silent, inscrutable, vengeful God who afflicts him find expression through exceptionally violent images in which the entire self is dismembered: "I was at ease, and he broke me asunder;/he seized me by the neck and dashed me to pieces;/he set me up as his target,/his archers surround me./He slashes open my kidneys, and does not spare;/he pours out my gall on the ground" (16:12–13). This is not the language of mere "mental" pain. Body and spirit are afflicted together.

What makes his affliction even worse is that Job understands his pain through the paradigm of divine punishment. In a larger sense, however, the Book of Job enacts a drama of multiple interpretations. How is Job's pain to be understood? This is the central question, and on one fundamental point Job and his comforters agree. Everyone understands his state as a punishment sent by God. Yet on a second, equally fundamental point Job and his comforters utterly disagree. The comforters reason that because Job is being punished he must therefore be guilty. They want to know what he has done wrong and why he will not admit it. Job, by contrast, knows that he is innocent. Thus he anguishes over questions to which nothing in his experience provides even the glimmering of an acceptable answer. Why would God punish an upright and guiltless man? Job will not let the question rest.

It is important to emphasize that Job and the comforters both accept the doctrine that pain represents divine punishment. They disagree only about *why* Job is being punished. The frame story, of course, offers us the explanation that Job suffers because God is testing him. This explanation provides another major paradigm for interpreting pain. The idea that pain is less a punishment than a divine test or trial has a long history, which clearly extends through the martyrdom of innumerable Christian saints. Yet, Job's pre-Christian experience and his agonized questioning make such an explanation seem finally a kind of historical afterthought, stuck on. Most biblical scholars, in fact, think that the frame story and its concept of pain as a divine test is a late addition to the narrative, designed to make it more palatable. The introductory wager between God and Satan, as well as the happy ending when God gives Job back twice his wealth, fourteen thousand sheep, and a brand new set of sons and daughters, reads like a Hollywood version of *Macbeth* in which the murder of King Duncan turns out to be just a bad dream.

The decisive moment in the original narrative comes when God confronts Job as a voice speaking out of the whirlwind. The Bible emphasizes that God is present as a voice only. Like Moses, Job does not look directly on God's face, but he nevertheless refers to his experience of God's voice as a form of seeing or vision. ("I had heard of thee by the hearing of the ear,/ but now my eye sees thee" [42:5].) This is probably a figurative way of comparing the immediacy of firsthand experience with secondhand or merely hearsay knowledge, but it also places God's visitation of Job in the context of mystical or visionary experience. Further, when God finally speaks to Job from the whirlwind, what Job receives is not a rational answer—no pat assurances about suffering as a punishment or test of faith—but rather a deluge of unanswerable questions. Where were you when I laid the foundations of the earth? Can you draw out Leviathan with a fishhook? The questions all repeat the brute facts of God's power and man's weakness. If we disregard the frame story, the original narrative from the sixth century B.C. presents the suffering of the upright, innocent man as an impenetrable mystery.

†

The Book of Job treats the question of innocent suffering as a matter of theological power. God's power simply puts the question beyond the limits of human understanding. If power is the raw material of politics, we might say that Job provides one of the earliest demonstrations that visionary pain is always implicitly political. Yet because ultimate power in the Book of Job resides with God, the story may seem disengaged from the more worldly politics of pain. This worldly politics will be easier to recognize if we examine several modern interpretations of Job's suffering.

We can pursue one such interpretation through the fiction of a fourth comforter. A second interpretation will take us—far from the upraised eyes of Saint Sebastian—to the defiantly earthward gaze of contemporary priests and clergy who fight for social justice with a theology of liberation.

It was no doubt simply an historical accident that prevented the Book of Job from including among the three famous comforters a behavioral psychologist. This omission is easy to repair. Indeed, pain clinics and centers employing behaviorist techniques and principles report good success in helping patients overcome long-established patterns that reinforce and even create chronic pain. Dr. Wilbert Fordyce, among the most respected pain specialists in America, employs flexible behaviorist modes of treatment in the University of Washington Multidisciplinary Pain Center (Seattle), and the resulting improvement in individual patients is often dramatic.[22] It is not unlikely that a modern Job, deprived of a culture-wide religious faith, would eventually find himself a patient in a pain center or clinic run by behavioral psychologists.

Behaviorists, of course, will not be fooled into granting Job's premise that pain is divine punishment. The behaviorist begins from the proposition that all pain can be redefined as pain behavior. Pain behavior— simply a special subclass of behavior—can be extinguished or modified (so the behaviorist believes) by withholding the "positive reinforcers" that underlie all human action. Here is how a modern pain specialist describes the behaviorist's view:

In practice, it usually develops that pain behavior is maintained or enhanced by attention, rest, and analgesics. For example, if a patient is lying quietly in his hospital room, he is likely to be ignored by the busy nursing staff, and he will begin to feel lonely and miserable and his pain will get worse. Pretty soon he will cry out, and immediately he will receive nursing attention, and perhaps medication. Thus, his pain behavior is positively reinforced, and is more likely to recur. As a consequence of this conditioning process, he will both experience and express more pain when next he needs company or medication.[23]

The behaviorist would ask what "positive reinforcers" are keeping Job on his dunghill. Could it be that Job feels guilty about his former wealth and unknowingly craves punishment, that he secretly enjoys provoking the comforters, or that he revels in all the attention he receives?

There are of course numerous schools and varieties of behavioral psychology, and many pain specialists employ selected behaviorist techniques without subscribing to a purist's underlying doctrine or credo. Let's imagine, however, that our fourth comforter is an altogether uncompromising behaviorist.[24] Pain, Job will be told, is simply the term we use to describe certain well-recognized social actions and signals: crying, screaming, limping, jumping up and down, staying home from work, rending your garments and pouring ashes on your head. Without these signals, we would not know that someone was in pain. In fact, if the person in pain simply stops performing the behavior associated with pain, including such common mental behavior as worrying and obsessive self-scrutiny, then for the behaviorist it is a uselessly abstruse, academic question whether the person truly feels pain. The behaviorist's immediate and pragmatic answer is clear: remove the pain behavior and you remove the pain.

Behaviorist treatment often rests on a distinction (widely shared within medicine) between pain and suffering. Pain, in this formulation, is understood not merely as pain behavior but, traditionally, as a sensory impulse communicated by the nervous system. Suffering is then defined as our emotional *response* to pain.[25] This distinction found support in a strange by-product of brain surgery. Several decades ago, when prefrontal lobotomies and leucotomies were an extreme but accepted tool for the control of intractable pain, clinicians observed an unexpected result. Lobotomized patients said they could still feel pain but that it no longer "bothered" them.[26] The pain persisted but, apparently, the quality of suffering was gone. Even if the behaviorists cannot remove the sensation of pain, they believe they can change the emotional response that (they claim) constitutes suffering.

There is much to be said in favor of behaviorist treatments for pain, despite the somewhat thin notion of suffering they entail. Because we come to understand our pain only within specific cultures and subcultures, it seems quite fair to describe our experience as, to a large degree, learned. Psychologists thus often write about "social modeling" as a process by which people come to adopt patterns of pain behavior that they see around them, like staying home from work when your back hurts.[27] The stoical Irishman learns to grit his teeth and keep silent. The Micronesian woman in labor gives so little evidence of pain that only by placing a hand on her abdomen can the visiting Western doctor know when a contraction occurs. Who can doubt that chronic pain involves patterns of learned behavior?

Behaviorists, in fact, share a broad basis of agreement with other pain specialists, despite sometimes wide differences in underlying philosophy.

Thus almost all authorities, from whatever school, recognize in chronic pain patients a complicated phenomenon called "secondary gain," which occurs when pain brings with it a hidden advantage that the patient is unwilling to give up. A middle-aged woman trapped in a sterile marriage finds that her pain kindles a caring, loving disposition in her otherwise indifferent spouse. A worn-out coal miner finds that undiagnosable low back pain brings a disability payment and a ticket out of the mines. Neither person consciously *chooses* pain. The pain remains a torment for which they continue to seek medical help. Yet the advantages they discover in pain—through a complex process that can only be called learning—create a behavior that, unchallenged, may well become ineradicable. The pain is unconsciously accepted, maintained, even vigorously and cagily defended against medical treatment because it appears to solve an otherwise insoluble dilemma.

Job's pain, if we may now return to the dunghill, does not solve a dilemma. More accurately, we could say that it expresses or represents a dilemma; it is the internal expression of his scandalous struggle with God. Further, far from encouraging a clear behaviorist division between pain and suffering, the biblical author seems to find them inseparable. "The Old Testament," writes one group of learned editors, "does not contrast physical and mental suffering, since man is seen in his totality." Another group of editors collects the various Hebrew and Greek terms in the Bible implying pain, adding: "None of these words allow any clear division between somatic and psychic pain."[28] The anguish that Job feels not only expresses itself through images of violent pain. Pain will not let him stop questioning and thus keeps his anguish alive. Job cannot shut off his pain except by heeding his wife's advice to curse God and die.

Suppose that Job rejects the clinical recommendation of a prefrontal lobotomy that would excuse him from being "bothered" by his pain. He might well respond testily that there is no better argument for the fusion of pain and suffering than the fact that it requires a prefrontal lobotomy to disentangle them. We may suppose nonetheless that Job agrees to take seriously the proposal that he must modify his pain behavior. He must stop sitting on that dunghill. Stop scratching those boils. Most of all, he must stop asking incessant and troublesome questions that simply upset him. No doubt a little marriage counseling would not be amiss. Maybe a support group. Through such common behaviorist treatments, Job could certainly be taught how to change his relation to pain.

Still, the most difficult question for a behaviorist to answer may be this: How can Job modify or remove his pain behavior and still remain Job? What Job craves is not so much release from pain as an acceptable *explanation* for his punishment. It is only after God speaks to him from the whirlwind that he can rest. It is only in the almost visionary encounter with God as the embodiment of a limitless, inscrutable power that Job comes to understand his pain as a mystery, as something that cannot be fully encompassed within human understanding. Job does not learn to change his behavior. Rather, his behavior changes only when he learns that his inseparable pain and suffering simply cannot be understood. "Therefore I despise myself," Job says in his final words, rejecting the fiction of a full, clear answer, "and repent in dust and ashes" (42:6).

†

The political status of Job's pain—understood in the light of his final repentance—is zero. God's omnipotence overwhelms not only human understanding but also human action. The city or polis of God, as Augustine would put it, is not of this world. Yet the Book of Job also leads to a very different understanding by which we can see how human pain is saturated in politics. Pain, in this political reading, belongs especially to the powerless. It is the poor and powerless who most often find themselves in pain. Why? Because poverty, ignorance, overwork, bad diet, wretched shelter, and nonexistent health care are major causes of illness and injury. Malnutrition, for example, is not simply the result of floods or bad harvests but ultimately has political causes. Surely, if they possessed political power, the children of third-world countries would not *choose* to starve. They live on an insufficient diet because they were born in impoverished lands—lands often split by civil wars, ruled by corrupt factions, exploited by foreign banks and corporations and governments who leave them at the mercy of each new natural disaster.

The pain felt by a starving child (or adult) results from the almost invisible distribution of political, social, and economic power. This thought, however, remains too abstract. Even the terrible photographs of mass starvation in Africa easily strike Western readers as somehow remote and inapplicable to our world. In America, pain surely cannot be contaminated by issues of political and economic power, can it? The short answer is yes. In 1978 Helen Neal published a book entitled *The Politics of Pain* in which, among other examples of politicized suffering, she examined the treatment of American children in hospital burn units. There are clearly special problems in assessing the pain that children feel, since their limited vocabulary and experience may not give doctors much help.[29] Yet adults who complain often enough and loudly enough usually get something to relieve their pain (or to shut them up). It was in 1977 that Joann M. Eland and Jane E. Anderson published their classic study showing that over half the children between four and eight years old who had major surgery—including amputations—received no medication for postoperative pain.[30] A recent study of Emergency Department records over a five-month period in 1987–1988 showed that children with painful conditions were twice as likely as adults to receive no medication. Apparently not much has changed. The pain of children in a hospital setting, as Helen Neal found, is too often dismissed as mere "noise level."[31]

These reflections may seem to take us far from the Book of Job. Yet the painful deaths of thousands of hungry children from Africa to Atlanta, like the pain of children in even the most humane burn units, returns us directly to the questions raised by Job. How can it happen that today thirty to forty children die every minute for want of food and inexpensive vaccines?[32] Do we think that it is somehow impossible to prevent masses of people from starving to death? We cannot truly face such questions, I think, without first recognizing that politics is always subtly at work shaping how we experience pain. Even as Job struggled to find a meaning for his pain, one of the most illuminating contemporary encounters with the Book of Job and its questions is the brief, powerful book by theologian Gustavo Gutierrez entitled *On Job: God-talk and the Suffering of the Innocent* (1986). It offers a compelling exploration of how our position inside or outside specific systems of power governs the ways in which we experience and interpret pain.

†

Gustavo Gutierrez, born and educated in Lima, Peru, is a Catholic theologian and activist often regarded as the founder of liberation theology. Liberation theology—while it extends today across numerous faiths and religions—is the name given to the movement that developed with great speed and intensity after the Second General Conference of Latin American Bishops (1968) in Medellín when the bishops proclaimed that the Catholic Church should exercise what Harvard theologian Harvey Cox describes as "a preferential option for the poor." Cox explains: "Liberation theology is an expression of this preference. It is the attempt to interpret the Bible and Christianity from the perspective of the poor. It is in no sense a liberal or modernist theological deviation. Rather, it is a *method*, an effort to look at the life and message of Jesus through the eyes of those who have normally been excluded or ignored."[33] The temperate but forceful language of the bishops includes a radical critique of the existing social order. The "agonizing problems" of Latin America, they declare, are not just evidence of growth or change but rather "signs of injustice that wound the Christian conscience."[34]

We must not think that liberation theology is only a method of reading—like the new academic theories of interpretation that seem to sprout up each year. This new way of reading scripture, as if through the eyes of the poor, implies a mode of direct action designed to assist the people wounded by injustice and to attack social oppression at its roots. Thus, while Gutierrez serves as professor of theology at the Catholic University in Lima, the liberation theology he expounds also reflects his life spent working among the poor people of Rimac, a Lima slum. Pain as a daily fact of life in the slums is something he knows intimately. Yet Gutierrez also insists that pain cannot be understood simply as a condition of solitary individuals. Liberation theology takes as its subject the immense *masses* of exploited poor who populate Latin America and the third world. It is the suffering of this entire group of people—a collective pain of almost unthinkable vastness—that for Gutierrez must be understood as deeply political.

Liberation theology differs from other theological movements in its emphasis on salvation as an event that occurs here and now. The focus is not on a heavenly city outside human time but rather on the very imperfect (not to say squalid) towns and villages of the present day. What gives Gutierrez his activist stance is the conviction that biblical faith must be, above all, faith in a God who reveals himself through events on earth, "a God who saves in history."[35] The emphasis is on salvation as something that must happen here, in this world. Thus among the first imperatives of liberation theology is the struggle to reject and to rectify the historical injustices of an immoral social order that creates and oppresses the poor.

The priests (and clergy of various denominations) who accept this imperative to fight an unjust social order live in effect as political activists. The oppression of the poor in Latin America, they believe, must be utterly repugnant to a God who saves in history. They are less concerned with correcting particular abuses than with reforming or even overthrowing the system that creates injustice. Further, they believe that a corrupt political and economic system survives only because it benefits specific classes and individuals, who must be identified and resisted. "An unjust situation," Gutierrez argues, "does not happen by chance; it is not something branded by a fatal destiny: there is human responsibility behind it."[36] Sin in this bold rethinking loses its traditional definition as something strictly private and individual—the forbidden, solitary acts of a single soul—and emerges instead as public and collective: a social, historical injustice that forces millions of people to live in misery.

For Gutierrez, then, the role of a modern priest ultimately requires putting himself in solidarity with the poverty-stricken Latin American masses and fighting the injustice—or, more precisely, the historical system of social and economic power—that oppresses them. Thus when he comes to read the Book of Job as if through the eyes of the poor, he understands the biblical story and its treatment of human pain in a profoundly contemporary, deeply political context. In fact, Gutierrez begins his study of Job by quoting from the South African opponent of apartheid, Archbishop Desmond Tutu. "All liberation theology," he quotes Archbishop Tutu as insisting, "stems from trying to make sense of human suffering when those who suffer are the victims of organized oppression and exploitation."[37] As Gutierrez sees it, the Book of Job is a basic text for anyone seeking to make sense of this "organized" or political pain.

The central fact about the Book of Job, for Gutierrez, is Job's innocence. It is his innocence that makes Job an archetype of the suffering multitudes in Latin America whose hunger and poverty Gutierrez sees as not a God-sent punishment or divine test of faith but rather as the direct result of organized exploitation and oppression. The solidarity with the poor that Gutierrez feels so deeply makes him especially sensitive to moments when Job and his comforters bring their sometimes abstract theological debate down to earth. Through Gutierrez we understand new meaning—or at least important new emphasis—in the lines where Job proclaims his uprightness: "I was eyes for the blind; and feet for the lame. / Who but me was father of the poor?"[38] Gutierrez finds in Job himself a model for solidarity with the poor. Job's long, circular exchanges with his comforters assume special significance for Gutierrez because they eventually reveal an inner change in Job. Job, according to Gutierrez, comes to recognize his own suffering as not simply private and personal but *akin* to the unjust suffering of the poor, whom he once assisted like a father.

The reading of pain that Gutierrez develops in analyzing Job's experience depends on a distinction between two different languages or visions. First, he identifies a prophetic language that denounces injustice and attacks oppression. As he shows, Job's words at times reflect the anger of the Old Testament prophets who railed against corruption. This prophetic outrage finds an echo among the liberation theologians determined to oppose and to denounce a corrupt social order, and for Gutierrez it takes on special urgency, even danger, as when he exposes how his own church and its hierarchy are directly implicated in the system of power that oppresses the poor. Second, he identifies in the Book of Job a very different language of contemplation and meditative speech. This meditative discourse is related to (but not identical with) prayer, which Gutierrez understands as a personal speech addressed *to* God. Unlike a personal address *to* God, the Book of Job in its contemplative mode offers a public way of talking *about* God. The crucial question for Gutierrez is not, abstractly, what general langauge is appropriate for discussing theologial issues, but, very concretely, how we can find a legitimate way to talk about God at a time when millions of innocent people suffer terrible pain as a result of systematic, organized social injustice. Job offers him one important model.

The pain of vast masses of Latin American poor confronts Gutierrez with a dilemma much like Job's. He needs to find a way to talk about God without the pat answers of our modern comforters—but also within a human history so oppressive that it seems almost godless or godforsaken. As he writes:

Our task here is to find the words with which to talk about God in the midst of the starvation of millions, the humiliation of races regarded as inferior, discrimination against women, especially women who are poor, systematic social injustice, a persistent high rate of infant mortality, those who simply "disappear" or are deprived of their freedom, the sufferings of peoples who are struggling for their right to live, the exiles and the refugees, terrorism of every kind, and the corpse-filled common graves of Ayacucho. What we must deal with is not the past but, unfortunately, a cruel present and a dark tunnel with no apparent end.[39]

The Book of Job articulates for Gutierrez the challenge facing everyone who does not simply turn away from human suffering but seeks to confront its specific historical roots in social injustice. The question is not merely how to speak about God amid a crushing cycle of pain, but how to mobilize an effective resistance to organized injustice.

It should be clear that Gutierrez does not, in behaviorist fashion, separate pain from suffering. The historical pain of hunger, poverty, illness, degradation, torture, and systematic brutalization in Latin America becomes the very substance of a spiritual anguish from which it cannot be neatly divided. Nor is the spiritual commitment to oppose the systematic oppression of the poor something that can be undertaken without grave personal danger: liberation theology lost six Jesuit priests to the death squads in El Salvador on the day I am writing this page. Despite his struggle, Gutierrez (like Job) cannot wrest a satisfactory rational answer to his questions about why God should permit millions of innocent people in Latin America to suffer. He has no otherworldly explanation to offer— no frame story about a trial of faith or divine bet. He knows, however, that inadequate answers are worse than unanswered questions. The serious politics of pain cannot be addressed by therapeutic behaviorist readjustments in an individual's emotional response to noxious sensations.

There is nevertheless one sense in which Gutierrez seeks to relieve pain by changing human understanding and behavior. He wants to awaken both the laboring masses and the ruling elite to the need for a political solution to injustices that are political and social in origin. Among the peasants of Latin America he frequently meets the fatalistic conviction— reinforced by centuries of religious teaching and folk belief—that their poverty and suffering is simply God's will. This is a belief he feels that he must both honor and challenge. The Book of Job reminds him that the mystery of why God permits such massive pain will not be solved with a pat explanation. But he also recognizes that the peasant's recourse to "God's will" is not necessarily a pat explanation: it is the compressed statement of a faith that nothing happens without God's permission. The dilemma for liberation theology, in refusing to acquiesce in a Job-like resignation, is how to transfer God's permission to the side of revolutionary justice.

The scandal of liberation theology—for traditionalists and for the church hierarchy—is that priests should meddle in politics. Gutierrez and his compatriots, however, see politics as the realm where the salvation of the poor must begin. The pain of the poor, he insists, is a spiritual issue that today's priests (and parishioners) must address through political means. Paradoxically, in Latin America it may be religion alone that holds

enough power to regenerate the social order. The Book of Job, as Gutierrez reads it, points the way to such a social regeneration by insisting
that pain is not merely an isolated, private, medical event, amenable to
analgesics or behavior modification. Unlike Sebastian with his eyes raised
to another order of being, Gutierrez pursues a spiritual vison that sees
pain as rooted in earth-bound, systematic, social and economic oppression. For Gutierrez such pain does not beckon beyond this world to a
paradise where all suffering has ceased. Nor does it stand as a universal
mark of original sin. It identifies rather the place where the work of salvation must begin. It stands at a specific time and place in human history
as the sign of organized injustice against the poor.

7
PAIN IS ALWAYS IN YOUR HEAD

When you feel a pain in a leg that has been amputated, where is the pain? If you say it is in your head, would it be in your head if the leg had not been amputated? If you say yes, then what reason have you ever for thinking you have a leg?

BERTRAND RUSSELL[1]

SOMETIMES THE MOST obvious questions, as Job discovered, prove hardest to answer. "Where does it hurt?" must be one of the oldest medical questions on record, and usually we can give a clear, if slightly annoyed, response. "It hurts *here!*"—and we point a finger to the spot. Obviously a headache refers to pain in the head, a backache refers to pain in the back. Common sense demands as much or else we might as well start playing croquet with flamingos. But common sense is notoriously weak when it comes to confronting a mystery. In fact, a mystery, as distinguished from a puzzle, might be defined as whatever refuses to yield up all its secrets to common sense. Sometimes we may encounter unexpected difficulty in saying exactly where it hurts. Sometimes a pain that starts in the lower back begins to slip around toward the hip, or suddenly shoots down the leg. Consider the strange case of phantom limb pain.

Phantom limb pain is one of the most elusive afflictions in the repertoire of human illness. It occurs in amputees. There would seem to be suffering enough in the events that surround the loss of a limb, yet for most amputees an even worse trial lies ahead. After surgery, almost all amputees report feeling an *invisible* limb in the empty space once occupied by the amputated hand or leg or foot. As Ronald Melzack explains: "The limb is usually described as having a tingling feeling, a definite shape, and capable of making a variety of movements."[2] The patient can see clearly that the leg, say, ends in a stump. The tingling is equally clear, however, and it has a specific location: in the unseen foot. For 5 to 10 percent of all amputees, this so-called phantom limb—composed of sheer blank space—hurts with an excruciating pain.

Patients usually describe the pain of phantom limbs as cramping, shooting, burning, or crushing, but ordinary language begins to fail in an experience so far beyond the reach of common sense. One man described his state as follows: "When the pain comes on I'd as soon be dead. It's like something trying to escape out of the end of the stump, it shoots down the end of your leg and feels as if someone's trying to pull your leg off . . . like an electric shock. . . . I could really scream at times with the pain. . . . It feels as if someone's sawing it off, very, very painful."[3] We come to trust that pain, among its most familiar traits, is *localizable*, unlike (say) anxiety. We can rub the spot that hurts and often it will feel better. Phantom limbs, against all the evidence of everyday experience, enclose their pain within parts of the body that no longer exist.

Phantom limb pain persists for a year or more in 3 to 7 percent of all amputees. Sometimes it lasts for decades. For example, amputees may feel the fingers of the missing hand turned inward and digging into the palm. Absent toes may seem twisted and cramped ("bunched up"). An entire missing leg can feel icy or burning. A nonexistent wedding ring may still supply its reassuring pressure around a nonexistent finger. We lack a widely accepted explanation for this enigmatic malady. Some researchers propose simple physiological causes, such as nerve entrapment in the stump, while others suggest complex psychological and psychosocial origins related to the trauma of loss.[4] Medical opinion now seems to favor the idea of multiple causes involving interaction among the peripheral, sympathetic, and central nervous systems. Meanwhile phantom limb pain remains for the person who suffers it an inexplicable catastrophe.

Phantom limb pain offers probably the most vivid and puzzling illustration of the perverse statement that pain is always in your head. In what follows, I want to explore several other contexts that help make such a claim seem less obviously irrational: an episode (from the modern history of childbirth) known as "twilight sleep"; an encounter with the meditations of the Roman emperor Marcus Aurelius; a visit to a pain clinic in

Durango, Colorado; and a return to the writing of well-known Viennese neurologist and psychiatrist, Viktor Frankl, who survived three years in Nazi death camps. The evidence from such diverse sources may serve to shake up or derail the automatic modern assumption, reinforced by at least two centuries of medical thought, that pain belongs strictly and solely to the mechanisms of the body. I am contending—to the contrary—that pain shows us how far body and mind are inextricably bound together.

We cannot appreciate the mind's contribution without first understanding how pain anchors itself in the human body.[5] The mind, after all, depends upon the brain, and the brain belongs to the central nervous system, which holds major responsibility for the transmission of pain impulses. Although we have learned an immense amount recently about the various interior pathways, no one can yet provide an absolutely perfect explanation of how pain impulses travel to the brain. Experiments show, however, that tissue damage creates three very different kinds of pain. This classification, which extends back to the time of Holmes and Head, would instruct us to distinguish the following broad types:

1. pricking pain (felt most commonly when we break or irritate the skin);
2. burning pain (also felt most commonly when the skin is involved);
3. aching pain (felt most commonly deep inside the body).

Pricking pain travels to the brain through small nerve fibers called A delta fibers. Aching pain and burning pain (which of course is not limited to actual burns) travel through even smaller, slower nerve fibers called C fibers; hence the lag between touching a stove and feeling the hurt.[6] We now have a pain impulse and a pain pathway, but we still do not have pain.

Pain most commonly occurs when the pain impulse travels across three crucial sites: the injured tissue, the spinal column, and the brain. Several important cautions are required, however, before we proceed to follow the pain impulse in its travels. First, we are talking here about acute pain only. What happens in chronic pain is far more complex and less well understood. Second, the pathways leading from the injured tissue to the brain are both multibranched and bidirectional. We cannot think of the nervous system as composed of the long, unbroken tubes that Descartes imagined running directly from the point of injury to the brain. The brain and spinal column, moreover, signal information back to the injured tissue in a two-way traffic. A highly simplified version of this complicated back-and-forth progress would include the following details.

At the site of injury, chemicals released by the damaged tissue trigger a series of events that amplify the pain signal. The most important of these chemical amplifiers are called prostaglandins and bradykinin. We now know that aspirin—for years a puzzle to science—works by inhibiting the operation of prostaglandins. Today, of course, researchers are looking hard for ways to block the operation of bradykinin, which is the most potent pain-producing substance yet discovered.[7] So long as it is unblocked, the chemical chain-reaction set in process at the site of injury sends the amplified impulses racing along the A delta or C fibers toward the spinal column.

At the exterior of the spinal column, the amplified pain impulse enters a crucial region known as the dorsal horn. What happens here and elsewhere in the spinal cord itself is not entirely clear. We know that the spinal cord releases chemicals called neurotransmitters that relay the message onward. There are two main tracks on which the pain impulse runs within the spinal cord: the neospinothalamic pathway (for sharp, localized pain) and the paleospinothalamic tract (for less localized, dull or burning pain). It is clear that the spinal column contains its own mechanisms—especially a neurotransmitter called Substance P—for reducing or blocking pain impulses, but let us assume that the nociceptive impulse, as it is technically called, continues to speed onward toward the brain.

The brain confronts researchers with abundant unanswered questions about pain, but we now know a number of clear facts. Sharp pain and dull pain proceed on different paths to the thalamus and then continue on to the cerebral cortex. At some point they connect with the limbic system, which controls our emotional responses. (Aristotle thus was not so far off in classifying pain as an emotion.) The most exciting recent breakthrough, as we have seen, concerns the discovery that the brain produces opiatelike peptides called endorphins, enkephalins, and dynorphins: natural analgesic substances that bind to receptors in the brain exactly like morphine. Thus the same impulse that reaches the brain to produce the perception of injury can also, under specific circumstances, trigger the release of a natural analgesic to erase it. Let us assume that the endorphins have gone on strike. When the well-traveled nociceptive impulse from the broken toe reaches the brain, suddenly you have just entered the familiar state called pain.

This simplified account, I must stress, concerns an episode of acute pain. We cannot assume that chronic pain follows exactly the same model. Further, it leaves out various other intersecting systems for transmitting, suppressing, and influencing pain, in particular the sympathetic and para-sympathetic systems that regulate circulation, breathing, digestion, and the genito-urinary functions. The pain impulse, further, far from always following a direct route to the brain, often seems to employ a path more like a complex network of crisscrossing highways. If you cut off the interstate route with a nerve block, the nociceptive impulse will frequently take to the back roads. Further, impulses *descending* from the brain may suddenly shut down all traffic, even to the point of inducing a profound analgesia. Ronald Melzack and Patrick D. Wall had something like this two-way model in mind when they proposed their well-known "gate-control" theory of pain.

What this artificial account lets us see clearly, first, is how far pain depends on the unseen biochemical processes within our bodies. Second, it emphasizes that pain does not exist until the nerves and neurotransmitters convey their information to the brain. It is the brain, ultimately, that allows us to feel pain. If we anesthetize the brain, the pain disappears. Indeed, researchers can produce pain behavior in rats without any side trips through the spinal column or through the peripheral nervous system. They simply attach their electrodes directly to the rat's brain and the pain flows. The brain of course does not suffer painful tissue damage in this process, as it contains no free nerve endings to communicate pain. (Thus brain surgery can proceed with the patient wide awake.) The pain flows because its point of origin lies within the very structure of the brain.

†

Our imperfect knowledge of pain impulses as they travel through the nervous system gets sketchy—and at points turns into educated guess-work—when we reach the higher centers of processing, especially the thalamus and cerebral cortex. The human brain is still a moonscape of uncharted fields. Research most often proceeds on animals such as cats and rats, where what we learn through counting tailflicks may not translate directly into a knowledge of human pain. Further, psychologists trained to analyze stimulus and response often find the cerebral cortex a black box full of mysteries that they prefer to leave alone. Thus, although we can now fill volumes with what we know about pain impulses as they travel toward the spine and enter the dorsal horn of the spinal column, we are still comparatively mute about the most important point in the entire process: the relation of pain to mind and brain.

Here is an idea guaranteed to set pain specialists on edge. Human brains, as if implanted with their own electrodes, seem able to produce pain in the absence of tissue damage. Such usually chronic pain is called (among other less explicit names) "psychogenic." Psychogenic pain means pain created or sustained by the mind. Traditional medicine, not surprisingly, does not know what to do with psychogenic pain, except to deny that it exists; the term itself is controversial. Quite naturally, patients resist the bizarre idea that they are somehow the cause of their own suffering.[8] How could it be that a pain spreading across the lower back like a firestorm does not reveal a steady stream of nociceptive impulses flowing from an injury to the lower back?

Although the concept of psychogenic pain normally implies that there is no identifiable organic cause, two eminent doctors remind their colleagues that psychogenic pain commonly expresses itself as "an elaboration" of pain already arising from tissue damage.[9] Perhaps an injury has healed, but the pain—for reasons unknown—simply refuses to stop, as if the brain had encoded it in a neural circuit that, once started, cannot be shut off. For Descartes, who provided one of the earliest descriptions, phantom limbs showed conclusively that pain could not be located "in" the body but only in the mind or soul.[10] Is it so hard to imagine that the same brain capable of turning the face blush-red at an indecent joke— the same brain that creates not only its own opioid analgesic but also the infinitely more bewildering product known as human thought—might on occasion fill the hand or foot or lower back with pain?

Perhaps the best way to deal with the difficult problems implied in the concept of psychogenic pain is to imagine a continuum. At one extreme we can locate the acute pain from a stubbed toe. Here the process of pain occurs almost too fast for thought; we need a conscious mind in order to perceive the injury, but otherwise the event belongs to the automatic and unthinking life of the body. Ideally, after a few minutes, the pain stops. At the other end of the continuum we can place the extreme variety of chronic pain called psychogenic. As in the couvade syndrome experienced by expectant fathers, which we will meet later, this pain generated or sustained by the mind needs the body mainly in order to give suffering a location. Once the pain begins it may continue potentially without end.

It is important to observe that neither extreme end of this continuum manages a complete separation of body and mind. Even though the source of each pain seems entirely distinct, as if they came from different countries, chronic psychogenic pain clearly requires a body (if only a phantom body) to give it a home, just as the acute pain of a simple stubbed toe cannot register its protest without a perceiving mind. What is true at the extreme ends of the continuum holds even more clearly and forcefully in the middle range. The carpenter who slips from a high roof and lands on his toolbox will suffer major injuries, but the pain may also enfold deep anxieties about whether he will ever again work, support his family, and lead a normal life. The real-time experience of pain always falls somewhere along a line where body and mind engage each other in an unending collaboration. We dream or sleepwalk in a nonconscious state, but nonconscious pain is a contradiction in terms.

†

All pain—especially all chronic pain—is an interdependent, inseparable, multidimensional union of the two elemental human forces that the Greeks called *psyche* (mind) and *soma* (body). The invisible interdependence of mind and body in the experience of pain is nowhere clearer than in a forgotten episode from American obstetrics known as "twilight sleep."[11] The name refers to a semiconscious state induced by a mixture of the drugs scopolamine and morphine. This combination, developed at the end of the nineteenth century in Germany, showed great promise in permitting safer childbirth. Safety, however, was only part of its public appeal. The combination of scopolamine and morphine blended an amnesiac with a narcotic, and it would take a philosopher to unravel the results fully. That is, the women who delivered their babies in a state of twilight sleep did not *remember* experiencing pain. As far as they were concerned, the experience had been absolutely painless.

Twilight sleep was quickly hailed, in the words of Dr. Bertha Van Hoosen, one of its foremost American medical advocates, as "the greatest boon the Twentieth Century could give to women."[12] Women were quick to celebrate its benefits. Most births at the end of the nineteenth century took place at home, attended by midwives or, less frequently, by a general practitioner. The modern specialty of obstetrics did not exist. Although to relieve pain women sometimes received the dubious benefit of opium, chloroform, chloral, cocaine, quinine, ergot, or nitrous oxide, effective anesthesia in the hands of competent experts had not yet arrived. Outside the hospital setting most doctors preferred not to meddle with tricky gases or drugs. Midwives worked without them. In the grip of labor, women were mostly on their own.

Anxiety is well known to increase pain, and women had good reason to be anxious when it came time to deliver. In 1924 George Clark Mosher reported that there had been over 16,000 maternity-related deaths per year for the past twenty years. About the time of World War I, for every 164 live deliveries one woman died in childbirth.[13] U.S. government statistics for 1915 show that this figure represents almost *half* of all female deaths.[14] In short, childbirth was the number one killer of young women, and most young women faced childbirth numerous times. The odds of surviving four or five deliveries were probably much worse than the chances of returning alive from combat. Reluctant doctors, who had doubts about scopolamine, who resisted change, or who believed (on biblical authority) that God intended labor to be painful, soon found themselves under pressure and even under attack from women determined to gain access to an anesthetic that promised to make childbirth both safer and free from pain.

There was only one small wrinkle that kept twilight sleep from achieving universal acclaim. Although women insisted that their deliveries had been painless, the screams from the delivery room at times resembled a grade-B horror film. According to one observer, the patient "gives every outward evidence during her confinement of acute suffering. She cries out as others do under suffering; tells the doctor perhaps that her pains are severe beyond endurance."[15] In Chicago, Dr. Van Hoosen invented a special crib for confining women during twilight sleep so that they would not injure themselves by thrashing and turning. The physicians had every right to assume, from the cries and struggles, that the woman in delivery was suffering something like the torments of the damned.

In her book *Scopolamine-Morphine Anaesthesia* (1915), Dr. Van Hoosen provides this remarkable transcript of an operation that took place with the patient in a state of twilight sleep. The patient was a woman aged sixty-three:

11:20 A.M. (Pulse 120.) First operation begins.

11:21 A.M. "Oh, dear me (mumbles). (Patient cringes with expectation of pain.) Yes, he comes. Oh, dear me. Please let me go. I can't stand that." (Moans.) "Oh, oh, my Lord."

11:25 A.M. "Oh, my! that hurts so." (Curettage.) "Oh, people, I never imagined—Oh, dear."

11:30 A.M. Operation finished.

11:30 A.M. Doctor V. H.: "How do you feel?" Patient: "Lovely."[16]

This exchange was followed by complete amnesia. After three days the woman still remembered nothing of the operation.

The public interest in scopolamine-morphine anesthesia grew so powerful that women who delivered under twilight sleep became celebrities and street-corner orators. Indeed, between 1914 and 1915 the number of women who testified to the wonders of twilight sleep swelled into the thousands. In refuting claims that scopolamine-morphine deliveries were dangerous to babies, Mrs. Francis Xavier Carmody of Brooklyn, one of the best-known leaders of the new movement promoting scopolamine-morphine anesthesia, took the unusual step of displaying her robust infant publicly at Gimbels Department Store. Her personal account was simple but disarmingly persuasive: "I experienced absolutely no pain."[17]

The twilight-sleep movement, which had thrived on publicity, crashed suddenly when in 1915 Mrs. Carmody died in childbirth. Twilight sleep, as her doctor testified, was not the cause of death, but the public clearly had its doubts, and the movement was irreparably damaged. Soon better anesthesia was available that avoided delivery-room screams and did not require confining cribs, so the episode passed from thought. It remains, however, like the use of hypnosis to block or to relieve pain, a fruitful subject for meditation. What can we say about a pain that somehow imprints its unmistakable signs upon the body—wild thrashings, contortions, moans, and cries—yet leaves absolutely no trace within the mind? Is pain we cannot remember still pain? Twilight sleep, however we respond to such questions, offers strong evidence that pain comes into existence only at the moment when it makes its way into our consciousness. Without the mind's contribution, there is no pain.

†

Our Western ideas of mind originate in ancient Greek and Roman philosophy. The Greek and Roman philosophers, as no doubt befits their sun-drenched climates, had far less to say about pain than about pleasure.[18] In these slave-owning, aristocratic cultures, pain belonged almost by default to the lower classes. Pleasure, by contrast, not only suited aristocratic temperaments but also supplied a topic full of troubling questions for thinkers searching for the "highest good." Was pleasure consistent with the good? antithetical? inseparable? Plato and Aristotle, for example, both devote extended discussions to the role of pleasure in a good life, and the philosophical sect known as hedonists unashamedly proposed pleasure as the *summum bonum*. Pain simply did not evoke such rich philosophical talk. Mostly, it was just something to be avoided.

It is with Marcus Aurelius and the Stoic philosophers that pain makes its way openly into Greco-Roman thought. Marcus Aurelius is a figure of great importance and paradox: the emperor who ruled Rome from 161 to 180, a period often taken to constitute the Golden Age of Roman imperialism. Rome in this Golden Age, however, had also turned into a supermarket of competing philosophies, religions, gods, quacks, and soothsayers, including the relatively new sect called Christians, and, in this confused time, the most powerful man in the Western world not only turned his hand to philosophy but also based his meditations on the thought of a former Greek slave, Epictetus, who had spent his life in ill health, lame, living in an unlocked house said to contain nothing except a pallet and a rush mat. From their opposite stations, Epictetus and Marcus Aurelius both came to see pain as always under the dominion of the mind.

With its bloody circus maximus and succession of short, violent reigns, the Roman empire had no lack of pain to go around, and the school of Stoic philosophy (to which both Epictetus and Marcus Aurelius belonged) came to see the wise man's relationship to pain as a crucial issue. Historians distinguish between the early Stoics and later Stoics, but for our purposes we can consider Stoicism a fairly unified body of thought that promised its adherents, when they attained the rare state of wisdom, a complete freedom from anxiety, dread, and evil. Freedom was not an idle metaphor or abstract idea to the former slave Epictetus. He held that we are all enslaved to the extent that we give up control over our lives. Such control, for Epictetus, came only from the will. He taught that by a supreme act of will we must in effect expel from our minds every possible distraction from what he repeatedly calls "the sphere of the moral purpose."[19]

Moral purpose for Epictetus did not refer to morality or rules of good behavior. The serene Stoic wise man, in fixing his thoughts on the sphere of the moral purpose, lived a life strictly according to reason, which for Stoics required a constant and utter contempt for the (irrational) passions. Only through the willed conquest of fear and passion, according to Epictetus, do we fully live out the inner truth of our own being. Only then are we truly free. Pain, of course, ranks among the most common sources of fear. Thus wisdom and moral purpose for Epictetus required that the individual should attain an absolute willed conquest over pain. This conquest did not depend on advances in Roman medicine. It was something the Stoic philosopher accomplished for himself.

Marcus Aurelius differs significantly from Epictetus in his darker tone and more somber images, as when he compares human life to a warfare and a sojourn in a strange land, but he picks up unchanged from Epictetus the conviction that pain represents a life of slavery.[20] Pain becomes both sign and source of our loss of freedom and of our falling away from wisdom. His strategy for opposing pain, in what amounts to an anticipation of modern medicine, is to regard it as entirely a phenomenon of the body. He views the body, with its diseases and passions, as continuously seeking to enslave us to its needs. The Stoic's willed conquest over pain thus entails an absolute victory of mind and will over body. Once we affirm the dominance of mind over body, pain for Marcus Aurelius confronts us with a simple, rational alternative: "If it is past bearing, it makes an end of us; if it lasts, it can be borne. The mind, holding itself aloof from the body, retains its calm, and the master-reason remains unaffected. As for the parts injured by the pain," he concludes contemptuously, "let them, if they can, declare their own grief."[21]

The disdain with which this pagan philosopher speaks of the body sounds like the severer excesses of medieval theology. (Marcus Aurelius cites approvingly, for example, the description of man composed by his master Epictetus: "A poor soul burdened with a corpse.")[22] Small wonder that the early Christians found this brand of Stoicism highly amenable to a system of thought that divided human beings into a perishable body and an immutable soul. The choice for Marcus Aurelius is clear:

Pain must be an evil either to the body—in which case let the body speak for itself—or if not, to the soul. But the soul can always refuse to consider it an evil, and so keep its skies unclouded and its calm unruffled. For there is no decision, no impulse, no movement of approach or recoil, but must proceed from within the self; and into this self no evil can force its way.[23]

Marcus Aurelius implicitly assumes here—as he explicitly states elsewhere—that the mind or soul attains true freedom only when retired to its own inwardness, untouched by the things of the world. The ultimate victory of soul over body thus finds its characteristic expression for Stoic philosophy in the triumph over pain.

Stoics, of course, sometimes found it difficult to live up to such an austere creed. Ancient literature records numerous moments of backsliding. Cicero in his *Tusculan Disputations* (II.xxv) writes that Dionysus of Herakleon, who learned his Stoicism from its founder, Zeno, suffered such agony in his kidneys that he was forced to cry out and confess how falsely he had understood pain. Even Marcus Aurelius unbends a bit. "When in pain," he writes, "always be prompt to remind yourself that there is nothing shameful about it and nothing prejudicial to the mind at the helm, which suffers no injury."[24] Stoicism did not teach that the mind's power over pain was easy to achieve, only that it was necessary. Yet this ideal gave special importance to aspects of life we might well take for granted. On his deathbed Marcus Aurelius deliberately recalled the pleasures of a philosophical friendship as a means of combatting a pain so terrible that he surely must have wondered whether mind possessed all the powers he had claimed.

The Stoic split between body and mind, like the Christian split between body and soul, indicates how ancient the desire is to assign pain wholly to the flesh. What makes Stoicism so germane to my argument, however, is the importance it assigns to mind. For Stoics such as Marcus Aurelius, the mind and will entirely reshape the experience of pain. Stoic writers were fond of describing philosophy as a medicine: a practical aid in the affairs of daily living. Like a medicine, the mind for the Stoic philosopher in effect uncreates or recreates the body's pain. The bodily pain of Stoicism, we might say, is paradoxically always in the head because the mind or reason or soul always possesses the power—as well as the duty—to erase or to overcome it.

No doubt today Stoicism seems too austere and remote to offer a credible medicine or philosophy for managing pain, although Freud used a variant of Stoic thinking when he described his cancer of the jaw as a "small island of pain in a sea of indifference." Yet Stoicism certainly suggests that the mind has powers over pain we have not sufficiently understood. We need not travel to ancient Rome, however, to encounter a philosophical medicine willing to recognize and to utilize the mind's crucial role in the experience of chronic pain. We might equally pay a brief visit to the pain center of Dr. Benjamin Crue in Durango, Colorado.

✝

Durango is a small, raw, Western town surrounded by mountains with strangely sawed-off, flat tops. The low buildings constructed out of orange-yellow brick give the impression that utility is prized here. It was originally a mining town, founded in 1880 by the Denver and Rio Grande Railroad, a no-nonsense place for ore and shipping. Yet beauty is all around: in the ancient stands of spruce, pine, and aspen dug into rock and crags, in the meadows that suddenly interrupt acres of dense woods. Half a millennium ago in the canyons of nearby Mesa Verde the mysterious Anasazi Indians ("the old ones") carved miniature stone cities high into the walls of overhanging cliffs. It is not where you would expect to encounter one of the world's finest specialists in chronic pain.

Dr. Benjamin L. Crue, Jr.—a rugged and gentle man in his sixties—seems at home both in the serene mountains around Durango and in the gritty, working-class town. This is surprising only because he spent most of his professional life in the affluent suburbs of Los Angeles where in 1960 he founded and directed one of the first multidisciplinary centers for the treatment of pain: the New Hope Pain Center. He is a distinguished neurosurgeon with a long train of publications and has specialized in chronic pain for the past thirty years. Among his many posts he has served as president of the American Pain Society and president of the American Academy of Algologists. Crue's approach to chronic pain was not just innovative. Within the world of medical thought and practice in place when he left medical school, it went profoundly against the grain.

Normal science has been described, in an influential book by Thomas Kuhn, as mostly a mopping-up exercise.[25] Kuhn means that during most periods and in most fields there is an accepted theoretical framework of scientific thought—a paradigm, as he calls it—that commands general acceptance, and scientists normally work on small, still unexplained problems (known as "puzzles") that explore and fill out and confirm the prevailing paradigm. When, fresh out of medical school, Benjamin Crue first began working on the specialized problem of facial pain called tic douloureux, the scientific paradigm that had prevailed for more than a century explained pain as a transmission of nerve impulses from the site of damage (the periphery) to the brain. In order to stop the pain, medicine, logically, set out to interrupt the transmission of pain impulses from the periphery. Anesthesiologists learned how to block specific nerves with chemical compounds. Neurosurgeons developed an array of exact operations with ominous names such as rhizotomy, cordotomy, and sympathectomy designed to cut the normal pain pathways. As an unsolved problem, tic douloureux offered a perfect opportunity for mopping up.

Crue discovered that in the case of tic douloureux the accepted paradigm was not working exactly right. Most of the time neurosurgeons could indeed stop the tic pain by blocking it at the periphery. The paradox was that, in a small percentage of cases, cutting the peripheral nerves or blocking them with alcohol did not stop the pain. None of the standard neurosurgical procedures provided lasting relief. It was this paradoxical exception to the rule that suggested something else must be going on. At last the moment of truth arrived. Crue finally decided that the pain of tic douloureux could not be fully explained through the accepted paradigm. Worse, it called the paradigm itself into question. Tic pain, Crue deduced, must not originate at the periphery but rather in the brain. Thus you could not always block the pain of tic douloureux at the periphery because it was always already in the head. This theory, since it opposed the accepted paradigm learned by all doctors in medical school, met with the fate of most new claims: instant disbelief.

There was more disbelief to come, however. In what he calls a "lyric leap," Crue soon recognized that many forms of intractable pain followed the pattern he proposed for tic douloureux. Not all forms. He recognized that cancer patients, for example, required a separate team of specialists, since their pain originated in specific tumors. Like cancer pain, what Crue called "recurrent acute pain"—such as the pain of arthritis—clearly had its origin in specific forms of peripheral tissue damage. Beyond these clear exceptions, however, Crue still confronted a large and growing population of patients whose pain could not be traced to a continuing, identifiable organic source. Crue described this specific, paradoxical illness as "benign chronic intractable pain syndrome" (BCIPS). The ultimate source of benign chronic pain syndrome, Crue decided, was not peripheral but central.

This new way of thinking about pain—while not so vast in its implications as the paradigm changes discussed by Kuhn—was revolutionary and explosive. In claiming a central origin, Crue absolutely did *not* mean that chronic pain was imagined or unreal or merely "mental." Indeed, he emphasized that most chronic pain started with an organic, peripheral injury. This pain, however, continued to persist long after the original lesion or injury had healed and thus transformed itself into a chronic condition that was entirely central and directed by the brain. Herein lay the bombshell. If much chronic pain was truly central rather than peripheral, it obviously required new methods of treatment and new avenues of research. Well-fortified boundaries would have to be crossed. For example, neurosurgeon Crue soon found he needed to hire a psychologist and later a psychiatrist and finally a full multidisciplinary team of specialists, including a neurologist, anesthesiologist, biofeedback technician, occupational therapist, neurophysiologist, dietician, and orthopedist.[26]

A polite, undeclared war broke out. A chronic pain that was central would not require the nerve blocks and operations so often prescribed to cut the peripheral pathways. (As it turned out, anterolateral cordotomies proved effective in only half the patients, often for just a short time, and almost 15 percent of patients suffered worse pain after the operation.)[27] Crue does not hesitate to blame his fellow physicians for clinging to an outworn peripheralist model that leads to useless, expensive, invasive mistreatment of patients with chronic pain. As he writes:

The overwhelming majority of patients we see with chronic intractable benign pain syndromes have had both their pain syndrome and their pain behavior iatrogenically reinforced over and over again. Many of them have been subjected to mutilating operative procedures, where the only reasonable expectation was, quite frankly, the placebo effect. . . . It is time that neurosurgeons, orthopedists, and anesthesiologists admit that with very few rare exceptions they are bankrupt when it comes to treating chronic intractable benign pain syndrome patients.[28]

Iatrogenic illness—to cite the worst euphemism in medical terminology—means illness caused by the physician (*iatros* in Greek). Understandably, Crue found himself at odds with powerful figures in the newly emerging specialty of pain treatment.

The two camps in this conflict of interpretations Crue has called the centralists and the peripheralists. In fact, he remembers first hearing the name "centralist" spoken dismissively by Dr. John J. Bonica, founder of the pioneering pain clinic at the University of Washington and the man almost universally regarded as the father of the pain clinic movement. Bonica was chairman of the Department of Anesthesiology and a proponent of various nerve blocks and surgical interventions designed to cut the pain pathways from the periphery. When Bonica at a meeting referred to "Crue and his group of centralists," the name sounded so right to Crue that he decided to ignore its apparently dismissive status. The lines were drawn. If Crue was a centralist, that made Bonica a peripheralist. He saw no middle ground.

The centralist and peripheralist models of chronic pain are absolutely distinct. The peripheralist model assumes that pain results from tissue damage and from continued "afferent nociceptive input." The centralist model rejects the need for any continued impulse from the periphery. It posits "a central generator mechanism" responsible for keeping the pain alive.[29] For a time, the conflict between centralist and peripheralist schools was red hot. Neither side would publish in the journals of the other side. Now the atmosphere seems more like an uneasy truce or compromise. Many specialists seem willing to grant that at least a few forms of chronic pain probably have an underlying central mechanism, just as patients with recurrent acute pain from underlying chronic pathologies (such as arthritis) may have long-lasting distress that results from a combination of peripheral and central causes. Crue points out that physicians already recognize comparatively rare pain syndromes that originate entirely within the central nervous system, as sometimes happens after a stroke.[30] But Crue goes far beyond the compromisers in asserting that a great deal of chronic pain—what he calls the benign chronic intractable pain syndrome—exists in the absence of a continuing, peripheral source of nociceptive input. The back or leg hurts now—whatever its original source of injury—simply because the central nervous system (and specifically the brain) tells it to.

Crue is unyielding in his conviction. "The centralist concept of pain is correct," he writes, "and the peripheralists are incorrect."[31] We will see, in the final chapter, that new research has uncovered in the brain a previously unknown pain-*enhancing* system of so-called "on-cells" that may well provide support for the centralist position. Crue meanwhile argues that most doctors remain dogged peripheralists, in part because medical schools for over a century have taught nothing else. Further, he would not agree that the conflict between centralists and peripheralists is subsiding into compromise or tacit agreement, even though some influential figures would like us to think so. It is, he contends, a still simmering and unresolved controversy. As a realist he recognizes that the public finds it hard or impossible to believe that their pain does not require a continuing peripheral, organic cause. "This certainly is not immediately acceptable to a majority of patients with chronic pain," Crue writes, adding with a jab at his colleagues, "and it seems not even conceivable to a majority of physicians."[32] We all secretly prefer the old Homeric notion of pain as the intrusion of an outside force: the arrows of the gods. Could it be that our brain alone really spins out a cycle of chronic suffering, like an endlessly replaying tape, with no continuing injury needed to keep it going?

✝

"It was my desire to find out more about human brain function in relation to the problem of free will," writes Benjamin Crue, "that led me into neurophysiology; then, during World War II, into neurosurgery." He wanted to know whether a knowledge of brain functions can support our normal belief—with its profound implications for thinking about good and evil—that "all things being equal, we could have done otherwise." Do we make truly free choices when we comfort the sick or rob a 7-Eleven store? Crue frankly confesses his failure to find a "scientifically acceptable hypothesis" to support his belief in free will.[33] Yet the desire of traditional medicine to flee such philosophical and theological questions may be precisely what limits many physicians in their understanding of chronic pain.

It took courage for Viktor E. Frankl to address the medical-scientific community in a text bearing the clearly unacceptable title *The Doctor and the Soul* (1955). Yet Frankl's courage is already well known to the several million readers of *Man's Search for Meaning* (1946).[34] In this brief book Frankl discusses both his approach to therapy and his experience as a prisoner in Nazi death camps. Although he afterward served as Professor of Psychiatry and Neurology at the University of Vienna Medical School, as head of the Department of Neurology at the Poliklinik Hospital in Vienna, and as president of the Austrian Medical Society of Psychotherapy, he is remembered among nonmedical readers as the man who survived for some three years the living hell of Auschwitz and Dachau.

The new explosion of interest in the Holocaust has not paid much attention to Frankl, which is unfortunate considering his importance in the postwar period. *Man's Search for Meaning*—which he had originally published under the title *From Death-Camp to Existentialism*—is not simply a personal memoir but a physician's cold-eyed calculation of what it costs to survive amid inhuman circumstances. "We who have come back," writes Frankl, "by the aid of many lucky chances or miracles—whatever one may choose to call them—we know: the best of us did not return."[35] This is not modesty. The best who did not return, in Frankl's words, were prisoners who sacrificed their lives so that other prisoners might live even a few days longer. The account that Frankl writes of his experience holds a unique place among narratives of the Holocaust because he writes both as a survivor and as a psychologist concerned with the question of what it was, beyond luck or miracle, that allowed some prisoners to survive scenes of unthinkable brutality.

Frankl believes he survived at least in part because, at a critical moment, when he felt absolutely overwhelmed by exhaustion, pain, and despair, he found a meaning that allowed him to go on. He suddenly imagined himself behind a lectern speaking to a large audience on the psychology of the concentration camps. Amid the wreckage of European civilization, this almost crazed vision of civilized, scientific inquiry recommencing its normal work in the aftermath of unprecedented disaster gave him a reason not to give in to his despair. It also provided an individual instance of the general principle he saw at work in the death camps and in the world beyond. For Frankl, the crucial key to survival—even in the face of an intolerable abyss of suffering—lies in our power to discover or to attribute a meaning to our existence.

Meaning—a term he leaves undefined and open to the varieties of human usage—is the key to Frankl's account of his protracted experience with pain. We perhaps lend his experience a false melodrama if we think of his pain through cinematic depictions of Nazi torture. Pain also belonged to the less graphic but backbreaking daily misery of the camps. For three years Frankl spent his days at unrelenting hard labor, in semi-starvation, under conditions so extreme that prisoners regularly collapsed and died, broken down from illness, exhaustion, and sometimes hourly beatings. Pain was not a sudden intruder but the medium in which he lived almost every minute of his three-year confinement.

Here is a fragment of Frankl's description of the ten-hour days he spent working at road repair in freezing temperatures without gloves— his only meal a thin, watery soup:

Like nearly all the camp inmates I was suffering from edema. My legs were so swollen and the skin on them so tightly stretched that I could scarcely bend my knees. I had to leave my shoes unlaced in order to make them fit my swollen feet. There would not have been space for socks even if I had had any. So my partly bare feet were always wet and my shoes always full of snow. This, of course, caused frostbite and chilblains. Every single step became real torture. Clumps of ice formed on our shoes during our marches over snow-covered fields. Over and again men slipped and those following behind stumbled on top of them. Then the column would stop for a moment, but not for long. One of the guards soon took action and worked over the men with the butt of his rifle to make them get up quickly.[36]

Even worse, according to Frankl, was the added agony of bearing insult, humiliation, and day-by-day injustice. It is hard to imagine a more intimate acquaintance with pain.

Frankl found himself living in a political version of the irrational universe that postwar existential philosophy came to describe as absurd: stripped of his identity, reduced to a number, denied his basic human dignity and rights, confined in a senseless routine, brutalized and tyrannized. Kafka invented nothing more terrifying than what Frankl faced every day. Yet this personal encounter with pain was for Frankl not a confirmation of existential nothingness. It was a turning point. The challenge he faced was to find a personal meaning in an apparently meaningless and inhuman existence. "Woe to him who saw no more sense in his life," he writes of his comrades in the camps, "no aim, no purpose, and therefore no point in carrying on. He was soon lost."[37]

Two crucial points need clarification before we return to Frankl's personal search for meaning amid the carnage and suffering of the concentration camp. First, meaning for Frankl is always plural and personal: there is no single, universal fountain of purpose. The meanings we discover in our lives will differ from person to person. The meanings an individual creates or discovers may differ from situation to situation, or simply change as we grow older. Frankl never tires of repeating that meaning must be discovered, not given, and he emphasizes that searching is more important than discovering. You may never find what you are searching for. Yet—on this point Frankl is adamant—if you block or deny the *search* for meaning, you ultimately annihilate the will to live.

The second point to clarify is this: the drive for meaning depends ultimately on our irreducible freedom of will. Frankl admits, readily, that we are never entirely free; social and biological limitations always constrain us. Yet he believes that no social system or biological constraint—from tyranny to death—is so powerful that it can overrule our freedom to take a stand: to choose at least our *attitude* toward pain. This emphasis on individual freedom of choice certainly links Frankl with a major theme of existential philosophy. (One of his many books is entitled *Psychotherapy and Existentialism*.) There is nothing abstract or abstruse, however, about his treatment of individual freedom. Even in the Nazi camps, Frankl believes, he still possessed the personal freedom to choose what gives his life—and his pain—its meaning.

Pain constitutes a major test for the mode of treatment called logotherapy that Frankl developed after his release from Dachau. He recognizes that we will avoid pain as long as avoidance is in our power.[38] But what about pain that we cannot avoid? This question returned to Frankl with particular urgency when he encountered patients who were terminally ill. When analgesics failed and cure was past hope, pain was then simply unavoidable. It faced such patients as a brute, existential fact, like the massive rock Sisyphus was doomed to push endlessly uphill. In fact, it was the unavoidable pain they faced—far more than the prospect of death—that seemed to plunge his patients into deepening despair.

Frankl's response to such hopeless pain came again from his experience in the death camps. There he discovered that meaning consists not only in statements but also in actions. It consists not only in asking questions or in seeking answers but in being questioned. "We needed to stop asking about the meaning of life," he writes of especially difficult moments in the camps, "and instead to think of ourselves as those who were being questioned by life—daily and hourly. Our answer must consist, not in talk and meditation, but in right action and right conduct. Life ultimately means taking the responsibility to find the right answer to its problems and fulfilling the tasks which it sets for each individual."[39]

The response to the question of unavoidable pain, for Frankl, is less a statement (a correct answer put into words) than a deed: suffering transformed from submission or defeat into right action. The phrase "right action" of course does not imply either moral behavior (Frankl freely confesses that he stole food in the camps) or a single, universally proper response applicable to everyone. It implies instead that crisis will ultimately confront us with the necessity to act, and our action, if it is right, will express the deepest level of our beliefs, beliefs we may not even know we hold or be able to put into words. In effect, Frankl discovered that his own protracted questioning by life brought him to understand his suffering as a task he was called upon to perform, well or poorly.

There is doubtless a strain or contradiction in Frankl's thought when he proceeds from personal experience to psychotherapy. He can never quite resist the temptation to make his own answer (that suffering is a task) universal. His language certainly embraces more than a strictly secular or medical point of view when he talks about the task of suffering as "taking up your cross." Perhaps he simply found in Christian tradition a metaphor consistent with his view that suffering, when understood as a task, holds out the possibility for redeeming a wasteland of meaninglessness pain. As he writes in this universalizing spirit:

When a man finds that it is his destiny to suffer, he will have to accept his suffering as his task; his single and unique task. He will have to acknowledge the fact that even in suffering he is unique and alone in the universe. No one can relieve him of his suffering or suffer in his place. His unique opportunity lies in the way in which he bears his burden.[40]

The vision of humankind as a solitary figure suffering in an empty landscape bears less resemblance to traditional Christian doctrine or to the Book of Job than to the plot of Beckett's existential classic *Waiting For Godot* (1952). Yet the difference is evident. Beckett's characters wait with no clear and articulate sense that pointless waiting might itself constitute their self-appointed task: might give a personally redemptive meaning to their meaningless pain. "If there is a meaning in life at all," Frankl writes, "then there must be a meaning in suffering."[41]

Frankl is a popular and moving speaker, and once he was asked to address the prisoners in San Quentin. There he encountered the same attentive audience that, in a now legendary performance, had understood almost instinctively the bleak avant-garde humor of *Waiting For Godot*. At the conclusion of his talk, an inmate asked Frankl to say a few words, publicly, over a speaker system, to a prisoner on death row who faced the gas chamber in four days. At Auschwitz Frankl too had lived in daily contact with the gas chamber. He told the condemned prisoner that man always holds the power to rise above himself, even in the last minute, and "by so doing retroactively invest meaning even in a wasted life."[42] Then he recounted for the prisoner Tolstoy's story about the death of Ivan Ilych.

†

Frankl's experience drew him into an unusual relationship with his patients. He wrote without embarrassment about what he called a "medical ministry," by which he meant that physicians cannot serve as mere technicians of the body but must also risk entering into the emotional and spiritual lives of their patients. Only by daring to cross such boundaries can the physician, in Frankl's view, attain maximum insight and thus offer maximum assistance. Today, of course, hospitals neatly divide the work of physician and chaplain into separate offices, as if needing a clear, bureaucratic structure to mark off the boundary between body and spirit. Yet this separation, maintained in the name of science, did not seem inevitable to the man often regarded as a father of the scientific revolution. Francis Bacon wrote in 1605:

I esteem it . . . to be clearly the office of a physician not only to restore health, but also to mitigate the pains and torments of diseases; and not only when such mitigation of pain, as of a dangerous symptom, helps and conduces to recovery; but also when, all hope of recovery being gone, it serves only to make a fair and easy passage from life.[43]

Modern doctors and patients who know little about chronic pain—and little about the mind's power to increase or to decrease the torment we experience—would do well to ponder Bacon's words and the life of Viktor Frankl.

8

THE USES OF PAIN

We are all bitched from the start and you especially have to be hurt like hell
before you can write seriously. But when you get the damned hurt use it—
don't cheat with it. Be as faithful to it as a scientist.
ERNEST HEMINGWAY TO F. SCOTT FITZGERALD[1]

*T*HE TRADITIONAL MEDICAL reading that derives
all pain from organic lesions and tissue damage
not only leads to unnecessary surgery and mis-
diagnosis but also has helped to create and to sustain our contemporary
(shrunken) understanding of pain as no more than a problem in biochemistry. The evening news assails us with innumerable scenes of human pain, from earthquakes in San Francisco to terrorist carnage in Bei-
rut, and then cuts to a commercial for aspirin. The vastly beneficial role
that medicine has played in the treatment of pain is of course evident to
anyone who has ever returned from a successful visit to the doctor. Yet
precisely because the role of medicine has lately come to seem all-
encompassing, we have lost the ability to recognize the ways in which the
entire fabric of our social lives is shot through with pain. As a consequence, we fail to notice the ways in which pain continually confronts us
with pressing questions of everyday ethical conduct.

Medicine unintentionally but implicitly depersonalizes pain by enfold-
ing it within its machinery of high-tech prowess. It removes its quirky
humanness and encourages us to forget that pain is not identical with
illness. The main difficulty in totally handing over to medicine the problem of pain, however, is that we act as if we can then stop thinking about
it. It becomes merely another complex issue we leave to specialists and
experts. The medical experts, as we have seen, know far less about pain
than most people assume. Often the advancement of scientific knowledge

demands that researchers occupy themselves with microscopic details, while clinicians face the pragmatic daily dilemmas of an overflowing practice. As a result, no one is really thinking about the changing place of pain in human life and culture. Yet when we fail to think about pain, we give up one of our main resources for dealing with it when suddenly pain has us, once again, in its grip.

Is pain merely a medical event? Is it simply a misfortune of the nerves and tissues that ambushes us, like a chunk of sky falling: an unexpected neurological event that interrupts our lives with its senseless clamor? Scholar Gerald Bruns, drawing on his Catholic education, writes of an old Jesuit ("a man of unspeakable cunning") who once told him: "All men are the servants of pain. We are its principal medium."[2] This line of thought has the benefit of acknowledging how often pain in effect *uses* us, much as we might say that a gene pool uses living organisms to strengthen and to perpetuate itself. Here I want to contend the reverse: that pain is something we implicitly or consciously mobilize for specific social and personal purposes. We use pain almost as regularly—and sometimes as cunningly—as pain uses us. The hope lies in learning how to use it to better purpose.

†

A good, if unusual, place to begin exploring the social uses of pain is satire. Satire helps to show how we are continually caught up in the cultural representations and displays of pain even when we are not immediately gripped by its affliction. It also illustrates how, in the wider culture beyond medicine, pain serves complex ethical and personal purposes. The difficulty we may experience in sensing the relevance of satire to pain reveals how far pain takes up residence within the changing field of human culture. We do not see a connection between satire and pain largely because pain no longer holds the same relation to language that characterized earlier periods. Satire, however tame and bookish today, was once almost as feared as the instrument to which satirists regularly compared it: the surgeon's knife.

Children seem to grasp at once the link between language and pain. They understand that soothing words can relieve pain, and they know too that harsh words can hurt as much as a bruise. Surely everyone has felt deeply "wounded" by a vicious taunt or a cutting remark. Is such pain merely metaphorical? Freud tells of a woman who suffered from an intense facial neuralgia. As part of her treatment, he asked her to recall a period when she had felt great irritation toward her husband. Freud continues: "She described . . . a remark of his which she had felt as a bitter insult. Suddenly she put her hand to her cheek, gave a loud cry of pain and said: 'It was like a slap in the face.' With this her pain and her attack were both at an end."[3]

Scholars have exploded the story that Keats pined away after an especially damaging review, but legends about the wounding power of language are not groundless. Satire in fact traces its origins to Archilochus of Paros, the mercenary soldier, poet, and the priest of Demeter, who lived in the seventh century B.C. Legend tells that Archilochus became engaged to a young woman named Neoboule, the daughter of Lykambes. For some unspecified reason—perhaps because his prospective son-in-law was not exactly an aristocrat—Lykambes broke off the engagement. Archilochus thereupon composed violent iambic verses, better described as metrical invective, which he recited publicly at the festival of Demeter. Such was the power of his words that Lykambes and his daughter, so the legend runs, obligingly hanged themselves.[4]

The historical truth of the legend of Archilochus finally matters less than its usefulness as a myth about the power of satire. Satire, as Robert C. Elliott shows in an important book, is in effect a modern survival of the ancient or primitive curse: a magical use of language that taps its hidden powers to inflict real damage. Children of course quickly memorize the singsong rhyme explaining that names will never hurt us, but their need for such often repeated reassurance suggests how much names really do hurt us, until we learn a song to ward off their power. Yet childhood and primitive cultures are not the only source of evidence linking words to wounds. In the great age of English satire, which dates roughly from the Restoration of Charles II (1660) to the death of Alexander Pope (1744), satirists openly confessed that they aimed to inflict injuries. These satirists saw their main task as learning how to transform the infliction of pain into an art.

The images that early satirists chose in describing their art helps to expose the deep attachment between language and pain. Poet laureate John Dryden wrote in the seventeenth century that satire was like a fine sword stroke that severed the victim's head from his shoulders but left it standing in place.[5] Lady Mary Wortley Montagu, writing a few years later, knew that the surest way to offend her implacable enemy Alexander Pope was to accuse him of composing satires that inflicted their injuries clumsily:

> *Satire* shou'd, like a polish'd Razor keen,
> Wound with a Touch, that's scarcely felt or seen.
> Thine is an Oyster-Knife, that hacks and hews.[6]

The almost surgical ideal of a touch "that's scarcely felt" should not be confused with painlessness. The art lies not in removing the pain but in inflicting it almost unnoticed. Pope, for example, retaliated against his arch-foe Colley Cibber by making him the hero of a poem entitled *The Dunciad* (1743). Comparing Cibber to a traditional figure called Zodiac Man who appeared in various almanacs with diagrammatic lines keyed to astrological signs, Pope exulted: "He will be stuck, like the man in the almanac, not deep, but all over" (fig. 21).[7]

The satirist's task to inflict pain seemed so clear that for centuries the standard emblem for satire was the lash. As there was no point in denying the pain of a satiric lashing, most apologists employed their arguments in justifying it. Renaissance theorists, for example, regularly compared the satirist to the surgeon, who inflicted a razorlike pain in the process of cure.[8] The image of the satirist as surgeon proved important because satirists liked to claim for their work the exalted social goal of correcting vice. Yet when satirists chose to attack individuals so powerful, unscrupulous, and so insulated from criticism that nothing short of divine intervention would change them, correction and cure were obviously futile goals. Would satire "cure" Richard Nixon? At such times, satirists begin to describe the pain of satire not as a means of cure but as a (quasi-legal) punishment.

The commonplace Renaissance image of satirist as surgeon gave way during the eighteenth century to an image of the satirist as judge. Satire thus justified the pain it caused by posturing as a kind of extension of the judicial system.[9] This justification succeeded in part because judicial punishments were so violent. Prisons were reserved mainly for pretrial detention and for debtors. Punishment for most eighteenth-century criminals did not involve loss of liberty but rather swiftly inflicted pain. The pain of such punishments was meant not to correct or improve the criminal, of course, but to deter the public.[10] Standard penalties included whipping, branding, and standing for hours in the stocks (locked into painfully contorted postures while spectators pelted the criminal with anything

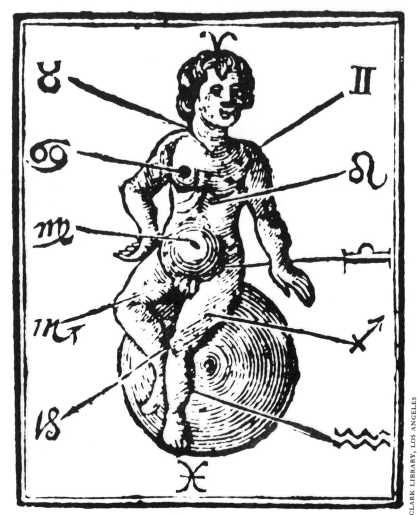

FIGURE 21. Zodiac Man. From *The Ladies' Almanac* (1725).

from garbage to rocks). The logic of judicial deterrence required that many punishments were public spectacles. Eighteenth-century hangings resembled carnivals, complete with crowds, vendors, speeches, and bleachers. Satire and the judicial system it claimed to uphold were in effect arenas for the civic display of pain.

The public, deterrent, even judicial purpose of satire, however, rarely succeeds in erasing its equally important personal purposes. Jonathan Swift claimed that his chief purpose in writing *Gulliver's Travels* (1726)—eviscerated and domesticated today as a children's book—was "to vex the world" rather than to "divert it." He urged his friend Pope to keep up similar attacks on complacency and vice. "When you think of the World," he advised, "give it one lash the more at my Request."[11] Indeed, we falsify Swift's life—including his temper, eccentricity, and deep disappointments—if we ignore the anger and indignation (his word was "hate") that burns within his great satiric masterpieces, despite their multilayered artifice. When Pope praised Swift for defending Irish interests against English oppression, Swift did not cite high-minded patriotic or literary motives. "What I do," he responded, "is owing to perfect rage and resentment, and the mortifying sight of slavery, folly, and baseness about me, among which I am forced to live."[12]

The thirty-second canto of Dante's *Inferno* offers a good summarizing image for the satirical traffic in pain. In a scene that summons up the primitive origins of satire, Dante finds himself walking among sinners who are buried up to their necks in ice. Incredibly, he kicks one of these immobilized creatures—a notorious traitor—in the face. ("Whether it was will or fate or chance I do not know," he says, disingenuously.)[13] "You advise me right not to trouble myself about the world," Swift wrote to Pope, adding, "But, Oppression *tortures* me."[14] Not every satirist is tortured with rage and resentment, of course. It is also essential to see that Swift's rage is not merely a fact of his temperament, as if he could not help flying off the handle. Satiric rage for Swift is an emotion based in an ethical response to organized stupidity and injustice. Without such pain, however, and without the almost visceral need to strike back because of it, satire surely would not exist.

Satire, we might say, is the civilized substitute for Dante's kick in the face. It finds various artful means of expressing the pain-triggered biological impulse to fight back. In a culture closer to the magical powers of language, the satirist's words could land with the force of an actual blow. The tameness of satire in our own language-poor age need not suggest that such impulses have vanished. Yet something has seriously changed in the relation between art and pain. In 1909, Bernard Shaw defended his practice as a playwright through a comparison that a half-century later would become simply unthinkable. As he wrote:

It is no more possible for me to do my work honestly as a playwright without giving pain than it is for a dentist. The nation's morals are like its teeth: the more decayed they are the more it hurts to touch them. Prevent dentists and dramatists from giving pain, and not only will our morals become as carious as our teeth, but toothache and the plagues that follow neglected morality will presently cause more agony than all the dentists and dramatists at their worst have caused since the world began.[15]

Today, as dentistry aspires to the pain-free condition of muzak, satire has been displaced by the harmless overblown rhetoric, ceremonial choke holds, and fake body slams dealt out by the self-parodic villains and heroes of professional wrestling. If the eighteenth century used public pain to attack injustice and to deter wrongdoing, we use it mostly for fun.

†

Satire, as a civilized adaptation of the primitive curse, shows how past cultures used pain by drawing it within the formal conventions of literary and cultural ritual. Not just any words will create an effective curse or satire but rather only carefully chosen words uttered in the correct order under just the right circumstances. The point is that pain seems to achieve a significant cultural power, as opposed to the random violence of fistfights, when it comes into contact with ritual. Ritualized pain is somehow made useful, even fruitful. Ronald Melzack introduced into modern research on pain the following curious example. As late as 1967 a few rural villages in India each year performed an ancient (but now discouraged, even outlawed) ceremony called *bagad*, or hook-swinging. The village elders would choose a young man to bless the fields at the time of the April full moon, which he did in a trancelike state while suspended from a long pole by two metal hooks inserted into the small of his back.[16] Although the young men chosen for this rite apparently experienced a kind of religious anesthesia, the *bagad* clearly proceeds on the understanding that fertility will be renewed through an act that normally would cost an unthinkable price in pain.

The ritualized use of pain is not restricted to such possibly archaic examples as satire or hook-swinging. Almost every culture includes rites and ordeals of initiation that mark the passage into adulthood, and pain constitutes one of the most important features of these varied rites. "The record clearly shows," writes anthropologist Alan Morinis of his research among various tribes and peoples, "that the delivery of a consistent, deliberate, direct experience of pain to participants in the ritual is a remarkably recurrent aspect of adolescent initiations." He goes on to argue that such pain cannot be dismissed as merely incidental or accidental: "Reports tell of initiands being beaten, bitten, starved, incised, scarified, pierced, tattooed, terrified, mutilated, circumcised, infibulated, cicatrized, bound, and subject to the removal of parts of their bodies (especially teeth and fingers)." Most anthropologists have simply ignored or explained away this consistent violence. Morinis convincingly argues that such ritually inflicted pain serves as a cultural mechanism for inducing and signaling a transformation of consciousness.[17]

A transformation of consciousness, however, might occur through mechanisms other than pain. Why is pain—rather than, say, music or drugs—the favored instrument? The answer, for Morinis, concerns the inherent bond between pain and sacrifice. Rites of initiation involve the passage into a state of full participation in a social group that requires a sacrifice of childhood freedoms. They in effect signal a change that we might describe as an acceptance of the more experienced, self-aware, responsible frame of mind that characterizes adulthood. Pain is the medium and mark of sacrifice. It takes away our independence. It binds us, however dimly we understand it, to the adult world in which our personal choices will inevitably acknowledge the overriding law of the group. Not coincidentally, pain tends to brand such an episode of initiation as unforgettable.

We might prefer to think that the pain of ritualized initiations belongs strictly to the practices of primitive cultures. The evidence, however, suggests that pain almost everywhere still continues to serve as a ritualized initiation. The novels of Ernest Hemingway offer probably the best literary illustration of how the modern entry into manhood involves rites of pain and danger. (As critic Leonard Kriegel puts it: "No other writer so consistently uses pain as a test of the capacity to endure.")[18] Certainly, John Wayne films, the cult of Rambo, and the popular hard-boiled detective novels all provide their own curious testament that the American definition of manhood requires an impassive immersion in pain. Ethics deals fundamentally with what we call character: the stuff someone is made of. From boot camp to football practice, we use pain today, in whatever diminished and misguided ethical sense, to know whether someone is a man—or to know what kind of man he is.

Pain inside a culture of manliness provides an apparently indispensable test of courage and machismo. If you are a man, you must be tough; if you are tough, you must be able to withstand pain. You must also be able to dish it out, particularly to women. Women, perceived as a threat to male toughness, offer a particular challenge to the culture of manliness, since the tough guy must be both sexually attractive and also indifferent to women. He needs women in order to show that he does not really need them. (Women who accept this crazed role are called broads.) Thus the typical hard-boiled detective earns his reputation by slugging or shooting almost as many broads as he beds. His maleness shows up as a variant of spouse abuse: a supreme indifference to female pain.

The dish-it-out approach to manliness still permeates American culture, especially in such cinematic enterprises as crime and sport. Sport, of course, is still mainly a male preserve, despite recent gains for women in such genteel, noncontact events as track and tennis. Appropriately, fans of one American professional football team have nicknamed its stadium The House of Pain, while media-hip linebackers and defensive ends promote themselves as brutal psychopaths bent on destruction. Street gangs, cults, and crime families initiate and discipline their members through rites that include—or simply consist in—pain. But our most commonplace ritualized use of pain may well be domestic violence. The male (although on rare occasions a woman takes over the male's role) schools his household in the unspoken rules of patriarchal culture by regularly beating them into submission. Modern families sometimes seem little less than machines for the production of pain.

Pain is not by any means confined simply to male rites. Women describing their first sexual intercourse—which undoubtedly holds in modern Western culture the status of a female rite of passage—commonly not only mention pain but also regard pain as central to the experience.[19] Certainly pain is also central to the modern Western experience of childbirth, although in non-Western cultures women do not invariably associate labor with pain. Despite our distance from hook-swinging ceremonies or finger-chopping rites of initiation, we have not entirely left behind the world in which pain is a kind of tunnel through which one passes to a new stage of being. Pain has always served—and continues to serve—specific social and ethical purposes. Indeed, as a species we show an endless ingenuity for discovering new uses for pain within the recurring structures of formal or informal rites.

†

The purposes for which we use pain sometimes prove inseparable from the methods or instruments we invent to deploy it. The modern world

employs pain with a detachment that reflects our need to distance ourselves from affliction at the same time we are fascinated by it and put it
to multiple uses, from selling newspapers to running marathons. The Roman crowd enjoyed its pain up close and personal; the wounded gladiator
died right before the eyes of the spectators who moments before condemned him to death. The psychopathic tyrant Vlad the Impaler—who
stands behind modern myths of Count Dracula—watched the bloody
death throes of his victims with absolute relish. The modern way with
pain, by contrast, is more often to produce it in private and by machine.
It is a clinical, sterile, high-tech pain that masks its violence as efficiency.
The American pilot who dropped the atomic bomb over Hiroshima says
he felt no remorse. Aerial technology had created its masterpiece of
detachment.

Kafka, as we might expect, is prophetic in depicting a future that uses
pain in the service of an almost surreal vision of mechanized control. His
story "In The Penal Colony" features an ingenious punishment called
"the Harrow"—a glass-cased apparatus with intricate cogwheels and
piercing, retractable needles that slowly executes a prisoner (who lies
bound and gagged) by writing an inscription appropriate to his crime
deeper and deeper into his flesh. In a deft stroke, Kafka sets the story in
an indistinct, reformist time when the Harrow has fallen out of favor. For
the officer who now serves as its lone defender and caretaker, this elegant
machine embodies a principle that perfectly befits Kafka's nightmare
world where the prisoner never knows what his crime is. "There would
be no point in telling him," explains the caretaker. "He'll learn it on his
body."[20]

In primitive tribes with their elaborate tatoolike designs etched over
the body, pain serves to inscribe a tribal knowledge directly into the flesh.
The scars and markings that result thereby enfold the individual within
the larger social order whose laws and customs are reflected in the visible,
written form of a bodily statement or design.[21] In Kafka's story, the Harrow purports to make the body not only a social text—in the sense of a
warning to others—but, more important, a medium of personal illumination. For the prisoner, the punishment supposedly leads to a moment
of absolute knowledge. Yet Kafka's world never seems more nightmarish
or modern than in the way its machines are continually breaking down.
Nothing quite works. At the crucial moment, the Harrow, with its mur-

derous, clicking needles, fails to perform exactly. It does not write but simply jabs repeatedly in an incomprehensible muddle of gears and needles and blood.

Kafka leaves us with the opposite of a lesson about the value of penal correction. There is no real enlightenment that comes through this socially administered punishment. What the Harrow creates is simply intolerable pain justified by the pretense of enlightened punishment. Instruction and correction are the very modern, humane uses *claimed* for pain in Kafka's dark tale. In truth, however, pain becomes simply the defining product and symbol of a futuristic, calculating rationalism run mad. Its use, unlike our quaint subterfuge in calling hard-core prisons "correctional institutions," is to demonstrate openly the implacable power of an inaccessible, unaccountable apparatus of bureaucratic reason.

Kafka's story serves to strip the civilized disguises from pain. The new commandant, we are led to believe, is no less committed to force but simply prefers more abstract, detached, and up-to-date punishments that make the Harrow look savagely old-fashioned. Disguised or hidden pain, like death by lethal injection, is now a more effective instrument of control because it is more acceptable to modern sensibilities. Kafka's maniacal Harrow in effect stands as a parodic exposure of our more subtle, more civilized modes of punishment and control. Its open, berserk cruelty helps to unmask the relation (which we so often labor to conceal) between pain and force. The Harrow might be said to represent the absolutist modern state stripped of its self-deceptive rhetoric about justice and compassion: it is nothing less than a technology designed to transform human pain into political power.

Pain, we might say, is the universal instrument of force. Force uses pain—or threatens to use it—in order to get its way. That is why, as far back as the rack, strappado, and thumbscrews of the late Middle Ages, torturers have relied on increasingly diabolical machines. The machine is an impersonal artifact for generating and multiplying force. Applied to the purpose of torture, it produces and intensifies pain. Equally important, as Elaine Scarry has argued, it represents the impersonal, mechanical power of whatever masked or unmasked authority stands behind its use. Without the state-sponsored machinery of secret police, sudden disappearances, torture chambers, and the ever-present threat of pain and death, most tyrannies would dissolve overnight. Like Kafka's bureaucratic officer, they use pain, in short, to enforce their own particular brand of social or political illumination.

Torture allows us to see with unusual clarity the link between force and pain. It is hard to believe, but torture in the late Middle Ages was actually *legal*.[22] It was an authorized means of gaining a confession at a time when confessions suddenly became crucial. The Fourth Lateran Council in 1215 had outlawed the older judicial practices of establishing guilt, such as duels, oaths, and ordeals, so that henceforth a legal conviction required either the testimony of two eyewitnesses or a confession. Legalized, judicial torture thus became indispensable for obtaining a conviction when two eyewitnesses were unavailable. It was also subject to an elaborate series of regulations concerning who could be tortured, under which circumstances, with what degree of damage.[23] Pain in this specific rethinking came to hold a new status in law as an essential condition for permitting the truth to emerge.[24] Yet Elaine Scarry is surely right that the pain of torture never serves only for extracting information.

Torture, Scarry argues, temporarily confers upon the states or regimes or movements or institutions that authorize it a reality and an omnipotence otherwise deeply in question.[25] Small wonder that it still finds multiple political uses today. Torture in fact is a highly developed, if obscene, contemporary art. Long after eighteenth-century reformers abolished the legalized torture of the Middle Ages, modern states and police and random militants continue to mutilate and torment, unofficially, in the name of some higher good or lesser evil. Amnesty International in a book entitled *Torture in the Eighties* (1984) documents the contemporary use of torture in Africa, the Americas, Asia, Europe, and the Middle East. It insists that we cannot dismiss torture as isolated, individual acts of sadism: "Torture does not occur simply because individual torturers are sadistic, even if testimonies verify that they often are. Torture is usually part of the state-controlled machinery to suppress dissent. Concentrated in the torturer's electrode or syringe is the power and responsibility of the state."[26]

Medicine might be thought far removed from such political uses of pain, but we should recall that a prisoner tortured by the Spanish Inquisition often suffered under strictest medical supervision. As the sixteenth-century Protestant hagiographer John Foxe reports: "A physician and surgeon attended, and often felt his temples, so as to judge of the danger he might be in. By these means his agonies were for a short time suspended, but only that he might have sufficient opportunity of recovering his vitality to sustain further torture."[27] Such medical complicity with state-sponsored torture is not merely a relic of past centuries. Amnesty International explains that today a doctor is sometimes present during torture "to ensure that the victim cannot escape the torment through losing consciousness or by dying."[28] Auschwitz, like all Nazi death camps, was run under the direct supervision of its medical staff. Doctors examined prisoners, made selections for the gas chambers, checked those about to die, and personally turned on the gas jets.

One example must, mercifully, suffice. At Auschwitz, from about September 1941, debilitated prisoners or longtime inmates on the medical block were killed by lethal injection. The injections were given in the same hospital room where surgery normally occurred. Eventually, doctors determined through human experiments that the most efficient death could be achieved by injecting phenol directly into the heart. Victims sat on a stool. The right arm was placed to cover the eyes. The left arm was raised sideways to expose the naked chest. The doctor then filled the syringe, thrust the needle through the chest wall, and emptied its payload into the heart. In his book *The Nazi Doctors* (1986), Robert Jay Lifton quotes an anonymous survivor of Auschwitz whose measured words apply far beyond the life of the Third Reich: "The doctor . . . if not living in a moral situation . . . where limits are very clear, . . . is very dangerous."[29]

†

Torture is so deplorable that it makes questions of ethics seem almost irrelevant. Most people would now say that torture under any circumstances is wrong. End of discussion. The danger is only that the quickness with which we condemn torture may prevent us from recognizing and discussing other uses of pain extending to the most casual, unnoticed details of our daily life, where ethical questions often go not only unanswered but unasked. We simply do not possess at present anything like an adequate ethics of daily practice. Philosophers and medical ethicists prefer to concentrate on gaudy, headline-grabbing issues such as abortion, euthanasia, genetic engineering, and the right to die. An ethics of daily practice, by contrast, would need to employ almost a novelist's eye in order to uncover the implications of acts and choices so small that we rarely stop to observe them.[30] It would take as its goal an examination of behavior that we automatically consider free from ethical content: what we read, what we wear, how we talk to our children, the furnishings we choose, even perhaps the daydream that passes unnoticed as we round a familiar corner.

Poet and physician William Carlos Williams in his brief story "The Use of Force" (1961) offers a good illustration of the complex questions that an ethics of daily practice can bring into focus. In its details, the story depicts the transformation of an ordinary house call into a contest of wills. The doctor arrives to examine a young girl who has been feverish for three days. Everyone suspects diphtheria, although the dreaded name remains unspoken. In its ordinariness, however, the examination begins like a scene from a Norman Rockwell painting. The girl refuses to cooperate, but the doctor proceeds with professional wisdom, "quietly and slowly."[31] She knocks his glasses off. The doctor addresses the child sternly, with no result. Then, with growing impatience, he explains her danger to the parents and says that he will forgo a throat examination if they accept "the responsibility." But the responsibilities soon become difficult to sort out.

The situation begins to change in ways that are not entirely clear. The girl breathes faster and faster in her struggle to resist. The doctor instructs her father to hold her. But it is his own professional self-control, the doctor senses, that has begun to slip. Williams leaves us unable to say exactly when this ordinary encounter between doctor and patient passes beyond the boundaries of medicine. The attempt to force open the child's mouth, however, signals a dramatic change. In the narrator's revealing metaphor: "Then the battle began."

A battle is a test of force, but the force exposed in this struggle between doctor and patient is not so much warlike as, however indirectly, sexual. "I had already fallen in love with the savage brat," the doctor confesses. It is her savagery—her uninhibited passion—that he identifies as the source of his excitement, "magnificent heights of insane fury of effort bred of her terror of me." The text also records, however, his initial observation of her "magnificent blonde hair" and "unusually attractive" features. Although medicine is the occasion for this passionate struggle, the struggle itself becomes central. Medicine seems merely the background for a sexualized encounter between male and female, between adult and child, between power and powerlessness.

The girl is soon screaming, hysterical. A wooden tongue depressor splinters in her mouth and blood begins to flow, but the brutal examination continues. "A man has to have a fever to write," Williams once said, promoting his own medical version of the inspired bard.[32] Here it is the doctor who seems possessed. We might as well be witnessing a scene of bacchic frenzy from Euripides. "I too had got beyond reason," the narrator explains, "I could have torn the child apart in my own fury and enjoyed it. It was a pleasure to attack her. My face was burning with it."

The brief account hurriedly concludes. The rapelike scene of resistance and penetration issues in triumph—"I forced the heavy silver spoon back of her teeth and down her throat till she gagged"—and the doctor's Dionysian "longing for muscular release" is satisfied, at great cost. The ends of power have been worthy, doubtless. The doctor's ultimate diagnosis of diphtheria will protect both the public and the child. Further, Williams understood that a pediatrician needed unusual resources that go beyond compassion. "I know you'll like the kids," he told the young medical student Robert Coles, who had proposed a residency in pediatrics. "They'll keep your spirits high. But can you go after them—grab them and hold them down and stick needles in them and be deaf to their noise?"[33]

The means and motives of power, however, are far more questionable than the doctor's worthy medical purpose. The doctor knows he has been at fault. ("Perhaps I should have desisted and come back in an hour or more. No doubt it would have been better.") His burning face and his sexualized pleasure in the struggle cannot be justified on medical grounds. What is at stake, in fact, goes beyond the protocol of a successful throat examination, beyond controversies about public health, legal definitions of battery, and the rights of minors. Williams's story raises questions that return us to the complex ethical issues always entangled in the uses of force and pain.

Pain, as the old Jesuit understood, uses us. Force takes on a life of its own. What has gone wrong when a well-meaning physician can "attack" a terrified child with such erotic violence? One answer is that Williams's doctor, like all of us, has limited patience and irrational impulses, but this tells us simply what was never in doubt: that doctors are human. For Williams, the dark regions of force are also the poet's special territory. Indeed, "The Use of Force" takes as its implicit subject the perils of confusing the doctor with the poet. As a doctor, Williams respected and followed what he called in his *Autobiography* "the humility and caution of the scientist."[34] Yet as a poet he also recommended what seems an incompatible approach. "Let yourself go completely," Williams advised poets, "—watching the effect, howbeit, with shrewd attention."[35]

The doctor in "The Use of Force"—who undoubtedly lets himself go—is in effect divided between the competing ethical imperatives of medicine and literature. In Williams's poet, the medical, scientific respect for detached observation is complemented (but also fatally compromised and subverted) by an egocentric, omnivorous, undiscriminating, sexualized appetite for experience that finds its most exuberant expression in the short poem he addressed to his nose, entitled "Smell!" ("What tactless asses we are, you and I boney nose/ always indiscriminate, always unashamed. . . .") The poet, unlike the doctor, is bound solely by the law of his own quickening desires and by the mandates of the imagination. As poet, Williams will not rest until he knows, or sniffs, everything.

"Sometimes I speak of imagination as a force, an electricity," Williams wrote.[36] Force, like contact, is a key concept to which he frequently returns. Poetry for Williams not only expressed wayward drives and desires in the poet but also took more impersonal energies—in man and in nature—as its recurrent theme. Unlike Hemingway, he saw no need to search in exotic places or in violent action to find expressions of this force. He could find it in the everyday responses of a crowd at the ballpark:

It is alive, venomous

it smiles grimly
its words cut—

The flashy female with her
mother, gets it—

The Jew gets it straight—it
is deadly, terrifying—

It is the Inquisition, the
Revolution

It is beauty itself
that lives

day by day in them
idly—[37]

The same force that flashes out as sexual attraction also, in Williams's poem, drives such opposing expressions of power as wars of liberation and inquisitorial torture. Williams here makes no ethical judgments about the uses of force. The poet, in fact, seems to occupy a position beyond good and evil. Force, like electricity or the imagination, obeys its own laws.

Williams's doctor in "The Use of Force" errs precisely at the point where he abandons the physician's detachment for the poet's impassioned contact. In his *Autobiography* Williams described himself as guided in his relations with patients by a code that keeps poetic impulses tightly in check. "Though I might be attracted or repelled," he writes of his encounter with individual patients, "the professional attitude which every physician must call on would steady me, dictate the terms on which I was to proceed."[38] "I smiled in my best professional manner," says the doctor-narrator in "The Use of Force," describing his initial encounter with his reluctant patient. The struggle that ensues certainly exposes the falseness of practiced, professional smiles, often employed as a kind of disguised prelude to force. It also exposes, however, the dangers of releasing our hold on the professional restraints that "steady" us in the face of powerful forces we cannot hope to master. Force, Williams's doctor shows us, is never merely instrumental, something we use for our own purposes. Like the crowd at the ballpark, we are its medium.

Doctors, according to Williams, have much to learn from literature. It can help them recognize the unnoticed ethical dilemmas that surround them in their daily practice. It can also help them to listen carefully to the language of the everyday people they treat. When an English professor— "an obvious Britisher"—slyly asked Williams where his poetic language came from, Williams shot back: "From the mouths of Polish mothers."[39] It was not the British literary tradition from Chaucer to Keats that inspired his best work but the words spoken by the patients he saw in his practice each day. Evidence shows that doctors need considerable help in learning how to listen to their patients. Yet the doctor who follows the poet *too* closely, Williams also reveals, will find that medicine lies on the border of forbidden territory. The doctor, unlike the poet, cannot afford to risk crossing fully into a region where there are no ethical restraints upon the uses of force: where pain in effect uses us.

†

Williams helps us recognize how far the everyday medical dealings with pain conceal unacknowledged ethical questions. Indeed, the ethics of pain management is an area of daily practice that, with a few exceptions, almost no one wants to talk about.[40] The tangled ethical questions surrounding the involuntary and very painful medical treatment of Donald "Dax" Cowart—a young man blinded and terribly disfigured in 1973 by deep burns over 60 percent of his body and who demanded the right to die—still occupy a squadron of medical ethicists.[41] But pain is not a central subject for most of those writing about "Dax's case," and medical education does not provide much help. Dr. John Bonica, past president of the IASP, says bluntly: "Physicians are poorly trained to manage pain properly. They rely on drugs which are often ineffective, prescribe too small doses, and often wait for pain before they do something."[42] One study shows that as patients feel increasingly more pain they are increasingly less likely to obtain adequate analgesics for relief. The catch-22 of hospital life: You receive adequate pain relief only when you don't need it.

The absence of adequate measures for relieving pain runs like a leitmotif through the sober study by Fagerhaugh and Strauss entitled *Politics of Pain Management* (1977). Their long case history of a woman dying of cancer ("Mrs. Abel") reveals how pain can create a massive rift dividing the patient from the hospital staff. Mrs. Abel claimed that she did not mind dying but was afraid of too much pain, and her fears of pain (possibly multiplied by a denial of her fears of dying) helped transform her into a woman whose unceasing complaints and unreasonable demands ultimately alienated everyone around her. Even the most empathetic nurse "pulled away," as the authors gently put it. Thus Mrs. Abel spent her last two months of life in "almost unendurable pain" and in "the almost total isolation which [the] staff had imposed on her."[43] The crucial point, beyond showing how fears of pain can destroy a person as effectively as cancer, is that *not* relieving pain brushes dangerously close to the act of willfully inflicting it.

Withholding an effective analgesic drug or prescribing less than an adequate dosage are certainly ways of using pain. It is only recently that the ethical implications of withholding adequate pain relief found a sharp, if limited, focus in debates over the medical use of heroin. In cases of intractable pain, British hospitals commonly employed a potent compound known as Brompton's Mixture—popularly, Brompton's Cocktail—containing both cocaine and heroin. Heroin, so British physicians argued, not only relieves pain better than morphine but also avoids its harmful side effects. Most important, heroin (so the argument ran) more effectively relieved anxiety and fear, left mental sharpness less impaired, and produced an extraordinary sense of well being.[44] In America, heroin passes like currency across the street corners of every major city. It also appears on Drug Schedule I of the Controlled Substances Act, which means that its medical use is strictly prohibited.

The question of whether to permit the medical use of heroin aroused a period of hot debate in the United States. In 1984 Senator Daniel Inouye and Representative Henry Waxman introduced the Compassionate Pain Relief Act, designed to legalize the medical use of heroin for relieving the intractable pain of dying patients. The measure failed to gather enough support. Subsequent efforts also failed, in part because the issue deeply divided the American medical community. Today, as we will see later, organized statewide groups calling themselves Cancer Pain Initiatives argue forcefully that (without heroin) we already possess adequate medication to relieve pain in 90 to 95 percent of cancer patients, if the drugs were used properly. (It is a big if.) Preliminary research indicates that heroin and cocaine do not provide superior pain relief or less severe side effects, although they are beneficial under some special circumstances.[45] Would heroin have helped in Mrs. Abel's special circumstances? Would it have made her final days less wretched? Was she among the small percent of patients whom properly administered morphine cannot reach? Was the terrible pain and isolation of her death unavoidable?

The prohibition of heroin in cases of terminal cancer—whether correct, prudent, or merely overcautious—undoubtedly constitutes a use of force. Unbelievably, American doctors regularly refuse to prescribe effective doses of narcotic painkillers to dying patients on the grounds that the patients might become addicted. The treatment of cancer pain, clearly, is still not based solely on scientific fact but draws on ignorance, fear, prejudice, and on an invisible, unacknowledged moral code expressing half-baked notions about the evil of drugs and the duty to bear affliction. The ethics of pain management, unfortunately, may not receive proper attention until the first doctor is successfully sued for failing to provide adequate relief. At that point, the need for a full and reflective dialogue on ethical questions about pain will be preempted—as so often happens in American life—in favor of the slowly grinding mills of the law.

†

Patients of course use pain. Chronic pain, as we have seen, sometimes proves the best available means for resolving a conflict that might otherwise prove insoluble. This "secondary gain" is one reason why effective treatment often proves so difficult. Dr. C. Norman Shealy describes such patients in his book *The Pain Game* (1976). "The patient may discover," he writes, "that there are coincidental, secondary rewards for suffering or that his pain provides a handle with which he can manipulate others." Examples of such manipulative gamesmanship are almost inexhaustible. A patient may find that pain wins approval. As Shealy continues:

He may take a sort of perverse pride in being the most unfortunate, the longest suffering, and his friends may unwittingly encourage him to establish his worth in this way. One of our patients took delight in letting us know that all of her friends kept telling her, "I don't know how you do it." With that kind of reinforcement for withstanding her pain, it will be hard to convince her that suffering is a frightfully high price for a few compliments.[46]

Such pain has obviously taken on both a meaning and a use that may completely escape the notice of the patient.

Patients sometimes use pain in ways that convert it to cash. Shakespeare's Falstaff boasted that he would "turn diseases to commodity," and the modern welfare state has created a system designed to do just that. In fact, pain is among the most common complaints in disability claims. Moreover, about 150,000 Americans each year apply for Social Security benefits because of disabling pain that cannot be fully explained by clinical findings.[47] Medical specialists contend that such patients normally are not faking sickness to avoid work—but a medical text for lawyers also advises that "pain is the most easily pretended symptom and among the most commonly feigned."[48] In this social debate, courts must confront at length such knotty questions as how much pain qualifies as disability, how it can be measured, and whether Workers' Compensation covers patients whose *sole manifestation* of disability is the subjective complaint of pain. We need not linger in this legal rat's nest. The point is that today chronic pain sometimes pays off with a disability check. The continuing check may make the pain almost impossible to remove.

Illness has its rituals, we know, and the habitual behavior of some chronic pain patients surely ranks among the familiar rites of modern illness. The rituals of secondary gain prove largely unproductive, it turns out, even when cash passes hands, because patients continue to walk the dreary round from specialist to specialist, seeking relief that never comes. The uses of pain outside of illness, however, are not always so fruitless. Ernest Hemingway's typically muscular advice to his far more fragile companion Scott Fitzgerald—"When you get the damned hurt use it"—suggests that we can sometimes invent truly creative uses for an unavoidable pain. Pain in this sense may serve as the raw material of personal and artistic triumph.

†

The creative uses of pain find no more flamboyant instance than the figure of the Romantic artist. The suffering artist (whom we will meet again in the next chapter) holds immense importance in the changing cultural history of pain and no doubt lurks somewhere behind Hemingway's modernist advice that Fitzgerald should be as faithful to his pain "as a scientist." Hemingway's advice no doubt draws less upon a respect for science than upon his preoccupation with rites of manhood, which underlie his well-publicized and complicated obsession with hunting and sport. Athletes, too, like artists, often learn to use pain in a testing and breaking of limits. George ("Sparky") Anderson, manager of the Detroit Tigers, received a lot of derisive press for his remark that "pain don't hurt."[49] Yet his meaning is not hard to fathom: the astonishing performances we witness almost daily in athletics occur only because the athlete has learned how to compete in pain. In professional sport, pain is in some sense the unchosen but inevitable medium of performance.

Dancers, like athletes, create performances that require the most extraordinary feats of grace. Certainly they would prefer to perform in perfect health. Yet an unavoidable price of the self-discipline required so that the dance may flow effortlessly through the dancer is, of course, pain. Toni Bentley, a former dancer with the New York City Ballet, writes:

Alongside the development of sheer physical prowess have come injuries as curious and chronic as their causes. At any given time any dancer, like any athlete, could list any number of aches and pains, both serious and transitory—sprains, tendinitis, ingrown toenails, blisters, pulled muscles, muscle spasms and stress fractures. Modern dancers, because they usually dance barefoot, can develop skin burns, bruised metatarsals, splits in the skin from excessive dryness and broken toes, injuries less common for pointe dancers whose feet are tightly bound in satin shoes.[50]

Pointe dancers, as she notes, have their own curious rites. A bloodied toe for the pointe dancer is considered a sign of good luck. Lucky or not, it is a clear example of how dancers do not just suffer pain but *use* it to their advantage.

Dancers sometimes speak of riding into their pain, as if it were a source of energy they could tap. The worst relation to pain for a dancer or athlete is simply to resist it: to stiffen the body, however slightly, in compensation. Significantly, such therapies as the Feldenkrais Method and the Alexander Technique work to counteract the muscular-skeletal stiffness common in chronic pain and to restore a dancelike fluidity of motion.[51] In a very practical sense, the dancer must accept pain, come to terms with it, and the dancer's use of pain thus lies in this willing acceptance. Such pain, according to Toni Bentley, is forgotten in the ecstasy of performance, although it returns with dull insistence when the curtain comes down. Perhaps the dancer's simultaneous acceptance and forgetfulness of pain offers a useful model. The art would lie in discovering how to avoid merely stiff, passive resistance and how to use pain as the medium for a fluid, creative performance, even if the performance were limited to walking downstairs for dinner or climbing behind the wheel of the car.

The distance between accepting pain and seeking pain is immense. Our view of art and artists still remains powerfully haunted by such portraits of self-mutilation as the bandaged Van Gogh.[52] European Romanticism beginning in the late eighteenth century made pain seem indispensable to the artist—a tormented, unworldly spirit tightrope-walking over the abyss—and such self-portraits in pain may prove irresistibly seductive to an artist who suffers great hardships. As poet John Berryman put it in an interview: "My idea is this: the artist is extremely lucky who is presented with the worst possible ordeal which will not actually kill him. At that point, he's in business. Beethoven's deafness, Goya's deafness, Milton's blindness, that kind of thing." "I hope," he concluded half-seriously, one year before his suicide in 1972, "to be nearly crucified."[53]

The saving word for Berryman is *nearly*. Yet the danger in such Nietzschean thinking ("What does not kill me makes me stronger") is that it can lead to a businesslike marketing of personal affliction and to self-fulfilling prophecies of doom. We should remain skeptical of psychoanalytic studies that seek to trace all creative activities, in whatever period, to self-torment in the artist or to aggression turned compulsively against the self.[54] Artists such as Berryman who have struggled with various demons, from alcohol and epilepsy to tuberculosis and insanity, do not demonstrate that pain provides the indispensable and eternal source of art but rather that the creative, transforming power of art can put anything to use, even pain.

FIGURE 22. Georgia O'Keeffe (1887–1986). *Drawing No. 9* (1915).

There is probably no ailment so common as a headache, and the artist's power to transform even pain into the raw material for art might take as its emblem an early charcoal drawing by Georgia O'Keeffe (fig. 22). As she wrote: "Drawing No. 9 is the drawing of a headache. It was a very bad headache at the time that I was busy drawing every night, sitting on the floor in front of the closet door. Well, I had the headache, why not do something with it? So—here it is."[55] Pain in this sense is more an occasion for art than a cause. At the extreme limit of art's transforming powers, however, we might say that such pain becomes, no matter how improbable the thought, not merely an occasion for art but even a possible source of beauty.

9
PAINFUL PLEASURES:
BEAUTY AND AFFLICTION

Beauty can pierce one like a pain.
THOMAS MANN[1]

I
T IS HARD to imagine the person so twisted as to discover beauty in pain. Not even the Marquis de Sade traveled so far in his own peculiar warp as to find pain beautiful. (Stimulating, yes. Beautiful, no.) Pain seems endowed with the power to pull the human figure out of alignment, to unform or de-form us, so that beauty is among its first casualties. The skin turns pale and clammy, the brow knotted, the eyes lusterless: such, according to one legal text, are the infallible signs of pain that malingerers cannot imitate. In addition, the person in pain may well experience a world from which beauty, like everything else that makes life valuable, seems simply drained away. Yet the history of cultural change contains few stranger revelations than the persistence with which humankind links affliction to beauty. It does not trivialize or deny suffering to inquire into the persistent alliance between beauty and pain. Rather, this unlikely alliance stands as a central instance of the principle we have been exploring: that pain continues to take on new meaning as it is drawn within the changing historical field of human culture.

Pain as a psychosocial creation is, as I have argued, something we experience not simply as private individuals but also as members of a culture or subculture. We therefore experience pain in ways shaped and reinforced by the images current around us. Family, friends, and community—in their behavior and values—supply the major representations of pain that shape our experience. Children at an early age begin to encounter images of pain in nursery rhymes, bedtime stories, and television cartoons. As we grow older, newspapers, novels, and films continue our education in pain. The advertising industry, with its unprecedented resources and power, may rank today as the most important force that shapes the ways in which we understand pain. The point to emphasize is that cultural changes in the representation of pain—from advertising to high art—both reflect and often help to create significant changes in our personal experience.

Three instances of change seem to me particularly useful for exploring the strange link between pain and beauty. These moments I will call the classical, the sentimental, and the postmodern. The term "moments" frees us from endless wrangling about the definition of historical periods and cultural movements. I mean simply that art at a specific time represents pain in ways that help to challenge and to shape the values of the surrounding culture. The link between beauty and pain that these three moments illuminate is thus far from solely a matter of aesthetics. Beauty, after all, even though it has almost vanished as a serious topic in contemporary thought, still influences our behavior in countless practical affairs of life, from choosing a mate to hearing a concert or taking a photo. Even without our knowing it, ideas of beauty hold a significant influence on the ways we come to experience pain.

†

The classical moment represents pain as something that ennobles even as it destroys. More precisely, pain in effect brings out or expresses a potential for nobility that is latent but often unrealized. This view of pain underwrites one of the most famous artifacts in the history of sculpture: the Late Hellenistic statue of Laocoön. Created in the first century B.C. by three sculptors from the Greek island of Rhodes (Hagesandros, Polydoros, and Athanadoros), this monument to the legendary Greek hero with the most unpronounceable name (Lay-ock-a-wan) depicts a scene described at length in Virgil's *Aeneid* (fig. 23). Indeed, the legend is inseparable from the sculpture and surrounds the visual form with its invisible web of meanings.

Virgil's retelling—almost exactly contemporary with the famous statue—dramatizes the scene in which Laocoön, a seer and priest of Apollo, gives the Trojans the only wise counsel they receive during the debate over whether to take inside the walls of Troy the prodigious

FIGURE 23. Hagesandros, Polydoros, and Athanadoros. *Laocoön* (*c.* 42–21 B.C.).

PAINFUL PLEASURES: BEAUTY AND AFFLICTION

wooden horse left behind (some say as a gift or offering) by the apparently departing Greeks. "I fear Greeks bearing gifts," Laocoön warns, famously, but no one listens.² Enraged, he hurls a spear at the wooden horse and surely would have discovered the Greek warriors hidden inside, but the sudden entrance of a (planted) Greek captive distracts the Trojans. Eagerly, they swallow the captive's lie that the wooden horse is indeed an offering left behind to placate an angry goddess.

Laocoön meanwhile withdraws to the shore preparing to sacrifice a bull to Neptune when two dragonlike serpents swim toward him. Their blood-red crests, gaping mouths, and blazing eyes strike terror into the Trojans, who watch the serpents churning straight toward Laocoön. "I sicken to recall it," says Virgil's hero, Aeneas, as he tells what happened next:

First each snake took one of his two little sons, twined round him, tightening, and bit, and devoured the tiny limbs. Next they seized Laocoön, who had armed himself and was hastening to the rescue; they bound him in the giant spirals of their scaly length, twice round his middle, twice round his throat; and still their heads and necks towered above him. His hands strove frantically to wrench the knots apart. Filth and black venom drenched his priestly hands. His shrieks were horrible and filled the sky, like a bull's bellow when an axe has struck awry, and he flings it off his neck and gallops wounded from the altar.³

Sources differ about whether Laocoön is punished for a broken vow of chastity or, as Virgil implies, for his unknowing opposition to the will of Zeus (by advising the Trojans to reject the horse). Interpreting Laocoön's grisly fate as punishment for bad advice and sacrilege, the Trojans almost instantly wheel the vast doom-machine inside the walls. At night Greek warriors spill out from the belly of the wooden horse and the bloodbath begins.

What matters most for our purposes is that the three Rhodian sculptors represent the destruction of Laocoön not simply as a spasm of terror or pain but as an occasion of heroic suffering. His herculean strength and stature certainly help to create a sense of colossal proportion, as does the contrast with his two small sons. Their bodies look less youthful than simply miniaturized: heroism flattened out and scaled down. Their calmly stylized faces (as if borrowed from earlier archaic Greek art) also provide a vivid contrast with Laocoön, whose agonized features make his knowledge of pain unmistakable. One son—his eyes already glazed over in death—is past such knowledge, the other not yet fully initiated. Virgil described the head and necks of the two serpents as towering above Laocoön (*capite et cervicibus altis*), but the sculptors instead give Laocoön the visibly heroic, superior position. His death is painful—and so appalling that the hero Aeneas grows sick even to recall it—but it is also, as in Greek tragedy, a pain that shows man elevated rather than crushed by defeat.

Pliny the Elder called the Laocoön greater than any other work in painting or sculpture.[4] Is such a terrifying scene, however, really an example of beauty? The question reveals the effects of a massive cultural change that separates us from the ancient Greeks. Beauty in Greek art is a matter of proportion, simplicity, and ideal form. More important, beauty achieves its power by appealing not to the senses alone but to the spirit or soul. "Man seeks to be near beauty," as the classical scholar Paul Friedländer summarizes the view of Socrates, "because the soul's wings grow at the sight of beauty."[5] The renowned classicist Johann Winckelmann understood this power in the statue of Laocoön. "The pain of the body and the greatness of the soul," he writes, "are distributed and, so to speak, balanced throughout the entire frame of the figure with equal strength. Laocoön suffers, but he suffers like the Philoctetes of Sophocles. His misery touches our soul, but we would wish to be able to bear misery like this great man."[6]

We might come closest to grasping the almost tragic spirit of the Laocoön statue through Yeats's phrase describing the death of the Irish patriots killed in the Easter Rebellion of 1916: "A terrible beauty is born."[7] This is not beauty for the faint-hearted, not beauty without loss and pain. On the contrary, such beauty demands that we confront and contemplate the mystery of human suffering as it plays itself out in the damaged, human flesh. So faithful is the Laocoön to the facts of bodily pain that Bernini believed he could observe the serpent's poison just beginning to take hold—by a stiffening in the thigh muscles. A nineteenth-century American physician discussed the statue at length in a doctoral thesis describing the "physiognomy of pain."[8] Anatomical detail certainly helps to authenticate the image of heroic suffering, but the suffering body in Greek heroic art always serves to make visible an internal greatness of spirit. Laocoön thus stands among the most strenuous examples of classical beauty: a beauty—mingling body with soul—that does not shrink from terror and pain.

The loss of this strenuous, classical understanding of beauty has required an enormous shift in cultural values, and nowhere is this shift more

FIGURE 24. Nicolas-Sébastien Adam (1705–1778). *Prometheus* (1763).

obvious than in imitations of classical art, such as the heroic statue of Prometheus by the eighteenth-century French neoclassical sculptor Nicolas-Sébastien Adam (fig. 24). Prometheus is in many ways a more impressive figure than Laocoön. Zeus chained him to a cliff for stealing fire from the gods and giving it to mankind. As additional punishment, Zeus also assigned an eagle to tear out his liver, which (to keep requiring fresh assaults) continually regenerated. In Adam's treatment, however, the frenzied, twisting flesh—not to mention an upside-down eagle perhaps distantly related to the gargoyle family—distracts attention from an interior drama of the spirit or soul. There is nothing of the added pathos or terror in Laocoön's helplessness as he watches the serpents attack his two young sons. In Adam's Prometheus, the heroic suffering of the Hellenistic age has given way to something like thinly classicized gothic horror.

The important point in comparing Prometheus with Laocoön is that already in Adam's work we can see pain abandoning the realm of beauty. For the neoclassical age, Adam's Prometheus is an example not of the beautiful but of the sublime. This distinction would perhaps be no more than a historical curiosity except that we are still living with the effects of the momentous split between sublimity and beauty. First popularized in the eighteenth century, the division between the beautiful and the sublime provides one main source of the utter demoralization of beauty in the modern world. Later we will return to this influential split, especially as defined and widely disseminated by Edmund Burke in his treatise *A Philosophical Enquiry into the Origin of Our Ideas of the Sublime and the Beautiful* (1757). Meanwhile, a second (related) moment awaits us in the changing cultural relations between beauty and pain: the sentimental.

†

Sentiment and sentimentalism have a bad reputation today, and it is easy to see why. Wordsworth showed what sentimentalism can do to defeat a great poet when at seventeen he published his "Sonnet on Seeing Miss Helen Maria Williams Weep at a Tale of Distress" (1787). Some of the lines are not just bad but memorably awful:

> She wept.—Life's purple tide began to flow
> In languid streams through every thrilling vein;
> Dim were my swimming eyes—my pulse beat slow,
> And my full heart was swell'd to dear delicious pain.[9]

The poem was Wordsworth's first published work. It appeared anonymously, and he never reprinted it. The style shows the young poet trapped within an outmoded neoclassical poetic diction he soon threw off. His subject, however, holds far more interest than his language. At a time when the father of philosopher John Stuart Mill was molding his solitary young son into a near robot of utilitarian reason, Wordsworth describes how pain (delicious or merely beautiful) draws us together in a great chain of feeling.

The sentimental movement, to which Wordsworth's lines belong, was already several decades old when he composed his sonnet upon the tears of Miss Williams. The sentimental Man of Feeling with whom the young Wordsworth allies himself is an invention of the late eighteenth century so important that he helped to set off social and political revolutions. This mawkish new hero—sometimes satirized, sometimes idealized, always teetering on the edge of self-parody—wept his way through numerous popular novels of the time, as if suffering (or about to suffer) perpetual punishment. The popular work of French painter Jean-Baptiste Greuze perfectly conveys an impression of individuals trapped by their encounter with a punitive world too harsh for their sensibilities, where pain and weeping become in fact almost signs of secular grace (fig. 25).

Literature, like painting, played an indispensable role in helping to popularize this new gospel of feeling. Yet literature was not simply a medium for spreading the news but rather an integral part of the sentimental transaction in which feeling serves to overcome the distance separating individuals. Such distance, under the pressures of a new industrial culture, seemed expanding to form an infinite gulf. Thus the simultaneously expanding rate of literacy is far more than an incidental social fact. Sentimentalism converts reading into a potent metaphor and instrument of human connectedness. It is significant that in Wordsworth's sonnet the source of Miss Williams's tears is a literary artifact: a tale of distress. Her tearful recitation, in turn, directly inspires not only the poet's slow pulse and brimming eyes but also the sentimental artifact that he composes in response. Further, his sonnet is no doubt meant to inspire similar tears in the feeling reader. In theory, there is no end to this artful circulation of pain.

It is useless to accuse sentimentalism of excess. Excess is exactly what sentimentalism is all about. Moreover, it is excess with a political and social purpose. The tears of sentimentalism are meant to confirm and to elicit an emotion in the human heart that contains the power, ultimately, to transform the world. The key to this radical program (implicit even in Wordsworth's youthful sonnet) is the idea of sympathy. Sympathy, strange to say, was a concept that occupied eighteenth-century physiologists and physicians almost as thoroughly as it captured the generation of readers who grew up weeping over Rousseau. It was used to explain how one

FIGURE 25. Jean-Baptiste Greuze (1725–1805). Study for *Le Fils Puni* (*c*. 1761).

PAINFUL PLEASURES: BEAUTY AND AFFLICTION

internal organ could influence another, just as it helped to validate the implicit kinship among individuals (*fraternité*) which became a founding principle of the French Revolution.[10] Physicians and philosophers alike agreed that the imagination worked through the structure of the human nervous system, and they concluded that it was the imagination that allowed our distress to create in another person sensations of sympathy that link us together in a chain of feeling.[11] The famous sentimental trust in natural goodness thus drew strength from a medically reinforced belief that our bodies in effect require us to share each other's pain.

Sympathy—as suggested by Wordsworth's overheated reference to "thrilling veins" and "swimming eyes"—brushes dangerously close to love. We need not speculate whether the young Wordsworth felt something beyond admiration for the still youthful Miss Williams. It is enough that her tearful response to a tale of distress marks her (in late eighteenth-century culture) as a fellow poetic soul. In fact, by age twenty she had already proved herself as a sentimental author with a well-received verse tale entitled *Edwin and Eltruda* (1782). The sonnet that Wordsworth composed in the year after she published her *Poems* (1786) shrewdly brews up as tribute an appropriate mixture of sentimental melancholy and distress. The "dear, delicious pain" that he celebrates no doubt adapts traditional expressions of the lover's anguish, an almost inexhaustible theme that runs back at least to the troubadours of twelfth-century France.[12] But in 1787—two years before the fall of the Bastille—it also hints at far-reaching cultural changes to come, changes that owe much of their force to the explosive mixture of sentiment, beauty, and pain.

It is Wordsworth's younger contemporary John Keats who turned the painfulness of beauty (an idea always implicit in sentimental fiction) into an explicit theme of Romantic poetry. In *Lamia* (1820), for example, the beautiful serpent/goddess and her earthly paramour—"murmuring of love, and pale with pain"—move through a tale of diabolic passion that repeatedly calls attention to the close link between bliss and torment. It is the famous "Ode on Melancholy" (1819), however, that develops Keats's most influential description of "the wakeful anguish of the soul" accompanying the Romantic experience of beauty. As the poet writes of his beloved:

> She dwells with Beauty—Beauty that must die;
> And Joy, whose hand is ever at his lips
> Bidding adieu; and aching Pleasure nigh,
> Turning to poison while the bee-mouth sips. . . .[13]

Beauty in its transience proves inseparable from death, just as pleasure (caught in this tangle of death and beauty) turns the very act of enjoyment into pain. The lover is melancholy not in the sense of being depressed but in the sense of feeling consumed by a passion for beautiful impermanence.

Havelock Ellis in his classic and exhaustive *Studies in the Psychology of Sex* (1897–1928) posed two weighty questions that concern us here. "Why is it that love inflicts, and even seeks to inflict, pain?" he asks. "Why is it that love suffers pain, and even seeks to suffer it?"[14] Ellis traces the pain of love through primitive courtship rituals (where brides are chased, captured, and sometimes beaten) to such curious expressions of civilized passion as flagellation, sadism, and love bites. After a lengthy and learned review of the evidence, he concludes: "Pain acts as a sexual stimulant because it is the most powerful of all methods for arousing emotion."[15]

The conclusion that Ellis reached, right or wrong, offers a useful contrast for understanding Keats. For Ellis the pain of love involves neither beauty nor the soul but only sexual excitement. Keats's work certainly generates a steady undercurrent of excited eroticism. For Keats, however, love and beauty do not owe their pain to the kind of bride-beating sexual stimulation that Ellis describes. Beauty fills the lover with painful pleasures in Keats's work because, as a passing state of exquisite fullness and perfection, it cannot be disentangled from death. Keats brings us face-to-face with the high Romantic *liebestod*: the union of love and death in an anguish of elevated passion. This is a pain to be desired: the pain *of* desire: the pain of reaching for an infinite perfection that always recedes, leaving us with an aching sense of loss.

Keats in a well-known letter opposing the traditional view of life as a vale of tears referred to human existence as a "vale of Soul-making." "Do you not see," he writes, "how necessary a World of Pains and troubles is to school an Intelligence and make it a soul? A Place where the heart must feel and suffer in a thousand diverse ways!"[16] Pain, in this Romantic view, is not an accidental property of human life but its essential and necessary core. It is what transforms mere minds into souls. Without pain, the Romantic doctrine runs, we live in the shallows. Pain, especially when mixed inseparably with love and beauty, takes us out of our depth. It draws us toward a higher level of experience in which conventional falsehoods and evasions drop away.

The link among pain, beauty, pleasure, and death finds its most influential expression in the myth of the Romantic artist. This isolated, brooding, tormented figure passes so quickly into self-parody that most Romantic writers—while promoting the image of an isolated, inspired, questing, bardic poet—maintain a wary distance through such devices as Byronic humor, Wordsworthian prosiness, or Keatsian detachment. A full genealogy of the Romantic artist would require a diagrammatic tree with more branches than the British royal family. If we seek a catalyst rather than a grandfather, however, probably no event is more important in the development of the Romantic artist than the sensational debut of the pained, sentimental, suicidal hero of Goethe's *Sorrows of Young Werther* (1774). It is Werther who makes the union of sentiment, beauty, and pain into a theme capable of transforming the map of Europe.

The Sorrows of Young Werther ranks among the first international bestsellers. It put literature unmistakably in the forefront of cultural change. Indeed, its tale of unrequited love swept out of Germany across Europe and England achieving the kind of instant celebrity we now reserve for movie stars and rock groups. Images of Werther and his beloved Lotte soon appeared on fans, gloves, jewelry, breadboxes, porcelain, and even in a wax museum.[17] Goethe's sensitive hero of inwardness wearing his distinctive yellow waistcoat and suffering his unconsummated passion for the rural earth-mother Lotte gave readers something more than an occasion for shedding a few tears. Werther is nothing less than a New Man: an unprecedented being so intoxicated with beauty and so tormented with longing that pain sometimes comes as a welcome relief, when it is not simply his everyday state.

Werther's sentimental melancholy is very different from the leaden affliction that Dürer and Burton depicted in the sixteenth and seventeenth centuries. *The Sorrows of Young Werther* requires a sense that the hero suffers not from such common Renaissance sources of melancholy as a sedentary lifestyle, overwork, or an imbalance of bodily humors but instead from his own nameless and infinite desire: an inner torment so excruciating that it makes injuries of the flesh both a tangible sign of his condition and a temporary release from his intangible woes. It is as if only by injuring the flesh can he somehow reestablish a lost concord between body and spirit. As Werther writes:

When my melancholy gets the better of me and Lotte grants me the miserable consolation of giving way to my anguish in a flood of tears, as happens some-times—then I have to get away, out, out . . . and I wander disconsolately in the fields. At moments such as these I like to climb a steep mountain or hack my way through uncleared forest, through hedges that hurt me, through brambles that scratch me. Then I feel a little better. A little better.[18]

The best resource for explaining Werther's influential version of senti-mental pain may well be the powerful theory that Freud developed in his essay "Mourning and Melancholia" (1917). In mourning, Freud wrote, we grieve for the loss of an explicit object, as in the death of a child, wife, husband, or lover. In melancholy, by contrast, we grieve without exactly understanding why. The object of loss remains unknown.

Werther in fact offers a good test case for a theory that locates senti-mental pain in grief for an object that remains lost to consciousness. Even Lotte understands that Werther magnifies her importance in large part because he *knows* he cannot possess her. Steadfastly engaged to the wor-thy Albert, she remains forever out of reach, not just unpossessed but un-possessable, a potent symbol for other infinite longings and indistinct losses to which Werther cannot assign a name. What drives him to frenzy and lacerates his feelings is not really an object at all. Indeed, Werther's pain expresses a loss that is finally not external and objective but subjective and internal.

It is not just the beautiful Lotte that eludes Werther but also the beauty of the world around him. "In mourning," Freud wrote, "it is the world which has become poor and empty; in melancholia it is the ego itself."[19] Werther's pain and the impoverishment of his world reflect the emptiness of his own creative spirit. As he writes less than a month before his suicide:

Suffice it to say that the source of all misery is within me just as I formerly bore within myself the source of all bliss. . . . I suffer much, for I have lost what was my singular joy in life—the sacred, invigorating power with which I could create worlds around me. It is gone. When I look out my window, . . . all magnificent nature stands still before my eyes like a glossy picture, and all this glory is in-capable of pumping one ounce of bliss from heart to brain—then the whole poor fellow that I am become stands before God like an exhausted fountainhead, a leaky pail run dry.[20]

What Werther has lost is not an object but a power: the internal creative impulse that the coming Romantic era would call imagination. Even na-ture for Werther becomes simply a panoramic setting for the interior drama of what he calls "my bliss and pain."[21] The famous suicide, which concludes his story, expresses an anguish that cannot find relief because its sources are entirely inward and inaccessible.

The suicide of Werther establishes a paradigm for the tormented, self-destructive artist who creates out of pain. Werther in fact is only more perfectly representative in being a failed artist—an artist who produces no art, beyond a few sketches which he soon abandons.[22] Within several decades, the Romantic movement in Germany, France, and England developed less suicidal versions of the same figure, who experiences the life of art—at least in its highest moments—as ecstatic suffering. What needs emphasis is that Goethe's portrait of the (failed) artist as a young man immersed in nameless bliss and pain would have struck earlier neoclassical writers as absurd. The cultural change signaled by the sorrows of Werther turned out to be so influential and lasting that today it takes special courage for an artist to *reject* the paradigm of suffering that society—in the case of poets Sylvia Plath and John Berryman, for example—seems almost to expect and to encourage, as if pain and suicide alone were what authenticates their art.

Sentimental pain challenged more than neoclassical ideas of the artist. It created instant enemies among people fixed in their devotion to robust good health and common sense. The burly Victorian novelist Thackeray ridiculed Werther as a weak-willed fool who shot "his silly brains out." Conservative opponents of the French Revolution tried to fix the blame for its bloody aftermath on sentimentalism run mad. British satirist James Gillray in a famous cartoon depicted Sensibility—a common code word for the sentimental movement—weeping over a dead bird, holding a copy of Rousseau, and treading underfoot the severed head of Louis XVI (fig. 26). Sentimental feeling did indeed possess revolutionary tendencies. It blurred traditional lines of class and gender; a footman or a milkmaid might possess it as well as a lord. Although Werther was insufficiently radical to imagine a new world wholly free from divisions of social class, it is significant that he chafed under the constraints of the old world. "I don't like subordination," he wrote ominously.[23] Gillray's cartoon shows how far sentimental pain seemed not just silly or subversive but dangerous.

Sentimental pain, even if at times it approaches bathos, always stood in implicit opposition to the unfeeling ways of the world. Later writers such as Dickens—who perfected the tearful deathbed scene—proved it

FIGURE 26. James Gillray (1756–1815). *New Morality* (1798).

to be a powerful instrument for social change. Popular American fiction in the nineteenth century, as Jane Tompkins and Philip Fisher have shown, employs sentimental feeling as a vehicle for radical protest and visionary politics. The tearful deaths and melodramatic encounters of *Uncle Tom's Cabin*, for example, support a massive indictment of slavery and hint at a complete relocation of power and value around the figure of the nurturing mother. Wordsworth boldly enlists our feeling for social outcasts such as his leech-gatherer, idiot boys, mad mothers, beggars, and ruined farmers. Their pain represents what Philip Fisher calls an "experimental extension of humanity" to dispossessed souls—prisoners, slaves, madmen, children—whom the surrounding culture has denied fully human status.[24] It implies a restoration of the rights and worth they have been denied.

The outcast's pain so central to sentimental art not only conferred a new humanity on such marginal, dehumanized figures as chimney sweeps, prostitutes, and factory hands but also nourished a passion for reform whose effects reach far beyond the genteel tears inspired by a tale of distress. For example, not long after the young Wordsworth commemorated her in verse, Helen Maria Williams left England to live permanently in France, where she sent back for publication influential and admiring accounts of the French Revolution. It was also in the age of sentimental pain that reformers succeeded in banishing legalized torture and in replacing violent corporal punishment with prison terms. Today we may find its literary excesses sometimes hard to digest, but sentimental feeling—with its inseparable union of beauty and pain—helped to reshape the modern world. Its shape, of course, is changing again right now with our own changing relations to beauty and pain.

The postmodern moment might be defined least restrictively as beginning sometime in the 1960s when Western society developed its international, late-capitalist, consumer-driven, eclectic style. As Jean-François Lyotard describes this new mélange of high fashion and popular culture: "One listens to reggae, watches a western, eats McDonald's food for lunch and local cuisine for dinner, wears Paris perfume in Tokyo and 'retro' clothes in Hong Kong."[25] A moment so far removed from the tears of Werther introduces us to yet another episode of cultural change that alters the strange relationship between beauty and pain. Our distance from the heyday of sentimentalism, however, is somewhat illusory. Much of the thinking (or lack of thinking) about beauty that constitutes the background for postmodernism takes its origin, however indirectly, in a treatise written just over a decade before Werther astonished Europe with his sorrows. In 1757 the young Edmund Burke—famous later as a prominent British statesman and political theorist—published an epoch-making book entitled *A Philosophical Enquiry into the Origin of Our Ideas of the Sublime and Beautiful*. Western ideas about beauty would never quite recover.

Burke's major innovation in his *Philosophical Enquiry*, aside from helping to found the modern discipline of aesthetics, lay in the logic-chopping rigor with which he divided previously fluid, if somewhat confused, concepts such as beauty, greatness, terror, delight, and sublimity into neatly packaged and contrasting units. In a split as sweeping as the dualism of Descartes, he rearranged all of art and nature into two separate and opposed categories: the sublime and the beautiful. The beautiful he associates exclusively with pleasure—and the sublime exclusively with pain. Not everyone agreed with him, of course, and within several generations his treatise lay buried beneath an avalanche of new writing on aesthetics which he helped to call forth. But the damage was done. The influential Burkean celebration of the sublime left beauty a demoralized, trivialized second best.

Burke effectively reinvented the sublime by insisting that it had only one source: terror. Terror, in turn, he defines with equal reductiveness as flowing solely from the apprehension of pain and death. As he sees death as merely pain in its ultimate degree, the Burkean sublime might be properly defined as an aesthetics of pain. Boundlessness and obscurity, he noted, were especially good sources of sublime terror, and almost on cue painters began to seek out frightening prospects where ice floes, earthquakes, infernos, and roaring seas threatened to overwhelm and demolish the puny human spectator. For example, the British artist John ("Mad") Martin (1789–1854) specialized in cataclysmic scenes and enormous biblical spectacles such as *The Great Day of His Wrath* (fig. 27). Werther's passion for rugged mountain scenery, stormy nights, and the obscure bardic verse of Ossian—not to mention his infinite yearning and drift toward death—mark him as an early and unabashed enthusiast for the sublime.[26] Our continuing fondness for art that features roaring seas and craggy mountains, as well as the modern taste for gothic paperbacks full

FIGURE 27. John Martin (1789–1854). *The Great Day of His Wrath*
(*c.* 1853). TATE GALLERY/ART RESOURCE, NEW YORK

of ghosts, catacombs, gruesome murders and ancient curses, cannot be traced *entirely* to Burke, but it belongs directly to the eighteenth-century reinvention of the sublime for which he was chief engineer and propagandist.[27]

Burke's fascination with sublime pain entailed an unexpected consequence for beauty. As the wild sublime took over the summit of aesthetic value, beauty suffered a related process of absolute domestication and diminishment. Beauty in Burke's *Philosophical Enquiry* loses all its ancient classical and Christian links with heroism, knowledge, truth, virtue, and wisdom. It reappears as little more than a facile charm. Plato, by contrast, had regarded beauty as crucial in the education of the philosopher because the desire for beauty leads directly to the love of truth. Keats pushed the relation even further: beauty is truth, truth beauty. In Burke's *Philosophical Enquiry* truth is nothing more than material fact. The soul has lost its wings, and the lover has lost his soul. "We must conclude," he writes in his dry, demystifying Enlightenment prose, "that beauty is, for the greater part, some quality in bodies, acting mechanically upon the human mind by the intervention of the senses."[28]

Beauty in the world after Burke's *Philosophical Enquiry* stands completely stripped of any moral, cognitive, or spiritual power. It is merely an external arrangement of matter: "some quality" in bodies. Further, whereas Burke sees the sublime as masculine and heroic, he views beauty with the eyes of Enlightenment gender as soft, small, pliant, and above all feminine. The beautiful—now empty, domestic, trivial—comes to occupy the sterile category we find reserved today for sunsets, postcards, swimsuit contests, and little fuzzy animals that do not bite. "Beauty in distress," adds Burke, as if winking toward the new entrepreneurs of melodrama, "is much the most affecting beauty."[29]

We should doubtless regard Burke more as symptom than cause of the vast cultural transformation of beauty that has accelerated since he wrote. With such a barren inheritance, however, it should not surprise us that toward the end of the nineteenth century the beautiful no longer ranked among the primary aims or subjects of serious art. Modernist writers and painters turn away from it entirely, finding the received ideas of beauty utterly bankrupt. Postmodernism, in its eclectic and accepting spirit, retains a fondness for the glossy, empty images of commercial art where beauty looks much as Burke left it. Yet there is more than one postmodern approach to beauty (as to almost everything). We should expect, then, that a serious postmodern rehabilitation of the beautiful would necessarily work against the grain of Burkean ideas. It will inevitably oppose the heritage that divides beauty from truth, virtue, wisdom, and—not incidentally—from pain.

✝

"There is no more beautiful sight in the world," writes surgeon Richard Selzer, "than that of a kindly, efficient doctor engaged in the examination of the body of a fellow human being."[30] Some readers may want to discount his statement as professional embellishment, yet Selzer (who has recently given up his surgical practice) is a powerful writer who draws sustenance from such diverse sources as Catherine of Siena and Sir Thomas Browne. He likely chooses his words with some care when he describes a medical examination as "beautiful"—not just beautiful but the height of beauty. To make sense of this heretical notion we need to reflect that the rehabilitation of beauty, in the post-Burkean world, will probably occur not in museums or art galleries but where we least expect it, even in the examining room. Vincent Van Gogh once wrote to his ever-supportive brother, Theo, "that I myself should always regret not being a doctor, and that those who think painting is beautiful would do well to see nothing in it but a study of nature."[31] True painters, he implies, like doctors, are engaged in the study of nature—not in the pursuit of beauty. Or, to turn his thought a little differently, it is our inherited and debased ideas of beauty that blind us to what is truly beautiful.

The inventors of modernism went a step further and declared in effect that beauty was dead as a subject for art. Nineteenth-century writers and painters, like the art patrons whom Van Gogh implicitly criticized, had ruined it for serious work. We can be pretty certain that Selzer would excuse himself from discussions of aesthetic theory. His prose suggests that he would far prefer any sensuous and solid act (say, palming a gall bladder) to an exploration of something as vague and unwieldy post-modernism. He is not a writer of isms and schools. Yet his work also reflects a serious return to beauty, and it thus shares in the wider post-modern effort to rehabilitate the beautiful. Pain, in fact, is the medium through which Selzer discovers and conveys something of the beauty that he encounters, among other unlikely places, in the daily practice of medicine.

Selzer did not begin to write until age forty, working at his fiction during the only time his schedule as a surgeon allowed, between one and three o'clock each morning. At three, he returned to bed, rising before dawn for the early hours of the operating room. (For years he also maintained a teaching position on the faculty at the Yale Medical School.) His writing often employs medical locales and tends to elude established categories, ranging widely from light essays to ambitious, extended prose narratives that lie somewhere in-between fiction and autobiography. At their best the direct, intense short stories—not notably experimental or arcane—introduce us to disturbing scenes of human passion and power.

Pain is among the subjects to which Selzer continually circles back, not so much like a musician developing a theme as like a scientist exploring an indistinct, unformulated field where his research nonetheless forces him to work. Indeed, Selzer knows the slipperiness of pain both as a writer and as a surgeon. In an essay entitled "The Elusive Language of Pleasure and Pain" he reflects openly on the familiar difficulties faced by doctor and patient as they try to communicate across the gulf of the body. The doctor runs through the standard questions and then translates the patient's halting responses into the clinical vocabulary of medicine. But the language of medicine cannot quite pin down the object it seeks, no doubt because it is not an object. "All these words," Selzer concludes, "remain at the periphery of the pain itself."[32]

Writing, however, offers Selzer an indispensable occasion and medium for pressing the search to understand pain. His aim is not to illuminate pain, as if disspelling its mysterious inwardness, but rather to illuminate what happens to us when we run up against its unseen presence, like an invisible stone wall. Selzer views the writer and the surgeon as natural partners because they both share in an almost priestly task of bearing witness to a truth from which humankind is normally shut out. Like the priest, the surgeon for Selzer is separated from the laity by the possession of an arcane knowledge and by the completion of an arduous training. "At last one emerges as celebrant," he writes of the novice surgeon, "standing close to the truth lying curtained in the Ark of the body." Yet the truths revealed to Selzer's surgeon, as he probes the forbidden interior of the human body, prove unremittingly secular: "There is no wine, no wafer. There are only the facts of blood and flesh."[33]

The writer in Selzer's work offers the surgeon a perspective on the facts of blood and flesh that in some sense transforms or redeems them. Writing thus provides a means for revealing a spiritual dimension *within* the secular. "The flesh," as he puts it on several occasions, "is the spirit thickened."[34] Here is a vision in which body and mind no longer proceed along separate tracks. Within the damaged and fragile interior of the body, in the space normally abandoned by metaphysics and outlawed by taboo, Selzer finds something more than the normally unseen organs, arteries, and coiled intestines which he describes like the poet of a rich inner landscape. As disease brings him into contact with our most intimate deformities, he finds in fat, fluid, tissue, and bone—in humankind as sheer matter and mass—the conditions for a revitalized understanding of beauty.

Brute and often painful facts always possess for Selzer the possibility that we will come to understand them anew, infused with a meaning that transforms and redeems them, much as mere events may reveal far more than the accidents of space and time. Even the most terrifying facts and events can yield a revised meaning if we know how to read them. "To *perceive* tragedy," as Selzer writes, "is to wring from it beauty and truth."[35]

Perception is the key. What constitutes beauty for Selzer is not external symmetry, proportion or ideal form ("some quality in bodies," as Burke puts it) but rather an internal act of understanding. He finds beauty not so much outside as *inside* the body. Like Walt Whitman, whose luxuriant rhythms and phrases occasionally surface in Selzer's prose, he brings us back to recognize the "body electric" as a primal mystery and (if we understand it aright) beauteous fact.

The action running through many of Selzer's stories might be described, abstractly, as an encounter in which we perceive the human body as if for the first time, like Adam in paradise. It is through this renewed encounter with the body—especially the body understood as the commonplace, unparadisial scene of pain—that Selzer requires us to question our normal canons of beauty. Beauty, he seems to say, exists here, deep in the black cavities of disease and matter, or nowhere. As we learn the contours of Selzer's aesthetic, we learn that the beautiful cannot separate itself from the vision of a bloodless limb turned rotten and festering. Pain is not itself beautiful in Selzer's work. But it serves as a force that somehow allows beauty to emerge. Pain, we might say, confers or reveals a beauty we ordinarily cannot see, feel, or understand. It is a beauty that has somehow recovered its ancient alliance with truth.

The struggle to understand beauty anew meets resistance at almost every point from everyday language. "Personally," says Selzer's narrator in "Textbook," "I suspect that truth is more accessible in 'ugliness' than it is in beauty."[36] The quotation marks around the word "ugliness" indicate the dilemma that Selzer faces in the world after Burke. What we normally call beauty is simply an exhausted and debased prettiness. Truth therefore would have to be located elsewhere, even in the opposite of Burkean beauty. For Selzer, the deformed and the diseased yield both a truth and a beauty we have lost the power to recognize. "When readers say to me, why do you write about these repulsive matters," he explained in an interview, "I would say that I write about them because I see beauty in them. The way Baudelaire wrote about a dead body that was decomposing and teeming with insects. . . ."[37]

Selzer sees the struggle to overhaul beauty as putting him in the company of other writers with a similar mission, as his reference to Baudelaire indicates. What sets him apart, however, is an almost mystical affirmation of spirit that he sees flashing out amid waste and pain. Selzer pointedly reminds modern readers about the ancient Greek belief that the gods often visited humankind disguised as mortals, although disguise is not quite the right term. In Greek literature the gods for a time *take over* human bodies: they are (temporarily) indistinguishable from normal, everyday mortals. In book one of the *Aeneid*, for example, Aeneas speaks at length with a young maiden who is dressed in hunting garb like a Spartan girl. Only as she leaves does he suddenly realize that she is really his mother, the goddess Venus. Perception again makes all the difference. In a numinous age, gods unexpectedly shone forth through ordinary human forms, and Selzer in a secular world repossesses something of this ancient vision. In patients crippled with deformities and ravaged by disease he is continually stunned by a sudden radiance resembling the appearance of a god. Such moments of beauty are not always comforting. There is a terror implicit in occasions that lift the veil from our ordinary world and show us that it is not what we think it is.

Selzer, like Keats, believes that beauty (once restored) must coincide with truth. For him, the brute facts of human life will always sustain us, even though the truths they reveal may also terrify. Thus the spiritualized beauty that Selzer sees radiating through or within the body makes its appearance even in such figures as the despairing, half-crazed father, fiercely protective of his blind, mute, malformed six-year-old son, a boy whose dead testicle (a kind of final link with normalcy) the surgeon must remove. The encounter concludes with the moment of revelation—or renewed perception—so typical in Selzer's work: "All at once I know that this man's love for his child is a passion. It is a rapids roiling within him. It has nothing to do with pleasure, this kind of love. It is a deep, black joy."[38]

"Disease," Selzer writes, "magnifies both the sufferer and those who tend him."[39] The arduous beauty that Selzer offers for our understanding has been rediscovered through the intensification of disease and pain. In such encounters, we glimpse something about human life that normally eludes us. We attain a kind of knowledge that, as in Greek tragedy, seems inaccessible except through suffering. Suffering, however, can also magnify aspects of life we do not really want to know about. It can show us, within our mundane world, another world that is not so much godlike as shadowy, primal, and threatening. In his short story "The Hartford Girl," Selzer takes his subject not from his medical practice but from the daily newspaper. Its revelation about the bond between beauty and pain, however, is no less disturbing to our ordinary sense of things.

"A sixteen-year-old girl slashed her wrists and arms and then rushed to the steps of a Roman Catholic church poking a razor to her throat while a crowd of three hundred persons cheered and screamed, 'Do your thing, sister.' "[40] So begins "The Hartford Girl" with a quotation from the local newspaper. Journalistic sensationalism or the casual violence of urban life, however, are not what draws Selzer to the incident. He describes how, after the girl is led away, the crowd lingers by the dark, blood-pooled steps, "strangely spent." He also records the mesmerized fascination that his narrator feels at an event that stirs ancient memories of human sacrifice and Dionysian rites. Even more disturbing than the crowd's archaic blood lust is the abstracted comment that the girl evokes from the narrator in the final two sentences of the story: "It is months later. Still, whenever I think of beauty, I think of her."[41]

What idea of beauty is it, we must ask, which coincides with the image of a dazed, bleeding, suicidal girl frozen in fear before a crowd excited—even slightly maddened—with blood lust? Certainly it is a beauty that cannot be disjoined from terror and from the darker truths of the human psyche. Yet Selzer, viewing such scenes with a surgeon's eye, may also recognize a strangely archaic beauty that belongs almost exclusively to the wound. Wounds, after all, are a crude form of incision. Further, the wound in Selzer's work at times contains the power to join people together, much like sentimental pain for Wordsworth. He thus retells to special purpose the Homeric episode in which Ulysses returns home in disguise after years of wandering and struggle. One person alone—his old nurse Eurycleia—sees through the disguise. "It was not his wife or his son who had recognized Ulysses," Selzer insists. "It was his nurse. It was the wound that had awakened the buried past, the wound that was the emblem of all the shared pain and despair, the disappointment and the exhilaration that are the measure of the tending relationship."[42]

In Selzer's retelling, the healed wound of Ulysses is not simply an accidental identifying sign, like a strawberry birthmark. It is the potent symbol of past pain, and it evokes the special bond that pain sometimes creates between patient and healer. Homer in fact includes a long description of the boar hunt on which the young Ulysses received both his wound and his name—a name that translates roughly as Man of Pain. The ten years that Ulysses spent fighting at Troy, followed by the ten more years he spent struggling to return home, certainly justify such a name. "Now, having suffered many pains, / I have come in the twentieth year to my fatherland," Ulysses tells Eurycleia.[43] The scar, like the pain it signifies, binds them together across the years.

Wounds, however, can also communicate a sense of outrage, exclusion, and impenetrable ambiguity that are equally common to pain. More than once Selzer compares the healed incision to a hieroglyphic whose meaning is lost. Its truth, if not frustratingly withheld, may fall outside the range of anything we can find understandable. Although pain and wounds sometimes join people together, the bond need not be permanent. Ulysses in fact coldly threatens to kill Eurycleia if she exposes his identity. Any revulsion we feel at his threat—directed at an old and faithful servant to whom he owes his life—might remind us just how far pain and its companion, fear, can undermine, undo, and destroy mutual understanding. The wound in its strange beauty may be at last simply incomprehensible.

In Selzer's brief story "Racoon" a surgeon visits a patient as she recovers from an abdominal operation. She ignores his tactful knock, secluding herself in the toilet stall engaged in some secret act. Worried, the surgeon intrudes and finds her seated, bent forward, with her arm plunged elbow-deep in her freshly opened incision. A razor blade lies on the floor. Appalled, he hurries her back to bed and hastily begins to resuture the wound, searching for explanations of the terrible scene he has unveiled. The woman remains calm. Then the surgeon experiences the moment of sudden breakthrough that typifies Selzer's fiction. The understanding he receives, however, is a revelation about the limits of knowledge. The story concludes: "All at once I know what it was, what she was reaching for, deep inside. It was her pain! The hot nugget of her pain that, still hissing, she would cast away. I almost had it, she said. You should have waited, she said."[44]

The slipperiness of the woman's pain mirrors for Selzer a more fundamental elusiveness in our understanding of truth and beauty. "Pain invents its own language," his narrator once says. In the same essay (entitled "An Absence of Windows") he also acknowledges that this unique language is a speech we cannot successfully learn. It remains closed off—or comes to us all at once. We live either wholly inside or wholly outside its domain. Outside pain, we can only observe, sympathize, and perhaps reply with a few inadequate cliches, like a tourist speaking from a phrasebook. Inside pain, we immediately attain full possession of a knowledge that defies accurate transmission. "Never mind," advises Selzer's narrator concerning our inability to speak this unknown tongue: "we shall know it in our time."[45] At such a difficult, bitter moment, when we are at last fully conversant in this archaic language, Selzer would suggest that we will also come into full understanding of the intimate, unseen connection that binds pain to truth and beauty.

10

SEX, PAIN, AND THE MARQUIS DE SADE

MADAME DE MISTIVAL, *opening her eyes*—Oh Heavens! Why do you recall me
from the grave's darkness? Why do you plunge me again into life's horrors?
DOLMANCÉ, *whipping her steadily*—Indeed, mother dear, it is because much
conversation remains to be held.
SADE, *PHILOSOPHY IN THE BEDROOM*[1]

I T SEEMS RIGHT that we have no portrait of the
Marquis de Sade and that his face remains a
blank. He knew very well how hateful his meth-
ods made him. He stipulated in his will that he should be buried in an
unmarked grave seeded with acorns. The site would soon be overgrown,
impassable, lost to human memory. Indeed, he spent most of his adult
life out of sight, imprisoned under five governments, at first as a justified legal punishment but later (with the connivance of his wife's
high-ranking family) as a means of keeping him locked away from polite
society. Sade once defended himself by explaining that while he had
imagined every possible form of sexual crime, he had not performed
everything he imagined. He was a libertine but not a criminal.[2] Yet he also
composed the speech in which a libertine—distressed that his crimes
would be limited to a single lifetime—is advised to consider writing: the
publication of corrupting fantasies (so the advice goes) will spread their
influence potentially without end.

Simone de Beauvoir in a famous essay asked whether it was necessary
to burn Sade. A harder question is why we should read the writings of a
man so deliberately resistant and offensive. One of Sade's best modern
critics seems to me entirely accurate when he described Sade's novels as
the most unbearable works ever written.[3] It is understandable that postwar
French writers and intellectuals have felt driven to confront Sade as an
almost unavoidable, monumental figure (however repellent) in their own

national literature and conscience. Anglo-American critics, however, mostly flee Sade as if he carried the plague. There are several reasons why it is essential here that we discuss rather than avoid Sade. Most important, Sade in some sense reinvented pain. At least, after Sade pain would never be quite the same again.

Sade's writing confronts us with one of the most important junctures in the history of human behavior: the moment when pain openly, violently, and irreversibly breaks into the arena of sexual pleasure. Sade of course is not the first writer to publish pornographic novels describing acts of cruelty, but the publication of Sade's massive fantasies makes pain and cruelty now an unavoidable presence in modern writing on sexuality. Sade in the name of sexual pleasure boldly assaults, degrades, defiles, and mutilates the human body with a thoroughness that can only be called encyclopedic. He does not merely write about cruelty; he anatomizes and celebrates it at epic length. His persecution in his own time and the subsequent censorship of his novels make him in some sense the archetypal fugitive-writer: the outlaw Homer and Virgil of sexual pain.

Pain draws us to Sade for yet another reason, however. Strangely, medicine proves as important as eroticism in shaping his treatment of sexualized cruelty. In fact, Sadean pain owes much of its distinctive character to the historical changes that pushed medicine in the eighteenth century toward its current status as a scientific discipline. His aristocratic torturers and renegade monks thus do not simply codify or give voice to bizarre sexual practices as old as Sodom. Sade's contribution to the remaking of pain belongs to the specific moment of cultural change when governments and long-established social orders—as well as intellectual disciplines from botany to philology—were being turned upside down and restructured.[4] Medicine too shared in these sweeping transformations. We will thus need to examine the changes in Enlightenment medicine as they contribute toward the reinvention of sexual cruelty. Like it or not, Sadean pain is pain as we have come to know it.

$\dagger$

Medicine is foundational for Sade. His use of medical knowledge cannot be dismissed as simply part of a general miscellaneous commerce between fiction and physiology in the Enlightenment.[5] Like theology in the Middle Ages, medicine in the Enlightenment approached the status of a master discourse that infiltrated and regulated all other communication.

The spectacular advances in medical knowledge had accelerated in Sade's time with special vigor in France.[6] French physicians (such as the polymath Pierre-Jean-Georges Cabanis) ranked among the most active reformers and philosophers, whose thought penetrated far beyond the limited spheres of medicine and public health into education, government, and law. It was common to hear such writers claim that medicine supplied the cornerstone for a whole new philosophy of man.[7] Medicine thus does not simply infuse Sade's novels with a technical vocabulary or miscellaneous insights. It provides him with a basis for utterly reorganizing our view of human nature.

Sade's erudition is legendary—he left some six hundred books behind in his cell when the authorities hastily transferred him a few days before the fall of the Bastille—but his interest in medicine was a widely shared excitement. Throughout France reformers were arguing forcefully for a new medical vision that renounced "hypothetical explanations" and "imaginary systems"—associated with the traditional education of doctors—in favor of scientific experiments and clinical observations.[8] Indeed, Sade's life coincided with the revolutionary series of events and discoveries in French medicine that Michel Foucault has called "the birth of the clinic." This bold restructuring of medical thought extended far beyond the vastly enlarged practice of clinical teaching, which rapidly displaced the moribund academic medicine centered in the Paris Faculty. It meant a new emphasis on the once subordinate arts of pharmacy and surgery. These vocations, formerly classed as mere trades, now enjoyed a vastly elevated status as possessing knowledge and techniques indispensable for penetrating the opaque surface of the body. A new medical space had opened up.

Not just a new space: the changed landscape of medicine proved inseparable from a new way of seeing and of speaking. The understanding of disease now proceeded through research that emphasized interior processes and conditions. "As autopsies became routine," one historian tells us, "the causes of illness came to be seen concretely in the tumors, abscesses, ulcers, inflammations, and hemorrhages located *inside* the body."[9] Monuments to this fresh clinical "gaze" (as Foucault calls it) include the free instruction in clinical surgery provided by Desault in the large amphitheater he obtained at the Hôtel-Dieu; Pinel's studies of mental illness, designed to reveal correlations between human passions and physiology;

Bichat's systematic study of tissue, which altered medical thinking about internal organs and helped to found the science of histology. Even—however utopian it sounds—the closing of all French medical schools in the postrevolutionary years between 1792 and 1794, like the practical demands of a changed battlefield medicine during the Napoleonic wars, helped to create a decisive break with the past. Paris during Sade's long imprisonment came to surpass both Leyden and Edinburgh as the international center of a new, modern medical knowledge.

Sade's novels in their treatment of pain and sexuality represent a pornographic extension of the new clinical gaze.[10] Sade, too, is probing beneath the surface, stripping the mask from sexual practices hidden beneath layers of politeness, hypocrisy, and superstition. He examines human sexual behavior like a slightly unhinged Linnaeus determined to identify and classify every possible permutation of lust. In seeking to exhaust the possibilities of sexual excess, he surrounds his monomaniacal reasoners and fuckers (as he calls them) with a verbal field in which no one ever has the last word. Victims must be replaced immediately—or revived—so that the unceasing discourse may go on. Rhetoric in Sade's fiction relentlessly sabotages logic: nothing can be left unsaid. At the end of the enormous novel that bears her name, the voracious libertine Juliette states this Sadean ideal with deceptive literalism: "It is necessary for philosophy," she observes, "to say everything."[11]

The attempt to leave nothing unsaid requires Sade to transgress every bound of bourgeois decency. But he violates far more than decorum. Sade extends his gaze into realms where the suppressed and the unspoken border, finally, on the unspeakable. As Maurice Blanchot writes of Sade: "Everything which is said is clear, but seems to be at the mercy of something left unsaid"; "Everything *is* expressed, is revealed, but also everything is plunged back again into the obscurity of unformulated and inexpressible thoughts."[12] The real issue in Sade is not whether the obscene can escape censorship in order to speak its (partial) truths. Such obscene truths remain thinkable and speakable. For Sade the obscene serves as a means to explore our participation in an irrationality that passes entirely beyond language. The eroticism he celebrates at such length embraces a horror that ordinarily deprives us of speech. Sade in effect refuses to let us suppress what we cannot speak or understand. He seeks to illuminate a darkness more impenetrable than the inside of the human body. It should not therefore surprise us that Sade's assault on the inexpressible and the unspeakable would find in pain—with its notorious silences—a fundamental resource.

✝

Sade might be construed as setting out to raze from human memory the sentimental myth (sweeping over Europe as he wrote) that associates pain with pleasing distress, fellow feeling, beauty, and the heart's truth. Sade, too, associates pain with truth, but it is a very different truth he has in mind. Although he certainly belongs among Enlightenment writers such as Voltaire who sought to demystify every form of superstition and intellectual humbug, he immediately resumes his isolated stance in equating truth not with a shared humanity or even with practical reforms but with desire and pain. Pain in effect defines for the libertine mind a realm of absolute certainty immune from dissembling. As the libertine monk Clément argues in *Justine*: "There is no more lively sensation than that of pain; its impressions are certain and dependable, they never deceive as may those of the pleasure women perpetually feign and almost never experience."[13]

Women and pleasure in Sade's work are far more than traditional images of deception that ruin male versions of paradise from Eden on. They belong in Sade to a larger category of radical falsehood that includes religion, language, and even reason itself. The libertine obsession with pain thus, as Sade assures us, cannot be reduced to merely an exotic, eccentric, sexual taste. It exposes both unexpressed male anxieties about women and openly expressed male needs to assert an absolute power and dominance. Most important, however, pain communicates an authenticity that Sade's libertine heroes and heroines see everywhere eluding them in a world dominated by deceit, custom, equivocation, timidity, and ignorance. In this sense, Sadean pain has already absorbed a range of historical meaning that distinguishes it from random, transient, universal sensations.

The meanings that Sade ascribes to pain not only absorb but also transform or transvalue traditional medical knowledge. The erotic tastes of his libertine heroes and heroines, for example, often seem so deranged (by normal standards) as to approach or attain the pathological. The medicine of his own day firmly diagnosed Sade as suffering from "sexual dementia" and thus justified his incarceration at the Asylum of Charenton. Sade's novels, however, rigorously subvert our estimations of what is normal.

Today—when it extends beyond a fashionable, middle-class taste for spanking, whips, and leather—sadism has passed securely into the lexicon of mental illness, explained through theories of childhood trauma, repression, passive-aggressive behavior, fears of impotence, or a reversal of the death wish. Sade, by contrast, refuses to represent even the most abnormal or self-destructive sexual behavior as illness. His libertines seem to derive an almost frightening health and robustness from the satisfaction of their cruel and chaotic desires.

Sade's transformation of medical knowledge is even more radical in rejecting the ancient, church-sponsored bond that places sexuality in the strict service of procreation. As Angela Carter has observed, Sade anticipates our own era with its unprecedented break between erotic pleasure and childbirth.[14] It is common for Sade's most discriminating male libertines to renounce all contact—even visual contact—with the vagina. ("Your authentic sodomist," explains Juliette, "will always come unerect at the sight of a cunt.")[15] Male libertines not only prefer male partners; their preference expresses a desire that sexuality should be not just infertile but deliberately sterile. Sadean eroticism is overwhelmingly anal, excremental, and bloody. Pain, released from its normal, medical contexts of childbirth or illness, serves as lubricant for a sexuality that finds its ultimate fulfillment in slow, cold, stimulating murders.

The disappearance of illness and childbirth in Sade's work creates a backdrop against which other calculated transvaluations of medical knowledge stand out sharply. For instance, the Enlightenment emphasis upon medicine as a science—a practice newly grounded in experiment and fact—becomes in Sade a pretense for creating new modes of erotic horror. The clinical gaze thus gives rise to a libertine medicine that, as in modern versions of Mary Shelley's *Frankenstein* (1818), finds its logical outcome in the figure of the mad scientist. Animal experiments common in Enlightenment medicine reappear in Sade's work as a sexualized form of torture. The libertine surgeon Rodin (a rationalist who extols "the progress of science") seeks to advance both the knowledge of anatomy and his own sexual pleasure by a protracted vivisection carried out on his own young daughter.[16] The balms and drugs often used to restore Justine and other long-suffering victims of libertinage link the new pharmacology with older, erotic traditions of black magic. Their Sadean purpose is simply to prepare the victim for fresh episodes of sexual pain.

Sadean medicine does more than help to create new scenes of sexual pain. The scientific prestige of medicine offers Sade a means to silence or to supersede other systems traditionally concerned with human suffering. Thus in its relentless appeal to the facts of anatomy and physiology, medicine as Sade employs it thoroughly dominates and displaces the speculative reasoning of philosophers ancient and modern. The Sadean libertine ultimately empties vice and virtue of their familiar status in philosophy, where for centuries our apparently natural aversion to pain and attraction to pleasure provided a bedrock for ethical thought. In Sade's sweeping redefinition, vice and virtue emerge as no more than meaningless names we give to whatever stimulus shows greater or lesser powers to excite the nervous system.

Theology fares even worse than philosophy at the hands of Sade's libertine medicine. Sade's contemptuous and relentless assault on Christianity as "incompatible with the libertarian system" includes his parodic exposure of Christian attitudes toward redemptive suffering.[17] "With his pain we are healed": for Christian readers the words of the prophet Isaiah (54:4) seemed to foreshadow Christ's role as savior. Sade's fullest response to the long Christian tradition of redemptive pain is simply the plot of *Justine*. Justine's faith in God and her love of virtue (all empty concepts for Sade) are the qualities that generate each new outrageous assault against her, as if the novel—far from reflecting picaresque randomness—served as a demonstration in logic. Sade contrives Justine's imitation of Christ to establish the *absence* of redemptive suffering. The world that she encounters inside the Church mirrors exactly the libertine cruelties she meets everywhere else. There is no inside, no outside. Even when she escapes from the debauched monks at St. Mary-in-the-Wood, Justine simply encounters their doubles wherever she turns.

Sade's transvaluations of Enlightenment medicine reshape it to serve his own needs. It is thus even possible, as Pierre Klossowski has argued, that Sade's godless, scientific materialism expresses his unacknowledged need for God.[18] Christianity is certainly indispensable to Sade in providing the raw material for an openly anti-Christian art. What draws Sade to Christianity, however, is not only what he sees as its errors and hypocrisies but also its historical interest in pain, from original sin, martyrdom, and flagellation to inquisitorial torture and the torment of the damned. The final scene of *The 120 Days of Sodom* appropriately concludes with the erotic carnage of a libertine pastime called "The Hell Game"—complete with impersonated demons and real agonies of those chosen as the damned. In Sade's work, theology, like philosophy, provides only a mocking, vacant, archaic language for interpreting pain, no match for the up-to-date, scientific physiology of nerve impulses and electrical fluids. As Justine innocently suffers each new episode of sexual abuse, her suffering leads nowhere, illuminates nothing, redeems no one.

†

The central question posed, endlessly, in Sade's work is what to make of the relationship between sexual pleasure and pain. Sade in effect has transformed the "dear, delicious pain" of the sentimentalists—drawing people together in a chain of fellow feeling—into an underground phantasmagoria of rape, incest, and murder. Not even Sade's libertines fully understand the strange compulsion they share. How is it, asks the libertine statesman Saint-Fond, that we can experience pleasure from watching others undergo pain or, stranger still, from undergoing pain ourselves? The reply from his fellow libertine Noirceuil, who begins by quoting the seventeenth-century Jansenist theologian Pierre Nicole, will help us appreciate the role of medicine in Sade's thought:

"Pain," logically defined, "is nothing other than a sentiment of hostility in the soul toward the body it animates, the which [sic] it signifies through certain movements that conflict with the body's physical organization." So says Nicole, who perceived in man an ethereal substance, which he called soul, and which he differentiated from the material substance we call body. I, however, who will have none of this frivolous stuff and who consider man as something on the order of an absolutely material plant, I shall simply say that pain is the consequence of a defective relationship between objects foreign to us and the organic molecules composing us; in such wise that instead of composing harmoniously with those that make up our neural fluids, as they do in the commotion of pleasure, the atoms emanating from these foreign objects strike them aslant, crookedly, sting them, repulse them, and never fuse with them. Still, though the effects are negative, they are effects nonetheless, and whether it be pleasure or pain brewing in us, you will always have a certain impact upon the neural fluids.[19]

This is the sort of writing that gives pornography a bad name, yet it is almost as typical of Sadean narrative as scenes of sexual cruelty.

The purpose of Sade's passage is to insist upon an absolute difference between two ways of thinking about pain. In quoting the words of Father Nicole, Noirceuil begins by setting up a god-centered model of pain that requires the concept of an eternal, immaterial soul at odds with a perishable, material body. Then, for assistance in demolishing this god-centered model, Noirceuil turns to modern physiology to promote his own secular, man-centered model of pain. Pain, in fact, becomes for Noirceuil the occasion for asserting a materialism so comprehensive that it collapses any significant differences between bodies and souls. As another Sadean libertine explains: "All we attribute to the soul is all simply the effect of matter."[20]

Sade, we might say, has recognized and seized upon the tendency in medicine to reduce the human being, which theology long held as created in the image of God, to a machine. Indeed, one of his favorite authors was the exiled physician-philosopher Julien Offroy de La Mettrie, whose subversive L'homme-machine (1747) developed at length the atheistic, materialistic implications of the new medical gaze. Although such materialist writers sometimes continue to talk of the soul, they no longer refer to the traditional theological concept of an immaterial essence that survives the death of the body. Instead, like the vitalist medicine centered at Montpellier, they refer to an in-dwelling, material power of the organism.[21] As Juliette's libertine instructor Delbène reports: "I am not aware of having any soul. . . . It is the body which feels, which thinks, which judges, which suffers, which enjoys." Sade's libertines move in a world where everything—including minds or souls—is material. "Body and soul," Delbène summarizes, "they are one."[22]

The crucial point is this: when Sade's libertines talk about pain as an event of hollow nerve fibers and neural fluids, they invoke a vision in which mind and soul have disappeared into matter. Sadean eroticism thus belongs to the same world of material fact as the modern medicine that has increasingly come to understand humankind as little more than unusually complex machinery in need of occasional repairs. Of course, fact plays a different role in Sadean narrative than in scientific and medical writing. His characters often mix concepts drawn from quite different systems of physiology. We will find pain discussed, depending upon the speaker, with reference to stinging atoms, excited animal spirits, stretched nerve fibers, or irritated tissue. There is some reason for feeling that Sade has brewed up a gigantic, simmering soup of fact. What matters for Sade is not whether his characters have access to a final correct answer (too much science remains unresolved) but whether their facts support a demystified, antitheological view of man. Pain is for Sade more than the sign of truth. It is the sign of a radically new and wholly secular truth: the truth of the material body.

†

The truth of the body is, in a limited sense, exactly what Enlightenment medicine undertook to disclose: a truth that took as its most potent instrument and symbol the newly routine practice of autopsy. Yet Sade did not stop with the eroticized versions of anatomy and surgery we have seen him employ to lay open the human body. The body constitutes for Sade not just the indispensable scene of erotic pleasure but, far more important, the force that defines and determines our sexuality. Thus Sade's work posits as a central dogma the belief that we live out a sexual fate imposed not by God, not by gender, not by culture, but solely by the nerves and tissues of our individual bodies. Sade gives revolutionary force to a view that seemed harmless enough when expressed in an earlier, prescientific medicine of bodily humors: physiology is destiny.

The role of the body in determining our sexual fate was clear to Sade from introspection. He once wrote to his wife that his scandalous manner of thought "holds with my existence and my constitution." He adds: "I do not have the power to change it."[23] The best gloss on this slightly enigmatic statement is probably the explanation that the Count du Bressac offers Justine in discussing the libertine preference for anal sex:

Do not suppose, Thérèse [as everyone calls Justine], we are made like other men. 'Tis an entirely different structure we have; and, in creating us, Heaven has ornamented the altars at which our Celadons sacrifice with that very same sensitive membrane which lines your temple of Venus; we are, in that sector, as certainly women as you are in your generative sanctuary; not one of your pleasures is unknown to us, there is not one we do not know how to enjoy, but we have in addition to them our own, and it is this delicious combination which makes us of all men on earth the most sensitive to pleasure, the best created to experience it; it is this enchanting combination which renders our tastes incorrigible, which would turn us into enthusiasts and frenetics were one to have the stupidity to punish us.[24]

The Count's delicacy as he encodes blunt sexual description in a mythological language of love perhaps explains why he is the single tormenter for whom Justine feels desire. Beneath his flowery rhetoric, however, lies the bedrock anatomy and physiology to which Sade always returns.

The material body for Sade determines everything else, even what moralists call virtue and vice. "Our constitution, our scheme, our organs, the flow of liquids, the animal spirits' energy," declares a typical Sadean libertine, "such are the physical causes which in the same hour make for the Tituses and the Neros."[25] The legendary virtue of Titus, like the infamous vice of Nero, is nothing more than the effect of "physical causes" hard wired in the body. As the dissolute monk Clément concludes, after laborious reference to the biomedical language of fluids, fibers, blood, and animal spirits: "When the study of anatomy reaches perfection they will without any trouble be able to demonstrate the relationship of the human constitution to the [sexual] tastes which it affects."[26] In Sade's world, a taste for pain—like the libertine delight in blaspheming a nonexistent God—may seem illogical or unnatural to outsiders, but it also expresses a new kind of truth: a truth inscribed in a personal biology of nerves, tissues, and membranes.

The truth of the body extends far enough, in fact, that for Sade it also includes whatever goes on in the mind and emotions. Although the body in Sade's work sometimes seems entirely separated from mind, like the adjacent blocks of pornographic description and of argumentative reasoning that make up the alternating structure of his books, the separation is only apparent. Sade, we have seen, does not oppose the mind to body, as if human beings were irreconcilably split. The body instead encompasses everything. It is the body, as Delbène had asserted, that feels, suffers, enjoys, judges, and even *thinks*. The concept of a "thinking body" is Sade's response to the Cartesian dualism that rigorously divides material bodies from immaterial thoughts. In Sade's libertine system, body and mind are both equally material, although they differ in the same degree as (for example) steam differs from ice. They are also mutually interactive. The mind, that is, relies for its contents—"all sensations, knowledge, and ideas," as Sade noted in *Justine*—upon the impulses that it receives through the nervous system. What complicates this commonplace empiricist psychology is Sade's insistence that the mind can alter our response to the impulses it receives. The mental-emotional powers of reason, imagination, and desire in effect can remake the libertine body.

Sade writes more like a centralist than a peripheralist when he argues that pain, like pleasure, expands or contracts according to the play of the libertine mind. Thus reason (the defining mental attribute of his cold antiheroes) makes its most notorious appearance in the endless Sadean dissertations justifying libertine erotic tastes, and for dedicated libertines like Juliette this incessant reasoning serves less as an excuse or rationale than as an aphrodisiac. Her sodomite activities with the Pope on the high altar of St. Peter's do not inflame her more than the thought of hearing his private lecture on the propriety of murder. As a mode of personal power, reason holds openly erotic attractions in Sade's work. "I loved Noirceuil for his libertinage," Juliette confesses, "for his mental qualities: I was not by any means captivated by his person."[27] Reason confers sensual enticements as palpable as any of Sade's impossibly rounded buttocks.

Like reason, imagination performs a very specific labor in Sade's erotic economy. As Saint-Fond puts it: "The imagination's fire must set the furnace of the senses alight."[28] The Sadean imagination, of course, is no less bodily than the senses that it inflames; matter merely acts on matter; and this imaginative power to inflame the senses finds its most pertinent expression for Sade in the process of reading. "Many of the extravagances you are about to see illustrated will doubtless displease you, yes, I am well aware of it," writes the narrator in *The 120 Days of Sodom*, "but there are amongst them a few which will warm you to the point of costing you some fuck, and that, reader, is all we ask of you."[29] Sade's pornographic forecast of reader-response criticism forces us to acknowledge that mere words on the page can wring a physical, sexual response from us, even against our will. Sade, a full century before Freud, demonstrates that the ego is not master in its own house.

The imagination also makes itself felt, literally, in the aesthetic arrangements inseparable from Sadean eroticism. Rarely do Sade's libertines satisfy their passions in a chaotic haste and tangle. Sexual partners and groups observe a carefully discussed choreography. Setting—like the elaborate theatrical scenes specially constructed at the chateau Silling— often require costly and ingenious preparation. Crimes are seldom merely perpetrated but rather lovingly premeditated and executed with an artistic attention to details, and libertines who survive long enough often develop a flair for spontaneous dramatic gestures, as when Juliette (after climbing to the summit of a volcano) decides to cast a tiresome companion into the bowels of the earth and then follows this gothic performance with impromptu copulations staged on the very brink of the glowing crater. As the dissolute monk Clément expresses Sade's dark version of Romantic idealism: "Objects have no value for us save that which our imagination imparts to them."[30]

Desire, of course, is the hidden master that Sadean imagination and reason always serve, directly or indirectly, and for Sade the body's truth leads ultimately to the concealed truth of desire. Sade's uniqueness, how-ever, does not lie in exposing unseen and unspoken desires—the regular fare of daytime television. The most shocking revelation in Sade's work is that desire, freed from its normal social restrictions, finds its deepest satisfaction in cruelty and pain. Sade in effect stands on its head the in-fluential Socratic argument that desire always presupposes a painful lack or absence, which disappears when desire attains its object, much as the pangs of hunger disappear after a satisfying meal. Pain for Sade not only arouses and accompanies desire but also fulfills it. Pain is simultaneously both the hunger and the food.

Metaphors of appetite seem perfectly appropriate to the world of Sade's voracious libertines, who do not stop at food—gulped down like gluttons—but consume almost any product of the human body, from blood to vomit, excrement, and flesh. Yet Sadean desire in seeking pain seeks more than the satisfaction of carnal appetites, which is why bodies alone are never enough. His heroes also require huge banquets of speech, reason, and meaning. The meanings that Sade's libertine reasoners assign to pain derive, as we have seen, from the demystified, scientific gaze that views pain strictly as an event of the central nervous system. This newly demystified pain, which strikes at the heart of earlier religious and ethical teaching, provides (or promises to provide) a reassuring sign of certainty, stability, and truth, especially as pain uncovers the suppressed, repressed, or openly denied truth of desire. Yet this picture is too stable. Desire holds the anarchic power in Sade to consume whatever it comes into contact with, including the truth it promises to supply. Not even the hyperrational libertine mind can successfully fix the meaning of pain. Pain, as we will see, unfixes everything.

†

In its power to unravel certainties, Sadean pain has political implica-tions that address not only the events of his own revolutionary era but also our own far from settled times. In fact, his devastating, biomedical critique of sentimentalism and natural goodness started pain on its un-finished journey through the twentieth century. Sade showed that the pol-itics of the nervous system lead not to the sentimentalist's utopia of moral reform and human fellowship but to a tyrannous, underground system of rape, sodomy, and murder.[31] Tyranny, however, was not for Sade the ideal state. Sade settled for tyranny, we might say, because it offered a durable substitute for the transient purity of revolution. It is revolution that provides the political metaphor best summarizing the meanings Sade found in pain.

Revolution for Sade gives a fleeting reality to the anarchic dream of absolute freedom. It introduces a temporary release from all law and all authority that confronts us with a condition of utter ambiguity. The existing political and social order dissolves into a primal, elemental chaos. Human relations seem ready to be wholly remade. Nothing stands on its former foundations. Nothing is sure anymore. "Lawful rule," as a Sadean libertine puts it, "is inferior to anarchy: the greatest proof whereof is the government's obligation to plunge the State into anarchy whenever it wishes to frame a new constitution. To abrogate its former laws it is driven to establish a revolutionary regime in which there are no laws at all."[32]

"No laws at all": it is this moment of complete freedom and utter ambiguity, when all ordinary structures fly apart, that fascinated Sade. Like the tumultuous moment of orgasm for Sadean libertines, it provides an image of the exhilarating vertigo that ensues when human beings live fully the consequences of their own lawless desire. Most readers, of course, rein in their fantasies far short of Sade and find the thought of such vertigo intolerable. It is Sade's distinction among writers of pornography, however, that he invites us to experience not just the description of a few suppressed sexual acts but an unstoppable flood of language aimed at showing in obscene and bloody detail the forbidden consequences that follow inevitably from our fantasies of letting go.

Pain, then, begins in Sade as a sign of certainty and truth but rapidly expands its meaning to include as well the vision of a dizzying, ambiguous void where nothing is certain. In Sade, there is finally no return to the normal world where pleasure and pain stand as the rock-solid opposites that his English contemporary Jeremy Bentham invoked in the first sentence of his *Principles of Morals and Legislation* (1789). "Nature," wrote Bentham, "has placed mankind under the governance of two sovereign masters, *pain* and *pleasure*. It is for them alone to point out what we ought to do, as well as to determine what we shall do." Sade shows how a reliance on pleasure and pain can just as easily undermine every principle of law and morality. In a process that is never simply or solely a reversal, pleasure for Sade implies pain, pain implies pleasure. Nothing remains separate once these two mighty opposites dissolve into an ambiguous mix, like the bodies in a Sadean mélange where even gender finally grows indistinct in the pursuit of an all-consuming sexuality that drives forward toward the undifferentiated embrace of death. Like revolution, pain for Sade leads away from clarities.

Sade is in many ways far more modern than we may want to admit. Pain, as we have seen, tends to open an almost impassable gulf between individuals, implicitly discrediting or questioning our usual pieties about brotherhood and the human community. How easy it is, apparently, to turn away from another's pain. Pain, in this sense, *is* the Other: utterly alien, even when it invades our own flesh. As Sade would contend, it both creates and symbolizes isolation. Words and knowledge carry poorly across this abyss. One modern treatment center advises its staff frankly that pain is "anything that the patient says it is."[33] The blankness, the anything-ness of pain, especially its power to summon up experience ultimately inaccessible to language, its power to evoke and engage ambiguities too slippery for even the slickest libertine reasoners: these are among the most radical meanings with which Sade endowed the mechanical rush of animal spirits through hollow, fibrous nerves.

†

Sade's treatment of pain is important, then, not simply because he provides an encyclopedia of abnormal sexual acts. "The history of civilization," writes Freud (another plague-carrier), "shows beyond any doubt . . . an intimate connection between cruelty and the sexual instinct."[34] We cannot separate Sade's offensiveness from a vision so comprehensive that it contradicts our most cherished values: our basis for understanding the world. In celebrating cruelty, Sade in effect reverses the gesture basic to all Western liberal democracies, which (as Judith Shklar has argued) put cruelty first among moral, social, and political outrages.[35] We count on waking up each day in a society where we cannot be dragged from our beds and tortured. The American Constitution—written while Sade was composing his dark epics of pain—officially forbids any punishment deemed "cruel and unusual." Sade, however, has described a world where the belief in justice simply marks you more clearly as a victim. What gives Sade both his power and his offensiveness is the obsessive exploration of a fact we prefer not to face. Sade forces us to acknowledge that the act of inflicting pain sometimes generates intense sexual excitement. He implicitly dares us to recognize how far his nightmarish counterworld of sexualized cruelty resembles a picture—distorted but therefore accurate—of our own renounced desire and violent times.

Sade's fiction in fact has proved chillingly prophetic. Hardly a month passes without news of a gruesome rape, mutilation, or murder that might be lifted directly from one of his novels. Even the sexual crimes well-documented within the American family—crimes of spouse abuse, child prostitution, battery, incest, sodomy, and murder—make Sade's work sound not so much fictitious as merely overdramatic, since domestic violence usually grinds on with a dullness Sade's libertines would never tolerate. Sade's pornographic vision of pain confronts us finally with social and sexual questions that are still deeply undecided. Some couples apparently find that whips and chains add zest to their sexual pleasure, and most video stores rent explicit sadomasochistic films with titles such as *Journey into Pain*. Indeed, the recent genre of "slice and dice" films combines horror and sex in ways that Sade could only envy for their technological advances in cruelty. His unreaderly novels—far too verbose for modern tastes—seem almost innocuous in a culture where subteens hold weekend parties to watch *The Texas Chain Saw Massacre*.[36]

What is at issue in this new proliferation of sadomasochistic pain? We may assume, first, that it is not new, just more open than ever before. Yet its openness has raised anew some very difficult questions. Questions, for example, about civil rights. What limits if any can be put on free expression? Questions about human desire. What do S&M clubs and magazines have to tell us about the human psyche? Such questions have predictable appeal both for demagogues and for legal or clinical researchers, but recently the discussion has received an unsettling jolt of reason and passion from the feminist movement. Many feminists see sadomasochistic pain, whatever its psychic sources or legal status, as posing an immediate threat to women. They would oppose Sade and others like him because the lives of women are at stake.

There is no single, uniform feminist position on pornography, of course. What we find instead is a dialogue among diverse points of view all focused on the central question of how far pornography supports or advances the oppression of women. British novelist Angela Carter believes that Sadean pornography actually serves women indirectly by its exposure of a brutal phallocentric structure: it strips away the mask of romance to reveal the sexual politics implicit in all male-female relations.

Carter's feminist interpretation of Sade as offering an indirect critique of bourgeois, male-centered ideology thus coincides with Susan Sontag's belief that "the pornographic imagination says something worth listening to, albeit in a degraded and often unrecognizable form."[37] Following Sontag and Carter, some feminist scholars are now exploring the obscene and pornographic in ways that other feminists can only deplore as misguided.

Certainly the most vocal feminist writers today vigorously deny pornography what Sontag calls "its peculiar access to some truth" and attack it as actively promoting the oppression of women.[38] This oppression, they argue, is ancient, ongoing, and relentless, and pornography simply fuels it. The proposals for resistance run from protest and boycott to censorship, legislation, and terrorism. What draws such feminists together, despite their differences about the means of resistance, is a belief that fictional images are not harmless. These opponents of pornography reject the claim that they should worry about *real* acts of oppression—not about books, films, and performances that merely *simulate* oppressive acts. Any image that simulates violence against women, they assert, helps to perpetuate a social order that ignores, excuses, or even encourages real violence against women. Such fictive images, they contend, are no less real (no less a part of the real world) than a rapist's knife. As novelist Monique Wittig says in attacking pornographic texts: "This discourse *is* reality for us."[39]

Sadean pain, so far from receding into the history of eighteenth-century fiction, confronts us with unavoidable controversy. How we decide these questions will strongly influence the shape of contemporary culture in the years ahead. Optimists might wish to see one hopeful sign in the strange novel *Venus in Furs* (1870), written by Sade's scholarly alter ego, the German novelist (and history professor) Leopold von Sacher-Masoch, whose name has given us our indispensable noun for people who enjoy feeling pain.[40] Unlike Sade, Sacher-Masoch creates soft-core fantasies in which cold, voluptuous, fur-clad women whip and humiliate various weak, hypersensitive males who crave such sexual stimulation. The decadent world of *Venus in Furs*, however, shares one important trait with Sade's anarchic novels. Both writers believe that men and women have only two roles available: tyrant or slave. Pain is a function of this fettered choice.

The pornographic imagination for Sade and Sacher-Masoch depends on social and erotic dominance. "In matters of love there is no equality," says the typical Sacher-Masoch male narrator of *Venus in Furs*: "If I were faced with the choice of dominating or being dominated, I would choose the latter. It would be far more satisfying to be the slave of a beautiful woman."[41] Sade's libertines, of course, make the opposite choice. They prefer to be tyrants rather than slaves, to inflict pain rather than to suffer it, although sometimes they find themselves disposed (from necessity or in search of change) to take pleasure in enslavement. What matters most, however, is that for both Sade and Sacher-Masoch, despite their significant differences, the erotic pain they seek and celebrate depends on a vision of radical inequality.

Venus in Furs is in its own way as curiously didactic as the novels of Sade. (Pornographers, it seems, may be frustrated schoolteachers at heart.) Thus Sacher-Masoch obligingly concludes his novel by pointing out the edifying lesson that readers, understandably, may have missed:

> The moral is that woman, as Nature created her and as man up to now has found her attractive, is man's enemy; she can be his slave or his mistress but never his companion. This she can only be when she has the same rights as he and is his equal in education and work. For the time being there is only one alternative: to be the hammer or the anvil.[42]

Masochism and sadism share this same historical origin. They emerge into literary prominence in a period when the choice between being the dominator or the dominated no longer seems wholly inevitable. Like Sade, Sacher-Masoch can now envision a radically egalitarian social order, which pornographers in their well-disguised conservatism implicitly oppose. What would happen to pornography, we might ask, if men and women were no longer stuck in a static culture where people must be either hammers or anvils? Would such a culture still have a place for sadism and masochism?

Perhaps. Some will argue (I think incorrectly) that sadist and masochist represent permanent dispositions of the human psyche. Psyches, like pains, however, always exist in people who inhabit specific cultures at particular historical moments. Paula J. Caplan has recently demolished arguments, strongly reinforced by Freud, that women are biologically disposed toward masochism.[43] A truly free and equal society which no longer divides men and women into (genteel) tyrants and slaves—or even into traditional husbands and wives or bosses and secretaries—may well discover that the psyche too has changed. In such a changed world, a sexual frolic with whips and chains (enjoyed like a Halloween stunt) might possibly provide a harmless, if retrograde, titillation. It seems useless to forbid anyone the right to suffer pain, especially if the pain brings pleasure. Nevertheless, people in a state of true equality who find pleasure in painful sadomasochistic fantasies may want to consider the second "moral" with which Sacher-Masoch concluded *Venus in Furs*: "Whoever allows himself to be whipped deserves to be whipped."[44]

✝

We may hope that the future will not belong to Sade. It is hard to see how a partnership culture—to use Riane Eisler's term—would find in Sade much more than a museum of bygone terrors. Yet such a future cannot somehow deny or forget what Sade has shown us. Moreover, Sade shows us that a truly just society would need to construct a new understanding of pain: an understanding that did not disavow but rather accepted and transformed the tendency in pain to isolate the individual and to plunge every human value into uncertainty. Meanwhile, the past and present still remain so gripped and haunted by Sade's vision of sexual pain that the tabloid press is often little more than a theater of Sadean cruelty. Our persisting social inequalities doubtless supply an indispensable precondition for such horrors, but Sade's world of sexual cruelty also depends upon a final (learned) trait that proves a distinctive feature of all his libertine heroes and heroines: apathy.[45]

The libertine taste for extracting pleasure from pain is not entirely, as Sade insists, a matter of anatomy and physiology. It also depends on a paradoxical deadening of the emotions in order that cruelty might be enjoyed to the utmost. Such willed apathy is the indispensable trait that allows the Sadean libertine to savor pain to the utmost. The libertine—like the Victorian hysteric— is paradoxically both hypersensitive and numb. Further, the apathy of Sadean eroticism differs significantly from the famous classical Stoic apathy, which expressed itself as a generalized rational indifference to all passion. Libertine apathy resembles a highly selective, local anesthesia, which eliminates only a specific band or zone of feeling, while thereby heightening the sensation that remains. There is no question that Sade's heroes and heroines possess this self-anesthetic power to an extraordinary degree. Of Madame Clairwil ("the most exceptional libertine of her century"), Sade writes that for lack of sensibility she had no equal: "She indeed prided herself on never having shed a tear."[46]

Madame Clairwil in her sublime apathy represents Sade's savage antidote to the eighteenth-century Man of Feeling. She stands in every possible way as an antitype of the sentimental hero. Her apathetic deadening of the emotions in the pursuit of heightened sensation, however, points far beyond Sade's murderous parody of sentimentalism. In almost every culture, a selective anesthesia is what permits us to tolerate the intolerable. The streets of every major American city contain hundreds of hungry, homeless, unemployed people whose pain we simply cannot face up to. Sade's libertine societies are unique not in their fictive brutality (as Auschwitz, Cambodia, and Vietnam attest) but only in their undeceived awareness and open enjoyment of the suffering they inflict. Sade shows us what can happen in any culture when pain—redefined as a mere shuttle of electrical impulses—has lost all memory of its contact with the tragic.

I I

TRAGIC PAIN

Affliction is an uprooting of life, a more or less attenuated equivalent of death, made irresistibly present to the soul by the attack or immediate apprehension of physical pain. If there is complete absence of physical pain there is no affliction for the soul, because our thoughts can turn to any object. Thought flies from affliction as promptly and irresistibly as an animal flies from death. Here below, physical pain, and that alone, has the power to chain down our thoughts. . . .

SIMONE WEIL[1]

T SEEMS PREPOSTEROUS to argue that medicine in general takes almost no account of human suffering. Yet Eric J. Cassell, a physician who has written extensively in the field of medical ethics, makes exactly this argument in an important essay entitled "The Nature of Suffering and the Goals of Medicine" (1982). "The obligation of physicians to relieve human suffering stretches back to antiquity," he writes. "Despite this fact, little attention is explicitly given to the problem of suffering in medical education, research, or practice." He then continues with personal observations about medical inattention to suffering that may strike the lay reader as slightly chilling. "My colleagues of a contemplative nature were surprised at how little they knew of the problem and how little thought they had given it," he reports, adding ominously for the next generation of patients, "whereas medical students tended to be unsure of the relevance of the issue to their work."[2]

Cassell's findings agree with those of psychiatrist Arthur Kleinman. Kleinman argues that the modern medical bureaucracy, when acknowledging it at all, treats human suffering as one might treat a malfunctioning car: as "a problem of mechanical breakdown requiring a technical fix." The failures of the medical bureaucracy to acknowledge or describe suffering extend to the laboratory as well. "Clinical and behavioral science research also possess no category to describe suffering," Kleinman writes, "no routine way of recording this most thickly human dimension of patients' and families' stories of experiencing illness. Symptom scales and survey questionnaires and behavioral checklists quantify functional impairment and disability, rendering quality of life fungible. Yet about suffering they are silent."[3] Suffering in effect proves too hard to measure. It does not lend itself conveniently to checklists and questionnaires. Its cash value is nebulous. Cassell concludes: "The relief of suffering, it would appear, is considered one of the primary ends of medicine by patients and lay persons, but not by the medical profession."[4]

The question that tragedy poses to medicine is what to make of human suffering. This is an inquiry that invites meditation and discussion rather than brisk true/false answers. Medicine seems to dislike such questions on principle, perhaps because most doctors are preternaturally busy and unavoidably practical, with always one more patient waiting at the door. Yet, like the physician who hastily retreats from the besieged castle after his conference with Macbeth, medicine seems instinctively to flee from tragedy. "Were I from Dunsinane away and clear," says the harried doctor, "Profit again should hardly draw me here."[5] Overwork and pragmatism cannot fully explain the tendency of medicine to pull away from the subject of suffering. Especially when pain is so central to the suffering that patients undergo, it is important that we should ask what tragedy can tell us about a realm medicine prefers to ignore.

†

Ralph Waldo Emerson (still among the most acute philosophers of American experience) argued that sickness is a major source of the tragic. "The swift penalty of torture acute or chronic on each abuse of the organs," he wrote in his essay on tragedy, "produces a very large proportion of the suffering in the world."[6] An understanding of tragedy offers a way to begin thinking about the pain and suffering so common to illness. One impediment to such thinking, strangely, is the tendency of scholars, critics, and teachers to focus on a mere handful of famous tragedies. As Northrop Frye observed: "Most theories of tragedy take one great tragedy as their norm: thus Aristotle's theory is largely founded on *Oedipus Tyrannus*, and Hegel's on *Antigone*."[7] Generations of high school students raised on a standardized syllabus might be excused for wondering if Shakespeare wrote only *Macbeth* and *Romeo and Juliet*. There is thus considerable merit in turning to less overworked texts not already absorbed into our thinking about tragedy. Here I want to examine two disparate, marginal works that appear on no one's list of the top ten: a neglected play by Sophocles entitled *Philoctetes* and a very brief book by novelist Joyce Carol Oates entitled *On Boxing*.

It is necessary to confess at once that definitions of tragedy are not notably more successful than definitions of pain. Each major theorist from Aristotle to Nietzsche seems compelled to produce a differing interpretation, which is not surprising when we consider the differences between, say, Athenian tragedy and Senecan tragedy, or between Shakespeare and Racine. We might begin, however, with a thought so basic that theorists often overlook it. Tragedy, I would offer (not as a definition but as a starting point), is the literary form that takes as its main social function an extended meditation on human pain and suffering. Everyday usage supports such a view. People routinely, if carelessly, attach the word "tragedy" to any great misfortune. The devastation from a flood that leaves thousands homeless will be called a terrible tragedy. The death of a child or spouse will be called a tragic loss. Scholars may regret a usage that takes no account of such revered literary concepts as catharsis, unity, and the tragic flaw. Yet our own everyday speech may be just as revealing as the distinctive understandings characteristic of earlier periods, as when writers in the Middle Ages (thinking about the fall of princes) defined tragedy as a plunge from high to low on fortune's wheel. Today, as in the Middle Ages, we employ the language of tragedy whenever we feel ourselves in the presence of great suffering.

Tragedy, then, we can provisionally think of as an extended meditation on human pain and suffering. But what constitutes suffering? Here everyday speech again proves helpful, since we refer to suffering in ways that imply a deep and long-lasting distress that does not confine its damage to the body alone. Suffering is a kind of damage that extends beyond the body to afflict the mind or soul or spirit too. A long, wasting struggle with cancer, for example, clearly takes its toll on more than the lung or pancreas. Behaviorist psychology at its most rigorous proposes to regard suffering as learned: action and emotion cleanly separable from the body and its "sensory" pain. Certainly in some cases pain may proceed without suffering, and suffering without pain. Yet tragedy argues for a less simplistic view of human life. It posits a crisis in which affliction works inseparably in body, mind, emotion, and spirit. Tragedy expresses a twofold or circular wisdom: to understand pain you must understand suffering, and to understand suffering you must understand pain.

There is good evidence to suggest that long-lasting, unresolved emotional distress finds a way of afflicting the body, just as chronic pain that drags on for months or years begins to take its toll on the emotions and spirit. A deep sorrow or grief that does not begin with pain very quickly produces it. Loss and isolation can cut like a knife. "Acute loneliness," writes psychoanalyst Rollo May, "seems to be the most painful kind of anxiety which a human being can suffer. Patients often tell us that the pain is a physical gnawing in their chests, or feels like the cutting of a razor in their heart region."[8] The emotional trauma of divorce, I can attest, often works its way into every crevice of the neck, heart, back, and bowels. It wrenches and twists the body until it creates what English-speaking people everywhere call pain. Simone Weil goes so far as to insist that every true affliction of the soul roots itself in the pain-filled human body.

Strict behaviorists are of course not the only source of the error that divides suffering from pain. While doctors tend to ignore the question of suffering, pain always seems the first thing to get lost when scholars and critics discuss the great tragic works of Western literature. The academic establishment often treats tragedy as too noble, too spiritual, too metaphysical for commerce with something so mundane as the human body with its chills, cramps, and fevers. A mere dysfunction in the flesh simply cannot command the almost reverential high-seriousness that now surrounds discussions of tragedy. Small wonder that much modern writing about tragedy sounds as if it were written by philosophers in disguise. (Often it *is* written by philosophers.) Tragedy, however, with its unflinching gaze at the pain-filled human body, offers us more than metaphysics.

Consider for a moment two icons of tragic pain: Oedipus and Lear. Near the conclusion of *Oedipus Tyrannus* the chorus and two messengers speak alone before the closed doors of the palace. Inside, hidden from view, King Oedipus has just learned the terrible truths he so stubbornly pursued: that he unknowingly killed his father and married his mother, the queen Jocasta. One of the messengers explains what happened next inside the palace. Just moments before, we are told, Jocasta hanged herself. Oedipus then tore the brooches from her dress and plunged them deep into his eyes. "No sluggish oozing drops," the messenger reports, "but a black rain and bloody hail poured down."[9] The flood of gore from his ruined eyes, the messenger says of Oedipus, even now runs down his face and stains his beard.

Only after this terrifying verbal preparation do the doors of the palace open. We behold the once mighty king now blind, broken, soaked in his own blood, and anguished with the guilt he feels for a crime he committed unknowingly. When Oedipus finally speaks, what we hear is not words but only a single, repeated cry of agony: speech rolled back into mere sound and torment. This is the stark revelation toward which every act and speech of the entire drama have been relentlessly aiming: a frozen moment of pain that contains nothing except the mutilated human body and its wordless suffering.

King Lear too brings us to such a moment. In the final act, after suffering almost every loss it would seem possible to absorb, the loss of power, loss of reason, loss of freedom, Lear suffers the final catastrophe he cannot survive. Shakespeare never lets us forget, from the opening scene, that the king is old and infirm. We now see him emerge, frail and in defeat, carrying in his arms his innocent, loyal daughter, Cordelia, whose love and honesty he had foolishly spurned. Like Jocasta, she too has just been hanged. Lear has cut down her body with his own hands. Still holding the corpse, Lear utters three words, but they are not so much words as sounds, less spoken than bellowed like an animal cry: "Howl, howl, howl."[10] As with Oedipus, we enter into an almost intolerable suspended moment when the eloquent field of tragic action—with its rich language of ceremony, wars, loves, and plots—suddenly drops away into the void. We witness simply the ruined human body and the sound of suffering. Nothing more.

The vision of Oedipus and Lear at their moments of deepest anguish ought to make it obvious that tragedy cannot dispense with the body and its pain. Tragedy, as I have argued, views suffering as intrinsically bound up with pain, pain as intrinsically bound up with suffering, in such a way that neither is fully comprehensible without the other. In effect, tragedy insists that what we call "being" cannot be understood apart from the body. The body in tragedy is not just something we possess, like an identifying birthmark or robe or kingdom, but what we *are*. It both defines us and, fatally, limits us. It opens us—with our very human greed, ambition, lust, and blindness—to disaster.

†

Sophocles's *Philoctetes* (c. 409 B.C.) demands our attention because it is so explicitly a tragedy of pain. Pain of course seems present almost by definition in tragic art, but *Philoctetes* is unique in that it takes pain as its explicit subject. Perhaps the choice of subject helps to explain why today the play remains generally unread, unperformed, and all but unknown.[11] Few ancient works seem more ripe for rediscovery in the postmodern era of chronic illness. Indeed, the action centers on a material fact that quickly assumes the dimensions of a major symbol. Philoctetes throughout the play suffers from a visible, festering, deeply painful wound.

The wound in Philoctetes' foot is far more than a simple injury. It lies at the root of the tragedy. Like Oedipus, whose name ("swell-foot") refers to the injury he suffered as an infant when abandoned to die on a hillside, Philoctetes erred without knowing it, walking by mistake into a sacred grove where a snake bit him on the foot. The subsequent pain proves so powerful, irresistible, and almost palpable that at one crucial point in the drama it literally knocks him to the ground senseless. Even more important than its shaping influence over the plot, however, is the power that pain holds to reshape Philoctetes. After nine years of unrelieved suffering, he in some sense *is* his wound. His character has become inseparable from his pain.

Philoctetes, of course, is not a household name, and we seldom remember him among the more famous Greeks who sailed for the ten-year siege of Troy. The ancient world, however, knew him well. He is the only character after whom all three of the classic Greek dramatists—Sophocles, Aeschylus, and Euripides—named a tragic drama. Perhaps the Greeks responded to him because his story takes place on a slightly less elevated plane than the heroic events at Troy, which it nonetheless decisively influences. When we first meet him, he seems more approachable than Oedipus or Antigone or Laocoön. His pain is more like our pain. Philoctetes in this sense embodies the everyday suffering that lies in wait not on an epic battlefield but concealed in a common domestic accident or hidden in the recesses of our own flesh. It is less the gods than our own vulnerable bodies, so the story suggests, that decree our isolation and suffering.

Sophocles' play dramatizes the occasion when Odysseus and Neoptolemeus (the young son of Achilles) arrive on the barren island of Lemnos where Philoctetes lives in unwilling exile as the sole inhabitant. They come to bring him back to join the Greek assault on Troy. A seer has foretold that the Greeks cannot take Troy without Philoctetes and his famous bow, which was given to him by the dying Hercules. Philoctetes, however, has no great love for Odysseus or the Greeks because nine years earlier (while they all sailed together to Troy) it was Odysseus and the Greeks who had abandoned him on Lemnos. Their reason for deserting Philoctetes tells us something important about pain. The snakebite on his heel had begun to fester. Its stench and his blasphemous cries finally grew unendurable. Early one morning, his shipmates slipped away, leaving him alone on the rocky, uninhabited island with nothing but a few garments and his bow.

The play in its spare geometry might be diagrammed as a triangle. At the apex stands the wounded, friendless, abandoned Philoctetes. Odysseus and Neoptolemeus stand at opposite ends of the base. Their opposition extends beyond the contrast of age and youth. Odysseus is the consummate politician: a chameleonic man of cunning, double-talk, and hardhearted pragmatism. He states his time-serving principles bluntly: "As the occasion/ demands, such a one am I."[12] Guile is the means he characteristically recommends for returning Philoctetes to Troy. Neoptolemeus, fired with youth and high birth, prefers noble deeds to deceitful words. "I have a natural antipathy," he tells the cunning Odysseus, "to get my ends by tricks and stratagems" (87–88). The Greek princes nonetheless have put Odysseus in charge, and Neoptolemeus at last defers to the older warrior and accepts his stratagem to "ensnare" Philoctetes by pretending to befriend him.

The play contains two scenes above all that demand the attention of anyone concerned with suffering and tragic pain. The first is the artfully delayed entrance of Philoctetes—described as an exile whose thoughts are "set continually on pain and hunger" (185)—whom we do not meet until he has been discussed at length. These long preliminary discussions give way to additional delays. Hearing a far-off footstep, the chorus asks for silence. As the sounds grow closer, it becomes clear they are not the sounds of a man walking, but crawling. Then a voice, "the voice of a man wounded" (209). Yet it is not really speech but more like the voice of a wound. Finally, as if all this off-stage absence and delay were compressed into a single image, the chorus hears a cry—twice specified as a "bitter cry" (219)—not simply a cry of pain but a cry expressing the bitterness of prolonged suffering. Only then do we at last see Philoctetes as he enters dragging his wounded leg.

This opening scene does more than simply build our anticipation. It also prepares us to recognize the heightened importance that Sophocles assigns to the paired human attributes of body and voice. We first meet Philoctetes only through his voice and through the words spoken about him. The play later reverberates with various references to words and language, sometimes embodied in the metaphor of speech as "tongue." "Friendliest of tongues!" (234) cries Philoctetes in rapture at hearing again after nine years the sound of his native Greek. (He does not know that the words are spoken to deceive him.) Odysseus openly states the politician's creed that words alone matter: "It is the tongue that wins and not the deed" (99). Words and voice, in short, rapidly come to suggest a realm of ambiguities and falsehood that Sophocles seems to oppose to the visible, certain truth of bodies and deeds.[13]

Voice and body—understood as paired opposites—have much to do with the subject of pain. They prompt some of Elaine Scarry's finest analysis in *The Body in Pain*, where she describes the relation between the disembodied torturer (at times no more than a voice) and the (speechless) victim who is all body: a repeating structure played out again in biblical history with a God who is all voice and in Marxist economic theory with its remote commands issued by a disembodied capitalist class. Sophocles—whose raw materials as a dramatist are the words and bodies he puts on stage—suggests in *Philoctetes* that the body alone is what allows us to grasp the undissembled truth of human affliction. This truth finds its most powerful expression in the second scene we need to examine: where a surge of pain knocks Philoctetes to the ground, unconscious, reducing him, like the victims of torture, to a creature who is all body.

The body, of course, functions like a verbal sign in Greek culture. It carries an unmistakable prestige and clear meaning. Simply by looking at him, Philoctetes knows that Neoptolemeus is of noble birth. The body in this sense cannot lie. It conveys, for example, the inner greatness of spirit that Aristotle saw as the proper endowment of tragic character. Laocoön merely by the heroic contours of his suffering expresses an inner nobility. The significance that the Greek world assigned to the body helps to enlarge the pathos and terror at stake when an overwhelming wave of pain from his festering wound drives the ragged but heroic Philoctetes to his knees, as if he were suddenly struck down like a sacrificial beast.

Scholars discussing *Philoctetes* have tended to concentrate on the meaning of the bow.[14] It is pain, however, that turns the bow loose to generate its meanings. In fact, often the characters refer to Philoctetes' pain through the Greek word for evil, *kakon*, a concept that belonged to the poets and dramatists long before Aristotle domesticated it for philosophy.[15] The moment when this compound pain-evil suddenly crushes Philoctetes to the ground constitutes the dramatic turning point when he hands over his sacred weapon to Neoptolemeus. "Take this bow," he says, "as you asked to do just now, until the pain,/ the pain of my sickness, that is now upon me, grows less" (762–764). Pain has given Neoptolemeus the prize that trickery failed to secure, yet the scene is not over. Neoptolemeus stands in silence as Philoctetes struggles with an agony so intense that it leaves him finally drained and unconscious. The image of Neoptolemeus—coveted bow in hand—standing silently over the fallen, stricken, wordless Philoctetes is, as classicist Charles Segal puts it, "one of the most powerful visual tableaux in Sophocles."[16]

What makes the scene so powerful is partly the invisible presence of pain. Philoctetes remains a formidable warrior. (Odysseus shrewdly stays hidden out of fear.) Suddenly, however, this dangerous warrior staggers under the force of a mysterious blow. The pain is so unendurable that Philoctetes first begs Neoptolemeus to cut off the festering limb. He next begs Neoptolemeus to burn his body on a funeral pyre, as Philoctetes had once done for Hercules when Hercules was similarly tormented with an unremitting pain. "Terrible it is, beyond words' reach" (756), says Philoctetes of his suffering. The silence implicit in pain—a shutting off of communication—could not be clearer. Indeed, in numerous places Sophocles writes dialogue indicating that one of the characters stands mute with overpowering emotion. It is a play composed of silences.

The scene of pain—as Neoptolemeus stands over the unconscious Philoctetes—concludes with a silence in which we are left alone with the damaged human body. The pained body and its sudden muteness in effect take on an iconic power, giving almost visual form to Philoctetes' inner exile. As he lies unconscious, his pain not only cuts him off from others but even from himself. This nearly visible pain is not merely like a static icon, however. It also serves a crucial dramatic function in helping to collapse the distance between Philoctetes and Neoptolemeus. As he stands witness to this painful exile within exile, Neoptolemeus begins to change in ways that finally turn him to action against the false-speaking and pragmatic Odysseus.

Neoptolemeus, in his response to Philoctetes, certainly demonstrates one possible way in which an encounter with suffering can change us. "I have been in pain for you," he says when Philoctetes regains consciousness; "I have been/ in sorrow for your pain" (805–806). Slightly later he tells the chorus: "A kind of compassion,/ a terrible compassion, has come upon me/ for him" (964–966). His vigil over the suffering Philoctetes transforms Neoptolemeus from a deferential youth, noble but inexperienced and unsure, into a mature young hero whose generosity of spirit now seems as evident as his noble body. Indeed, the plot turns on this pivotal change in Neoptolemeus. His new compassion brings him from simulated friendship to genuine concern, from speech to embodied deeds. He decides to give back the bow.

It is a mistake, however, to read *Philoctetes* simply as a play that endorses an uplifting moral about how suffering naturally leads to compassion. Oedipus, it is true, once states that suffering leads to wisdom. His own suffering certainly leads Oedipus on a journey to a new kind of knowledge. Yet Sophocles as dramatist also recognizes that compassion in the audience is not identical with suffering in the hero. Someone *else's* suffering does not necessarily make us wise—or even compassionate. Odysseus, for example, feels nothing but scorn for Philoctetes. Moreover, Neoptolemeus and Philoctetes change in different ways. Pain has not only ennobled Philoctetes but also embittered him until he has grown finally almost as hard as Odysseus.

The sternest wisdom of Greek tragedy may be that suffering cannot be shared: only witnessed. The chorus expresses the awe and terror that the Greek world felt at the prospect of the life that Philoctetes has been forced to lead, in exile from family, friends, and community:

> There is wonder, indeed, in my heart
> how, how in his loneliness,
> listening to the waves beating on the shore,
> how he kept hold at all
> on a life so full of tears (685–690).

When Philoctetes discovers the plot against him, his friendliness turns instantly into implacable defiance. He absolutely refuses to help the Greeks, and his refusal threatens to bring human history to a standstill. Troy, without his help, will not fall. In fact, it takes a literal *deus ex machina* to resolve the action when, in the final scene, the demigod Hercules descends from Olympus and in effect orders Philoctetes to set sail for Troy.

Aristotle explained that one class of tragedies ends happily, but the absurdist happy ending of *Philoctetes* simply demonstrates how far the action is deadlocked beyond human resolution. Pain—compounded by the treachery of Odysseus and the hardness of Philoctetes—has created an impasse that neither persuasion nor compassion can unblock. It literally takes a god to put things right. The tacked-on happy ending, however true to legend, cannot erase our knowledge that pain and suffering have transformed Philoctetes into a broken man who remains an exile even after his rescue: alone, bitter, suspicious, friendless. What then do readers both medical and nonmedical have to gain from this literary encounter with tragic pain?

Nietzsche believed that tragedy held a cognitive function; it could teach us about ourselves and about the world.[17] What we learn from tragedy, however, does not always resemble a nugget of portable wisdom ("the moral of the story"). It is sometimes more like an experience that changes you in ways you cannot exactly explain. *Philoctetes* makes us feel the power of pain to reduce a life to utter emptiness and misery. It unweaves the self until the self is nothing but pain. This is what Simone Weil understood so well:

Affliction is anonymous before all things; it deprives its victims of their personality and makes them into things. It is indifferent; and it is the coldness of this indifference—a metallic coldness—that freezes all those it touches right to the depths of their souls. They will never find warmth again. They will never believe any more that they are anyone.[18]

Philoctetes has fallen into this ice-cold living tomb. In his despairing speech addressed to the wild crags of Lemnos, he describes himself as already passed beyond the limits of the human world, "one that is dead, a kind of vaporous shadow, a mere wraith."[19]

Tragic drama may contain and evoke moments of individual change, such as the compassion that sweeps over Neoptolemeus, but the vision of tragedy is bitter. Doctors and patients cannot expect tragedy to offer the kind of therapeutic benefit that comedy provides. Only an idiot would stage *Hedda Gabler* in a cancer ward. Yet tragedy takes as its function to show us what it is to live in a universe of inexplicable suffering: to endure the unendurable. In this scene, it may approach an understanding of what it means to live with chronic illness.[20] Philoctetes, we must remember, does not suffer because of a flaw in his character. He simply wandered into a sacred grove where a snakebite fatally changed his life. Tragedy, according to George Steiner, shows us a vision of humankind as unwelcome guests in the universe; it exposes a force inside or outside the self that leads us relentlessly toward a final catastrophe. "Call it what you will," Steiner writes: "a hidden or malevolent God, blind fate, the solicitations of hell, or the brute fury of our animal blood. It waits for us in ambush at the crossroads. It mocks us and destroys us. In certain rare instances, it leads us after destruction to some incomprehensible repose."[21]

What tragedy offers us is not consolation but, at times, the almost incomprehensible knowledge of a human being who has suffered so long and so deeply that (like the aged outcast Oedipus exhausted from his ceaseless exile or like political prisoners released after years of unspeakable torture) they move among us with a kind of holiness, as if they have come back from the dead. Such knowledge holds the power to shake us and to change us as we experience a dimension of human life we normally do not acknowledge. Doctors, of course, need a certain self-protective dispassion. They must move amid the businesslike routines of hospital and office, where each day pain casts up its new exiles. We cannot expect them to do their work well if they are shaken to the core by each fresh encounter with human suffering. Still, perhaps what medicine can profitably relearn from tragedy is a sense of awe, even reverence, at the extraordinary struggles it is sometimes called upon to attend. Pain on occasion becomes the site of encounters we can do nothing except witness in respect.

†

The reason why doctors and writers and all of us should think about tragic pain is because, as a culture, we are rapidly losing an understanding of tragedy—which means that we are losing one important way of thinking about human life. It is easy today to regard tragedy as merely a vanished literary form: an oversized fossil, like epic. Certainly what George Steiner calls "the dry and private character of modern suffering" has given little encouragement for a contemporary art that rivals the tragic drama of Sophocles or Racine.[22] It is quite possible, as Steiner suggests, that the ruling systems of thought in our time are inherently antitragic, in the sense that, like medicine, they draw strength from the vision of continuing progress toward a utopian future. As a culture we do not take kindly to the tragic vision. We tacitly reject it, even as medicine almost blindly resists the biological fact of death, strapping terribly damaged, infirm, or unconscious bodies onto machines that pump the blood and keep the cells alive until it takes a court order to allow death to reenter the world. Yet tragedy, as Emerson wrote, is all around us.

The real problem is not that tragedy has vanished or become impossible. It is worse than that. We no longer recognize tragedy when we encounter it. Richard Selzer wrote that to perceive events as tragic is to wring from them beauty and truth. The corollary is also true: *not* to perceive tragedy (not to recognize a certain situation as tragic) is to wring from it next to nothing. We simply gaze with a numbed fascination at a meaningless set of actions we cannot comprehend—then shift our attention elsewhere. One strong reason for reading Sophocles or Shakespeare is so that we can recognize tragedy when it enters our lives. The modern flight from tragedy thus gives special importance to the few contemporary writers who, like Selzer, seek to show us fragments or traces of the tragedy that continues to surround us. One such writer is Joyce Carol Oates.

Joyce Carol Oates—best known as a novelist but skilled in many genres from poetry to criticism—offers unique assistance in helping us address the question of what has happened to tragedy. Tragedy is a subject that has long preoccupied her. One of the first reliable studies of her fiction, by Mary Kathryn Grant, is entitled *The Tragic Vision of Joyce Carol Oates* (1978). Further, Oates has published an entire collection of critical essays on tragedy, *The Edge of Impossibility: Tragic Forms in Literature* (1972). There she includes Melville and Dostoevski among writers working with tragic forms and themes, so clearly she does not regard tragedy as having vanished with the Greeks or Shakespeare. Still, Melville and Dostoevski both belong to a world of fiction now at least a century old. Where in the public arena do we find tragedy unfolding today? Oates's answer is something of a shock. "Boxing," she writes in the provocative, final sentence of a remarkable little book she published in 1987, "has become America's tragic theater."[23]

The proposal to regard boxing as America's contemporary tragic theater seems guaranteed to arouse resistance. One pious male reviewer unfairly compared Oates to the women called Jenny Wrens, who were hired or lured by boxing promoters years ago to attend matches and thus to soften the image of an uncivilized sport.[24] No one reading Oates's *On Boxing* with an open mind, however, will conclude that it ignores or glamorizes brutality. Oates seems right to protest a sexist bias in reviewers who criticize women writers for their violence.[25] Boxing is a fit subject for Norman Mailer or for Samuel Johnson but not, apparently, for Joyce Carol Oates. Still, it is tempting to think that Oates simply fell into a moment of careless or concluding hyperbole when she described boxing in her final sentence as America's tragic theater. Is boxing really something we can understand in the way we understand, say, *King Lear*?

It is simple fairness to one of our most impressive contemporary writers to look carefully at her claims about the relation between boxing and tragedy. Resistance, as Freud taught us, often conceals something we do not wish to admit, and I believe that we resist Oates's claims about boxing in the same way that we resist the claims of tragedy. We prefer to inhabit a world of happy endings—that sure box-office formula Hollywood revives each season. We flee tragedy and we implicitly denigrate boxing (even if we can't help watching it) for the same underlying reason: because they both confront us with something we desperately wish to keep concealed. Oates offers to show us what it is we have resisted and concealed in our flight from tragedy.

We must begin, in Oates's view, with the acknowledgment that tragedy has changed. It is not today exactly what Aristotle described in the fourth century B.C. Her own novels, for example, create dark tales of aborted tragedy: action and characters unable to measure up to classic tragic stature. These failures, however, do not prove that tragedy has vanished. Rather, Oates chronicles what she calls "remnants" of classical tragedy "amid the chaos of a post-Copernican world." She gives us tragedy transformed and diminished as it reenters our thinner atmosphere. Her analysis of Shakespeare's *Troilus and Cressida*, for example, provides an apt description of what she sees as a typically modern dilemma. "This is tragedy of a special sort," she observes, "the 'tragedy' the basis of which is the impossibility of conventional tragedy."[26]

Conventional tragedy, then, is impossible. Classical drama remains important, however, because it provides a standard for recognizing modern transformations and echoes. Indeed, Mary Kathryn Grant argues that the greatest mistake in Oates's fictional world is not to succumb to the tragic but to fail to recognize it.[27] Oates sees the absence of conventional tragedy as in effect opening up new space for unconventional tragic forms. Our memory of classical tragedy is what makes such unconventional modern versions comprehensible (no matter how fragmentary or flawed) as something more than chaos and blind suffering. Oates acknowledges that boxing cannot provide an Aristotelian catharsis of pity and fear (93), but in a 1971 review she also insisted that modern tragedy takes as its distinctive characteristic the *lack* of cathartic effect.[28] Some people will doubtless claim a culture that finds its most elevated tragic spectacle in boxing is inherently lost. Yet Oates sees boxing as something darker and fiercer than we know. It is an example—even a public prototype—of the tragedy all around us that we cannot perceive.

Aristotle, despite his limitations for a contemporary account of tragedy, proves helpful in illuminating a sense in which boxing, like illness, holds a commerce with the tragic. The Greek word *pathos* is the term Aristotle used to describe one of the three crucial elements of tragic plot, and it is pathos that constitutes the foundation of the tragic structure.[29] "A *pathos*," Aristotle writes, "is a destructive or painful act, such as deaths on stage, paroxysms of pain, woundings, and all that sort of thing."[30] It is difficult to see how tragedy could exist without such acts of *pathos*. Yet what Aristotle does not say directly—perhaps because it seemed obvious—is that deaths, woundings, and paroxysms of pain all throw our attention on the vulnerable human body.

Oates in her discussion of boxing helps us recover the ancient sense, so clear in *Philoctetes*, that what occupies the center of the tragic stage is the human body and the mute fact of the body's vulnerability to pain. While the comic body is invulnerable, the body in tragedy is intrinsically open to injury. As in the famous paintings by George Wesley Bellows, boxing strips the individual down to an elemental level where our attention is fixed not only on the body but also on its approaching doom (figs. 28 and 29). Boxing, Oates writes, "forces our reluctant acknowledgement that the most profound experiences of our lives are physical events—though we believe ourselves to be, and surely are, essentially spiritual beings" (99). The body in boxing holds a status that we do not recognize in everyday life. "Like a dancer," as Oates put it, "a boxer 'is' his body, and is totally identified with it" (5). The body has become the main actor in the drama: it is through the body that we will come to know such qualities as grace, speed, courage, discipline, and generosity of spirit.

The boxer for Oates is not just an actor but—crucially—a tragic actor. She again cites Aristotle in order to emphasize how far boxing conforms to the requirements that tragic action should be serious, complete, and of significant magnitude. She also emphasizes that the action in the ring must be, like classical tragedy, removed from everyday life and utterly ritualized. The action thus requires a special place of performance, as well

FIGURE 28. George Wesley Bellows (1882–1925). *Stag at Sharkey's* (1909).
THE CLEVELAND MUSEUM OF ART, HINMAN B. HURLBUT COLLECTION, 1133.22

as an audience whose will it expresses. In the boxing ring as on the stage, the ordinariness of place is erased by an action that transcends it. The action in its speed and complexity takes the place of language. "So much happens so swiftly," she writes, "and with such heart-stopping subtlety you cannot absorb it except to know that something profound is happening and it is happening in a place beyond words" (11).

This is not glamorizing rhetoric. Oates does not hide the brutality of boxing. She is candid about her own quite visceral revulsion. "I feel it as vertigo—breathlessness—a repugnance beyond language," she writes, "a sheerly physical loathing" (102). Yet tragedy too confronts us with a brutal spectacle. Think of the bloody beard and blinded eyes of Oedipus, or Lear cradling the body of his murdered daughter. The real (if stylized)

FIGURE 29. George Wesley Bellows (1882–1925). *Both Members of This Club* (1909). NATIONAL GALLERY OF ART, WASHINGTON, CHESTER DALE COLLECTION

violence in the ring—in contrast to the fictive violence on stage—certainly distinguishes boxing from tragic drama, but also distinguishes it from every other sport. (Only in boxing do you win by knocking out your opponent.) As Oates observes shrewdly: "One *plays* football, one doesn't *play* boxing" (19).

Oates's emphasis on the violence of boxing helps to illuminate the idea I want to explore: that tragic pain continues to exist all around us. Violence matters to her for one reason. It matters because violence constitutes the only mode we know for confronting death. After the work of Ernest Becker, it would be hard to underestimate how far the modern world is committed to a denial of death.[31] The violence of boxing, however, becomes for Oates one of the rare occasions when our culture allows us (indirectly) to contemplate death. It is a spectacle in which the body encounters its double or dark other: nemesis, fate, annihilation. "The boxer," she writes, "meets an opponent who is a dream-distortion of himself in the sense that his weaknesses, his capacity to fail and to be seriously hurt, his intellectual miscalculations—all can be interpreted as strengths belonging to the Other" (12). This Other—with a capital O—is not just another fighter. The real fight is never simply Dempsey versus Firpo, or Ali versus Frazier. The boxer stands face-to-face with the embodiment of his own deepest fears and hidden weaknesses suddenly given menacing, destructive force. This powerful confrontation is what Oates calls "the body's dialogue with its shadow-Self—or Death" (18).

The stylized confrontation with violence and death that we witness in the ring makes boxing for Oates a modern remnant of ancient tragic drama. Boxing in this sense resembles writing. "Art is built around violence, around death," she says in her book on tragedy, and "at its base is fear."[32] Boxing concentrates this fear with almost primitive power in the small public space of the ring, and the fear always intensifies as the fight nears its conclusion, reminding Oates of "the bloody fifth acts of classical tragedies" (60). Boxing also resembles tragedy in that the conclusion, at some point, becomes inescapable. Death in tragedy is not accidental but, if such a metaphor can be allowed, almost mathematical. It follows inevitably from a relentless sequence of events already set in motion, like the adding up of a sum.

Boxing, of course, seeks to prevent real deaths. No doubt the few, well-publicized, accidental fatalities in the ring linger somewhere in the spectator's mind and lend an added tension to every match. The possibility of death is always present. But for Oates the emotional power of boxing depends less on the possibility of accidental death than upon the necessity of defeat. Here is how she describes her own response to the closing moments of a match:

The moment of visceral horror in a typical fight, at least as I experience it, is that moment when one boxer loses control, cannot maintain his defense, begins to waver, falter, fall back, rock with his opponent's punches which he can no longer absorb; the moment in which the fight is turned around, and in which an entire career, an entire life, may end. It is not an isolated moment but *the* moment— mystical, universal. The defeat of one man is the triumph of the other: but we are apt to read this "triumph" as merely temporary and provisional. Only the defeat is permanent (60–61).

Permanent defeat is the vision of tragedy. What redeems tragedy from utter bleakness is a sense that amid inescapable defeat we may sometimes rise to moments of awesome fortitude, grandeur, and almost inconceivable endurance.

The body is always the site of defeat in tragedy. It is not the body split from mind or spirit but rather, in Richard Selzer's phrase, the spirit thickened. Other forms of loss take in a wider sweep—ships sunk, cities burnt, whole armies put to the sword—but, no matter how wide its implications for a community or state, tragedy always shows us the defeat of the solitary human figure. Tragic pain nevertheless is not simply a spectacle of defeat: a medium for approaching, however indirectly, the repressed mystery of our own individual deaths. Oates sees pain in boxing as also a medium for fashioning a tragic-heroic resistance to defeat. Boxing, she claims, is less about hitting the opponent than about being hit.

Tragedy allows us to experience and to contemplate the paradox that inescapable defeat, with its approach toward death, may bring us close to grasping something essential that eludes us in the ordinary events of life. Only in pain—immersed in what Joseph Conrad called the destructive element—does the boxer, like the tragic hero, truly live. This is the thought that medicine finds so intolerable, why it must resist the tragic at all costs. "One sees clearly from the 'tragic' careers of any number of boxers," Oates writes, "that the boxer prefers physical pain in the ring to the absence of pain that is ideally the condition of ordinary life" (25). She sees boxing as a self-destructive pursuit that the boxer cannot avoid because avoiding pain means avoiding the exaltation that lifts him above the plane of everyday life. Tragic pain cannot be reduced to mere waste and loss. It affirms that even inescapable defeat may not wholly crush us.

An awareness of tragic pain will not merely alert us to its remnants in an everyday world that seems utterly removed from the regal arenas of Oedipus or Lear. It also reminds us that pain can serve a creative as well as destructive function. Oates argues, for example, that writers resemble boxers in their "systematic cultivation of pain in the interests of a project, a life-goal" (26). Such pain is less chosen or accepted than inseparably bound up with the combination of talent and obsession that drives some writers to write and some fighters to fight. Oates concedes that her own work is preoccupied with what she once called "the imagination of pain." Yet she returns to this subject so often, she explains, simply because "people need help with pain, never with joy." Thus what interests her is not pain itself ("it's a dead-end") but the human powers of compassion, survival, and creation which pain can elicit. In the midst of pain, she points out, people are "very often, irrationally, quite happy." Pain, she says, "has got to point beyond itself."[33]

Tragic pain, in pointing beyond itself, does not point to an optimistic world of Hollywood happy endings. Oates describes tragedy as "a therapy of the soul" in the sense that the tragic embrace of violence, suffering, and destruction shows us the (suppressed) reverse of our everyday lives.[34] "The terrible silence dramatized in the boxing ring," she writes, "is the silence of nature before man, before language, when the physical being alone was God" (69). Boxing takes us back to a ritualized world of bodies in action. It acquaints us with a silence that can be heard only in such moments of high tragic drama as Lear's howl, the agony of Oedipus, or the wounded cry of Philoctetes. We cannot linger or live in this world, but writing and boxing—in their contact with the tragic—can keep us from suppressing it entirely. "The use of language," Oates said in accepting the National Book Award, "is all we have to pit against death and silence."[35] Tragic pain, we might say, resists death and silence by acknowledging their presence. It places us in touch with the primal, unspoken world of the body where our answers and explanations always seem somehow beside the point. For Oates, the violence of boxing matters precisely because, like tragedy, it "cannot be assimilated into what we wish to know about civilized man" (99).

†

How could medicine benefit from what Oates and Sophocles have to show us? Certainly what we do not wish to know about civilized man includes the knowledge of our own deaths. We recognize we must die, of course, in the general way we accept other abstract or far-off truths, such as the information that one day the sun will burn out. Our own actual deaths, however, belong to the class of truths we simply do not want to know about. Not even the unconscious, as Freud once wrote, can accept the knowledge of our own deaths. Nowhere, indeed, is death so powerfully unacknowledged as in traditional modern medicine.

The medical resistance to death may seem entirely laudable, since we expect doctors to enhance health and to preserve life. Yet before the late nineteenth century, most deaths—like most births—occurred at home. We have effectively sequestered death in hospitals and other medical settings where it has lost contact with noninstitutional life. The impersonal and institutional character of modern death, which is simply another form of denial, seems so inescapable today that psychiatrist Elisabeth Kübler-Ross almost singlehandedly invented a new field with her book *On Death and Dying* (1969). Like the recent hospice movement she helped to inspire, Kübler-Ross sees death not as a last occasion for heroic medical labors but as a meaningful action that takes place in a rich setting of human relations and natural events. As she summarized:

It has been our life's work to help our patients view a terminal illness not as a destructive, negative force, but as one of the windstorms in life that will enhance their own inner growth and will help them to emerge as beautiful as the canyons which have been battered for centuries.[36]

Clearly, as the images of windstorm and canyon suggest, Kübler-Ross has invested the pain of terminal illness with a distinctive meaning, which includes its link to the beauty of natural process. Such images suggest a powerful contrast with the technologies that now enable medicine to delay death and to protract dying almost indefinitely. Tragedy tells us that the body must go down to defeat. Medicine cannot endure this thought.

It is consistent with our cultural resistance to tragedy that in 1984 the prestigious American Medical Association, after years of study and debate, passed a resolution calling for the abolition of boxing.[37] The AMA case against boxing expresses a praiseworthy desire to protect fighters from probable and measurable brain damage. Although there are far fewer accidental deaths from boxing than from football or baseball, the injury rate is high.[38] The most debilitating injuries to boxers, moreover, come not from knockout punches but from repeated subconcussive blows to the head. Studies show that an increased number of fights directly increases a boxer's likelihood of developing severe encephalopathy.[39] The so-called "punch-drunk" syndrome is unfortunately not a cinematic myth but accurately describes the slurred speech, ataxia, impaired memory, dementia, broad-based gait, and parkinsonian-like facial features that await many professional boxers.

The AMA is not alone in its call to ban boxing. The same call comes from the American Academy of Pediatrics, the American Association of Neurological Surgeons, the American Neurological Association, and the American Academy of Neurology. It comes from the British, Canadian, and Australian medical associations. It comes from the World Medical Association. Professional boxing is already banned in Sweden and Norway. There is no other way to say it: medicine and boxing are now mortal enemies.

The medical call to ban boxing, while undeniably sensible and humane, does not rest entirely on issues of health. For example, the AMA possesses reliable statistics about the far vaster damage to public health that tobacco and alcohol cause, and certainly *JAMA* has devoted many pages to exposing the dangers of smoking and drinking. Significantly, however, the AMA has never called for a ban on the sale of cigarettes or liquor. Why single out boxing? Does this selective ban perhaps express the special interests of members willing to give up Saturday night fights but unwilling to give up the cocktail hour? Is the boxing lobby less well funded than the alcohol and tobacco industries? Undoubtedly there is a covert moral argument at work. Its opponents depict boxing as a sport *about* violence, while defenders of violent sports such as football argue that the relentless damage to football players is merely incidental. The moral argument—brought out into the open—would run like this: violence is bad, boxing is about violence, therefore we should ban boxing.

The medical resistance to boxing, whatever its basis in logic, also reflects a fundamentally antitragic point of view. Medicine simply cannot carry out its work gripped by a vision of permanent defeat. The abolition of boxing proposed by the AMA offers a clear example of social power used to promote values and practices intended for our benefit. No one would dispute the good intentions of the AMA. Tragedy, however, reminds us that the best motives and intentions—such as Lear's scheme to divide his kingdom, or the plan by Oedipus to discover who killed his father—cannot cancel out the terrible suffering that life thrusts upon us. In tragedy, it is often good intentions that *create* suffering.

Medicine prolongs life and advises us how to live well. We are obviously lucky to have it around, even if perhaps slightly weary of measuring cholesterol levels and downing oat bran. Tragedy, like a dark alter ego, strips away the illusion that living well or eating well offers any protection against the destructive forces within ourselves and within our world that we cannot control or defeat but only endure, until endurance itself becomes too terrible to bear. Tragedy forces us to confront the suffering we normally evade, avert, or deny—a suffering that medicine too (as Cassell and Kleinman argue) turns away from. The body that medicine works so hard to keep healthy sooner or later goes down to defeat.

People continue to make self-destructive choices in pursuing goals that give their lives meaning. We may suffer for no reason except that we are mortal and therefore vulnerable. Boxing, like tragedy, accepts these stark facts.

The great heavyweight champion Muhammad Ali now suffers from what his physician calls "Parkinson syndrome secondary to pugilistic brain syndrome." Translated: Ali's tremor and slightly slurred speech result from brain damage received in boxing. Fortunately, there is no evidence of deterioration in his ability to think. Ali is still sharp, sly, still a consummate actor. He is also a deeply religious man scarred by his upbringing in the racist South. The man born Cassius Clay says that he sought fame as a boxer in order to help his race: "I saw Negroes being put out of white restaurants, I saw Negroes being hung, a boy named Emmett Till, castrated and burned up. I said I'm gonna be a boxer and I'm gonna get famous so I can help my people." The costs to his health have been high. But he is adamant. Referring to his current impairments, he says simply: "If you told me I could go back in my life and start over healthy and that with boxing this would happen—stay Cassius Clay and it wouldn't—I'd take this route. It was worth it."[40]

Joyce Carol Oates is right: the victory is always temporary in boxing, only defeat is permanent. She is also right that tragic pain differs from ordinary waste or senseless suffering. It brings with it the possibility of subordinating or transcending pain in the pursuit of a choice or goal, even if pursuing such a goal is unwise and unhealthy, even if (like Ahab's quest of the white whale) it ultimately assures destruction. Her analysis of boxing matters finally because it is not merely about boxing. It is about the possibilities for understanding contemporary pain in such a way as to recognize it as meaningful. Tragic choices and tragic events are by definition unhealthy. Yet tragedy would tell us that we might be much healthier as a culture if we did not turn away from suffering, if we stopped trying to cancel pain and to prolong life at all costs, and if we gave up trying to ban or to remove from sight everything that frightens us with the premonition of our own death.

12
THE FUTURE OF PAIN

The critical (in the literary sense) and the clinical (in the medical sense) may be
destined to enter into a new relationship of mutual learning.
GILLES DELEUZE[1]

T HERE IS NO conclusion to the study of pain. The
neuroanatomy and neurophysiology of pain still
remain imperfectly understood. More important,
the cultural contexts in which we experience pain continue to change. It
is thus impossible to close the door: to say that pain henceforth means
exactly this or this and no more. Yet, if we cannot reach a conclusion in
the sense of securing a decisive feeling of closure, it is possible to attain
a kind of summarizing perspective from which the past and future begin
to look clearer. That is my purpose here. Not somehow to settle pain, once
and for all, but to suggest where it is going, what its direction will be.
The best way to gain this perspective, I think, is through several concluding images that seem to capture—as if recapitulating or condens-
ing—the argument I have been presenting that pain is never simply a
matter of nerves and neurotransmitters but always requires a personal
and cultural encounter with meaning. The question at issue is whether
these meanings in the future will be ample and sustaining or thin and
sterile. Will the meanings we discover in pain help us or merely increase
our feeling of affliction?

†

The immediate past should now be coming into focus. It is certain that
for the past four or five generations we have been living with an organic
model of pain inherited from the mid-nineteenth century. "It is astonish-

ing," wrote George L. Engel in 1959 in the *American Journal of Medicine*, "how little discussions of pain in standard textbooks of medicine have changed in the past hundred years."[2] Indeed, almost everything else in medicine has undergone dramatic transformations since the Civil War. Birth now takes place in gleaming, skyscraper hospitals under the care of obstetricians whose profession did not exist before the turn of the century. Death is a clinical phenomenon measured out in brain waves. Most important, we have seen medicine transformed from a household practice, usually supervised by wives or aunts, into a high-priced, high-tech commodity produced by specialists, regulated by government agencies, and sold to consumers by massive corporations. As historian Paul Starr writes:

In early American society, medicine was relatively insignificant as an economic institution. Insofar as care of the sick remained within the family and communal circle, it was not a commodity: It had no price in money and was not "produced" for exchange, as were the trained skills and services of doctors. But when people in sickness and distress resorted to physicians, paid for hospital care, or bought patent medicines instead of preparing their own remedies, medical care passed from the household into the market.[3]

The dominance of the organic model during the last hundred years doubtless owes much to the way in which pain, too, has passed irrecoverably from the household into the marketplace.

The marketing of pain since the Civil War has certainly helped to disseminate a general belief that pain operates solely through the transmission of nerve impulses from the site of tissue damage to the brain. The scientific discoveries supporting this organic model in the nineteenth century were so impressive that any other hypothesis seemed simply out-of-date. Today the most innovative work in contemporary pain treatment suggests, however, that the old organic model needs a major overhaul. One researcher examined records of 10,533 back injuries from 1977 in the state of Washington. Patients with low back pain accounted for over one-third of all compensation payments and received some $63.5 million. It would be hard to deny that pain has entered the marketplace. Astonishingly, in 75 percent of these patients there was no finding of organic damage.[4]

The old organic model—keyed to an understanding of acute pain—simply will not account for the waves of chronic pain now sweeping over the modern world. It sputters and wheezes when forced to work with the new idea that pain is not a sensation but a perception: an experience in which consciousness, emotion, meaning, and social context all play an important part. It is clear that research conducted on cats and rats, however helpful, cannot tell us much about the cognitive and psychosocial dimension of chronic pain in humans. Specialists, as we have seen, now emphasize how far chronic pain eludes therapies that presuppose a simple sensory mechanism for transmitting nociceptive impulses from the site of tissue damage to the brain. The body, we are learning, contains multiple pain pathways. Its resources include not only the central nervous system but the sympathetic and parasympathetic systems as well, which influence the limbic system governing our emotions and thus make chronic pain always a psychological state. We still do not understand fully what happens to the nociceptive impulse at the level of the cerebral cortex, but it is certain that the thalamus relays the signal it receives to the higher cerebral centers of consciousness. Pain, in effect, is no mere physiological event. It is simultaneously emotional, cognitive, and social.

The future is likely to see large numbers of doctors and patients supplement or replace the old one-dimensional organic model with a new multidimensional model that encompasses the intersecting physiological, emotional, cognitive, and social aspects of pain. Pain, as I have been claiming, is not a simple, static, universal code of nerve impulses but an experience that continues to change as it passes through the complicated zones of interpretation we call culture, history, and individual consciousness. We need to start listening to the specialists in pain centers who are arguing (on the basis of striking new research) what various patients and writers have been saying, implicitly, for years: that anything beyond the most commonplace acute pain is a complex perceptual experience taking place not strictly within the individual nervous system but also within the open-ended, social field of human thought and action. Pain, we are slowly beginning to recognize, is far more than merely a medical issue. It exists within us only as it wraps itself up, for better or worse, in meaning.

†

The future will look clearer if we contrast two very different pictures of pain. The first is the well-known kneeling figure that Descartes in the seventeenth century included in his *Treatise of Man* (fig. 30). Cartesian physiology still employed the idea that the body moved with the assistance of small organisms called "animal spirits" that were produced and stored in the brain. These minute rarefied particles traveled through nerves sup-

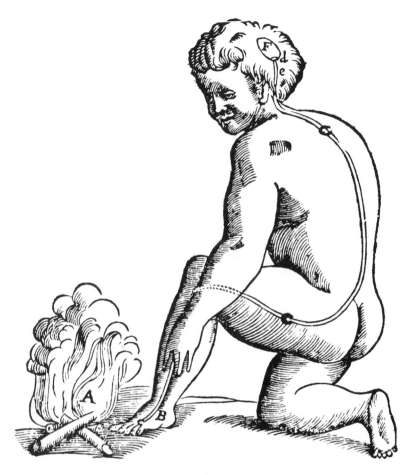

FIGURE 30. René Descartes (1596–1650). Illustration from *De l'homme* (1664).

posed to resemble hollow tubes containing tiny filaments that terminate in the brain.[5] The bodily response to pain, as Descartes described it, worked like a simple mechanism. The fast-moving particles of fire disturb the filaments in the nerve. The disturbance passes along the length of the nerve filament until it reaches the brain, where it activates the animal spirits. The animal spirits in turn travel down through the nerves to the muscles, producing the movement that removes, say, foot from flame. The direct, causal relation that Descartes understood between the injury and the pain is reflected in his mechanistic analogy. The impulse traveling from the site of injury to the brain, he explains, produces pain "just as, pulling on one end of a cord, one simultaneously rings a bell which hangs at the opposite end."[6]

Descartes's rope-pull model of pain is a direct predecessor of the organic model developed in the mid-nineteenth century. Doctors and researchers adhering to the organic model now talk about nociceptive impulses and endorphins rather than about filaments and animal spirits, but the basic idea is the same. They view pain as the result of a universal, internal mechanism that sends a signal from the injury to the brain. The implications of this mechanistic view will prove most revealing if we observe what is absent from the Cartesian diagram. Notice how Descartes suspends his human figure in a limbo without time or space. There is literally no ground to stand on. The diagram cannot tell us whether the figure is French or English, whether he is a Christian, Moslem, or Jew. Its blankness probably reflects a desire to situate scientific truth in an abstract or universal realm beyond the irrelevant historical accidents of a specific time and place. But the vacancy of the drawing is exactly the point. Descartes, in this early version of the organic model, gives us what amounts to a picture of pain in a vacuum.

There is one more important omission that we should notice in the diagram. Descartes deliberately leaves out any details that would indicate whether the figure belongs to the aristocracy or to the lower classes. "One of the effects of civilization (not to say one of the ingredients in it)," wrote the nineteenth-century philosopher John Stuart Mill, "is, that the spectacle, and even the very idea, of pain, is kept more and more out of the sight of those classes who enjoy in their fullness the benefits of civilization."[7] Civilization, that is, not only insulates the upper classes from discomfort but is built upon the pain of the masses. This distasteful idea, of course, has nothing to do with Descartes's diagram, but that is because the diagram on principle excludes it. A detached, blank, scientific representation of pain allows us to believe that pain is simply a mechanical response like pulling a bell-rope. The Cartesian model allows us to think that the bitter lives of the poor and homeless are merely an irrelevant historical accident, cut off from questions of pain. The diagram conveniently allows us to forget altogether about poverty, fear, hunger, and oppression in favor of scientific talk about nerve filaments and animal spirits.

Scientific theories, as scholars now emphasize, are not timeless but rather rooted in a very human history of science. The organic model of pain in fact reflects a deliberate assault, in the manner of Sade, on earlier ways of understanding that nineteenth-century scientists judged wholly

FIGURE 31. Piero della Francesca (*c.* 1420–1492). *The Flagellation*
(*c.* 1450). GALLERIA NAZIONALE DELLE MARCHE, PALAZZO DUCALE, URBINO, ITALY

inadequate. It will be useful, thus, to consider a second illustration suggesting just how far Descartes and his modern successors have managed to strip away the complex fabric of human cultural experience that once enfolded pain. The enigmatic painting *The Flagellation* by Piero della Francesca, created some two hundred years before Descartes, about 1460, ranks among the most famous artifacts of the early Renaissance (fig. 31).

The Flagellation sets pain within a rich field of social and psychological meaning. What first attracted art historians to the painting was Piero's brilliant architectural treatment of space. Unlike earlier medieval painters, Piero treats spatial perspective in ways that allow an exact estimate of heights, widths, and distances. For our purposes, however, the visual accuracy matters mainly as it proves appropriate for a complex drama played out in historical space and time. In fact, the painting depicts *two* specific and vastly different spaces and times. The trio of figures standing to the right clearly inhabits the contemporary world of quattrocento Italy. Within the interior, we see another trio of figures: the two torturers who stand on either side of Jesus with their whips upraised, as Pontius Pilate and a mysterious turbaned figure look on.

The painting indeed is full of mysteries. Who are the three well-dressed contemporary figures? What are they doing at this biblical scene of flagellation? Why should the flagellation (whose theological importance is paramount) proceed in the background? Such questions have sparked a variety of ingenious and often conflicting explanations. It is not surprising—given the current split between medicine and the arts—that none of the commentators directly addresses the question we need to ask here. How does the painting invite us to think about pain? The answer turns out to be closely entwined with an account of Piero's strange mixture of disparate historical places and times.

The best explanation of the painting (so far) has been proposed by Marilyn Aronberg Lavin.[8] She identifies the contemporary group on the right as portraying two powerful Renaissance figures: Ludovico Gonzaga, a nobleman, and Ottaviano Ubaldini della Carda, a famous astrologer. (As befits his occult profession, Ottaviano wears an exotic, Eastern-style hat.) Both men, she shows, had each recently lost a son, one to death, the other to crippling disease. The barefoot youth standing between the two bereaved fathers thus represents an idealized, angelic "son"—whose loss brings them together. Their loss, meanwhile, is also what helps explain why Piero should represent them as if standing alongside the biblical scene of flagellation. The subject of the painting, we might say, is pain ancient and modern, visible and invisible. The presence of pain is what draws the two disparate historical scenes into a single field of thought.

There is something very peculiar, however, about this scene of loss and flagellation. What strikes a modern viewer at once is the apparent absence of emotion. The faces in the painting appear impassive, almost expressionless. An effort to explain—not just shrug off—this strange representation of pain must take us back to the flagellation. Jesus in effect accepts the blows of the two torturers with a calm that provides a model for the two bereaved fathers. It is as if Piero had set out to dramatize—in biblical Judea and in quattrocento Italy—a Christian understanding of pain. Ludovico and Ottaviano accept their loss in the spirit of an imitation of Christ. Their grief and the suffering of their sons becomes comprehen-

THE FUTURE OF PAIN

sible, no matter how painful, through the parallel with the suffering inflicted on the Son of God, which Piero depicts Jesus accepting as God's will. The painting serves both as a memorial and as a meditative source of consolation. Lavin shows that it would have fit directly in front of the altar in Ludovico's private chapel.

Piero and Descartes, then, offer two very different perspectives on pain. Piero seeks to make pain comprehensible by placing it within a complexly layered historical world of religious meaning, social values, and personal loss. Descartes purposely strips away the social and psychological meanings of pain to expose almost an x-ray picture of a universal human nervous system. It is probably high time that the flagellation of Descartes should stop, because he distinguishes himself from his later mechanistic followers by insisting that we do not feel pain until the physical motion of the nerve fibers and animal spirits is perceived by the mind or soul. (This insistence explains his otherwise bizarre claim that animals do not feel pain; Descartes believed that animals, by definition, cannot possess minds or souls.) Whatever his role in the origin of the modern organic model, the post-Cartesian world has very successfully out-descarted Descartes. It has perfected a pain so stripped down that it has almost no meaning and no social value at all.

†

The meanings and social implications concealed in our everyday encounters with pain came clear to me quite powerfully as I talked with chronic-pain patients. I remember two patients who especially opened my eyes. One was a middle-aged woman, short, overweight, timid. She endured the examinations of the medical staff without comment and without question. Everything in her manner suggested that she put complete faith in their expertise, but for this reason she grew increasingly depressed as week after week passed with no progress. She had worked as a drill-press operator in a factory where she stood beside the same machine eight hours each day. Now her elbow hurt so badly that she could not work. She had no immediate family and always came alone to her appointment at the pain clinic.

One day after her appointment we talked for more than an hour. I made the mistake of asking if her injury had caused major changes in her life. Suddenly this composed, quiet woman, who had sat through her treatment almost in total silence, sobbed and sobbed. She told me that the high point of her life was playing the organ for her church choir. She lived for the twice-a-week practices and Sunday performances. Now, with pain immobilizing her elbow, she could no longer manage the keyboard. Her days held nothing that she looked forward to. The constant aching had robbed her of any hope. Life seemed empty of everything except pain. When I asked her if she had explained this to the staff of the clinic, she replied that they had not asked. Her medical history, as one might expect, read exactly like the history of an elbow.

The second patient was a burly young construction worker in his mid-thirties. When I met him at the pain clinic he was wearing cut-off jeans over a full leg cast, although he was not complaining about his leg but about chronic headaches and back pain. He was starting his second week of treatment and understood the clinic's philosophy that chronic pain was often reinforced or sustained by unresolved emotional and psychological trauma. He cheerfully introduced himself to me as "the nut," and during the two hours of group therapy he seemed to play a self-appointed, unofficial role as jester. His comic, offhand comments suggested a deep skepticism toward the view that his pain could be influenced by psychological or emotional states. As the discussion turned to the question of fear, however, he suddenly stopped joking and his face turned pale. What did fear have to do with pain?

The story he told explained a lot. His young daughter needed an expensive operation. The only way he could pay for the operation was to work at a job where he drove a truck packed with explosives through a network of tunnels so narrow that one false move would kill him instantly. He was unable to sleep. Every day on the job was a terrifying ordeal. The obvious solution was to change jobs. "I'm a laborer," he said. "There's nowhere else I can earn this kind of money." So he risked his life each day to pay for his daughter's operation, and the pain just kept coming.

These two patients are quite typical in the personal and social histories attached to their chronic pain. Many of the patients treated in a pain center are covered by Workers' Compensation, but an on-the-job injury may not account for all the pain they experience. Sociologist Lillian Breslow Rubin gave her impressive study of life in the American working-class family the appropriate title (borrowed from poet John Masefield) *Worlds of Pain*.[9] It is easy to understand why the specific pain for which an individual receives treatment may prove difficult to cure when patients live in a world dominated by multiple forms of hardship and distress over which they have little control.

The social histories of working-class pain patients often read like especially brutal soap operas. Women may live with violent alcoholic husbands who beat or sexually abuse them. They may feel trapped in menial jobs under harsh employers. Their health begins to deteriorate and they put on weight. One day, as surely as overwork leads to injury, they simply wear out as the chief caretakers for chaotic and unappreciative families. Men too often have a concealed social history of trauma backing up their chronic pain. It may begin with abusive or negligent parents and continue through military combat with its delayed shock and nightmares. Like their wives, they often feel simply worn out after years of hard labor at low pay. A list of conditions that frequently accompany chronic pain would include divorce, rape, spouse-abuse, incest, depression, child-abuse, grief, alcoholism, obesity, suicide, bankruptcy, drug addiction, unemployment, dead-end jobs, and quarrelsome, impossible families. The serious question in some cases is why the individual should *not* feel pain.

The social history of an individual's pain is often compounded by an equally complex psychological history. Patients who are angry and afraid steadfastly deny feeling anger or fear. Often deeply felt emotions of grief and guilt, for example, find no outlet or resolution. Sometimes the trauma is quite idiosyncratic. A woman who had survived a highway crash that killed her husband later suffered inexplicable chronic pain after a runaway car crashed through the window of a convenience store and nearly struck her. We should not doubt our (unconscious) ingenuity in producing whatever pain we need in order to give expression to woes of the spirit that may be explicit or highly inexplicit. One emotionally troubled patient I interviewed said of her pain: "I can only describe it vaguely because, after you've lived with it so long, it kind of spreads and gets vague." Such pain no doubt has a lot of ground to cover.

Chronic pain, of course, is far more than a working-class problem. It knows no boundaries of class, race, gender, or profession. Executives, lawyers, accountants, teachers, stockbrokers, managers—anyone living in the fast-paced, fast-buck societies of the Western world—can suddenly fall into the hell of an inexplicable pain that will not end. (It is easy to speculate on the multiple reasons why chronic pain does not constitute a significant medical problem in non-Western cultures.) Upscale lives have their own impasses and trauma. Moreover, the well-to-do may find it particularly hard to break free from the cycle of endless referrals from specialist to specialist. As long as we cling to the belief that somewhere hidden in the maze of the body an overlooked organic injury is sending out its electrochemical code for pain, we are likely to remain prisoners of nineteenth-century medicine. The future of pain requires that we move on to a new, less certain way of thinking.

†

The future, as I have been contending, will no longer think of rigidly separate categories called physical pain and mental pain. We might represent The Myth of Two Pains as two closed fists. Now imagine that the hands are open and the fingers interlaced. Pain, especially chronic pain, calls forth some such interlacing of mind and body. It is physiological, to be sure. But, as Richard A. Sternbach was arguing as far back as 1968, the physiology of pain is also powerfully adjusted by broadly cognitive influences such as meaning, emotion, and culture.[10] Clinical treatment that concentrates on body alone or mind alone is unlikely to succeed with difficult cases of chronic pain. When the nerve block wears off, when the analgesic loses its potency, when the electrical stimulation grows familiar, the pain may return even more deeply entrenched for its power to overcome all of our technological prowess.

We can say of pain in general what neurologist Oliver Sacks says of the distinctive and peculiarly debilitating form of headache called migraine. "A migraine," he writes, "is a physical event which may also be from the start, or later become, an emotional or symbolic event. A migraine expresses both physiological and emotional needs: it is the prototype of a psychophysiological reaction."[11] This complex (psychophysiological) understanding of illness is exactly what led Sacks toward an almost novelistic writing that, as he says, deepens a case history into a narrative or tale. Pain, as Sacks writes of migraine, becomes a symbolic event whenever it overlaps with our personal and cultural needs to discover a meaning in our affliction, which is to say that it is almost always a symbolic event, even when pain (as initially for Ivan Ilych) symbolizes merely the meaninglessness of everyday bumps and bruises. The meaninglessness we attribute to such pain helps us to deal with it. If the flesh heals but the ache persists, our fears about the meaning of this abnormal turn of events can transform a mere bruise into a crisis.

We might take as a final summarizing example of the underground, symbolic meanings intrinsic to pain the curious practice known as couvade. Couvade (from the French verb meaning "to hatch") refers to a set of customs surrounding childbirth in cultures both ancient and modern.[12] In its more colorful version, the woman gives birth with often no more than a brief pause from her work in the fields. The father meanwhile takes to his bed. He groans and writhes at great length. Sometimes the newly delivered mother returns to wait on her bedridden husband, as relatives drop by to offer him their congratulations. This practice has appeared in societies so far flung as to suggest that couvade is more than an isolated curiosity. We can trace its impact on world literature from the *Argonautica*, written by Apollonius of Rhodes in the first century, to James Joyce's *Ulysses* (1922).[13]

Explanations for the custom vary. Some theories emphasize the establishment of a patriarchal bond between child and father, while other theories (no doubt concocted by male anthropologists) suggest that its function is somehow to ease the physical ordeal for the mother. The practice of couvade, however, cannot be relegated to the hinterlands of anthropology. Medical journals today describe a condition known as "couvade syndrome" affecting, at a minimum, some 10 to 20 percent of all expectant fathers.[14] While the woman is pregnant, the father experiences numerous ailments related to pregnancy, including nausea, vomiting, weight gain, or anorexia. Not surprisingly, abdominal pain ranks among the most common symptoms.[15]

The pain of couvade syndrome is sometimes quite severe. One father, an ex-infantryman who had served in Vietnam, experienced a sharp, constant, squeezing, incapacitating torment in the lower abdomen with radiation to the low back and sacral area.[16] Several researchers sensibly propose that such pains are owing in large part to anxiety or to severe psychological disturbance. Certainly, the men suffering from couvade syndrome are not willing to accept suggestions that their pain is "unreal," "imaginary," or "all in the head." The pain, like the pain of hysteria, is as real as a brick. As Sacks says of migraine, we are dealing with a physical event that is also a symbolic event—or, more accurately in this case, events that are inseparably physical and symbolic.

The men suffering from couvade syndrome understand the meaning of their pain in different, often curious, ways. One husband interpreted his symptoms as evidence that he was the biological father, and he worried during his wife's pregnancies when he did *not* experience them.[17] The crucial point is that the pain of couvade syndrome—like pain in general—holds numerous meanings, sometimes not only personal but absolutely unique. The point, so easily ignored in examples less exotic than couvade syndrome, has profound implications for the future of pain. We need to acknowledge that pain can serve multiple purposes and hold multiple meanings beyond its basic function as a signal of tissue damage. Such an acknowledgment is hard to make, especially for doctors faithful to their training, because it completely revises our understanding of pain. Yet it can also help us construct a future vastly different from the present and the past.

The most limiting feature of the old organic model is its implication that—outside the narrow limits of medical knowledge—pain is simply meaningless: no more than the effect of nociceptive impulses speeding through the nervous system. This nineteenth-century model so completely superseded other ways of thought, as we have seen, that questions about the meaning of pain became entirely irrelevant. What possible meaning does a neurotransmitter possess? It simply is. Yet, as it has turned out, for patients who must live daily with the presence of an unremitting chronic affliction, the concept of a truly meaningless pain rapidly begins to approach the inhuman. Meaninglessness now adds its weight to the burden of affliction.

One important contribution of this study, I hope, is to suggest that the meaninglessness of modern pain is not an unchanging or permanent fact but rather belongs to a specific historical time and place. We might consider it among the founding cultural myths of modernism. In effect, ever since the middle of the nineteenth century we have been living through the era of modernist pain. Modernist pain is not simply the invention of doctors and researchers but has received the endorsement, to varying degrees, of numerous writers from Samuel Beckett through Joseph Heller. It is affliction stripped of its previous cultural and personal significance until it emerges as nothing more than a meaningless sensation shooting along the nerves. Modernist pain is meaningless pain: the expression of a grand theory that reduces all affliction not merely "mental" to the dimensions of a mechanistic event taking place solely within the circuits of the human nervous system.

The future will not completely reject the old organic model. It explains a great deal about acute pain, and we have much yet to learn about the ascending and descending systems within the body for transmitting and for modifying nociceptive signals. But the limitations of the organic model have been clear for several decades. The resulting breakdown has not yet emerged as front-page news, but the word is spreading, and it cannot be stopped. We are living through a transition that has some years to run before the change in thinking about pain is complete. Transitions, of course, are almost always confusing. This is in some ways an especially difficult time to suffer chronic pain. Still, change is coming. It is thus critical to ask what lies ahead when the transition has run its course. What, we need to ask, would it be like to enter an entirely new era of postmodern pain?

†

We can be certain to see new research and new rules in the arena of medical treatment. The most immediately practical research has shown that various drugs act at different sites in the central nervous system. Thus researchers are able to map new strategies for providing drugs in combination, so that they can act simultaneously on separate parts of the body's far-flung pain control network. Another important innovation—introduced in 1984, but still too expensive for general use—is called "patient-controlled analgesia" (PCA). It often involves a computerized pump (containing a solution of morphine or some other opioid analgesic) attached by an intravenous line to the patient's arm. By pushing a button, the patient delivers a premeasured dose from the pump. The computer sets safety limits, so that the patient cannot receive too large a dose, but the safeguards most often prove unnecessary. Studies show that PCA patients experience a diminished perception of pain, use less medication, and have shorter hospital stays than patients receiving analgesics through normal modes of delivery.[18] Patients clearly feel better as their sense of control increases. Pain no longer looms as a towering menace when we know we are not wholly at its mercy.

Much of the research currently in progress does not yet show practical applications, but our growing knowledge of the brain will surely lead to new therapies for pain. Among the discoveries most exciting in its implications is the work on rat brainstems by Howard L. Fields and his colleagues. Their research shows that the rat brainstem contains not only a well-known type of neuron that blocks the transmission of pain ("off" cells) but also—here is the surprise—a previously unknown type of neuron that *facilitates* pain transmission ("on" cells). The survival value of a system to block pain seems clear. It is less clear at first why animals might need the "on" cells that constitute a pain-enhancing system. Fields offers one explanation for the presence of these newly discovered "on" cells. "By attending to the pain, or the possibility of pain," he suggests, "you are juicing up the pain pathway. . . ."[19] A pathway juiced up by the action of pain-enhancing "on" cells, if they exist in humans, would provide us with a supersensitive warning system when there is danger. It also may help to account for the vicious circle inhabited by a person in chronic pain, whose "on" cells would continue to fire and to enhance the perception of pain because the danger he or she now anticipates is the peril of uninterrupted chronic pain.

It is not necessary to wait for the practical applications of such current research in order to recognize that recent work is now generating a series of new rules on pain. Long-standing medical habits are under direct attack. For example, the pioneering pain specialist Ronald Melzack recently published an essay entitled "The Tragedy of Needless Pain," in which he argues at length against the myths and misconceptions that prevent doctors from prescribing adequate doses of morphine.[20] The traditional hospital prescription for painkilling medication gives the charge PRN (*pro re nata*, or "as needed"). Yet, unlike "patient-controlled analgesia," medication dispensed PRN by the hospital staff comes only after understandable delays; it may not be administered intravenously and thus not get immediately into the bloodstream; and it often actually increases the patient's discomfort, anxiety, and dangers of dependence. Today specialists recommend that patients receive pain medication at regularly scheduled invervals: ATC (around the clock).

Some cancer patients (though too few) now benefit directly from the efforts of an innovative group called the Wisconsin Cancer Pain Initiative.[21] These bold individuals have set up a statewide system designed to educate physicians and patients about cancer pain, and their work has given rise to similarly vigorous groups in Vermont and Pennsylvania. They deliver the message that pain is the most common symptom in advanced cancer and that in almost all cases it can be effectively controlled with the proper use of available drugs, especially morphine. They are fighting mainly the ingrained habits of doctors for whom questions about pain never appeared on medical school exams. It takes hard work to convince physicians and state regulatory commissions that prevention of pain is as important as relief, that pain tolerance varies greatly among individuals, that narcotic drugs are not addictive in a hospital population, that large doses can be given safely without damaging side effects, and that the need for medication differs significantly at different stages in the process of an unstable disease such as cancer. Clearly this is a message that needs to be heard in more than three states.

The new rules for the treatment of pain find an especially clear statement in an article appearing in *The New England Journal of Medicine* entitled "The Physician's Responsibility Toward Hopelessly Ill Patients" (1989). The twelve doctors listed as coauthors (banded together perhaps for the safety or authority of number) side with the many patients and families who fear that physicians allow dying patients to suffer needless pain. They insist that "textbook doses" recommended for short-term pain are "grossly inadequate" for long-term pain in the patient dying of cancer. They pull no punches about how much medication to prescribe. "The proper dose of pain medication," they say plainly, "is the dose that is sufficient to relieve pain and suffering, even to the point of unconsciousness." The authors in effect signal a new day in medical thinking about pain. Indeed, they no longer treat pain as simply an object of scientific knowledge but as the subject of pressing moral inquiry. Their unequivocal conclusion reaches far beyond the realm of the hopelessly ill to articulate a founding principle of postmodern medicine: "To allow a patient to experience unbearable pain or suffering is unethical medical practice."[22]

†

We can look a little further into our postmodern future with the help of French philosopher Jean-François Lyotard.[23] Lyotard defines postmodernism as the condition in which vast, overarching, general systems of explanation (he calls them "metanarratives") lose their power. Christianity stands as one example of a metanarrative, in the sense that it tells an overarching story that runs from the creation of the universe to the end of time. (Indeed, as a metanarrative it automatically encompasses a large number of smaller narratives, such as the story of the Last Supper and the Resurrection.) Marxism is another example of a metanarrative, in the sense that it tells an overarching story about the development of society from its agrarian past to its utopian post-capitalist future. The organic model of pain certainly constitutes another overarching metanarrative. It tells us that all pain, of every kind, is merely the result of nociceptive impulses traveling along neural pathways between the site of tissue damage and the brain. Such pain—no matter how full of sound and fury—means only one thing: nothing. Within the metanarrative of the organic model, pain is always and completely meaningless.

Postmodern pain, if we follow Lyotard's scheme, would be pain that cannot be enfolded within a single overarching metanarrative or system of explanation. It is a pain that has recovered or discovered its multiple voices.[24] The old organic model remains one of these voices, of course, not only because of its longevity but also because it contains a very potent element of truth. That indeed is why it has been so successful in silencing or subjugating all other cultural discourse on pain. In a postmodern world, however, the organic model can no longer hold sway as the sole or even dominant voice. Instead, postmodern pain calls into being multiple systems or subsystems of explanation, each with its own distinctive language or discourse, none of which holds absolute priority. It promises not so much a chaos or babel of competing tongues as the possibility that we may learn how to enrich our knowedge of pain by listening to more than one voice.

The transition to a more ample knowledge of pain is certainly under way. We have already seen how contemporary theologian Gustavo Gutierrez proposes to understand the pain of Latin American masses as a sign of organized sin and injustice against the poor. Surgeon-writer Richard Selzer has recovered and revitalized an understanding that links pain with beauty. His fellow writer Joyce Carol Oates provides a different but related view of pain as a medium for tragic struggle. Writers clearly will have an important role in a postmodern understanding of pain because they deal so directly with questions of meaning. But meaning is not the exclusive province of writers. Doctors and patients, advertisers and manufacturers, athletes and dancers, theologians, housewives, and philosophers will all have a significant role in developing a new awareness of the meanings of pain.

A multiplicity of understandings, of course, implies that your pain and my pain might have totally different explanations and meanings. Postmodern pain could still be meaningless, for example, but only if an individual chose or came to understand it so (in which case, paradoxically, meaninglessness would count as a kind of meaning—not just a blindly suffered condition). For someone else, affliction might contain several different meanings—even meanings that threatened to contradict or to cancel each other out. We would be living amid a multitude of alternative explanations for pain. The resulting uncertainty may bring its own discomforts. The most important compensation for an inevitable uncertainty, however, is that pain will have reestablished the link with meaning that ties it to culture, history, and individual lives. It will be a more human pain.

There are voices already present in our culture—however muted or subjugated—that suggest what such a postmodern multiplicity of narratives might contain. Nietzsche, so often ahead of his time, offers one illustration. His failing health forced him into retirement in 1879, yet he managed his ailments in a manner both idiosyncratic and typically shrewd. "I have given a name to my pain," he wrote, "and call it 'dog.' It is just as faithful, just as obtrusive and shameless, just as entertaining, just as clever as any other dog—and I can scold it and vent my bad mood on it, as others do with their dogs, servants, and wives."[25] "Dogs, servants, and wives" is a category that carries the musty odor of a previous century, even if employed here in a comic vein. The useful point to grasp, however, is that Nietzsche has in effect taken charge of his pain. He has assigned it a personal place and meaning. His crucial move, in fact, is to assign his pain a position of inferiority. He may be inescapably bound to pain, as if to an obnoxious pet, but he still claims the power to define the relationship. Nietzsche decides, typically, that he will be the master rather than the slave.

The accounts written by numerous patients today indicate that the master/slave relationship still dominates our experience of pain. Too many patients implicitly accept a definition of their illness that enslaves them and makes pain the master. A postmodern vision would undermine a sense that we are slaves to pain (or even occasionally masters) by encouraging alternative ways of thinking. Paul Valéry, for example, another writer ahead of his time, created the portrait of a semiautobiographical character named Monsieur Teste. Teste—a hero of intellect—lived a life committed to pure reason. A sudden illness, however, brought him abruptly up against the undeniable fact of his own body. He looked at his pain with eyes of wonder. "This is very odd," he began:

Suddenly, I can see into myself. . . . I can make out the depths of the layers of my flesh; I feel zones of pain . . . rings, poles, plumes of pain. Do you see these living forms, this geometry of my suffering? There are certain flashes that are exactly like ideas. They make me understand—from here, to there. . . . Yet they leave me uncertain. "Uncertain" is not the word. . . . When *it* is coming on, I find something confused or diffused inside me. Inside my *self* . . . foggy places arise, there are open expanses that come into view.[26]

The pure rationalist comes to understand pain through a visual experience whose strange rings and flashes bring a new insight into the limits of understanding: an unexpected recognition of how far the mind shares its power with the mysteries of our bodily life—mysteries that bring us into contact with whatever is uncertain or diffused or foggy within ourselves.

The geometrical abstractness that Monsieur Teste sees in pain bears a striking resemblance to the vision of another extraordinary figure. This anonymous man, studied for years by the eminent Russian neurologist A. R. Luria, had a memory so tenacious that he could effortlessly recall vast pages of print. Anything he could visualize he not only remembered but also—this was the curse—could not forget. It was a power, like Edward Gibson's strange insensibility to pain, that finally left him unfit for normal human life. In an entry for 1935 he writes that his greatest difficulty comes in understanding and in remembering words he is unable to visualize. "When I hear the word *pain*, for example," he explains, "I see bands—little round objects, and fog. It's the fog that has to do with the abstractness of the word."[27]

We are not used to thinking of pain as abstract. But perhaps we should begin to try. In one sense, there is nothing less abstract than a sharp stab in the abdomen that can bring us, like Philoctetes, to our knees. Yet, as we have seen, humankind has continued to remake pain into meanings that change over time and across cultures, as if pain were a clay ready to be refashioned into different shapes. A postmodern pain would be a pain in which we at last recognize and consciously employ our power to create and to reshape its meanings. It is a pain in which we would avoid the traps that confine us, unknowingly, to the role of slaves or of passive, hopeless "thick-folder" patients. It is a pain we may choose finally, in the terms proposed by Norman Cousins, to defy rather than to deny.[28]

✝

Defiance is among the most important stances that may come to characterize the new postmodern attitudes toward pain. "Fuck pain," says the black novelist Ishmael Reed. "The crying towel doesn't show up in my writing."[29] A similar tone runs through the searing elegies composed by writer Paul Monette on the death of his lover, Roger Horwitz. The poems proceed in a raw, unpunctuated rush of grief and rage, as in the elegy entitled "Gardenias," which begins:

> pain is not a flower pain is a root
> and its work is underground where the moldering
> proceeds the bones of all our joy winded
> and rained and nothing grows a whole life's love
> that longed to be an orchard forced to lie
> like an onion secret sour in the mine of pain

The poet explains that he went out into the garden "to die of the pain" when he unexpectedly encounters a gardenia. It revives the memory of other gardenias associated with their love and with the anguish of Roger Horwitz's nineteen-month struggle with AIDS. These flowers, however, do not offer consolation:

> but for all the spunk of the three gardenias
> still the pain is not a flower and digs like
> a spade in stony soil no earthly reason
> not a thing will come of it but a slag heap
> and a pit and the deepest root the stuff of witch
> banes winds and winds its tendril about my heart[30]

Pain here is simply useless and destructive: nothing but slag and poison.

Still, pain defiantly reshaped by rage and grief as a poisonous waste—not even a flower of evil but simply a sour blind root—already sets affliction within a context that separates it from the medical metanarrative of meaningless tissue damage. Here is a pain for which hospitals and pharmacies have no remedy. Such pain for Monette takes its bitter meaning only in relation to a specific cultural and historical moment of late twentieth-century life that has confronted us with an epidemic disease threatening, as he says, to destroy an entire generation of gay men. The stance of defiance and rage is not merely an expression of personal anguish. It expresses an emotion capable of being transformed into militant political action directed against the high-priced drug companies and slow-footed government agencies that have found the pain of gay men so easy or expedient to ignore.[31]

The concept of postmodern pain implies not just the risk of a possibly random proliferation of meanings. It also implies that we can work to change the understandings of pain that prevail in our own culture. Happily, a few philosophers are returning to the subject of pain after the long analytic epoch in which philosophy regarded pain (shrunk to the firing of C fibers) mainly as an example of mind and as an illustration in the endless arguments about private language. Emmanuel Levinas in his essay "Useless Suffering" (1982) proposed a way of understanding that begins from the premise that pain is utterly negative, absurd, and evil. Yet he also allows one way in which an individual's useless suffering might be transformed. Suffering, he proposes, opens up an ethical dimension of the "inter-human." My own uselessness suffering, that is, takes on a changed meaning if it becomes the occasion for your empathetic, even suffering response. This is what Levinas calls a suffering for the suffering of someone else. "Already within an isolated consciousness," he writes, "the pain of suffering can take on the meaning of a pain which merits and hopes for reward, and so lose, it seems, in diverse ways, its modality of uselessness."[32]

It was Albert Schweitzer, in his autobiography, who perhaps best described the ethical ("inter-human") perspective on pain that Levinas proposes to recover. As he wrote:

Whoever among us has through personal experience learned what pain and anxiety really are must help to ensure that those who out there are in bodily need obtain the help which came to him. He belongs no more to himself alone; he has become the brother of all who suffer. On the "Brotherhood of those who bear the mark of pain" lies the duty of medical work. . . .[33]

Schweitzer wrote these words in 1933. It is worth remembering that he wrote about the "Brotherhood of those who bear the mark of pain" in the context of his medical ministry to the blacks of equatorial Africa. It was a radical and practical—not nominal—kinship that he imagined: feeling that reaches out to assert our solidarity with those despised or feared or rejected as the Other. Like Levinas, who might be considered our major contemporary philosopher of the Other, Schweitzer implies that pain can transform us—and transform our different cultures—when we come to understand its claims. The modern denial of pain is in the largest sense a denial of the claims pain implicitly makes upon us.

Levinas's return to the interhuman meanings of pain—within a mechanistic, medicalized, post-Holocaust culture that the sentimental age never imagined—is an encouraging sign. It will take more than doctors to help reshape our experience of pain in the years ahead. Doctors at the best pain clinics have already begun to show the way, but they are still a small minority within medicine, sometimes mistrusted by their colleagues, many of whom remain wedded to the old organic model. The problem is not simply that physicians are wedded to an outmoded model of pain, as if the issue at stake were merely whether to adjust an intellectual theory. Doctors committed to the organic model cannot help but respond inadequately to a number of the patients who come to them with chronic pain. We need more than a handful of drugs, a booklet of exercises, and a fresh referral slip. Doctors will change decisively only when patients demand a change, and we will make such a demand only when we have at last begun to think for ourselves about pain.

†

What does the immediate future hold for the person struggling with chronic pain? Pain clinics, alas, are not a sure answer because they differ so greatly in philosophy, staff, and methods of treatment. Licensing and accreditation are still at an early stage of development. The risk of quacks cannot be dismissed since pain is a big money-maker. Many insurance programs now pay for up to six or more months of treatment. Not every clinic is well run by a competent director with a skilled, multidisciplinary staff. Patients need to think carefully about the treatment they receive. Some clinics will frankly—and I think rightly—inform patients that real progress depends largely upon the patient's will to improve.

A postmodern pain will very likely be a pain of which the patient takes charge. Taking charge does not imply rejecting good medical help. It also does not imply that we are responsible for our pain in the sense of having, deliberately or unwittingly, caused it. The origin of chronic pain is often a murky question. Once pain has taken up residence in the psyche for six months or more, it is never exactly the same pain we experienced at the beginning. Six months of unremitting pain (with no end in sight) has inevitably changed us, too. We have learned new patterns of behavior and thought and feeling. Many people find that this new learning involves a disheartening education in the difficulties of getting effective medical treatment for chronic pain. Here is the point at which taking charge of our pain becomes crucial. It may very well turn out that relief or improvement will come only when we take responsibility for changing patterns of living and thinking—from diet and exercise to job and marriage—that have proved unhealthy and even destructive. Pain is a magnet for any unresolved dilemma. We may need to resolve the dilemma before we can let go of the pain.

Taking charge of our pain can also include assuming personal responsibility for its meaning. For over a century our culture has encouraged us to abandon this burden. Unquestionably it is burdensome to confront, almost on ground zero, the issue of how we are to understand our pain. The point is, however, that (even without thinking about it) we *already* understand our pain within the organic model we have inherited from nineteenth-century medicine. For many people the question of understanding pain will seem compelling only at the moment when this official biomedical explanation sanctioned by our culture has failed them. At that point, the best way to take charge may be to listen to the voices in our culture that medicine has succeeded in drowning out. These subjugated voices—audible if we will only take the trouble to hear—will be saying in numerous ways that how we experience pain has almost everything to do with how we understand it.

†

"*Learn to think with pain*": these words appear in Maurice Blanchot's book of meditations on the Holocaust entitled *The Writing of the Disaster*.[34] It is a statement with multiple meanings. In pain, we must nonetheless learn to think. Pain is something we must learn to use in our thinking. Thinking is somehow learned or born or created out of pain. The deliberate proliferation of meanings in Blanchot's statement constitutes a kind of metaphor describing the future of pain. It suggests that successful treatment for chronic pain will require a medicine that seeks to work within—not against or in disregard of—each patient's individual system of belief. Sometimes, when the belief system simply mirrors the limitations or entrenched errors of nineteenth-century medicine, the first task of doctors may lie in reeducating the patient about the nature of pain.

We certainly cannot succeed as a culture by continuing to deny and ignore pain, as if we could silence it beneath a mountain of pills. That clearly does not work. Nor can we help each other by continuing to place unblinking faith in an outworn organic model as limited in its way as the theory that attributes pain to the arrows of the gods. We are more than bundles of neurons. We must recover a sense of the importance of minds and cultures in the construction of pain, and we must begin to proliferate the meanings of pain in order that we do not reduce human suffering to the dimensions of a mere physical problem for which, if we could only find the right pill, there is always a medical solution.

Pleasure comes and goes, sometimes within a single instant, but pain has real staying power. Chronic pain inevitably changes the world we inhabit, like a permanent winter. Medicine alone cannot possibly resolve all the questions raised by pain. The fault lies in asking doctors to assume the entire burden of a condition that stretches far beyond the borders of medical practice. Pain, in Blanchot's summarizing phrase, must become something with which, and through which, we learn to think for ourselves. We really have no choice: if we fail to rethink our pain we must automatically accept the worn-out cultural thinking that is already in place and only aggravating our torment. The opportunity for a major shift in our relationship to pain is at hand. Indeed, the new thinking that lies ahead—when we learn what pain can teach us, when we apply what we learn to the arena of cultural change—may just lead to a future worth the pain it takes to create.

NOTES

INTRODUCTION

1. Paul Valéry, *Monsieur Teste* (1896–1946), trans. Jackson Mathews (Princeton: Princeton University Press, 1973), 68. Valéry's final text evolved over a period of some fifty years.

2. The best general introduction to modern medical research on pain is by Ronald Melzack and Patrick D. Wall, *The Challenge of Pain* (New York: Basic Books, 1983). For a convenient supplement, see the three essays by Allan I. Basbaum, Macdonald Critchley, and John D. Loeser collected under the general title "Unlocking the Secrets of Pain," in *1988 Medical and Health Annual*, ed. Ellen Bernstein (Chicago: Encyclopedia Britannica Inc., 1987), 84–131. Among the various books written for general readers, see Peter Fairley, *The Conquest of Pain* (1978; rpt. New York: Charles Scribner's Sons, 1980); and H. B. Gibson, *Pain and its Conquest* (London: Peter Owen, 1982). For more philosophical studies, see J. L. Cowan, *Pleasure and Pain: A Study in Philosophical Psychology* (London: Macmillan, 1968); Rem B. Edwards, *Pleasures and Pains: A Theory of Qualitative Hedonism* (Ithaca, N.Y.: Cornell University Press, 1979); and Thomas S. Szasz, *Pain and Pleasure: A Study of Bodily Feelings*, 2d ed. (New York: Basic Books, 1975). Other relevant studies will be cited in subsequent notes. A fuller bibliographical introduction is available in my essay "The Languages of Pain," in *Exploring the Concept of Mind*, ed. Richard M. Caplan (Iowa City: University of Iowa Press, 1986), 89–99.

3. Of course, we possess various fragments toward an eventual (if incomplete) history of pain. See, for example, the excellent study by K. D. Keele, *Anatomies of Pain* (Oxford: Blackwell Scientific Publications, 1957). Also useful are K. D. Keele, "Some Historical Concepts of Pain," in *The Assessment of Pain in Man and Animals*, ed. C. A. Keele and Robert Smith (London: Livingstone, 1962), 12–27; Daniel de Moulin, "A Historical-Phenomenological Study of Bodily Pain in Western Man," *Bulletin of the History of Medicine* 48 (1974): 540–570; H. Mersky, "Some Features of the History of the Idea of Pain," *Pain* 9 (1980): 3–8; P. Procacci, "History of the Pain Concept," in *Pain and Society*, ed. H. W. Kosterlitz and L. Y. Terenius (Deerfield Beach, Fla.: Verlag Chemie, 1980), 3–12; and (more specialized) *The History of the Management of Pain: From Early Principles to Present Practice*, ed. R. D. Mann (Park Ridge, N.J.: The Parthenon Publishing Group, 1988).

4. René Leriche, *La Chirurgie de la douleur* (1937), 3d ed. (Paris: Masson, 1949), 15. The phrase "la douleur vivante" is translated literally as "living pain" in the English translation by Archibald Young.

5. "L'homme est un apprenti, la douleur est son maître": Alfred de Musset, "La Nuit d'octobre" (1837), in *Oeuvres complètes*, ed. Philippe van Teighem (Paris: Seuil, 1963), 158. Translation mine.

6. For a fuller response to Scarry's fine book, see my review essay "How to Read *The Body in Pain*," *Literature and Medicine* 6 (1987): 139–155.

7. Immanuel Kant, "Der Streit der Facultäten in drey Abschnitten" (1798), iii.2 ("Vom Schlafe"), in *Werke in Sechs Bänden*, ed. Wilhelm Weischedel (Wiesbaden: Insel-Verlag, 1960), 6: 382–383. The episode is discussed by J. H. van den Berg, *Divided Existence and Complex Society: An Historical Approach* (Pittsburgh, Pa.: Dusquesne University Press, 1974), 227–228. The chapter "Pain in a Plural Existence" develops van den Berg's thesis that the modern experience of pain derives from a complex nineteenth-century social process that Marxist theory would call alienation.

ONE: LIVING PAIN

1. Plato, *Philebus*, 21d–e, in *The Dialogues of Plato* (1871), trans. B. Jowett, 4th ed., 4 vols. (Oxford: Clarendon Press, 1953), 3: 573.

2. See George Van Ness Dearborn, "A Case of Congenital General Pure Analgesia," *Journal of Nervous and Mental Disease* 75 (1932): 612–615. Another classic study—far more detailed—is Gordon A. McMurray, "Experimental Study of a Case of Insensitivity to Pain," *Archives of Neurology and Psychiatry* 64 (1950): 650–667. For a review of these and other such cases in the medical literature, see Richard A. Sternbach, "Congenital Insensitivity to Pain: A Critique," *Psychological Bulletin* 60 (1963): 252–264.

3. Dearborn, "A Case of Congenital General Pure Analgesia," 614.

4. *Philosophical Investigations* (1953), trans. G. E. M. Anscombe, 3d ed. (New York: Macmillan, 1970), 8e.

5. On the various terms and systems for describing pain both in English and in other natural languages, see D. C. Agnew and H. Mersky, "Words of Chronic Pain," *Pain* 2 (1976): 73–81; Horacio Fabrega, Jr., and Stephen Tyma, "Culture, Language and the Shaping of Illness: An Illustration Based on Pain," *Journal of Psychosomatic Research* 20 (1976): 323–337; and Anthony Diller, "Cross-cultural Pain Semantics," *Pain* 9 (1980): 9–26.

6. "The concept of meaning is every bit as problematic as the concept of mind" (*The Oxford Companion to The Mind*, ed. Richard L. Gregory [New York: Oxford University Press, 1987], 450). For a sample of different approaches, see Thomas E. Hill, *The Concept of Meaning* (New York: Humanities Press, 1971); Stephen R. Shiffer, *Meaning* (Oxford: Clarendon Press, 1972); Brian Lear, *Mind and Meaning* (Cambridge: Cambridge University Press, 1981); Algirdas Julien Greimas, *On Meaning: Selected Writings in Semiotic Theory* (Minneapolis: University

of Minnesota Press, 1987); and *The Theory of Meaning*, ed. G. H. R. Parkinson (London: Oxford University Press, 1988). My own preference is for the broadly personal and cultural analysis in Michael Polanyi and Harry Prosch, *Meaning* (Chicago: University of Chicago Press, 1975).

7. See, for example, Stephen A. Cooper et al., "The Analgesic Efficacy of Suprofen in Periodontal and Oral Surgical Pain," *Pharmacotherapy* 6, no. 5 (1986): 267–276. Much of Cooper's recent research uses the pain caused by removal of impacted third molars as a model for testing various analgesics.

8. "Pain Terms: A List with Definitions and Notes on Usage," *Pain* 6 (1979): 249.

9. Paul Feyerabend describes the technique of *anamnesis* by which revolutionary scientists such as Newton described their findings in a traditional language designed to shield them from charges of radicalism (*Against Method: Outline of an Anarchistic Theory of Knowledge* [1975; rpt. London: Verso Edition, 1978], 89–90).

10. Quoted in Claudine Herzlich and Janine Pierret, *Illness and Self in Society* (1984), trans. Elborg Forster (Baltimore, Md.: Johns Hopkins University Press, 1987), 87.

11. Ronald Melzack, "The McGill Pain Questionnaire: Major Properties and Scoring Methods," *Pain* 1 (1975): 277–299. William Fordyce et al., however, found that the language of patients was not a strong diagnostic tool ("Relationship of Patient Semantic Pain Descriptions to Physician Diagnostic Judgments, Activity Level Measures and MMPI," *Pain* 5 [1978]: 293–303). Some basic diagnostic uses are described by Fannie Gaston-Johansson and Jens Allwood, "Pain Assessment: Model Construction and Analysis of Words Used to Describe Pain-like Experiences," *Semiotica* 71, nos. 1 and 2 (1988): 73–92.

12. In addition to Herzlich and Pierret (*Illness and Self in Society*), see, for example, Leon Eisenberg, "The Physician as Interpreter: Ascribing Meaning to the Illness Experience," *Comprehensive Psychiatry* 22 (1981): 239–248; and Arthur Kleinman, *The Illness Narratives: Suffering, Healing, and the Human Condition* (New York: Basic Books, 1988). Especially pertinent to my concerns is Byron J. Good and Mary-Jo Delvecchio Good, "The Meaning of Symptoms: A Cultural-Hermeneutic Model for Clinical Practice," *The Relevance of Social Science for Medicine*, ed. Leon Eisenberg and Arthur Kleinman (London: Reidel, 1981), 165–196.

13. Michael Bury, "Meanings at Risk: The Experience of Arthritis," *Living with Chronic Illness: The Experience of Patients and Their Families*, ed. Robert Anderson and Michael Bury (London: Unwin Hyman, 1988), 115. The material in this paragraph is based on Bury's essay. For an eloquent description of her illness (as it affects many different aspects of her life) by someone who suffered for years with rheumatoid arthritis, see Grace Stuart, *Private World of Pain* (London: Allen & Unwin, 1953).

14. The most valuable work is undoubtedly by Ferdinand Sauerbruch and Hans Wenke, *Pain: Its Meaning and Significance* (1936), trans. Edward Fitzgerald, 2d ed. (London: Allen & Unwin, 1963). Their preface to the first German edition insists that pain "is a physical feeling but it is nevertheless not confined to the

sphere of the physical; indeed, it affects all areas of the psyche and mind" (7). For another medical text full of sage observations, delivered from the perspective of existential philosophy, see W. Noordenbos, *Pain* (Amsterdam: Elsevier, 1959).

15. Physician Steven F. Brena emphasized the extent of the dilemma in *Chronic Pain: America's Hidden Epidemic*, ed. Steven F. Brena (New York: Atheneum/SMI, 1978). For the most comprehensive introduction to medical knowledge, see *Textbook of Pain*, ed. Patrick D. Wall and Ronald Melzack, 2d ed. (New York: Churchill Livingstone, 1989). It was Melzack and Wall who, in 1965, first proposed the widely respected "gate control" theory of pain (see "Pain Mechanisms: A New Theory," *Science* 150 [1965]: 971–979).

16. See *Chronic Pain: Hope Through Research*, NIH Publication no. 82–2406 (April 1982), 2–3. For figures suggesting that over 30 percent of all households contain at least one person with persistent pain, see Joan Crook, Elizabeth Rideout, and Gina Browne, "The Prevalence of Pain Complaints in a General Population," *Pain* 18 (1984): 299–314.

17. See John J. Bonica and C. Richard Chapman, "Biology, Pathophysiology, and Therapy of Chronic Pain," *American Handbook of Psychiatry*, ed. Silvano Arieti, 2d ed., vol. 8 (New York: Basic Books, 1986), 721–722. Similarly staggering figures are collected by Dennis C. Turk, Donald Meichenbaum, and Myles Genest in *Pain and Behavioral Medicine: A Cognitive-Behavioral Perspective* (New York: Guilford, 1983), 73–74.

18. See G. S. Rousseau, "Literature and Medicine: The State of the Field," *Isis* 72 (1981): 406–424. Two key events in the rise of the new discipline known as medical humanities were publication of *Literature and Medicine: An Annotated Bibliography* (1975), ed. Joanne Trautmann and Carol Pollard—now in a revised edition (Pittsburgh, Pa.: University of Pittsburgh Press, 1982); and publication in 1982 of the new journal *Literature and Medicine*. See also *Reflections: A Subject Guide for Fiction and Biography on Illness and Disability* (1981), ed. R. B. Tabor and J. Stephenson, 3d ed. (Southampton: Wessex Regional Library Information Service, 1989).

19. The most important specialized journal dealing with current research on pain is undoubtedly *Pain: The Journal of the International Association for the Study of Pain* which commenced publication in 1975. A sample of other related periodicals includes *The Clinical Journal of Pain*; *Pain Management*; *Pain Control in Dentistry*; *Journal of Pain and Symptom Management*; and *Back Pain Monitor*.

20. In *Advances in Neurology*, vol. 4, ed. John J. Bonica (New York: Raven Press, 1974), vii.

21. See, for example, the article "Douleur" in *Dictionnaire encyclopédique des sciences médicales* (1884), which quotes from more than twenty academic theses on pain from the seventeenth and eighteenth centuries (30: 465–511).

22. In Richard S. Weiner, "An Interview with John J. Bonica, M. D.," *Pain Practitioner* 1 (Spring 1989): 2.

23. The pioneering study on the subject is by Richard M. Marks and Edward J. Sachar, "Undertreatment of Medical Inpatients with Narcotic Analgesics," *Annals of Internal Medicine* 78, no. 2 (1973): 173–181. On the continuing dilemma, see John P. Morgan, "American Opiophobia: Customary Underutilization of Opioid Analgesics," *Advances in Pain Research and Therapy*, vol. 2, ed. C. Stratton Hill, Jr., and William S. Fields (New York: Raven Press, 1989), 181–189.

24. See Samuel W. Perry, "Undermedication for Pain on a Burn Unit," *General Hospital Psychiatry* 6 (1984): 308–316. On hospital-induced addiction, see Jane Porter and Hershel Jick, "Addiction Rare in Patients Treated with Narcotics," *New England Journal of Medicine* 302 (1980): 23; and Barry Stimmel, *Pain, Analgesia, and Addiction: The Pharmacologic Treatment of Pain* (New York: Raven Press, 1983).

25. Quoted in *New York* 18, no. 8 (25 February 1985): 48.

26. According to Solomon Snyder, of Johns Hopkins, who discovered the existence of opiate receptors in the brain and was among the discoverers of enkephalins in 1975: "It is now realistic to believe that serious pain can be conquered" (in Herbert Burkholz, "Pain: Solving the Mystery," *New York Times Magazine* [27 September 1987]: 35).

27. See, for example, J. Louwrens Menges, "Pain: Still an Intriguing Puzzle," *Social Science and Medicine* 19 (1984): 1257–1260.

28. For a discussion of the distinction between puzzle and mystery, see Gabriel Marcel, *The Mystery of Being*, trans. G. S. Fraser, 2 vols. (London: The Harvill Press, 1950–1951), 1: 211–215.

29. Heidegger, "What Are Poets For?" (1950), *Poetry, Language, Thought*, trans. Albert Hofstadter (New York: Harper & Row, 1971), 96: "Das Geheimnis des Schmerzes bleibt verhüllt." On Heidegger's view of pain, see Orville Clark, "Heidegger and the Mystery of Pain," *Man and World* 10 (1977): 334–350.

30. Two recent books by physicians—Howard Brody's *Stories of Sickness* (New Haven: Yale University Press, 1987) and Arthur Kleinman's *The Illness Narratives: Suffering, Healing, and the Human Condition* (New York: Basic Books, 1988)—explore the new medical interest in what illness "means" to the patient. On the cultural meanings of pain, an especially valuable study is Ivan Illich's chapter "The Killing of Pain," *Medical Nemesis: The Expropriation of Health* (New York: Pantheon Books, 1976), 133–154. Other relevant studies include Joseph A. Kotarba, *Chronic Pain: Its Social Dimensions* (Beverly Hills, Calif.: Sage Publications, 1983); Donald S. Ciccone and Roy C. Grzesiak, "Cognitive Dimensions of Chronic Pain," *Social Science and Medicine* 19 (1984): 1339–1345; and Thomas M. Johnson, "Contradictions in the Cultural Construction of Pain in America," *Advances in Pain Research and Therapy*, vol. 11, ed. Hill and Fields, 27–37.

31. Macdonald Critchley, a neurologist, makes consistent use of literary sources in his essay "Unlocking the Secrets of Pain: The Psychology," in *1988 Medical and Health Annual*, ed. Ellen Bernstein, 104–119. There are a few critical studies that tend to work around the topic of pain, not directly on it, as, for example, James H. Averill, *Wordsworth and the Poetry of Human Suffering* (Ithaca, N.Y.:

Cornell University Press, 1980); Walter J. Slatoff, *The Look of Distance: Reflections on Suffering and Sympathy in Modern Literature—Auden to Agee, Whitman to Woolf* (Columbus: Ohio State University Press, 1985); and, a classic earlier work, Edmund Wilson's *Patriotic Gore: Studies in the Literature of the American Civil War* (New York: Oxford University Press, 1962).

32. René Leriche, *The Surgery of Pain* (1937), trans. Archibald Young (London: Ballière, Tindall and Cox, 1939), 29. Leriche insists: "Everything in pain is subjective."

33. *The Surgery of Pain*, trans. Young, 40. Leriche insists that what he calls the "pain-malady" calls into play the entire person and not simply a set of neural pathways.

34. *The Surgery of Pain*, trans. Young, 40, 483. Modern research bears out Leriche's claims about the artificial character of laboratory pain. See "Sensitivity to Pain Greater in a Clinical Than in a Laboratory Setting," *JAMA* 250 (August 1983): 718.

35. William Blake, "The Grey Monk," in *The Poetry and Prose of William Blake*, ed. David V. Erdman, commentary by Harold Bloom (Garden City, N.Y.: Doubleday, 1965), 481. For a helpful pondering of Blake's line, see Jerome Neu, "'A Tear Is an Intellectual Thing,'" *Representations* 19 (1987): 35–61.

36. On the importance of perception, see, for example, John M. Luce, Troy L. Thompson II, Carl J. Getto, and Richard L. Byyny, "New Concepts of Chronic Pain and Their Implications," *Hospital Practice* 14 (April 1979): 113–123.

37. Allan I. Basbaum, "Unlocking the Secrets of Pain: The Science," *1988 Medical and Health Annual*, ed. Ellen Bernstein, 86.

TWO: THE MEANINGS OF PAIN

1. *Philosophical Investigations* (1953), trans. G. E. M. Anscombe, 3d ed. (New York: Macmillan, 1970), 178e.

2. For a learned and encyclopedic treatment, see Walter Addison Jayne, *The Healing Gods of Ancient Civilizations* (New Haven, Conn.: Yale University Press, 1925).

3. See I. M. Lewis, *Ecstatic Religion: An Anthropological Study of Spirit Possession and Shamanism* (Harmondsworth: Penguin, 1971)—especially chapter three, "Affliction and Its Apotheosis."

4. The Hippocratic writings until the Renaissance were transmitted mainly through Galen. On the modern rediscovery of Hippocrates, disentangled from Galen, see Wesley D. Smith, *The Hippocratic Tradition* (Ithaca, N.Y.: Cornell University Press, 1979). On medicine and illness in antiquity, see Paul Ghalioungui, *Magic and Medical Science in Ancient Egypt* (London: Hodder and Stoughton, 1963); *Diseases in Antiquity*, ed. Don Brothwell and A. T. Sandison (Springfield, Ill.: Charles C. Thomas, 1967); Fred Rosner, *Medicine in the Bible and the Talmud: Selections from Classical and Jewish Sources* (New York: Yeshiva Univer-

sity Press, 1977); *Disease in Ancient Man: An International Symposium*, ed. Gerald D. Hart (Toronto: Clarke Irwin, 1983); and Mirko D. Grmek, *Diseases in the Ancient Greek World* (1983), trans. Mireille Muellner and Leonard Muellner (Baltimore, Md.: Johns Hopkins University Press, 1989).

5. On the mixture of ancient religion and medicine, see Steven M. Oberhelman, "The Hippocratic Corpus and Greek Religion," *The Body and the Text: Comparative Essays in Literature and Medicine*, ed. Bruce Clarke and Wendell Aycock (Lubbock: Texas Tech University Press, 1990), 144–163.

6. David Bakan, *Disease, Pain, and Sacrifice: Towards a Psychology of Suffering* (Chicago: University of Chicago Press, 1968), 57–58.

7. James Boswell, *Life of Johnson* (1791), ed. R. W. Chapman, corrected by J. D. Fleeman, 3d ed. (New York: Oxford University Press, 1970), 333.

8. *The Complete Poems of Emily Dickinson*, ed. Thomas H. Johnson (Boston: Little, Brown and Company, 1960), 479 (no. 1049).

9. Edmund Burke, *A Philosophical Enquiry into the Origin of Our Ideas of the Sublime and Beautiful* (1757), ed. J. T. Boulton (New York: Columbia University Press, 1958), 131.

10. Leo Tolstoy, *The Death of Ivan Ilych and other stories*, trans. J. D. Duff and Aylmer Maude (New York: New American Library, 1960), 155. The word *bol*, which Tolstoy employs here, is the common Russian word for pain.

11. S. Weir Mitchell, "Civilization and Pain," *The Annals of Hygiene* 7, no. 1 (1892): 26. This very brief piece appears to be a report of remarks delivered by Mitchell—cited as if in his own words.

12. Quoted in Martin S. Pernick, *A Calculus of Suffering: Pain, Professionalism, and Anesthesia in Nineteenth-Century America* (New York: Columbia University Press, 1985), 156. I am indebted to Pernick's fine study.

13. See James Turner, *Reckoning with the Beast: Animals, Pain, and Humanity in the Victorian Mind* (Baltimore, Md.: Johns Hopkins University Press, 1980).

14. Harriet Beecher Stowe, *Uncle Tom's Cabin* (1852) (New York: Random House, 1985), 440–441 (chaps. xxxiii and xxxiv).

15. *The Iliad of Homer*, trans. Richmond Lattimore (1951; rpt. Chicago: University of Chicago Press, 1961), 417 (XX.474–483). The Greek text, with an archaic English prose translation by A. T. Murray, is available in the Loeb Classical Library series (1924; rpt. Cambridge, Mass.: Harvard University Press, 1963).

16. *The Iliad of Homer*, trans. Lattimore, 151 (V.859–863).

17. *The Iliad of Homer*, trans. Lattimore, 366 (XVII.446–447). On the differences between men and gods, see Jasper Griffin, *Homer on Life and Death* (Oxford: Clarendon Press, 1980).

18. See psychologist Julian Jaynes, "Sensory Pain and Conscious Pain," *The Behavioral and Brain Sciences* 8 (1985): 61–63. Jaynes, who does not discuss Ares and Aphrodite, observes that ancient Proto-Indo-European (before 2000 B.C.) had no word for pain, and he argues that the modern experience of pain commenced

only with the invention of human consciousness, which (amid much controversy and uncertainty) he dates as occurring sometime after 1000 B.C. See Jayne's *The Origin of Consciousness in the Breakdown of the Bicameral Mind* (Boston: Houghton Mifflin, 1976).

19. *The Iliad of Homer*, trans. Lattimore, 344 (XVI.527–528). The Homeric word for pain here is *odunas*. For a discussion of Homeric war wounds, see Mirko D. Grmek, *Diseases in the Ancient Greek World* (1983), trans. Mireille Muellner and Leonard Muellner (Baltimore, Md.: Johns Hopkins University Press, 1989), 27–33.

20. Henry K. Beecher, "Pain in Men Wounded in Battle," *The Bulletin of the U.S. Army Medical Department* 5 (April 1946): 445. For an updated version of Beecher's pioneering analysis, see Patrick D. Wall, "On the Relation of Injury to Pain," *Pain* 6 (1979): 253–264.

21. Beecher, "Pain in Men Wounded in Battle," 448. See also Beecher's article "Relationship of Significance of Wound to the Pain Experience," *JAMA* 161 (1956): 1609–1613.

22. On the influence of fear on the perception of pain, see Kenneth S. Bowers, "Pain, Anxiety, and Perceived Control," *Journal of Consulting and Clinical Psychology* 32 (1968): 596–602. On the likelihood of opioid analgesia in cases of shock, see John W. Holaday and Alan I. Fadan, "Naloxone Treatment in Shock," *Lancet*, 25 July 1981: 201. The relation of stress to analgesia is discussed by Jean Rossier et al., "On the Mechanisms of the Simultaneous Release of Immunoreactive B-Endorphin, ACTH, and Prolactin by Stress," *Neural Peptides and Neuronal Communications*, ed. Erminio Costa and Marco Trabucchi (New York: Raven Press, 1980), 363–375.

23. Beecher, "Pain in Men Wounded in Battle, " 451, punctuation slightly altered.

24. Blaise Pascal, "Prière pour demander a dieu le bon usage des maladies," in *Oeuvres complètes*, ed. Louis Lafuma (Paris: Seuil, 1963), 363–364 (translation mine). Lafuma dates the *Prayer* as probably late 1659.

25. For an excellent study that treats Christianity and other major religions, see John Bowker, *Problems of Suffering in Religions of the World* (Cambridge: Cambridge University Press, 1970). On the comparison between theological and scientific understandings, see Steven Brena, *Pain and Religion: A Psychophysiological Study* (Springfield, Ill.: Charles C. Thomas, 1972).

26. See F. P. Lisowski, "Prehistoric and Early Historic Trepanation," in *Diseases in Antiquity: A Survey of the Diseases, Injuries and Surgery of Early Populations*, ed. Don Brothwell and A. T. Sandison (Springfield, Ill.: Charles C. Thomas, 1967), 651–672; and Edward L. Margetts, "Trepanation of the Skull by the Medicine-men of Primitive Cultures, with Particular Reference to Present-day Native East African Practice," in *Diseases in Antiquity*, ed. Brothwell and Sandison, 673–701.

27. In W. G. Lambert, *Babylonian Wisdom Literature* (Oxford: Clarendon Press, 1960), 7.

28. See Giles Constable, *Attitudes Toward Self-Inflicted Suffering in the Middle Ages* (Brookline, Mass.: Hellenic College Press, 1982).

29. C. S. Lewis, *The Problem of Pain* (New York: Macmillan, 1944), 103–104: "There is no such thing as a sum of suffering, for no one suffers it. When we have reached the maximum that a single person can suffer, we have, no doubt, reached something very horrible, but we have reached all the suffering there ever can be in the universe. The addition of a million fellow-sufferers adds no more pain."

30. Mark Zborowski, *People in Pain* (San Francisco: Jossey-Bass, 1960). The book develops ideas presented in Zborowski's earlier study, "Cultural Components in Responses to Pain," *Journal of Social Issues* 8, no. 4 (1952): 16–30.

31. Zborowski, *People in Pain*, 20. Asenath Petrie in *Individuality in Pain and Suffering* (Chicago: University of Chicago Press, 1967) emphasizes that tolerance for pain varies from person to person. Yet her measurements also indicate that individuals nonetheless fall into three main groups. She describes the three main groups as "augmenters" (who perceive any stimulus as increased), "reducers" (who perceive any stimulus as decreased), and "moderates" (who perceive any stimulus as neither increased nor decreased). "The results of the study reported here," she writes, "suggest a neurological or physiological basis for this variation in tolerance of pain" (2).

32. Zborowski, *People in Pain*, 193.

33. Zborowski, *People in Pain*, 99.

34. Zborowski, *People in Pain*, 21. Several authors tend to confirm the general direction of Zborowski's research by studying the narrow issue of tolerance for pain. See Charles C. Josey and Carroll H. Miller, "Race, Sex, and Class Difference in Ability to Endure Pain," *Journal of Social Psychology* 3 (1932): 374–376; Richard A. Sternbach and Bernard Tursky, "Ethnic Differences among Housewives in Psychophysical and Skin Potential Responses to Electric Shock," *Psychophysiology* 1 (1965): 241–246. Other studies, however, have failed to show significant differences in tolerance for pain. See H. Merskey and F. G. Spear, "The Reliability of the Pressure Algometer," *British Journal of Social and Clinical Psychology* 3 (1964): 130–136; and B. Winsberg and M. Greenlick, "Pain Response in Negro and White Obstetrical Patients," *Journal of Health & Social Behavior* 8 (1967): 222–227. Significant differences, however, may not emerge in laboratory experiments that measure tolerance alone. Artificially induced pain owing to heat, pressure, or electrical shock necessarily removes pain from its cultural setting.

35. See Cecil Helman, "Pain and Culture," *Culture, Health and Illness: An Introduction for Health Professionals* (Bristol: John Wright & Sons, 1984), 95–105. B. Berthold Wolff and Sarah Langley review in detail the studies before 1968 that support or refute Zborowski's findings ("Cultural Factors and the Response to Pain" [1968], rpt. *Culture, Disease, and Healing: Studies in Medical Anthropology*, ed. David Landy [New York: Macmillan, 1977], 313–319). For a more recent, detailed review of research, see James A. Lipton and Joseph J. Marbach, "Ethnicity and the Pain Experience," *Social Science and Medicine* 19 (1984): 1279–1298. Thomas M. Johnson explores some implications of Zborowski's approach in "Contradictions in the Cultural Construction of Pain in America," *Advances in Pain Research and Therapy*, vol. 11, ed. Hill and Fields, 27–37.

THREE: AN INVISIBLE EPIDEMIC

1. *The Complete Poems of Emily Dickinson*, ed. Thomas H. Johnson, 323 (no. 650). For a good discussion, see Suzanne Juhasz, "'But most, like Chaos': Emily Dickinson Measures Pain," *American Transcendental Quarterly* 43 (1979): 225–241.

2. Guido Majno in *The Healing Hand: Man and Wound in the Ancient World* (Cambridge, Mass.: Harvard University Press, 1975) reproduces this photograph (fig. 9) and remarks that the arrow "came from the rear, passed between two ribs, and crossed the whole chest: a deadly wound." Professor Robert I. Sundick, a forensic anthropologist specializing in the identification of bone fragments, asserts on the contrary that the arrow could only have struck the chest from in front.

3. See Peter Fairley, *The Conquest of Pain* (New York: Charles Scribner's Sons, 1978), 139–142.

4. For these and similarly alarming statistics on the consumption of painkilling medication, now more than a decade out of date, see Richard Hughes and Robert Brewin, *The Tranquillizing of America: Pill-Popping and the American Way of Life* (New York: Harcourt Brace Jovanovich, 1979).

5. The marketing periodical *Prospects* (December 1988) estimates 1989 U.S. costs for prescription analgesics at $1 billion and costs for prescription tranquilizers at $1.1 billion. The periodical *Chain Drug Review* (31 July 1989) estimates 1988 retail costs for over-the-counter analgesics at $2.2 billion. We should also add a percent of costs for prescription antidepressants, since tricyclic antidepressants are commonly prescribed for chronic pain. The Food and Drug Administration reports that in 1986 retail pharmacies filled over 35 million prescriptions for antidepressant drugs.

6. The letter describing her mastectomy is available in *The Journals and Letters of Fanny Burney (Madame D'Arblay)*, ed. Joyce Hemlow et al., 12 vols. (Oxford: Clarendon Press, 1972–1984), 6: 596–616. For an excellent discussion, see Julia L. Epstein, "Writing the Unspeakable: Fanny Burney's Mastectomy and the Fictive Body," *Representations* 16 (1986): 131–166. Burney adds concerning her harrowing surgical ordeal: "Even now, 9 months after it is over, I have a head ache from going on with the account. . . . I dare not revise, nor read, the recollection is still so painful."

7. John M. T. Finney, *The Significance and Effect of Pain* (Boston, Mass.: Griffith-Stillings Press, 1914), 4.

8. See W. Schupbach, "Sequah: An English 'American Medicine'-Man in 1890," *Medical History* 29 (1985): 272–317.

9. See the novelistic but reliable account of these events by René Fülöp-Miller, *Triumph Over Pain*, trans. Eden and Cedar Paul (New York: The Literary Guild of America, 1938).

10. S. Weir Mitchell, "The Life and Death of Pain," *The Wager and Other Poems* (New York: The Century Company, 1900), 18.

11. *Pain and Disability: Clinical, Behavioral, and Public Policy Perspectives*, ed. Marian Osterweis, Arthur Kleinman, and David Mechanic (Washington, D.C.:

National Academy Press, 1987), 11. The Institute of Medicine was chartered in 1970 by the National Academy of Sciences.

12. On the notion of a crime that defines or typifies a specific historical period, see Pat Rogers, *The Augustan Vision* (London: Weidenfeld and Nicolson, 1974), 99.

13. Susan Sontag, *AIDS and Its Metaphors* (New York: Farrar, Straus and Giroux, 1989). Sontag's *Illness as Metaphor* (New York: Farrar, Straus and Giroux, 1978) provides a pioneering study of the cultural myths surrounding cancer and tuberculosis. For other studies related to the representation of illness, see Michel Foucault, *Madness and Civilization: A History of Insanity in the Age of Reason* (1961), trans. Richard Howard (New York: Random House, 1965); and Saul Nathaniel Brody, *The Disease of the Soul: Leprosy in Medieval Literature* (Ithaca, N.Y.: Cornell University Press, 1974).

14. Quoted in Sandy Rovner, "Headaches: Portraits of Pain," *Washington Post Health*, 26 September 1989: 12.

15. John D. Loeser, "Unlocking the Secrets of Pain: The Treatment: A New Era," in *1988 Medical and Health Annual*, ed. Ellen Bernstein, 129.

16. See, for example, Steven F. Brena and Stanley Chapman, "Acute versus Chronic Pain States: The 'Learned Pain Syndrome,'" *Chronic Pain: Management Principles*, ed. Steven F. Brena and Stanley L. Chapman, *Clinics in Anesthesiology*, vol. 3, no. 1 (Philadelphia: W. B. Saunders, 1985), 41–55.

17. For an authoritative guide to the varieties of pain considered chronic, see the book-length special issue edited by Harold Merskey, "Classification of Chronic Pain: Description of Chronic Pain Syndromes and Definitions of Pain Terms," *Pain*, supp. 3 (1986).

18. Lawrence LeShan, "The World of the Patient in Severe Pain of Long Duration," *Journal of Chronic Diseases* 17 (1964): 119.

19. Quoted in Richard A. Sternbach, *Pain Patients: Traits and Treatment* (New York: Academic Press, 1974), 7.

20. *The Notebooks of Leonardo da Vinci*, ed. Edward MacCurdy (1939; rpt. Garden City, N.Y.: Garden City Publishing Co., 1941), 66.

21. Ronald Melzack, "The Personal Pain," in *Essays of Our Time I*, ed. Leo Hamalian and Edmond L. Volpe (New York: McGraw Hill, 1960), 172–177.

22. Bernard Shaw, *You Never Can Tell* (1899), in *Complete Plays with Prefaces*, 6 vols. (New York: Dodd, Mead & Company, 1962): 6:638. Shaw sets the play in 1896, which means that the patient, Crampton, would have been born well before the surgical use of ether. On the importance and nature of learning in our responses to pain, see Wilbert E. Fordyce, "Learning Processes in Pain," *The Psychology of Pain*, ed. Richard A. Sternbach, 2d ed. (New York: Raven Press, 1986), 49–66. Related work by Fordyce is cited in chapter six, note 22.

23. Virginia Woolf, "On Being Ill," in *The Moment and Other Essays* (New York: Harcourt Brace Jovanovich, 1948), 11.

24. Aristotle, *Nicomachean Ethics*, in *The Complete Works of Aristotle*, ed. Jonathan Barnes, 2 vols. (Princeton: Princeton University Press, 1984), 2: 1767.

25. Technically, a pain *clinic* implies outpatient care only, whereas a pain *center* covers both inpatient and outpatient treatment. (I will use the terms interchangeably.) Dr. John J. Bonica, describing the years that preceded the advent of the multidisciplinary pain clinic, says: "Between when I began in 1944 and 1970, nothing of any real significance really happened" (in *Pain Practitioner* 1, no. 2 [1989]: 1–3). For accounts of important developments since 1960, see *New Approaches to Treatment of Chronic Pain: A Review of Multidisciplinary Pain Clinics and Pain Centers*, ed. Lorenz K. Y. Ng, NIDA Research Monograph 36 (Washington, D.C.: Department of Health and Human Services, 1981). For a current description of the Center founded by Dr. Bonica, see *Managing the Chronic Pain Patient: Theory and Practice at the University of Washington Multidisciplinary Pain Center*, ed. John D. Loeser and Kelly J. Egan (New York: Raven Press, 1989).

26. Quoted in Gretchen Fields, "Winning the Pain Game," *West Michigan* 15 (August 1986): 7.

27. For the most recent listing, see *Directory of Pain Treatment Centers in the U.S. and Canada* (Phoenix, Ariz.: Oryx Press, 1989).

28. For a fascinating addition to the contemporary protests against mind/body dualism, see Mark Johnson, *The Body in the Mind: The Bodily Basis of Meaning, Imagination, and Reason* (Chicago: University of Chicago Press, 1987).

29. Herman Melville, *Moby-Dick or, The Whale* (1851), ed. Charles Feidelson, Jr. (New York: Bobbs-Merrill, 1964), 253–255.

FOUR: THE PAIN OF COMEDY

1. *The Will to Power* (1901–1906), trans. Walter Kaufmann and R. J. Hollingdale (New York: Random House, 1967), 517. Even a briefly annotated bibliography of modern scholarship on comedy runs well over three hundred pages. See James E. Evans, *Comedy: An Annotated Bibliography of Theory and Criticism* (Metuchen, N.J.: The Scarecrow Press, Inc., 1987). Other useful collections include *The Philosophy of Laughter and Humor*, ed. John Morreall (Albany: State University of New York Press, 1987); and *Theories of Comedy*, ed. Paul Lauter (Garden City, N.Y.: Doubleday, 1964). On the value to doctors of a comic perspective, see the lecture by Joanne Trautmann Banks, *Medicine and the Comic Spirit* (New Orleans, La.: American Osler Society, 1988).

2. On the "green world" of romantic comedy, see Northrop Frye, *Anatomy of Criticism* (Princeton: Princeton University Press, 1957), 182–183. I will disregard the various useful (but always too tidy) distinctions sometimes proposed in order to separate humor from comedy from the comic.

3. Plato, *Laws* (644*d*), in *The Collected Dialogues of Plato*, ed. Edith Hamilton and Huntington Cairns (Princeton: Princeton University Press, 1963), 1244.

4. Quoted by Peter W. Kaplan, "David Letterman's Shtick Shift," *Rolling Stone* 538 (3 November 1988): 75. This number is entitled "The Comedy Issue" and deals with recent changes in contemporary comic practice.

5. Matthew Arnold, "The Study of Poetry" (1880), *The Complete Prose Works of Matthew Arnold*, ed. R. H. Super, 11 vols. (Ann Arbor: University of Michigan Press, 1960–1977), 9: 177.

6. Norman Holland in *Laughing: A Psychology of Humor* (Ithaca, N.Y.: Cornell University Press, 1982) is among the few literary scholars to write about the anatomy and physiology of laughter. For other accounts, see Frederic R. Stearns, *Laughing: Physiology, Pathophysiology, Psychology, Pathopsychology and Development* (Springfield, Ill.: Charles C. Thomas, 1972); Herbert J. Levowitz, "Smiles and Laughter: Some Neurologic, Developmental, and Psychodynamic Considerations," in *Comedy: New Perspectives*, ed. Maurice Charney (New York: New York Literary Forum, 1978), 109–116.

7. See *Fragments for a History of the Human Body*, ed. Michel Feher, 2 vols. (New York: Zone Books, 1989).

8. Shakespeare, *Henry the Fourth, First Part* (1598), II.iv.242–243. All quotations refer to *The Riverside Shakespeare* (Boston: Houghton Mifflin, 1974). For an excellent study of Falstaff and company, see Jonathan Hall, "Falstaff, Sancho Panza and Azdak: Carnival and History," *Comparative Criticism* 7 (1985): 127–145.

9. *The Spectator*, no. 249 (1711), ed. Donald F. Bond, 5 vols. (Oxford: Clarendon Press, 1965), 2: 466. Norman Holland's *Laughing* surveys current research into laughter and infancy.

10. See, for example, Mahadev L. Apte, *Humor and Laughter: An Anthropological Approach* (Ithaca, N.Y.: Cornell University Press, 1985), 29–66.

11. See Francis MacDonald Cornford, *The Origin of Attic Comedy* (1934), ed. Theodore H. Gaster (Gloucester, Mass.: Peter Smith, 1968).

12. In the tradition of Bakhtinian views of laughter, Hélène Cixous in "The Laugh of the Medusa" (1975) foresees a "feminine text" that is subversive and seeks "to shatter the framework of institutions, to blow up the law, to break up the 'truth' with laughter" (trans. Keith Cohen and Paula Cohen, in *New French Feminisms*, ed. Elaine Marks and Isabelle de Courtivron [New York: Schocken Books, 1981], 258). See also the various essays in *Last Laughs: Perspectives on Women and Comedy*, ed. Regina Barreca (New York: Gordon and Breach, 1988).

13. Shakespeare, *King Lear* (1605), III.iv.106–108.

14. See, for example, Lane Cooper, *An Aristotelian Theory of Comedy* (1922; rpt. New York: Kraus, 1969); Richard Janko, *Aristotle on Comedy: Towards a Reconstruction of "Poetics" II* (Berkeley: University of California Press, 1984); and Leon Golden, "Aristotle on Comedy," *The Journal of Aesthetics and Art Criticism* 42 (1984): 283–290. Golden also offers a helpful discussion in "Eco's Reconstruction of Aristotle's Theory of Comedy in *The Name of the Rose*," *Classical and Modern Literature: A Quarterly* 6 (1986): 239–249.

15. *Aristotle's Poetics: A Translation and Commentary for Students of Literature*, trans. Leon Golden, commentary by O. B. Hardison (1968; rpt. Tallahassee: University Presses of Florida, 1981), 9 (chap. 5): italics added.

16. For a modern restatement and development of the traditional view, see "Comedy: The World of Pleasure" in Christopher Herbert's *Trollope and Comic Pleasure* (Chicago: University of Chicago Press, 1987), 10–31.

17. *Symposium* (216e), in *The Collected Dialogues of Plato*, ed. Hamilton and Cairns, 568. The Victorian classicist Benjamin Jowett writes of Plato: "These dialogues are in the great comic tradition, and Socrates is one of three of the greatest comic characters of all time; the others, that I am thinking of, are Don Quixote and Falstaff" ("Introduction," *The Republic*, trans. Benjamin Jowett [1871; rpt. Cleveland: Fine Editions Press, 1946], 7).

18. *Philebus* (50d), in *The Collected Dialogues of Plato*, ed. Hamilton and Cairns, 1132.

19. *The Notebooks of Leonardo da Vinci*, trans. Edward MacCurdy (1939; rpt. Garden City, N.Y.: Garden City Publishing, 1941), 1097.

20. Sigmund Freud, *Jokes and Their Relation to the Unconscious* (1905), in *The Standard Edition of the Complete Psychological Works of Sigmund Freud*, trans. and ed. James Strachey et al., 24 vols. (London: Hogarth Press, 1966), 8: 236.

21. See Richard Keller Simon, "Freud's Concepts of Comedy and Suffering," *The Psychoanalytic Review* 44 (1977): 391–407.

22. *The Diary of a Writer* (1873–1881), trans. Boris Brasol, 2 vols. (New York: Charles Scribner's Sons, 1949), 2: 836. Dostoevski was deeply drawn to the ridiculous heroism of Cervantes's knight: "Of all the noble figures in Christian literature, I reckon Don Quixote the most perfect. But Don Quixote is noble only by being at the same time comic" (*Letters of Fyodor Michailovitch Dostoevsky to His Family and Friends*, trans. Ethel Colburn Mayne [New York: Horizon Books, 1961], 142).

23. *The Adventures of Don Quixote*, trans. J. M. Cohen (Baltimore, Md.: Penguin Books, 1950), 317 (I.xxxv).

24. *Don Quixote*, trans. Cohen, 317 (I.xxxv).

25. *Don Quixote*, trans. Cohen, 317 (I.xxxv).

26. *Don Quixote*, trans. Cohen, 69–70 (I.vii). The best Spanish edition is *El Ingenioso Hidalgo Don Quijote de la Mancha*, ed. Vicente Gaos, 3 vols. (Madrid: Gredos, 1987).

27. Leon Golden in "Aristotle on Comedy" (285–287) argues that Aristotle's *Poetics* establishes a running parallel between comedy and tragedy. On the basis of this parallelism, he proposes "indignation" as the comic counterpart of tragic "pity." Golden does not, however, propose a counterpart for fear (which Aristotle in discussing tragic *catharsis* consistently links with pity). Like Plato, Aristotle understands fear as the anticipation of pain. Extended passages where Aristotle discusses fear (*Problems*, xxvii; *Rhetoric*, ii.5) suggest that its comic opposite

would be a courageous disregard for pain that approaches fearlessness or a conviction of invulnerability.

28. See Mikhail Bakhtin, *Rabelais and His World* (1965), trans. Hélène Iswolsky (Bloomington: Indiana University Press, 1984), 91–94. As a supplement and occasional corrective to Bakhtin, see also Peter Burke on "The World of Carnival" in *Popular Culture in Early Modern Europe* (New York: New York University Press, 1978), 178–204.

29. On the comic and burlesque traditions at work in *Don Quixote*, see P. E. Russell, *"Don Quixote* as a Funny Book," *Modern Language Review* 64 (1969): 312–326; and Anthony Close, *The Romantic Approach to "Don Quixote": A Critical History of the Romantic Tradition in Quixote Criticism* (Cambridge: Cambridge University Press, 1977). More controversial in his treatment of masochistic elements in the text is Louis Combet, *Cervantès ou les incertitudes du désir: Une approche psychostructurale de l'œuvre de Cervantès* (Lyon: Presses Universitaires de Lyon, 1980).

30. Shakespeare, *The Tempest* (1611), I.ii.368–371.

31. Here I am much indebted to Glending Olson, *Literature as Recreation in the Later Middle Ages* (Ithaca, N.Y.: Cornell University Press, 1982).

32. Quoted by Olson, *Literature as Recreation*, 58, 173. This tradition of therapeutic laughter can be traced back to the Hippocratic writings, especially "On Epidemics." Rabelais certainly encountered this tradition in his studies at the Montpellier Medical School and described it in the epistle that begins book four of his comic masterpiece *Gargantua and Pantagruel* (1532–1552).

33. Robert Burton, *Anatomy of Melancholy* (1621), ed. Floyd Dell and Paul Jordan-Smith (New York: Tudor Publishing Company, 1927), 368 (I.iv.1).

34. Burton, *Anatomy of Melancholy*, ed. Dell and Jordan-Smith, 482 (II.ii.6.4). The entire section ("Mirth and Merry Company, Fair Objects, Remedies") discusses the therapeutic values of merriment. On "the English malady," see Vieda Skultans, *English Madness: Ideas on Insanity, 1580–1890* (London: Routledge & Kegan Paul, 1978), 26–51. For the vaster history of this condition, see Stanley W. Jackson, *Melancholia and Depression: From Hippocratic Times to Modern Times* (New Haven: Yale University Press, 1986).

35. For an excellent study of this tradition of therapeutic humor, see Stuart M. Tave, *The Amiable Humorist: A Study in the Comic Theory and Criticism of the Eighteenth and Early Nineteenth Centuries* (Chicago: University of Chicago Press, 1960). The continuing medical and literary responses to melancholy can be traced in John F. Sena, *A Bibliography of Melancholy, 1660–1800* (London: Nether, 1970).

36. Laurence Sterne, *Tristram Shandy, Gentleman*, ed. Ian Watt (Boston: Houghton Mifflin, 1965), 225.

37. *New England Journal of Medicine* 295, no. 26 (23 December 1976): 1463–1485.

38. *Anatomy of an Illness as Perceived by the Patient: Reflections on Healing and Regeneration* (New York: W. W. Norton, 1979), 37, 89.

39. *Anatomy of an Illness*, 39–40.

40. *Anatomy of an Illness*, 47.

41. "Thirty to forty percent seems to be the baseline frequency with which pain is relieved by most placebos. . . . In controlled clinical trials of duodenal ulcer therapy, placebo effectiveness seldom falls below 35 or 45 percent, although it may rise as high as 60 percent depending upon the circumstances" (Howard M. Spiro, *Doctors, Patients, and Placebos* [New Haven, Conn.: Yale University Press, 1986], 86–87). On the self-healing powers engaged by placebos, see William B. Plotkin, "A Psychological Approach to Placebo: The Role of Faith in Therapy and Treatment," *Placebo: Theory, Research, and Mechanisms*, ed. Leonard White, Bernard Tursky, and Gary E. Schwartz (New York: The Guilford Press, 1985), 237–254.

42. See Kathleen M. Dillon, Brian Minchoff, and Katherine H. Baker, "Positive Emotional States and Enhancement of the Immune System," *International Journal of Psychiatry in Medicine* 15 (1985): 13–18. The authors found that the concentration of salivary immunoglobulin A (IgA) increased significantly after subjects viewed a humorous videotape, but did not change significantly after subjects viewed a didactic videotape.

43. See William F. Fry, Jr., "Humor, Physiology, and the Aging Process," *Humor and Aging*, ed. Lucile Nahemow, Kathleen A. McCluskey-Fawcett, and Paul E. McGhee (New York: Academic Press, 1986), 81–98; and Kaye Herth, "Contributions of Humor as Perceived by the Terminally Ill," *American Journal of Hospice and Palliative Care* 7 (January/February 1990): 36–40.

44. Jon D. Levine, Newton C. Gordon, and Howard L. Fields, "The Mechanism of Placebo Analgesia," *Lancet*, 23 September 1978: 655–657.

45. See Joel Davis, *Endorphins: New Waves in Brain Chemistry* (Garden City, N.Y.: Doubleday, 1984), especially 97–118 ("Endorphins and Pain"). Davis cites research that indicates the need for caution in attributing the placebo response to endorphins—or to endorphins alone (229). For a more technical account, see Allan I. Basbaum and Howard L. Fields, "Endogenous Pain Control Systems: Brainstem Spinal Pathways and Endorphin Circuitry," *Annual Review of Neuroscience* 7 (1984): 309–338.

46. Norman Cousins, *Head First: The Biology of Hope* (New York: E. P. Dutton, 1989), 150–153. The list does not consist entirely of humorous materials, but they clearly dominate.

47. Lars Ljungdahl, "Laugh If This Is a Joke," *JAMA* 261, no. 4 (1989): 558. See also *The Handbook of Humor Research*, ed. Paul E. McGhee and Jeffrey H. Goldstein, 2 vols. (New York: Springer-Verlag, 1983); and Herbert M. Lefcourt and Rod A. Martin, *Humor and Life Stress: Antidote to Adversity* (New York: Springer-Verlag, 1986).

48. Viktor E. Frankl, *Man's Search for Meaning: An Introduction to Logotherapy* (1946), trans. Ilse Lasch (New York: Pocket Books, 1963), 68. See also Terrence Des Pres, "Holocaust *Laughter?*", in *Writing and the Holocaust*, ed. Berel Lang (New York: Holmes & Meier, 1988), 216–233.

49. See, for example, Marjorie Garber, "'Wild Laughter in the Throat of Death': Darker Purposes in Shakespearean Comedy," in *Shakespearean Comedy*, ed.

Maurice Charney (New York: New York Literary Forum, 1980), 121–126; and Linda Anderson, *A Kind of Wild Justice: Revenge in Shakespeare's Comedies* (Newark: University of Delaware Press, 1987).

50. Christopher Fry, "Comedy" (1951), in *Comedy: Meaning and Form*, ed. Robert W. Corrigan (San Francisco: Chandler Publishing Company, 1965), 15.

51. Quoted in the excellent essay by B. H. Fussell, "A Pratfall Can Be a Beautiful Thing," *Comedy: New Perspectives*, ed. Maurice Charney (New York: New York Literary Forum, 1978), 243–257.

FIVE: HYSTERIA, PAIN, AND GENDER

1. *Epistolary Dissertation* (1681), in *The Works of Thomas Sydenham, M.D.*, trans. R. G. Latham, 2 vols. (London: The Sydenham Society, 1848–1850), 2: 85.

2. A. M. Rankin and P. J. Philip, "An Epidemic of Laughing in The Bukoba District of Tanganyika," *The Central African Journal of Medicine* 9, no. 5 (1963): 167–170. The episode is cited by William B. Bean, *Rare Diseases and Lesions: Their Contributions to Clinical Medicine* (Springfield, Ill.: Charles C. Thomas, 1967), 101. On recent work in related cases, see Donald W. Black, "Pathological Laughter: A Review of the Literature," *Journal of Nervous and Mental Disease* 170, no. 2 (1982): 67–71.

3. See Roberta Satow, "Where Has All the Hysteria Gone?", *Psychoanalytic Review* 66 (1979–1980): 463–477; and J. Laplanche, "Panel on 'Hysteria Today,'" *International Journal of Psycho-Analysis* 55 (1974): 459–469.

4. See Samuel B. Guze, "The Validity and Significance of the Clinical Diagnosis of Hysteria (Briquet's Syndrome)," *American Journal of Psychiatry* 132 (1975): 138–141; and George E. Murphy, "The Clinical Management of Hysteria," *JAMA* 247, no. 18 (1982): 2559–2564.

5. *Diagnostic and Statistical Manual of Mental Disorders*, 3d ed. rev. (Washington, D.C.: American Psychiatric Association, 1987), 257–259. It is a sign of changing attitudes that in the earlier, unrevised *DSM-III* (1980) the entry on hysterical neurosis was followed immediately by a related entry on "Psychogenic Pain Disorder." Seven years later psychogenic pain has been replaced by a condition called "Somatoform Pain Disorder": a "preoccupation with pain in the absence of adequate physical findings to account for the pain or its intensity" (264). "The disorder," as the entry explains, "is diagnosed almost twice as frequently in females as in males" (265). For recent medical texts, see *Hysterical Personality*, ed. Mardi J. Horowitz (New York: Jason Aronson, 1977); Alan Krohn, *Hysteria: The Elusive Diagnosis* (New York: International Universities Press, 1978); and *Hysteria*, ed. Alec Roy (New York: John Wiley & Sons, 1982).

6. *Doctor and Patient*, 3d ed. (Philadelphia: Lippincott, 1901), 83.

7. *Doctor and Patient*, 84.

8. For recent studies, see Eli Robins, James J. Purtell, and Mandel E. Cohen, "'Hysteria' in Men," *New England Journal of Medicine* 246 (1952): 677–685; and

Phillip Kroll, Kenneth R. Chamberlain, and James Halpern, "The Diagnosis of Briquet's Syndrome in a Male Population," *Journal of Nervous and Mental Disease* 167 (1979): 171–174. Robins et al. conclude that hysteria as diagnosed in men is probably not the same disease as hysteria in women. Kroll et al. see a very different range of symptoms separating men and women who are diagnosed as hysterical. On the counterpart of hysteria, see Susan Baur, *Hypochondria: Woeful Imaginings* (Berkeley: University of California Press, 1988).

9. On early ideas about hysteria, see Ilza Veith, *Hysteria: The History of a Disease* (Chicago: University of Chicago Press, 1965).

10. See Veith, *Hysteria*, 210. Ann Douglas Wood observes that uterine cauterization involved applying nitrate of silver, hydrate of potassa, or a white-hot iron. "In a successful case, the uterus was left 'raw and bleeding' and the patient in severe pain for several days; in an unsuccessful one, severe hemorrhage and terrible pain might result. It should be noted that the cauterization process, whether by chemicals or by the iron, had to be repeated several times at intervals of a few days" ("'The Fashionable Diseases': Women's Complaints and Their Treatment in Nineteenth-Century America," *Journal of Interdisciplinary History* 4 [1973]: 30–31).

11. *Epistolary Dissertation* (1681), in *The Works of Thomas Sydenham*, trans. Latham, 2: 90.

12. *Epistolary Dissertation*, in *The Works of Thomas Sydenham*, trans. Latham, 2: 85.

13. *The Major Symptoms of Hysteria*, 2d ed. (New York: Macmillan, 1920), 272.

14. *Traité de l'hystérie* (1859), in Francois M. Mai and Harold Merskey, "Briquet's Treatise on Hysteria: A Synopsis and Commentary," *Archives of General Psychiatry* 37 (December 1980): 1404. For an excellent discussion of hysteria and neurasthenia beginning with Victorian England, see Elaine Showalter, *The Female Malady: Women, Madness, and English Culture, 1830–1980* (New York: Pantheon Books, 1985).

15. *Traité de l'hystérie*, in Mai and Mersky, "Briquet's *Treatise*: Synopsis and Commentary," 1403.

16. In *The Standard Edition of the Complete Psychological Works of Sigmund Freud*, trans. and ed. James Strachey et al., 2: 72. For an extensive discussion of Freud's understanding of hysterical pain, see Monique David-Ménard, *Hysteria From Freud to Lacan: Body and Language in Psychoanalysis* (1983), trans. Catherine Porter (Ithaca, N.Y.: Cornell University Press, 1989), 17–20 and 25–54.

17. Thomas Inman, "On So-Called Hysterical Pain," *British Medical Journal*, 9 January 1858: 24.

18. The sexual politics and family warfare implicit in hysteria, when the sick woman in effect declined to perform her traditional household duties, is described by Carroll Smith-Rosenberg, "The Hysterical Woman: Sex Roles and Role Conflict in 19th-Century America," *Social Research* 39 (1972): 652–678. Mary Poovey offers an analysis of the similar politics implicit in nineteenth-century debates over the use of chloroform in childbirth ("'Scenes of an Indel-

icate Character': The Medical 'Treatment' of Victorian Women," *The Making of the Modern Body: Sexuality and Society in the Nineteenth Century*, ed. Catherine Gallagher and Thomas Laqueur [Berkeley: University of California Press, 1987], 137–168]). Also helpful in illuminating the sexual politics of nineteenth-century medicine is Lorna Duffin, "The Conspicuous Consumptive: Woman as an Invalid," *The Nineteenth-Century Woman: Her Cultural and Physical World*, ed. Sara Delamont and Lorna Duffin (New York: Barnes and Noble, 1978), 26–56; and "The Sexual Politics of Sickness" in Barbara Ehrenreich and Deirdre English, *For Her Own Good: 150 Years of the Experts' Advice to Women* (New York: Doubleday, 1978), 91–126.

19. Joan M. Romano, Judith A. Turner, and Mark D. Sullivan, "What Are Some Basic Guidelines for the Primary Care Practitioner's Management of Chronic Nonmalignant Pain?", *American Pain Society Newsletter*, Winter 1989: 4. The list of recommendations starts with an insistence on the necessity of distinguishing between acute and chronic pain.

20. *An Essay on Hysteria* (Philadelphia: Haswell, Barrington, and Haswell, 1840), 96.

21. Charlotte Perkins Gilman, *The Living of Charlotte Perkins Gilman: An Autobiography* (New York: D. Appleton-Century, 1935), 95.

22. See Ellen L. Bassuk, "The Rest Cure: Repetition or Resolution of Victorian Women's Conflicts?", *The Female Body in Western Culture: Contemporary Perspectives*, ed. Susan Rubin Suleiman (Cambridge, Mass.: Harvard University Press, 1986), 139–151.

23. *The Living of Charlotte Perkins Gilman*, 96.

24. *The Yellow Wallpaper*, afterword by Elaine R. Hedges (Old Westbury, N.Y.: The Feminist Press, 1973), 10. It was first published in *The New England Magazine* for May 1892. William Dean Howells, who had recommended it (unsuccessfully) to the editor of *The Atlantic Monthly*, reprinted it in 1920 in his anthology *Great Modern American Stories*.

25. *The Yellow Wallpaper*, 23. Feminist critics have written a number of studies of Gilman's narrative. For a complex analysis of *The Yellow Wallpaper* that discusses the merits and shortcomings of earlier work, see Mary Jacobus, *Reading Woman: Essays in Feminist Criticism* (New York: Columbia University Press, 1986), 229–248.

26. *The Living of Charlotte Perkins Gilman*, 121.

27. Gilman, *The Yellow Wallpaper*, 10, 14, 34, 25.

28. Gilman writes of her return from Dr. Mitchell's rest cure: "I went home, followed those directions rigorously for months. . . . The mental agony grew so unbearable that I would sit blankly moving my head from side to side—to get out from under the pain. Not physical pain, not the least 'headache' even, just mental torment, so heavy in its nightmare gloom that it seemed real enough to dodge" (*The Living of Charlotte Perkins Gilman*, 96).

29. See Charles L. Dana, "A Study of the Anaesthesias of Hysteria," *American Journal of the Medical Sciences* 101 (October 1890): 365–376.

30. Janet, *The Major Symptoms of Hysteria*, 2d ed. (New York: Macmillan, 1920), 272. See J.-M. Charcot, *Lectures on Diseases of the Nervous System* (1872–1883), trans. G. Sigerson and T. Savill, 3 vols. (London: The New Sydenham Society, 1877–1889).

31. Janet, *The Major Symptoms of Hysteria*, 273.

32. Janet, *The Major Symptoms of Hysteria*, 276.

33. Here is a brief fragment of an interview in which Duras discusses the voices that call to her women: "Desire is the biggest voice. . . . So the pain, all that, is very, very, very close" (Marguerite Duras and Xavière Gauthier, *Woman to Woman*, trans. Katharine A. Jensen [Lincoln: University of Nebraska Press, 1987], 159). The Duras/Gauthier interviews were published in French under the title *Les Parleuses* (Paris: Éditions de minuit, 1974). In the passage above (*Les Parleuses*, 215), as throughout her work, the word that Duras employs for pain is *douleur*.

34. See the chapter "La maladie de la douleur: Duras" in Julia Kristeva's *Soleil noir: Dépression et mélancolie* (Paris: Gallimard, 1987). The essay is translated as "The Pain of Sorrow in the Modern World: The Works of Marguerite Duras," *PMLA* 102 (1987): 138–152. Kristeva notes in Duras's work "the frigid insignificance of a psychic numbing, which is the minimal but also the ultimate sign of pain and ravishment" (141).

35. *The Complete Poems of Emily Dickinson*, ed. Thomas H. Johnson, 294 (no. 599).

36. *The Malady of Death* (1982), trans. Barbara Bray (New York: Grove Press, 1986), 45.

37. *The Ravishing of Lol Stein* (1964), trans. Richard Seaver (New York: Pantheon, 1966), 15. For the French text, see *Le Ravissement de Lol V. Stein* (Paris: Gallimard, 1964), 25.

38. Duras and Gauthier, *Woman to Woman*, trans. Jensen, 8.

39. *The Ravishing of Lol Stein*, trans. Seaver, 3.

40. *The Vice-Consul* (1966), trans. Eileen Ellenbogen (New York: Pantheon Books, 1968), 158.

41. Duras and Gauthier, *Woman to Woman*, trans. Jensen, 6.

42. Duras and Gauthier, *Woman to Woman*, trans. Jensen, 127.

43. Dianne Hunter, "Hysteria, Psychoanalysis, and Feminism: The Case of Anna O." (1983), rpt. *The (M)other Tongue: Essays in Feminist Psychoanalytic Interpretation*, ed. Shirley Nelson Garner, Claire Kahane, and Madelon Sprengnether (Ithaca, N.Y.: Cornell University Press, 1985), 113–114.

44. Mitchell, *Fat and Blood*, 155.

45. Duras, "Baxter, Vera Baxter," *Marguerite Duras* (1976), trans. Nancy J. Peters and Amy Scholder (San Francisco: City Lights Books, 1987), 95; also Duras and Gauthier, *Woman to Woman*, trans. Jensen, 119–120.

46. Duras and Gauthier, *Woman to Woman*, trans. Jensen, 120.

47. As Duras says: "'feminine literature' is an organic, translated writing . . . translated from blackness, from darkness. Women have been in darkness for centuries. They don't know themselves. Or only poorly. And when women write, they translate this darkness" (in Susan Husserl-Kapit, "An Interview with Marguerite Duras," *Signs* 1 [1975]: 425).

48. *Reading Woman: Essays in Feminist Criticism* (New York: Columbia University Press, 1986), 201.

49. *Women: The Longest Revolution* (New York: Pantheon Books, 1984), 289–290. Mary Jacobus quotes not only this passage from Mitchell but also an equally famous statement by Julia Kristeva that women's writing is "the discourse of the hysteric."

50. Patricia Fedikew, "Marguerite Duras: Feminine Field of Hysteria," *Enclitic* 6 (1982): 78–86.

51. For a good example of recent feminist readings of Lol Stein, see Alice A. Jardine, *Gynesis: Configurations of Woman and Modernity* (Ithaca, N.Y.: Cornell University Press, 1985); Sharon Willis, *Marguerite Duras: Writing on the Body* (Urbana: University of Illinois Press, 1987); and Trista Selous, *The Other Woman: Feminism and Femininity in the Work of Marguerite Duras* (New Haven, Conn.: Yale University Press, 1988).

52. In Husserl-Kapit, "An Interview with Marguerite Duras," 432.

53. Duras, *The War: A Memoir* (1985), trans. Barbara Bray (New York: Pantheon Books, 1986), 115. The English title completely misses the implications of the French title *La Douleur*.

SIX: VISIONARY PAIN AND THE POLITICS OF SUFFERING

1. *The Political Unconscious: Narrative As a Socially Symbolic Act* (Ithaca, N.Y.: Cornell University Press, 1981), 102.

2. Jacobus de Voragine, *The Golden Legend*, trans. Granger Ryan and Helmut Ripperger (New York: Longmans, Green and Co., 1941), 108–109. The Latin text was first translated into English by William Caxton as *The Legende named in Latyn Legenda aurea that is to say in Englisshe The golden legende* (1493), based in part on the French translation by Jean de Vignay.

3. See the entries in *The Book of Saints*, compiled by The Benedictine Monks of St. Augustine's Abbey, Ramsgate, 5th ed. (New York: Thomas Y. Crowell, 1966); and *Butler's Lives of the Saints*, ed. Herbert Thurston and Donald Attwater, 4 vols. (New York: P. J. Kenedy & Sons, 1962). It was not until the tenth century that saints were canonized by popes. The early church had no formal process of canonization, but local cults abounded, and the translation of a martyr's relics from the burial site to a church was equivalent to canonization.

4. See E. Hoade, "St. Sebastian," *New Catholic Encyclopedia* (Washington, D.C.: Catholic University of America, 1967), 13: 18.

5. W. H. Auden, "Musée des Beaux Arts" (1938), in *Collected Poems*, ed. Edward Mendelson (New York: Random House, 1976).

6. Yukio Mishima, *Confessions of a Mask* (1949), trans. Meredith Weatherby (New York: New Directions, 1958), 39–40. Mishima's fascination with Sebastian is discussed in John Nathan's *Mishima: A Biography* (Boston: Little, Brown and Company, 1974), 95–97.

7. *Vida de Santa Teresa de Jesus* (1611), in *Obras Completas*, ed. Luis Santullano (Madrid: Aguilar, 1963), 233. I have employed the translation by Kieran Kavanaugh and Otilio Rodriguez, *The Collected Works of St. Teresa of Avila*, 3 vols. (Washington, D.C.: Institute of Carmelite Studies, 1976–1985), 1: 193–194.

8. Richard Crashaw, "A Hymn to the Name and Honor of the Admirable Sainte Teresa" (1652), *The Poems of Richard Crashaw*, ed. L. C. Martin, 2d ed. (Oxford: Clarendon Press, 1957).

9. *Life of the Mother Teresa of Jesus*, in *Works*, trans. Kavanaugh and Rodriguez, 1: 131 ("The body feels it along with the soul, and both seem to have a share in it"). Teresa contrasts this rapturous mixed pain ("pena") of body and soul with a far more desolate pain that concerns the soul alone and that attends the state of prayer.

10. "Portando ànno diletto e non portando ànno pena" (*Il Dialogo della Divina Provvidenza ovvero Libro della Divina Dottrina*, ed. Giuliana Cavallini [Rome: Edizioni Cateriniane, 1968], 191). I have used the translation by Suzanne Noffke, *The Dialogue* (New York: Paulist Press, 1980), 155.

11. M. Starr Costello, "Catherine of Siena and The Eschatology of Suffering," *Vox Benedictina* 5 (1988): 49. For two studies of the medieval acetic tradition within which Catherine's spirituality must be understood, see Rudolph M. Bell, *Holy Anorexia* (Chicago: University of Chicago Press, 1985); and Caroline Walker Bynum, *Holy Feast and Holy Fast: The Religious Significance of Food to Medieval Women* (Berkeley: University of California Press, 1987).

12. Giles Constable, *Attitudes Toward Self-Inflicted Suffering in the Middle Ages*, The Ninth Stephen J. Brademas, Sr., Lecture (Brookline, Mass.: Hellenic College Press, 1982), 20.

13. *The Dialogue*, trans. Noffke, 29.

14. *The Dialogue*, trans. Noffke, 323.

15. *The Dialogue*, trans. Noffke, 30.

16. See Raymond Crawford, *Plague and Pestilence in Literature and Art* (Oxford: Clarendon Press, 1914).

17. Daniel Defoe, *A Journal of the Plague Year* (1722), ed. Louis Landa (New York: Oxford University Press, 1969), 76. Medicine was of little help against such an adversary, which it sometimes inadvertently aided. As Defoe continues: "The Pain of the Swelling was in particular very violent, and to some intollerable [*sic*]; the Physicians and Surgeons may be said to have tortured many poor Creatures, even to Death" (81–82).

18. *The Diary of Samuel Pepys*, ed. Robert Latham and William Matthews, 11 vols. (Berkeley: University of California Press, 1970–1983), 6: 170–171. Spelling normalized.

19. For a helpful review of recent scholarship, see *Studies in the Book of Job*, ed. Walter E. Aufrecht (Waterloo, Ontario: Wilfrid Laurier University Press, 1985).

20. For an overview of recent work on Blake's *Job*, see the review essay by Mary Lynn Johnson in *The English Romantic Poets: A Review of Research and Criticism*, ed. Frank Jordan (New York: MLA, 1985), 246–249. I am relying here on the traditional interpretation by S. Foster Damon.

21. On Job as scapegoat, who bears the violence of the entire community, see René Girard, *Job: The Victim of His People* (1985), trans. Yvonne Freccero (Stanford: Stanford University Press, 1987). Girard's reading of *Job* develops the thesis of his classic work *Violence and the Sacred*. As he writes: "Violence is the heart and secret soul of the sacred" (*Violence and the Sacred* [1972], trans. Patrick Gregory [Baltimore, Md.: Johns Hopkins University Press, 1977], 31).

22. Wilbert E. Fordyce, "Pain Viewed as Learned Behavior," *Advances in Neurology*, vol. 4, ed. John J. Bonica (New York: Raven Press, 1974), 415–422; and, most important, Wilbert E. Fordyce, *Behavioral Methods for Chronic Pain and Illness* (St. Louis, Mo.: C. V. Mosby, 1976). See also the comprehensive and balanced account in Dennis C. Turk, Donald Meichenbaum, and Myles Genest, *Pain and Behavioral Medicine: A Cognitive-Behavioral Perspective* (New York: Guilford, 1983).

23. Richard A. Sternbach, *Pain Patients: Traits and Treatment* (New York: Academic Press, 1974), 100.

24. For a rigorous development of behaviorist thinking, see Howard Rachlin, "Pain and Behavior," *The Behavioral and Brain Sciences* 8 (1985): 43–53. His essay inspired an additional thirty pages of expert commentary.

25. See the distinction between "sensory" and "psychological" pain in Rachlin, "Pain and Behavior," 43–53.

26. See, for example, Asenath Petrie, *Personality and the Frontal Lobes* (New York: Blakiston, 1952); and John C. Nemiah, "The Effect of Leukotomy on Pain," *Psychosomatic Medicine* 24 (1962): 75–80. On the philosophical and cultural implications of such now outdated psychosurgery, see Roger Trigg, *Pain and Emotion* (Oxford: Clarendon Press, 1970), 125–142; and Elliot S. Valenstein, "The History of Lobotomy: A Cautionary Tale," *Michigan Quarterly Review* 27 (1988): 417–427.

27. See, for example, Kenneth D. Craig, "Social Modeling Influences: Pain in Context," *The Psychology of Pain*, ed. Sternbach, 67–96.

28. *The Interpreter's Dictionary of the Bible*, ed. George Arthur Buttrick et al., 4 vols. (Nashville, Tenn.: Abingdon Press, 1962), 4:451; and *The International Standard Bible Encyclopedia*, ed. Geoffrey W. Bromiley et al., 4 vols. (Grand Rapids, Mich.: Eerdmans Publishing Company, 1979), 3: 628.

29. See Mary M. McBride, "Assessing Children with Pain," *Pediatric Nursing* 3, no. 4 (1977): 7–8; and Margo McCaffery, "Pain Relief for the Child: Problem

Areas and Selected Nonpharmacological Methods," *Pediatric Nursing* 3, no. 4 (1977): 11–16.

30. Joann M. Eland and Jane M. Alexander, "The Experience of Pain in Children," in *Pain: A Sourcebook for Nurses and Other Health Professionals*, ed. Ada Jacox (Boston: Little, Brown and Company, 1977), 453–476.

31. Steven M. Selbst and Mark Clark, "Analgesic Use in the Emergency Department," paper presented at the 29th Annual Meeting of the Ambulatory Pediatric Association, Washington, D.C. (May 1989); and Helen Neal, *The Politics of Pain* (New York: McGraw-Hill, 1978).

32. Ruth Sivard, *World Military and Social Expenditures 1983* (Washington, D.C.: World Priorities, 1983), 5.

33. "Liberation Theology vs. Cardinal Ratzinger," *Tikkun* 3, no. 3 (1988): 19–20. For useful introductions, see Roger Haight, *An Alternative Vision: An Interpretation of Liberation Theology* (New York: Paulist Press, 1985); and Ricardo Planas, *Liberation Theology: The Political Expression of Religion* (Kansas City, Mo.: Sheed & Ward, 1986).

34. "The Church in the Present-Day Transformation of Latin America in the Light of the Council" (1968), in *Liberation Theology: A Documentary History*, ed. Alfred T. Hennelly (Maryknoll, N.Y.: Orbis Press, 1990), 90.

35. Gustavo Gutierrez, *A Theology of Liberation: History, Politics and Salvation* (1971), trans. Caridad Inda and John Eagleson (Maryknoll, N.Y.: Orbis Books, 1973), 154.

36. *A Theology of Liberation*, trans. Inda and Eagleson, 175.

37. Quoted in Gustavo Gutierrez, *On Job: God-Talk and the Suffering of the Innocent* (1986), trans. Matthew J. O'Connell (Maryknoll, N.Y.: Orbis Books, 1987), xiv–xv.

38. Quoted in Gutierrez, *On Job*, trans. O'Connell, 40.

39. *On Job*, trans. O'Connell, 102.

SEVEN: PAIN IS ALWAYS IN YOUR HEAD

1. "The Cult of 'Common Usage,'" *The British Journal for the Philosophy of Science* 3 (1952–1953): 306.

2. Ronald Melzack, "Central Neural Mechanisms in Phantom Limb Pain," in *Advances in Neurology*, vol. 4, ed. John J. Bonica, 319.

3. In C. Murray Parkes, "Factors Determining the Persistence of Phantom Pain in the Amputee," *Journal of Psychosomatic Research* 17 (1973): 99. On the localized nature of pain—as opposed to the nonlocal nature of pleasure—see Gilbert Ryle, "Pleasure," in *Dilemmas* (Cambridge: Cambridge University Press, 1954), 54–67.

4. See Richard A. Sherman, Crystal J. Sherman, and Glenda M. Bruno, "Psychological Factors Influencing Chronic Phantom Limb Pain: An Analysis of the

Literature," *Pain* 28 (1987): 285–295; and Norman Postone, "Phantom Limb Pain: A Review," *International Journal of Psychiatry in Medicine* 17 (1987): 57–70.

5. For a highly technical but nonetheless clear explanation, see David Bowsher, "The Anatomo-physiology of Pain," *Persistent Pain: Modern Methods of Treatment*, vol. 1, ed. Sampson Lipton (New York: Grune & Stratton, 1977), 1–20. Also clear and excellent is Ronald Melzack's "Neurophysiological Foundations of Pain," in *The Psychology of Pain*, ed. Sternbach, 1–24. On recent research into the chemical compound called bradykinin released at the site of tissue damage, see Kevin McKean, "Pain," *Discover* 7, no. 10 (October 1986): 82–92.

6. See Hoyle Leigh and Morton F. Reiser, *The Patient: Biological, Psychological, and Social Dimensions of Medical Practice*, 2d ed. (New York: Plenum Medical Book Company, 1985), 212.

7. See McKean, "Pain," 82–92.

8. See the classic article by George L. Engel, "'Psychogenic' Pain and the Pain-Prone Patient," *American Journal of Medicine* 26 (1959): 899–918. Another equally classic article by Thomas S. Szasz helped to emphasize the ways in which chronic pain depends on consciousness ("The Psychology of Persistent Pain: A Portrait of L'Homme Douloureux," *Pain*, ed. A. Soulairac, J. Cahn, and J. Charpentier [New York: Academic Press, 1968], 93–113). As Szasz writes: "Feeling pain depends on whether a person has a reason for the experience; if he does have a reason, he will have pain, even if he has no bodily lesion 'causing' it" (94).

9. Leigh and Reiser, *The Patient*, 233.

10. "Pain in the hand is felt by the soul not because the soul is present in the hand but because the soul is present in the brain" (*Principles of Philosophy* [1644], in *The Philosophical Writings of Descartes*, trans. John Cottingham, Robert Stoothoff, and Dugald Murdoch, 2 vols. [Cambridge: Cambridge University Press, 1985], 1: 284). Phantom limb pain thus helped confirm Descartes's belief that the soul was located in the brain (in the pineal gland, to be exact). I have clarified ambiguous pronouns in the translation.

11. For a thorough account, see Lawrence G. Miller, "Pain, Parturition, and the Profession: The Twilight Sleep in America," in *Health Care in America: Essays in Social History*, ed. Susan Reverby and David Rosner (Philadelphia: Temple University Press, 1979), 19–44.

12. *Scopolamine-Morphine Anaesthesia* (1915), quoted in Judith Walzer Leavitt, "Birthing and Anesthesia: The Debate over Twilight Sleep," *Signs* 6 (1980): 149.

13. Margarete Sandelowski, *Pain, Pleasure, and American Childbirth: From the Twilight Sleep to the Read Method, 1914–1960* (Westport, Conn.: Greenwood Press, 1984), 37. The ratio Sandelowski cites is 61 deaths for every 10,000 live births.

14. *Historical Statistics of the United States: Colonial Times to 1970*, 2 vols. (Washington, D.C.: U.S. Department of Commerce, 1975), 1: 63. The actual figure is 13.7 deaths per 1,000 women.

15. Quoted in Miller, "Pain, Parturition, and the Profession: Twilight Sleep in America," *Health Care in America*, ed. Reverby and Rosner, 20.

16. Bertha Van Hoosen, *Scopolamine-Morphine Anaesthesia* (Chicago: House of Manz, 1915), 114.

17. Quoted in Leavitt, "Birthing and Anesthesia: The Debate over Twilight Sleep," 154.

18. See C. J. De Vogel, *Greek Philosophy: A Collection of Texts with Notes and Explanations*, 3 vols. (Leiden: E. J. Brill, 1963–1964). Only in volume three are there any references to pain in the index, and then only a handful. The proportions are roughly the same in A. A. Long and D. N. Sedley, *The Hellenistic Philosophers*, 2 vols. (Cambridge: Cambridge University Press, 1987).

19. *Arrian's Discourses of Epictetus*, IV.vi.10, in *Epictetus*, trans. W. A. Oldfather, 2 vols. (Cambridge, Mass.: Harvard University Press, 1925), 2: 349. As Epictetus asks an imagined opponent: "Are not things now upside down? Is this what you have been in earnest about? Not to learn how to get rid of pain, and turmoil, and humiliation, and so become free? Have you not heard that there is but a single way which leads to this end, and that is to give up the things which lie outside the sphere of the moral purpose, and to abandon them, and to admit that they are not your own?"

20. For differences between Marcus Aurelius and Epictetus, as well as a survey of relevant historical and philosophical backgrounds, see R. B. Rutherford, *The Meditations of Marcus Aurelius: A Study* (Oxford: Clarendon Press, 1989). For a discussion of attitudes toward pain in ancient thought, including Stoicism, see *Theological Dictionary of the New Testament*, ed. Gerhard Kittel and Gerhard Friedrich, trans. and ed. Geoffrey W. Bromiley, 10 vols (Grand Rapids, Mich.: Eerdmans Publishing Company, 1964–1976), 4: 313–324.

21. Marcus Aurelius, *Meditations*, VII.33, trans. Maxwell Staniforth (New York: Viking Penguin, 1964), 33. The Greek text, with English translation, is available under the title *The Meditations of the Emperor Marcus Antonius*, trans. and ed. A. S. L. Farquharson, 2 vols. (1944; rpt. Oxford: Clarendon Press, 1968). For a discussion of Stoic attitudes toward pleasure and pain, particularly in the writings of the Stoic philosopher Chrysippus, see J. M. Rist, *Stoic Philosophy* (Cambridge: Cambridge University Press, 1969), 37–53.

22. Marcus Aurelius, *Meditations*, IV.41, trans. Staniforth, 73.

23. *Meditations*, VIII.28, trans. Staniforth, 127. Here and elsewhere in Marcus Aurelius the Greek term for pain is *ponos*. For a convenient discussion of some of the main themes of Stoic philosophy, see *The Stoics*, ed. John M. Rist (Berkeley: University of California Press, 1978). The ancient attitudes toward pain vary, often confusingly. According to Cicero, the Stoics deny that pain is an evil, unlike the Epicureans. The Peripatetics say that pain is an evil, but (like the Stoics) they teach that bearing pain with fortitude is a duty (*De Finibus* V.xxxi).

24. *Meditations*, VII.64, trans. Staniforth, 116.

25. Thomas S. Kuhn, *The Structure of Scientific Revolutions*, 2d ed. (Chicago: University of Chicago Press, 1970). Kuhn's book, which first appeared in 1962, has generated a quarter-century of controversy and discussion. For opposing views of how science works, see, for example, *Criticism and the Growth of Knowl-*

edge, ed. Imre Lakatos and Alan Musgrave (London: Cambridge University Press, 1970); and Paul Feyerabend, *Against Method: Outline of an Anarchistic Theory of Knowledge* (1975; rpt. London: Verso Edition, 1978).

26. See B. L. Crue et al., "What is a Pain Center?", in *Chronic Pain: Further Observations from City of Hope National Medical Center*, ed. Benjamin L. Crue, Jr. (New York: SP Medical & Scientific Books, 1978), 3–12.

27. Allan I. Basbaum, "Unlocking the Secrets of Pain: The Science," *1988 Medical and Health Annual*, ed. Ellen Bernstein, 97.

28. B. L. Crue, "The Courage To Risk Being Wrong," *Bulletin of the Los Angeles Neurological Societies* 26 (1981): 5.

29. Benjamin L. Crue, Jr., "The Centralist Concept of Chronic Pain," *Seminars in Neurology* 3 (1983): 331.

30. The classic text is by Valentino Cassinari and Carlo A. Pagni, *Central Pain: Neurological Survey* (Cambridge, Mass.: Harvard University Press, 1969). Stroke, multiple sclerosis, and spinal cord injuries—to name the most common sources of central pain syndromes—all produce evident or easily verifiable lesions of the central nervous system. The controversy heats up when researchers ask whether other chronic pain patients might suffer through a central mechanism that cannot be described in terms of traditional organic *lesions*.

31. Crue, "The Courage to Risk Being Wrong," 5.

32. Crue, "The Centralist Concept of Chronic Pain," 331.

33. Crue, "The Courage to Risk Being Wrong," 10–11.

34. The text first appeared under the title *Ein Psycholog erlebt das Konzentrationslager* (1946). Subsequent editions added new materials. The English version first appeared in 1959 under the now discarded title *From Death-Camp to Existentialism: A Psychiatrist's Path to a New Therapy*. *The Doctor and the Soul* was first published in 1946 under the title *Ärtzliche Seelsorge*.

35. Viktor E. Frankl, *Man's Search for Meaning: An Introduction to Logotherapy*, trans. (part one) Ilse Lasch (New York: Pocket Books, 1963), 7. Frankl's account stands alongside the untold stories of over five million Jews who perished in the Holocaust, as described in Raul Hilberg's definitive three-volume study *The Destruction of the European Jews*, rev. ed. (New York: Holmes & Meier, 1985).

36. Frankl, *Man's Search for Meaning*, 41–42.

37. Frankl, *Man's Search for Meaning*, 121. On the difficulties of discovering language and meaning appropriate to an event so catastrophic, see Maurice Blanchot, *The Writing of the Disaster* (1980), trans. Ann Smock (Lincoln: University of Nebraska Press, 1986); and *Writing and the Holocaust*, ed. Berel Lang (New York: Holmes & Meier, 1988).

38. Frankl, *The Will to Meaning: Foundations and Applications of Logotherapy* (1969; rpt. New York: New American Library, 1970), 72.

39. Frankl, *Man's Search for Meaning*, trans. Lasch, 122.

40. Frankl, *Man's Search for Meaning*, trans. Lasch, 123–124.

41. Frankl, *Man's Search for Meaning*, trans. Lasch, 106.

42. Frankl, *The Will to Meaning*, 76–77.

43. Francis Bacon, *The Advancement of Learning* (1605), IV.ii, in *The Works of Francis Bacon*, ed. James Spedding, Robert Leslie Ellis, and Douglas Denon Heath, 15 vols. (London: Longman and Co.: 1860–1864), 4: 387.

EIGHT: THE USES OF PAIN

1. Ernest Hemingway, *Selected Letters, 1917–1961*, ed. Carlos Baker (New York: Charles Scribner's Sons, 1981), 408.

2. Gerald L. Bruns, "Language, Pain, and Fear," *The Iowa Review* 11, no. 2 (1980): 132.

3. Freud, *Studies on Hysteria* (1895), in *The Standard Edition of the Complete Psychological Works of Sigmund Freud*, trans. and ed. Strachey et al., 2: 178. Freud does not assume that the insult *created* the pain; he insists that often an existing organic pain is "merely used, increased and maintained" by the neurosis (2: 174).

4. See Robert C. Elliott, *The Power of Satire: Magic, Ritual, Art* (Princeton: Princeton University Press, 1960), 7.

5. "A Discourse Concerning the Original and Progress of Satire" (1693), in *Essays of John Dryden*, ed. W. P. Ker, 2 vols. (New York: Russell & Russell, 1961), 2: 93.

6. Lady Mary Wortley Montagu, *Verses Address'd to the Imitator of Horace* (London, 1733), 4.

7. In Joseph Spence, *Observations, Anecdotes, and Characters of Books and Men* (1820), ed. James M. Osborn (Oxford: Clarendon Press, 1966), 1: 149. For additional discussion, see my book *Alexander Pope: The Genius of Sense* (Cambridge, Mass.: Harvard University Press, 1984), 214–240.

8. See Mary Claire Randolph, "The Medical Concept in English Renaissance Satiric Theory" (1941), in *Satire: Modern Essays in Criticism*, ed. Ronald Paulson (Englewood Cliffs, N.J.: Prentice-Hall, 1971), 135–170.

9. See Alexander Pope, "Epilogue to the Satires. Dialogue I" (1738). On the Italian tradition of punitive art, called "pitture infamanti," see Samuel Y. Edgerton, Jr., *Pictures and Punishment: Art and Criminal Prosecution during the Florentine Renaissance* (Ithaca, N.Y.: Cornell University Press, 1985).

10. Two crucial works for understanding changes in attitudes toward punishment are Michel Foucault's *Discipline and Punish: The Birth of the Prison* (1975), trans. Alan Sheridan (New York: Pantheon Books, 1977); and Michael Ignatieff's *A Just Measure of Pain: The Penitentiary in the Industrial Revolution* (New York: Pantheon Books, 1978). On the theory and practice of legal punishment, see Leon Radzinowicz, *A History of English Criminal Law and Its Administration from 1750*, 4 vols. (New York: Macmillan, 1948–1968), especially volume one.

11. In *The Correspondence of Jonathan Swift*, ed. Harold Williams, 5 vols. (Oxford: Clarendon Press, 1963), 3: 102–103 (29 September 1725).

12. In *The Correspondence of Jonathan Swift*, ed. Williams, 3: 289 (1 June 1728).

13. *Inferno*, xxxii.76–78, in *The Divine Comedy*, trans. Charles S. Singleton, 3 vols. (Princeton: Princeton University Press, 1977), 1: 343. On this incident, see Gerald L. Bruns, "Allegory and Satire: A Rhetorical Meditation," *New Literary History* 11 (1979): 121–132.

14. In *The Correspondence of Jonathan Swift*, ed. Williams, 4: 383 (3 September 1735)—italics added.

15. Bernard Shaw, *The Shewing-Up of Blanco Posnet* (1909), in *Complete Plays with Prefaces*, 6 vols. (New York: Dodd, Mead & Company, 1962), 5: 236.

16. See D. D. Kosambi, "Living Prehistory in India," *Scientific American* 216, no. 2 (1967): 105–114. For similar rites in which the body is pierced with needles, hooks, and skewers, see Coleen Ward, "Thaipusam in Malaysia: A Psycho-Anthropological Analysis of Ritual Trance, Ceremonial Possession and Self-Mortification Practices," *Ethos* 12, no. 4 (1984): 307–333.

17. Alan Morinis, "The Ritual Experience: Pain and the Transformation of Consciousness in Ordeals of Initiation," *Ethos* 13, no. 2 (1985): 150–174.

18. See Leonard Kriegel, "Hemingway's Rites of Manhood," *Partisan Review* 44 (1977): 421–422.

19. See David L. Weis, "The Experience of Pain during Women's First Sexual Intercourse: Cultural Mythology about Female Sexual Initiation," *Archives of Sexual Behavior* 14 (1985): 421–438.

20. "In The Penal Colony" (1914), in *Selected Short Stories of Franz Kafka*, trans. Willa and Edwin Muir (New York: Modern Library, 1952), 96.

21. See Pierre Clastres, "De la torture dans les sociétés primitives," *L'Homme* 13, no. 3 (1973): 114–120.

22. For the history of legalized torture and its aftermath, see John H. Langbein, *Torture and the Law of Proof: Europe and England in the Ancien Régime* (Chicago: University of Chicago Press, 1977); and Edward Peters, *Torture* (Oxford: Basil Blackwell, 1985). Langbein's distinction between pain used to extract a confession (torture) and pain used to penalize a criminal (punishment) is no doubt sound in theory, but in practice the lines are less clear.

23. As Foucault writes: "Judicial torture was not a way of obtaining the truth at all costs; it was not the unrestrained torture of modern interrogations; it was certainly cruel, but it was not savage. It was a regulated practice, obeying a well-defined procedure; the various stages, their duration, the instruments used, the length of ropes and the heaviness of the weights used, the number of interventions made by the interrogating magistrate, all this was, according to the different local practices, carefully codified" (*Discipline and Punish*, trans. Sheridan, 40).

24. On the new status of pain in judicial torture, see Talal Asad, "Notes on Body Pain and Truth in Medieval Christian Ritual," *Economy and Society* 12 (1983): 287–327.

25. Scarry, *The Body in Pain*, 56.

26. *Torture in the Eighties* (London: Amnesty International Publications, 1984), 4.

27. *Foxe's Book of Martyrs* (1563–1583), ed. Marie Gentert King (New York: Jove Publications, 1968), 64. This famous book of Protestant martyrology—officially entitled *Actes and Monuments of These Latter Perilous Times Touching Matters of the Church*—was first published at Strasbourg in Latin in 1559, and the English text went through four editions in Foxe's lifetime. For a scholarly view, see Edward Peters, *Inquisition* (New York: The Free Press, 1988).

28. *Torture in the Eighties*, 97.

29. *The Nazi Doctors: Medical Killing and the Psychology of Genocide* (New York: Basic Books, 1986), 430. My paragraph is based on details in Lifton's book. The racial theories behind such atrocities were thoroughly integrated into German medical education. See Robert Proctor, *Racial Hygiene: Medicine under the Nazis* (Cambridge, Mass.: Harvard University Press, 1988).

30. Martha Craven Nussbaum raises crucial questions about how far novels might constitute a form of ethical inquiry ("Flawed Crystals: James's *The Golden Bowl* and Literature as Moral Philosophy," *New Literary History* 15 [1983]: 25–50). The current activism of ecologists and animal-rights groups suggests that we are entering a period when an ethics of daily practice—questioning such matters as what we eat, what we wear, what we throw away, what we do in the name of fashion or consumer safety—is increasingly important.

31. "The Use of Force," *The Farmer's Daughters: The Collected Stories of William Carlos Williams* (Norfolk, Conn.: New Directions, 1961), 132. The story is so short that I will omit page numbers for subsequent quotations. For a more detailed exposition of the reading I propose here, see my essay "Williams's Force," *Literature and Medicine* 5 (1986): 122–140.

32. In Paul Mariani, *William Carlos Williams: A New World Naked* (New York: McGraw-Hill, 1981), 416.

33. William Carlos Williams, *The Doctor Stories*, compiled by Robert Coles (New York: New Directions, 1984), viii. The quotation comes from Coles's "Introduction."

34. *The Autobiography of William Carlos Williams* (New York: Random House, 1951), 58. For a discussion of "The Use of Force"—with citations to relevant scholarly studies—see Barbara Currier Bell, "Williams's 'The Use of Force' and First Principles in Medical Ethics," *Literature and Medicine* 3 (1984): 143–151. Joanne Trautmann provides an excellent discussion of the points of contact between Williams as poet and doctor in "William Carlos Williams and the Poetry of Medicine," *Ethics in Science and Medicine* 2 (November 1975): 105–114.

35. Quoted in Thomas R. Whitaker, *William Carlos Williams* (New York: Twayne, 1968), 26.

36. Williams, *Spring and All* (1923), in *Imaginations*, ed. Webster Schott (New York: New Directions, 1970), 150. Earlier in *Spring and All* Williams writes: "The imagination is an actual force comparable to electricity or steam, it is not a plaything but a power" (120).

37. "At the Ball Game," *Collected Earlier Poems of William Carlos Williams* (New York: New Directions, 1951).

38. Williams, *Autobiography*, 357.

39. Williams, *Autobiography*, 311. Physician Eric J. Cassell has written extensively on problems of communication within medicine. See, for example, Cassell's "Language As a Tool in Medicine: Methodological and Theoretical Framework," *Journal of Medical Education* 52 (March 1977): 147–203; and his two-volume study *Talking with Patients* (Cambridge, Mass.: MIT Press, 1985).

40. An important exception is Rem B. Edwards, "Pain and the Ethics of Pain Management," *Social Science and Medicine* 18 (1984): 515–523.

41. See *Dax's Case: Essays in Medical Ethics and Human Meaning*, ed. Lonnie D. Kliever (Dallas, Texas: Southern Methodist University Press, 1989). Sally Gaddow's "Remembered in the Body: Pain and Moral Uncertainty" (151–167) makes particularly good use of Elaine Scarry's work for an illumination of problems in medical ethics.

42. Quoted in *Newsletter of the National Committee on the Treatment of Intractable Pain* 2, no. 3 (1979): 3. See also Charles S. Cleeland, "The Impact of Pain on the Patient With Cancer," *Cancer* 54 (1984): 2635–2641. A majority of physicians and nurses interviewed in Cleeland's study believed that cancer patients are undermedicated for pain.

43. Shizuko Y. Fagerhaugh and Anselm Strauss, *Politics of Pain Management: Staff-Patient Interaction* (Menlo Park, Calif.: Addison-Wesley Publishing Co., 1977), 28–55. The authors conclude, a little too hastily: "Nobody is to blame for this downward spiral in events. The organization itself is at fault" (55).

44. Peter Sternlieb, "Coping with the Pain of Terminal Cancer Patients," *Newsletter of the National Committee on the Treatment of Intractable Pain* 2, no. 2 (1979): 2.

45. See research sponsored in part by the Memorial Sloan-Kettering Cancer Center. For example, R. F. Kaiko et al., "Relative Analgesic Potency of Intramuscular Heroin and Morphine in Cancer Patients with Postoperative Pain and Chronic Pain Due to Cancer," *National Institute of Drug Abuse Research Monograph Series* 34 (February 1981): 213–219; Charles E. Inturrisi et al., "The Pharmacokinetics of Heroin in Patients with Chronic Pain," *New England Journal of Medicine* 310 (1984): 1213–1217; Robert F. Kaiko et al., "Cocaine and Morphine Interaction in Acute and Chronic Cancer Pain," *Pain* 31 (1987): 35–45.

46. C. Norman Shealy, *The Pain Game* (Berkeley: Celestial Arts, 1976), 4. See also Richard A. Sternbach, "Varieties of Pain Games," *Advances in Neurology*, vol. 4, ed. John J. Bonica, 423–432. For a personal account by one of Dr. Shealy's patients, see Judith A. Helmker, *The Autobiography of Pain* (New York: New Voices Publishing Co., 1976).

47. See *Pain and Disability: Clinical, Behavioral, and Public Policy Perspectives*, ed. Osterweis, Kleinman, and Mechanic, 6.

48. Quoted in Deborah A. Stone, *The Disabled State* (Philadelphia: Temple University Press, 1984), 135.

49. Quoted by David Mayo, "Tigers' Sparky Sly and Successful," *Kalamazoo Gazette*, 2 April 1989: G2. The remark concerned an arm injury to shortstop Alan Trammell.

50. Toni Bentley, "Dancers: The Agony and the Ecstasy," *New York Sunday Times*, 31 May 1987, 2: 32.

51. See Wilfred Barlow, *The Alexander Technique* (New York: Alfred A. Knopf, 1973); and Moshe Feldenkrais, *Awareness Through Movement* (1972; rpt. New York: Harper & Row, 1977).

52. For an illuminating study of the persistent phenomenon of self-mutilation, see Armando R. Favazza, with Barbara Favazza, *Bodies Under Siege: Self-Mutilation in Culture and Psychiatry* (Baltimore, Md.: Johns Hopkins University Press, 1987).

53. Interview with John Berryman, *Paris Review* 53 (1971): 207.

54. For an approach I distrust, see Leo Schneiderman, *The Literary Mind: Portraits in Pain and Creativity* (New York: Insight Books, 1988).

55. Georgia O'Keeffe, *Some Memories of Drawings*, ed. Doris Bry (1974; rpt. Albuquerque: University of New Mexico Press, 1988), n.p. The classical medical text is Harold Wolff's *Headache and Other Head Pain*, 3d ed., rev. by Donald J. Dalessio (New York: Oxford University Press, 1972).

NINE: PAINFUL PLEASURES: BEAUTY AND AFFLICTION

1. Thomas Mann, *Buddenbrooks* (1902), trans. H. T. Lowe-Porter (1924; rpt. New York: Modern Library, 1935), 305 (XI.ii).

2. "Timeo Danaos et dona ferentis" (*Aeneid* II.49).

3. Virgil, *The Aeneid*, trans. W. F. Jackson Knight (Baltimore, Md.: Penguin Books, 1958), 57–58, (II.109 ff).

4. Pliny, *Natural History* XXXVI.37. For a very helpful collection of responses to the Laocoön group, see Margarete Bieber, *Laocoön: The Influence of the Group Since Its Rediscovery*, rev. ed. (Detroit, Mich.: Wayne State University Press, 1967).

5. Paul Friedländer, *Plato: An Introduction*, 2d ed., trans. Hans Meyerhoff (1954; rpt. Princeton: Princeton University Press, 1969), 196.

6. Johann Winckelmann, *Reflections on the Imitation of Greek Works in Painting and Sculpture* (1754), quoted in Bieber, *Laocoön*, 20–21.

7. "Easter 1916," in *The Collected Poems of W. B. Yeats* (New York: Macmillan, 1956).

8. Winckelmann in his *Reflections* recounts the story about Bernini. On the "physiognomy" of pain, see Frank Spencer, "Samuel George Morton's Doctoral Thesis on Bodily Pain: The Probable Source of Morton's Polygenism," *Transactions and Studies of the College of Physicians of Philadelphia* 5, no. 4 (1983): 333.

9. In *The Poetical Works of William Wordsworth*, ed. E. de Selincourt and Helen Darbishire, 5 vols. (Oxford: Clarendon Press, 1940–1949).

10. See John Mullan, "Hypochondria and Hysteria: Sensibility and the Physicians," *The Eighteenth Century: Theory and Interpretation* 25 (1984): 141–174; John B. Radner, "The Art of Sympathy in Eighteenth-Century British Moral Thought," in *Studies in Eighteenth-Century Culture*, vol. 9, ed. Roseann Runte (Madison: University of Wisconsin Press, 1979), 189–210; and David Marshall, *The Surprising Effects of Sympathy: Marivaux, Diderot, Rousseau, and Mary Shelley* (Chicago: University of Chicago Press, 1988).

11. On the medical, philosophical, theological, and literary backgrounds of sentimentalism, see G. S. Rousseau, "Nerves, Spirits, and Fibres: Towards Defining the Origins of Sensibility," *The Blue Guitar* 2 (1976): 125–153; Stephen D. Cox, *"The Stranger Within Thee": Concepts of the Self in Late-Eighteenth-Century Literature* (Pittsburgh, Pa.: University of Pittsburgh Press, 1980); John K. Sheriff, *The Good Natured Man: The Evolution of a Moral Ideal, 1660–1800* (University, Ala.: University of Alabama Press, 1982); Janet Todd, *Sensibility: An Introduction* (New York: Methuen, 1986); and John Mullan, *Sentiment and Sociability: The Language of Feeling in the Eighteenth Century* (Oxford: Clarendon Press, 1988).

12. See the classic text by Denis de Rougemont, *Love in the Western World* (1939), trans. Montgomery Belgion, rev. ed. (New York: Pantheon Books, 1956); and John C. Moore, *Love in Twelfth-Century France* (Philadelphia: University of Pennsylvania Press, 1972). Overtly sexual traditions of the lover's pain, visible in Ovid and Catullus, are transformed by the more spiritualized (but still erotic) medieval tradition of courtly love. Later the well-recognized bond between love and pain gives rise to medical-philosophical tracts on illness such as Jacques Ferrand's *A Treatise on Lovesickness* (1610), originally written in French and translated into English in 1640 under the short title *Erotomania*.

13. In *The Poems of John Keats*, ed. Jack Stillinger (Cambridge, Mass.: Harvard University Press, 1978).

14. Havelock Ellis, *Studies in the Psychology of Sex* (1897–1928), 3d ed., 2 vols. (New York: Random House, 1936), 2: 66.

15. Ellis, *Studies in the Psychology of Sex*, 2: 172.

16. *The Letters of John Keats*, ed. Hyder Edward Rollins, 2 vols. (Cambridge, Mass.: Harvard University Press, 1958), 2: 102 (21 April 1819). The "Ode on Melancholy" was composed a month later, in May 1819.

17. See Stuart Pratt Atkins, *The Testament of Werther in Poetry and Drama* (Cambridge, Mass.: Harvard University Press, 1949). For a thorough study of the book's somewhat slower start in England among the especially important group of women readers, see Syndy McMillen Conger, "The Sorrows of Young Charlotte: Werther's English Sisters 1785–1805," *Goethe Yearbook*, vol. 3, ed. Thomas P. Saine (Columbia, S.C.: Camden House, 1986), 21–56.

18. Johann Wolfgang von Goethe, *The Sorrows of Young Werther and Selected Writings*, trans. Catherine Hutter (New York: New American Library, 1962), 65–66.

19. "Mourning and Melancholia," in *The Standard Edition of the Complete Psychological Works of Sigmund Freud*, trans. and ed. Strachey et al., 14: 246.

20. Goethe, *The Sorrows of Young Werther*, trans. Hutter, 92–93.

21. Goethe, *The Sorrows of Young Werther*, trans. Hutter, 67 ("Seligkeit und Schmertz"). On the mixture of pain and bliss, see Mario Praz, *The Romantic Agony* (1933), trans. Angus Davidson, 2d ed. (New York: Oxford University Press, 1951).

22. Werther's interest in art and artists is unmistakable. Rejecting earlier neo-classical codes, he commits himself entirely to nature, saying that nature alone is "capable of developing a great artist" ("sie allein bildet den grossen Künstler"). His heroes are such overheated, eighteenth-century bards of feeling as Klopstock and Ossian. He longs for an expressive writing that would be "the mirror of my soul." In typical Romantic fashion, he scorns the cautious, middle-class, rule-bound artist in favor of the untutored genius who breaks all bonds (*The Sorrows of Young Werther*, trans. Hutter, 25, 30).

23. Goethe, *The Sorrows of Young Werther*, trans. Hutter, 52. Werther earlier states: "I know that we human beings were not created equal and cannot be" (26). The best analysis of social class in the novel is the essay on *Werther* written in 1936 by the eminent Marxist critic George Lukács (in *Goethe and His Age*, trans. Robert Anchor [New York: Grosset & Dunlap, 1969], 35–49).

24. Philip Fisher, *Hard Facts: Setting and Form in the American Novel* (New York: Oxford University Press, 1987), 100. On the subversiveness of sentimental fiction, Jane Tompkins writes: "Out of the ideological materials at their disposal, the sentimental novelists elaborated a myth that gave women the central position of power and authority in the culture; and of these efforts *Uncle Tom's Cabin* is the most dazzling exemplar" (*Sensational Designs: The Cultural Work of American Fiction, 1790–1860* [New York: Oxford University Press, 1985], 125).

25. Jean-François Lyotard, "Answering the Question: What Is Postmodernism?" (1982), in *The Postmodern Condition: A Report on Knowledge* (1979), trans. Geoff Bennington and Brian Massumi (Minneapolis: University of Minnesota Press, 1984), 76. Frederic Jameson provides a helpful discussion in "Postmodernism, or The Cultural Logic of Late Capitalism," *New Left Review* 146 (1984): 53–92. On the struggles of various theorists to define the postmodern, see C. Barry Chabot, "The Problem of Postmodernism," *New Literary History* 20 (1988): 1–20.

26. See Clark S. Muenzer, "Turning Toward the Sublime: Reflexivity and Self-worth in *Die Leiden des jungen Werthers*," *Figures of Identity: Goethe's Novels and the Enigmatic Self* (University Park: Pennsylvania State University Press, 1984), 5–36. On the relation of Burke and the sublime to the emerging gothic novel, see my essay "Gothic Sublimity," *New Literary History* 16 (1985): 299–319.

27. Fifty years of scholarly literature on the sublime originates with Samuel H. Monk's *The Sublime: A Study of Critical Theories in XVIII-Century England* (1935; rpt. Ann Arbor: University of Michigan Press, 1960). Peter de Bolla, who provides a bibliography covering much of the work since Monk, is the most recent contributor with *The Discourse of the Sublime: History, Aesthetics and the Subject* (Oxford: Basil Blackwell, 1989).

28. Edmund Burke, *A Philosophical Enquiry into the Origin of Our Ideas of the Sublime and Beautiful* (1757), ed. J. T. Boulton (New York: Columbia University Press, 1958), 112.

29. Burke, *Philosophical Enquiry*, ed. Boulton, 110.

30. Richard Selzer, "Textbook," *Letters to a Young Doctor* (New York: Simon and Schuster, 1982), 20. For a discussion of Selzer's work, with reference to recent scholarship, see Charles Anderson, *Richard Selzer and the Rhetoric of Surgery* (Carbondale: Southern Illinois University Press, 1989).

31. In *The Complete Letters of Vincent Van Gogh*, trans. anon., 2d ed., 3 vols. (Greenwich, Conn.: New York Graphic Society, 1952), 3: 121 (17 January 1889).

32. Richard Selzer, "The Elusive Language of Pleasure and Pain," *New York Times Book Review*, 5 April 1987: 38.

33. Richard Selzer, "The Knife," *Mortal Lessons: Notes on the Art of Surgery* (New York: Simon and Schuster, 1976), 94.

34. In Keiko Beppu and M. Teresa Tavormina, "The Healer's Art: An Interview with Richard Selzer," *The Centennial Review* 25 (Winter 1981): 40; and Selzer, "Textbook," *Letters to a Young Doctor*, 14.

35. Selzer, "Lessons from the Art," *Mortal Lessons*, 46.

36. Selzer, "Textbook," *Letters to a Young Doctor*, 15.

37. In Beppu and Tavormina, "The Healer's Art: An Interview with Richard Selzer," 36.

38. Selzer, "Witness," *Letters to a Young Doctor*, 124.

39. Selzer, "Rounds," *Letters to a Young Doctor*, 80.

40. Selzer, "The Hartford Girl," *Confessions of a Knife* (New York: Simon and Schuster, 1979), 206.

41. Selzer, "The Hartford Girl," *Confessions of a Knife*, 210.

42. Selzer, "Rounds," *Letters to a Young Doctor*, 82. On wounds and their relation to language, see Geoffrey H. Hartman, "Words and Wounds," *Medicine and Literature*, ed. Enid Rhodes Peschel (New York: Neal Watson Academic Publications, 1980), 178–188.

43. Homer, *The Odyssey*, trans. Albert Cook (New York: W. W. Norton, 1967), XIX.483–484. George E. Dimock calls his chapter on the boar hunt and on the naming of Odysseus "The Man of Pain." He notes "the phonetic similarity" that links the name Odysseus to the Greek noun *odune* ("pain") and conducts a book-by-book reading of *The Odyssey* that demonstrates its continuous emphasis on pain (*The Unity of the "Odyssey"* [Amherst: University of Massachusetts Press, 1989], 257).

44. Selzer, "Racoon," *Confessions of a Knife*, 34.

45. Selzer, "An Absence of Windows," *Confessions of a Knife*, 18.

1. Marquis de Sade, *The Complete Justine, Philosophy in the Bedroom, and Other Writings*, trans. Richard Seaver and Austryn Wainhouse (New York: Grove Press, 1965), 362 (9:586). When citing the Grove Press translations of Sade, I will also provide (in parentheses following the page number) reference to the volume and page number of the standard French text, *Oeuvres complètes du Marquis de Sade*, ed. Gilbert Lély et al., 16 vols. (Paris: Cercle du Livre Précieux, 1966–1967). An essential tool for work on Sade is Colette Verger Michael's *The Marquis de Sade: The Man, His Works, and His Critics: An Annotated Bibliography* (New York: Garland Press, 1986).

2. Sade, *Correspondance*, in *Oeuvres complètes*, ed. Lély, 12: 276.

3. See Georges Bataille, *Literature and Evil* (1957), trans. Alastair Hamilton (London: Calder & Boyars, 1973). Simone de Beauvoir's essay "Must We Burn Sade?" (1951–1952) is reprinted in Sade's *The 120 Days of Sodom and Other Writings*, trans. Austryn Wainhouse and Richard Seaver (New York: Grove Press, 1966), 3–64. Among the other major French figures to write on Sade are, to name a few, Blanchot, Klossowski, Paulhan, Camus, Lacan, Barthes, and Sollers. The relatively few Anglo-American scholars who have written well on Sade include Lester G. Crocker, Ihab Hassan, Nancy K. Miller, and Joan De Jean. For a general introduction, see Maurice Charney, "Sexuality at the Edge of the Abyss: The Marquis de Sade," *Sexual Fictions* (New York: Methuen, 1981), 32–51.

4. Michel Foucault writes: "Sadism is not a name finally given to a practice as old as Eros; it is a massive cultural fact which appeared precisely at the end of the eighteenth century, and which constitutes one of the greatest conversions of Western imagination: unreason transformed into delirium of the heart, madness of desire, the insane dialogue of love and death in the limitless presumption of appetite" (*Madness and Civilization: A History of Insanity in the Age of Reason* [1961], trans. Richard Howard [New York: New American Library, 1965], 210).

5. See, for example, James Rodgers, "'Life' in the Novel: *Tristram Shandy* and Some Aspects of Eighteenth-Century Physiology," *Eighteenth-Century Life* 1 (1980): 1–20. Particularly relevant to the admixture of "medical language" in erotic or pornographic texts is G. S. Rousseau, "Nymphomania, Bienville and the Rise of Erotic Sensibility," in *Sexuality in Eighteenth-Century Britain*, ed. Paul-Gabriel Boucé (Manchester: Manchester University Press, 1982), 95–119.

6. See Michel Foucault, *The Birth of the Clinic: An Archaeology of Medical Perception* (1963), trans. A. M. Sheridan Smith (New York: Pantheon Books, 1973); Erwin H. Ackerknecht, *Medicine at the Paris Hospital, 1794–1848* (Baltimore, Md.: Johns Hopkins University Press, 1967); David M. Vess, *Medical Revolution in France, 1789–1796* (Gainesville: University Presses of Florida, 1975); *Medicine and Society in France*, ed. Robert Forster and Orest Ranum, trans. Elborg Forster and Patricia M. Ranum (Baltimore, Md.: Johns Hopkins University Press, 1980); and John E. Lesch, *Science and Medicine in France: The Emergence of Experimental Physiology, 1790–1855* (Cambridge, Mass.: Harvard University Press, 1984).

7. Cabanis develops the connections linking medicine and physiology with mind and culture in his *Rapports du physique et du moral de l'homme* (1802). For a fine discussion of his thought, see Martin S. Staum, *Cabanis: Enlightenment and Medical Philosophy in the French Revolution* (Princeton: Princeton University Press, 1980). The *Rapports* is available in English translation under the title *On the Relations Between the Physical and Moral Aspects of Man*, ed. George Mora, trans. Margaret Duggan Saidi, 2 vols. (Baltimore, Md.: Johns Hopkins University Press, 1981). For similar links between physiology and culture, see the treatise "Discours sur les rapports de la médecine avec les sciences physiques et morales" (1798) by Jean-Louis Alibert—a young colleague of Cabanis.

8. Phrases in quotation marks cite remarks by Philippe Pinel and François Percy in 1812 (in Lesch, *Science and Medicine in France*, 12).

9. Vess, *Medical Revolution in France*, 189 (italics added).

10. For two essays (relevant to Sade) on the medicalization of erotic passion, see Christine Birnbaum, "La vision médicale de l'amour dans *L'Encyclopédie*," in *Aimer en France 1760–1860*, ed. Paul Viallaneix and Jean Ehrard, 2 vols. (Clermont-Ferrand: Association des Publications de la Faculté des Lettres et Sciences Humaines de Clermont-Ferrand, 1980), 2: 307–313; and Paul Hoffman, "Le discours médicale sur les passions de l'amour, de Boissier de Sauvages à Pinel," in *Aimer en France*, ed. Viallaneix and Ehrard, 2: 345–356. Sade of course utterly divorces sexuality from love.

11. "La philosophie doit tout dire" (*Juliette* [1797], in *Oeuvres complètes*, 9:586). Wainhouse translates: "Philosophy must never shrink from speaking out." Juliette, however, is not implicitly comparing timid speech with bold speech; she is comparing traditional (circumscribed) philosophies to a radically new philosophy that dares to be all-encompassing. On Sadean extravagance both verbal and nonverbal, see Marcel Hénaff, "Tout dire ou l'encyclopédie de l'excès," *Obliques* 12–13 (1977); 29–37.

12. Maurice Blanchot, "Sade" (1949), in *Justine*, trans. Seaver and Wainhouse, 39. Georges Bataille and Simone de Beauvoir offer similar views on Sade and the "incommunicable" or "inexpressible."

13. *Justine* (1791), trans. Seaver and Wainhouse, 606/3:206. There are three separate versions of *Justine*, which was first published in 1791. The earliest version, entitled *Les Infortunes de la vertu*, Sade composed in 1787; the vastly expanded, final version, entitled *La Nouvelle Justine*, was published in 1797.

14. Angela Carter, *The Sadeian Woman and the Ideology of Pornography* (New York: Pantheon Books, 1978), introductory note.

15. *Juliette*, trans. Wainhouse, 681/9:87.

16. *Justine*, trans. Seaver and Wainhouse, 551–552/3:150–151. Rodin's libertine accomplice remarks concerning the human victims required by medical science: "In those hospitals where I worked as a young man I saw similar experiments by the thousand" (552/3:151).

17. *Philosophy in the Bedroom*, trans. Seaver and Wainhouse, 301/3:483.

18. Pierre Klossowski, *Sade mon prochain* (Paris: Seuil, 1947).

19. *Juliette*, trans. Wainhouse, 267/8:255–256.

20. *Juliette*, trans. Wainhouse, 386/8:372.

21. The movement from a mechanistic to a vitalist-dynamic physiology is discussed by Robert E. Schofield, *Mechanism and Materialism: British Natural Philosophy in an Age of Reason* (Princeton: Princeton University Press, 1970). The materialist body was not a "lifeless machine" but a galvanic organism. In the controversies surrounding late eighteenth-century physiology, some writers combined a theological view of the soul with vitalist understandings of the nervous system. See, for example, Elizabeth L. Haigh, "Vitalism, the Soul, and Sensibility: The Physiology of Théophile Bordeu," *Journal of the History of Medicine and Allied Sciences* 31 (1976): 30–41.

22. *Juliette*, trans. Wainhouse, 44, 50/8:52, 59. For Descartes, who encouraged such mechanistic views, thinking (*cogitans*) is of course the defining attribute of the soul. It distinguishes soul from body. Sade collapses the distinction between body and soul.

23. "Ma façon de penser est le fruit de mes réflections; elle tient à mon existence, à mon organisation. Je ne suis pas le maître de la changer" (in *Oeuvres complètes*, 12:409). A portion of Sade's correspondence is available in *Selected Letters*, ed. Margaret Crosland, trans. W. J. Strachan (London: Peter Owen, 1963).

24. *Justine*, trans. Seaver and Wainhouse, 512/3:111–112.

25. *Philosophy in the Bedroom*, trans. Seaver and Wainhouse, 254/3:438.

26. *Justine*, trans. Seaver and Wainhouse, 606/3:203. On the eccentricity of libertine sexual tastes, the same speaker says: "Sa singularité est le résultat de ses organes" (3:202). For the most important studies of relations between Sadean eroticism and physiology, see Jean Deprun, "Sade et la philosophie biologique de son temps," in the anonymously edited collection *Le Marquis de Sade* (Paris: Armand Colin, 1968), 189–203; and Marcel Hénaff, *Sade: L'invention du corps libertin* (Paris: Presses Universitaires de France, 1978).

27. *Juliette*, trans. Wainhouse, 159/8:157. On the aesthetics and semiotics of Sadean eroticism, see Roland Barthes, *Sade/Fourier/Loyola* (1971), trans. Richard Miller (New York: Farrar, Straus and Giroux, 1976).

28. *Juliette*, trans. Wainhouse, 341/8:329. On the mind as aphrodisiac, see Pierre Fedida, "Les exercices de l'imagination et la commotion sur la masse des nerfs: Un éroticism de tête," in Sade's *Oeuvres complètes*, 16:613–625.

29. *The 120 Days of Sodom* (1785), trans. Wainhouse and Seaver, 254/13:61.

30. *Justine*, trans. Seaver and Wainhouse, 599/3:200.

31. On the political implications of the nervous system in Sade's time, see Christopher Lawrence, "The Nervous System and Society in the Scottish Enlightenment," in *Natural Order: Historical Studies of Scientific Culture*, ed. Barry Barnes and Steven Shapin (Beverly Hills, Calif.: Sage Publications, 1979), 19–40. Jean-Pierre Faye discusses Sade's political thought in "Changer la mort (Sade et la politique)," *Obliques* 12–13 (1977): 47–57.

32. *Juliette*, trans. Wainhouse, 733/9:137.

33. B. L. Crue et al., "Observations on the Taxonomy Problem in Pain," *Chronic Pain: Further Observations from City of Hope National Medical Center*, ed. Benjamin L. Crue, Jr. (New York: SP Medical & Scientific Books, 1978), 20.

34. *Three Essays on the Theory of Sexuality* (1905), in *The Standard Edition of the Complete Psychological Works of Sigmund Freud*, trans. and ed. Strachey et al., 7: 159.

35. Judith Shklar, *Ordinary Vices* (Cambridge, Mass.: Harvard University Press, 1984), 7–44.

36. For a lucid discussion of the complex layers of cinematic violence, see Linda Williams, "Power, Pleasure, and Perversion: Sadomasochistic Film Pornography," *Representations* 27 (1989): 37–65. I share Williams's view that sadism and masochism, although theoretically distinct, often mingle in ways that justify the term "sadomasochism."

37. Susan Sontag, "The Pornographic Imagination," in *Styles of Radical Will* (New York: Farrar, Straus and Giroux, 1966), 70. Angela Carter's argument appears in *The Sadeian Woman and the Ideology of Pornography* (1978).

38. Sontag, "The Pornographic Imagination," in *Styles of Radical Will*, 70–71. On the argument that pornography promotes the oppression of women, see, for example, *Take Back the Night: Women on Pornography*, ed. Laura Lederer (New York: William Morrow, 1980); and Susan Griffin, *Pornography and Silence: Culture's Revenge Against Nature* (New York: Harper & Row, 1981).

39. "The Straight Mind," *Feminist Issues* 1 (Summer 1980): 106. For a helpful discussion, see Donna Landry, "Beat Me! Beat Me! Feminist Appropriations of Sade," *Enclitic* (forthcoming). Landry devotes major attention to the feminist-Lacanian studies by Jane Gallop, *Intersections: A Reading of Sade with Bataille, Blanchot, and Klossowski* (Lincoln: University of Nebraska Press, 1981) and *The Daughter's Seduction: Feminism and Psychoanalysis* (Ithaca, N.Y.: Cornell University Press, 1982).

40. Theodor Reik argues that masochists do not enjoy pain itself but only what the pain "buys" (*Masochism in Sex and Society*, trans. Margaret H. Beigel and Gertrude M. Kurth [1941; rpt. New York: Grove Press, 1962], 28). Some philosophers strongly agree that enjoyable pain is self-contradictory. See, for example, R. M. Hare, "Pain and Evil" (1964), rpt. *Moral Concepts*, ed. Joel Feinberg (New York: Oxford University Press, 1970), 29–42; and George Pitcher, "The Awfulness of Pain," *The Journal of Philosophy* 67 (1970): 481–492. Such reasoning would not impress Sade and Sacher-Masoch, however; their work strikes at the heart of logic and normal experience.

41. Leopold von Sacher-Masoch, *Venus in Furs* (1870), in *Masochism*, trans. Jean McNeil (1971; rpt. New York: Zone Books, 1989), 163. The best introduction to Sacher-Masoch's work is Gertrud Lenzer, "On Masochism: A Contribution to the History of a Phantasy and Its Theory," *Signs* 1 (1975): 277–324. For a survey of the fine art of spanking, see William B. Ober, *Bottoms Up! A Pathologist's Essays on Medicine and the Humanities* (Carbondale: Southern Illinois University Press, 1987), 3–39.

42. Sacher-Masoch, *Venus in Furs*, in *Masochism*, trans. McNeil, 271.

43. Paula J. Caplan, *The Myth of Women's Masochism* (London: Methuen, 1986).

44. Sacher-Masoch, *Venus in Furs*, in *Masochism*, trans. McNeil, 271.

45. For Enlightenment ideas on apathy, which Sade (as usual) transvalues and subverts, see Max Horkheimer and Theodore W. Adorno, *Dialectic of Enlightenment* (1944), trans. John Cumming (New York: Herder and Herder, 1972), 96.

46. *Juliette*, trans. Wainhouse, 1042/9:440 and 274/8:262.

ELEVEN: TRAGIC PAIN

1. Simone Weil, *Waiting for God* (1957), trans. Emma Craufurd (New York: G. P. Putnam's Sons, 1951), 118. For Weil, affliction ("le malheur") is inseparable from physical pain ("la douleur physique"). She dismisses as unimportant, however, a pain that is *only* physical. As she writes: "Une douleur seulement physique est très peu de chose et ne laisse aucune trace dans l'âme" (*Attente de Dieu* [Paris: La Colombe, 1957], 82).

2. Eric J. Cassell, "The Nature of Suffering and the Goals of Medicine," *New England Journal of Medicine* 306, no. 11 (1982): 639–640. See also Laurel Archer Copp, "The Spectrum of Suffering," *American Journal of Nursing* 74 (1974): 491–495. Cassell's book-length study *The Nature of Suffering* (New York: Oxford University Press, 1990) unfortunately appeared too late for me to consult.

3. Arthur Kleinman, *The Illness Narratives: Suffering, Healing, and the Human Condition* (New York: Basic Books, 1988), 28.

4. Cassell, "The Nature of Suffering and the Goals of Medicine," 640.

5. Shakespeare, *Macbeth* (1606), V.iii.61–62.

6. "Tragedy" (1839), in *The Early Lectures of Ralph Waldo Emerson*, vol. 3, ed. Robert E. Spiller and Wallace E. Williams (Cambridge, Mass.: Harvard University Press, 1972), 107.

7. Northrop Frye, *Anatomy of Criticism* (Princeton: Princeton University Press, 1957), 212.

8. Rollo May, *Love and Will* (New York: W. W. Norton, 1969), 151.

9. Sophocles, *Oedipus the King*, ll. 1278–1279. All quotations refer to the translation by David Grene in *The Complete Greek Tragedies*, ed. David Grene and Richmond Lattimore, 3 vols. (Chicago: University of Chicago Press, 1959).

10. Shakespeare, *King Lear* (1605), V.iii.258.

11. The Greek text is available conveniently, with English translation, in volume four of the 1932 Cambridge University Press edition of Sophocles (*The Plays and Fragments*, trans. and ed. Sir Richard C. Jebb [rpt. Amsterdam: Adolf M. Hakkert, 1966]). Scholarship on *Philoctetes* is relatively sparse compared with work on other Greek tragedies. Probably the most influential account of the play was in Edmund Wilson's *The Wound and the Bow: Seven Studies in Literature* (New

York: Oxford University Press, 1941), 272–295. There are, of course, obligatory chapters on *Philoctetes* by writers treating all or most of Sophocles' works, as in C. M. Bowra, *Sophoclean Tragedy* (Oxford: Clarendon Press, 1944); and in A. J. A. Waldock, *Sophocles the Dramatist* (Cambridge: Cambridge University Press, 1966).

12. *Philoctetes*, ll. 148–149. All quotations refer to the translation by David Grene in *The Complete Greek Tragedies*, ed. David Grene and Richmond Lattimore, 3 vols. (Chicago: University of Chicago Press, 1959). Subsequent quotations will be documented by line number, in parenthesis. Martha Nussbaum resists a moralistic reading of Odysseus and calls him a utilitarian, "a man who accords ultimate value to . . . the state of affairs which seems to represent the greatest good of all citizens" ("Consequences and Character in Sophocles' *Philoctetes*," *Philosophy and Literature* 1 [Fall 1976]: 30).

13. Sheila Murnaghan strangely does not discuss *Philoctetes* in her helpful essay "Body and Voice in Greek Tragedy," *The Yale Journal of Criticism* 1, no. 2 (1985): 23–43.

14. See Cedric H. Whitman, *Sophocles: A Study of Heroic Humanism* (Cambridge, Mass.: Harvard University Press, 1951), 172–189; Philip Whaley Harsh, "The Role of the Bow in the *Philoctetes* of Sophocles," *American Journal of Philology* 81 (1960): 408–414; Bernard M. W. Knox, *The Heroic Temper: Studies in Sophoclean Tragedy* (Berkeley: University of California Press, 1964), 117–142; and R. P. Winnington-Ingram, *Sophocles: An Interpretation* (Cambridge: Cambridge University Press, 1980), 280–303. For an excellent general study, despite its technical-sounding title, see Peter W. Rose, "Sophocles' *Philoctetes* and the Teachings of the Sophists," *Harvard Studies in Classical Philology* 80 (1976): 49–105.

15. F. E. Peters, *Greek Philosophical Terms: A Historical Lexicon* (New York: New York University Press, 1967), 94.

16. Charles Segal, *Interpreting Greek Tragedy: Myth, Poetry, Text* (Ithaca, N.Y.: Cornell University Press, 1986), 122. Of the same scene David Seale says: "It is a spectacular display which has no parallel in extant Greek tragedy. The very length of the episode (760–866) puts it in a category of its own" (*Vision and Stagecraft in Sophocles* [Chicago: University of Chicago Press, 1982], 37–38).

17. Friedrich Nietzsche, *The Birth of Tragedy* (1870–1871), trans. Walter Kaufmann (New York: Vintage Books, 1967), 1. For helpful discussion of Nietzsche's views beyond *The Birth of Tragedy*, see Francis Nesbitt Oppel, *Mask and Tragedy: Yeats and Nietzsche, 1902–10* (Charlottesville: University Press of Virginia, 1987), 118–122.

18. Weil, *Waiting for God*, trans. Craufurd, 125.

19. *Philoctetes*, ll. 946–947.

20. See Daniel J. Anderson, *Living with a Chronic Illness* (Center City, Minn.: Hazelden Foundation, 1986). Anderson includes a section entitled "The Tragedy of Chronic Illness" and emphasizes the phrase "to bear the unendurable" from an essay about narratives of illness and impending death by Edwin J. Kenney, Jr. ("Death's Other Kingdom," *Commonweal*, 19 November 1982: 627–632).

21. George Steiner, *The Death of Tragedy* (1961; rpt. New York: Oxford University Press, 1980), 9. If it were necessary to choose among rival theorists of tragedy, Steiner would be my choice.

22. Steiner, *The Death of Tragedy*, 303.

23. Joyce Carol Oates, *On Boxing* (Garden City, N.Y.: Doubleday, 1987), 116. Page numbers will follow quotations in parentheses. For her numerous publications in poetry, drama, criticism, and fiction, see Francine Lercangée, *Joyce Carol Oates: An Annotated Bibliography* (New York: Garland Press, 1986).

24. Garry Wills, "Blood Sport," *The New York Review of Books* 35, no. 2 (18 February 1988): 5–7.

25. Oates, "Why Is Your Writing So Violent?", *New York Times Book Review*, 29 March 1981: 15, 35.

26. Oates, *The Edge of Impossibility: Tragic Forms in Literature* (New York: The Vanguard Press, 1972), 12, 65. For an example of the tragic impossibility of tragedy, see her poem "Lines for Those to Whom Tragedy Is Denied," *Anonymous Sins and Other Poems* (Baton Rouge: Louisiana State University Press, 1969).

27. Grant, *The Tragic Vision of Joyce Carol Oates*, 118.

28. Oates: "Tragedy does not seem to me to be cathartic, but to deepen our sense of the mystery and sanctity of the human predicament" ("An American Tragedy," *New York Times Book Review*, 24 January 1971: 2).

29. Aristotle, *Poetics*, trans. Gerald F. Else, 84. For an expanded treatment of *pathos*, see Else's *Aristotle's Poetics: The Argument* (1957; rpt. Cambridge, Mass.: Harvard University Press, 1967), 414–424.

30. Aristotle, *Poetics*, trans. Gerald F. Else, 37.

31. See Ernest Becker, *The Denial of Death* (New York: Free Press, 1973).

32. Oates, *The Edge of Impossibility*, 7.

33. "Transformations of Self: An Interview with Joyce Carol Oates," *The Ohio Review* 15 (1973): 57–58.

34. Oates, *The Edge of Impossibility*, 4. As she says: "Tragedy always upholds the human spirit because it is an exploration of human nature in terms of its strengths. One simply cannot know strengths unless suffering, misfortune, and violence are explored quite frankly by the writer" (Leif Sjöberg, "An Interview with Joyce Carol Oates," *Contemporary Literature* 23 [1982]: 272).

35. Quoted in Grant, *The Tragic Vision of Joyce Carol Oates*, 4.

36. Elisabeth Kübler-Ross, with photographs by Mal Warshaw, *To Live Until We Say Good-bye* (Englewood Cliffs, N.J.: Prentice-Hall, 1978), 12–13. For the growing literature on thanatology, see Michael A. Simpson, *Dying, Death, and Grief: A Critical Bibliography* (Pittsburgh, Pa.: University of Pittsburgh Rress, 1987).

37. *Proceedings of the House of Delegates*, 38th Interim Meeting (Chicago: American Medical Association, 1984), 371.

38. Thomas A. Gonzales, "Fatal Injuries in Competitive Sports," *JAMA* 146 (1951): 1506–1511. Gonzales used statistics for New York City from 1918 through 1950. Statistics provided by *Ring* magazine show 335 deaths worldwide in amateur and professional boxing in the thirty-three years between 1946 and 1979 (Mike Moore, "The Challenge of Boxing: Bringing Safety into the Ring," *The Physician and Sportsmedicine* 8, no. 11 [1980]: 101–105).

39. For a fine review of research, see Robert Glenn Morrison, "Medical and Public Health Aspects of Boxing," *JAMA* 255, no. 18 (1986): 2475–2480.

40. Quoted in Peter Tauber, "Ali: Still Magic," *New York Times Magazine*, 17 July 1988, 23 +. The quotations and details in this paragraph all come from Tauber's article.

TWELVE: THE FUTURE OF PAIN

1. Gilles Deleuze, "Coldness and Cruelty" (1967), in *Masochism*, trans. Jean McNeil (1971; rpt. New York: Zone Books, 1989), 14. The hidden passages connecting science and literature have been explored recently by Michel Serres (see, for example, Serres's *Hermes: Literature, Science, Philosophy*, ed. Josué V. Harari and David F. Bell [Baltimore, Md.: Johns Hopkins University Press, 1982]).

2. George L. Engel, " 'Psychogenic' Pain and the Pain-Prone Patient," *American Journal of Medicine* 26 (1959): 916. Engel adds: "In a textbook published in 1858 Wood discusses pain in terms which differ only in details from what appears in Harrison's 'Principles of Internal Medicine' published in 1954."

3. Paul Starr, *The Social Transformation of American Medicine* (New York: Basic Books, 1982), 60–61. Starr emphasizes as well the ways the public and physicians partly (if unsuccessfully) resisted the transformation of medicine into a commodity.

4. John D. Loeser, "Low Back Pain," in *Pain*, ed. John J. Bonica, Research Publications: Association for Research in Nervous and Mental Disease, vol. 58 (New York: Raven Press, 1980), 363–377.

5. See Edwin Clarke, "The Doctrine of the Hollow Nerve in the Seventeenth and Eighteenth Centuries," in *Medicine, Science, and Culture: Historical Essays in Honor of Owsei Temkin*, ed. Lloyd G. Stevenson and Robert P. Multhauf (Baltimore, Md.: Johns Hopkins University Press, 1968), 123–141. On the origin and development of the term "animal spirits," see Walther Riese, *A History of Neurology* (New York: MD Publications, 1959), 50–52.

6. René Descartes, *Treatise of Man*, trans. Thomas Steele Hall (Cambridge, Mass.: Harvard University Press, 1972), 34. The treatise *De l'homme* was published posthumously—and imperfectly—in 1662.

7. "Civilization" (1836), in *Collected Works of John Stuart Mill*, vol. 18, ed. J. M. Robson (Toronto: University of Toronto Press, 1977), 130. Mill continues: "All those necessary portions of the business of society which oblige any person to be the immediate agent or ocular witness of the infliction of pain, are delegated by

common consent to peculiar and narrow classes: to the judge, the soldier, the surgeon, the butcher, and the executioner" (131).

8. Marilyn Aronberg Lavin, *Piero della Francesca: The Flagellation* (London: Allen Lane; The Penguin Press, 1972). The strongest competing interpretation is by John Pope Hennessy ("Whose Flagellation?", *Apollo* 124 [September 1986]: 162–165). Hennessy uncovers a striking parallel with a nearly contemporary work by Matteo di Giovanni entitled *The Dream of St. Jerome*. (In Jerome's dream— a popular subject in the Renaissance—the saint imagined that he was punished for preferring Cicero to the Bible.) Piero as humanist, however, would doubtless view the flagellation of Saint Jerome as connected, through biblical typology, with the flagellation of Christ. In any case, the treatment of pain would remain securely within the Christian tradition of acceptance.

9. Lillian Breslow Rubin, *Worlds of Pain: Life in the Working-Class Family* (New York: Basic Books, 1976).

10. Richard A. Sternbach, *Pain: A Psychophysiological Analysis* (New York: Academic Press, 1968).

11. Oliver Sacks, *Migraine: Understanding a Common Disorder*, exp. ed. (Berkeley: University of California Press, 1985), 8. For an explanation of the new ("novelistic") mode of clinical writing that such a view of illness entails, see the preface to Sacks's best-selling book *The Man Who Mistook His Wife for a Hat and Other Clinical Tales* (New York: Summit Books, 1985).

12. For the classic study, see Warren R. Dawson, *The Custom of Couvade*, Publications of the University of Manchester, no. 194, Ethnological Series, no. 4 (Manchester: The University Press, 1929).

13. See L. F. Newman, "Some References to the Couvade in Literature," *Folk-Lore* 53 (1942): 148–157; and R. Barrie Walkley, "The Bloom of Motherhood: Couvade as Structural Device in *Ulysses*," *James Joyce Quarterly* 18 (1980): 55–67.

14. See M. Lipkin, Jr., and G. S. Lamb, "The Couvade Syndrome: An Epidemiologic Study," *Annals of Internal Medicine* 96 (1982): 509–511; and L. Y. Bogren, "Couvade," *Acta Psychiatrica Scandinavica* 68 (1983): 55–65—where almost 20 percent of the men who participated in the study (16 out of 81) fulfilled the criteria for couvade syndrome.

15. J. O. Cavenar, Jr., and W. W. Weddington, Jr., "Abdominal Pain in Expectant Fathers," *Psychosomatics* 19 (1978): 761–768.

16. See Allan A. Maltbie et al., "A Couvade Syndrome Variant: Case Report," *North Carolina Medical Journal* 41, no. 2 (1980): 90–92. For a possible explanation of such phenomena, see Francis T. Twiggs, "Expectant Fathers: Couvade Syndrome and Stress" (Ph.D. diss., Temple University, 1987).

17. Wayland D. Hand, "American Analogues of the Couvade," *Studies in Folklore*, ed. W. Edson Richmond (1957; rpt. Westport, Conn.: Greenwood Press, 1972), 213–229.

18. Patrick N. Catania, "PCA: Why Is It Popular?", *Pain Practitioner* 1, no. 4 (1989): 5; and Elisabeth Rosenthal, "Powerful New Weapons Change Treatment of Pain," *The New York Times*, 13 February 1990, B5+.

19. Quoted in "UCSF News," University of California, San Francisco, dated for release 30 March 1990. This research by Fields and his UCSF colleagues Joshua B. Bederson and Nicholas M. Barbaro has been reported at the 6th World Congress on Pain (April 1–6, 1990) and in the journal *Somatosensory and Motor Research* 7, no. 2 (1990).

20. Ronald Melzack, "The Tragedy of Needless Pain," *Scientific American* 262, no. 2 (1990): 27–33.

21. See June L. Dahl, David E. Joranson, and David E. Weissman, "The Wisconsin Cancer Pain Initiative: A Progress Report," *American Journal of Hospice Care* 6 (November/December 1989): 39–43; and Michael H. Levy, "Pain Management in Advanced Cancer," *Seminars in Oncology* 12, no. 4 (1985): 394–410.

22. Sidney H. Wanzer et al., "The Physician's Responsibility Toward Hopelessly Ill Patients: A Second Look," *New England Journal of Medicine* 320, no. 13 (1989): 844–849.

23. See Jean-François Lyotard, *The Postmodern Condition: A Report on Knowledge* (1979), trans. Geoff Bennington and Brian Massumi (Minneapolis: University of Minnesota Press, 1984). A conveniently condensed version is available as "The Postmodern Condition," in *After Philosophy: End or Transformation?*, ed. Kenneth Baynes, James Bohman, and Thomas McCarthy (Cambridge, Mass.: MIT Press, 1987), 73–94.

24. For an excellent account of the multiple voices characteristic of postmodern culture, see Jim Collins, *Uncommon Cultures: Popular Culture and Post-Modernism* (New York: Routledge, 1989).

25. Friedrich Nietzsche, *The Gay Science* (1882), trans. Walter Kaufmann (New York: Random House, 1974), 249–250.

26. Paul Valéry, *Monsieur Teste* (1896–1946), trans. Mathews, 20. For a helpful analysis, see Jean Starobinski, "Monsieur Teste Confronting Pain," *Fragments for a History of the Human Body*, ed. Michel Feher, with Ramona Naddaff and Nadia Tazi (New York: Zone Books, 1989), 2: 371–405.

27. A. R. Luria, *The Mind of a Mnemonist*, trans. Lynn Solotaroff (New York: Basic Books, 1968), 134.

28. Norman Cousins, *Head First: The Biology of Hope* (New York: Dutton, 1989), 79–96. Cousins is not writing here specifically about pain, but what he says applies to pain especially well.

29. Ishmael Reed, quoted by Darryl Pinckney, "Trickster Tales," *New York Review of Books*, 12 October 1989: 20.

30. Paul Monette, *Love Alone: Eighteen Elegies for Rog* (New York: St. Martin's Press, 1988), 8–9. See also Monette's powerful prose account of his last months with Roger Horwitz (*Borrowed Time: An AIDS Memoir* [New York: Harcourt Brace Jovanovich, 1988]).

31. D. A. Miller rejects Susan Sontag's recommendation that the military metaphors surrounding AIDS be "retired" and argues that AIDS activism requires a fighting posture ("Sontag's Urbanity," *October* 49 [Summer 1989]: 91–101). Issue 43 of *October* (Winter 1987) is entirely devoted to the subject "AIDS: Cultural Analysis and Cultural Activism."

32. Emmanuel Levinas, "Useless Suffering" (1982), in *The Provocation of Levinas: Rethinking the Other*, ed. Robert Bernasconi and David Wood (London: Routledge, 1988), 159.

33. *Out of My Life and Thought: An Autobiography*, trans. C. T. Campion (1933; rpt. New York: Henry Holt, 1949), 193–194.

34. *The Writing of the Disaster* (1980), trans. Ann Smock (Lincoln: University of Nebraska Press, 1986), 145.

INDEX

Levine, Jon, 99
Lewis, C. S., 51, 299n
L'homme-machine (La
  Mettrie), 232
Liberation theology, 146–
  151
Lifton, Robert Jay, 186
Little Shop of Horrors
  (film), 79–80, 87
Luria, A. R., 285
Lyotard, Jean-François,
  213, 282–283

Macbeth (Shakespeare), 245
Madness: and hysteria,
  103–124; women and,
  121–122. *See also*
  Melancholy; *The Yellow
  Wallpaper*
*Major Symptoms of
  Hysteria* (Janet), 109,
  116
Malady of Death (Duras),
  118
Manliness: rituals of, 181–
  182. *See also* Hemingway
Mann, Thomas, 198
Man's Search for Meaning
  (Frankl), 168–172
Marcus Aurelius, 161–163
Martin, John ("Mad"),
  214–215
Martin, Steve, 79–80
"Martyrdom of Saint
  Sebastian" (Pollaiuolo),
  127–129
May, Rollo, 247
McGill-Melzack Pain
  Questionnaire, 16–17, 73
Meaning: definitions of,
  15; role in pain, 18, 26–
  27, 31–56; meaningless-
  ness, 77–78; logotherapy,
  168–173; multiplicity
  of, 282–290
*Medical and Chirurgical
  Review* (British), 40
Medicine: ancient, 20, 33,
  45–47, 74; iatrogenic
  illness, 166; and torture,
  185–186; Enlighten-
  ment, 226–227;
  nineteenth-century, 267–

269. *See also* AMA;
  Madness; Pain (all
  entries)
*Meditations of Marcus
  Aurelius* (Marcus
  Aurelius), 161–163
Melancholy: mirth vs., 94–
  96; Keats and, 207–209;
  Freud on, 208; Goethe
  and, 209–211. *See also*
  Burton; Dürer
Melville, Herman, 77, 256,
  266
Melzack, Ronald, 23, 72,
  152–153, 156, 180, 281
Migraine, 16, 66, 277
Mill, John Stuart, 204, 271
Mishima, Yokio, 129–131
Mitchell, Juliette, 122
Mitchell, S. Weir, 39, 64–
  65, 105–107, 110,
  113–115, 121
Moby Dick (Melville), 77,
  256, 266
Monette, Paul, 285–286
Monsieur Teste (Valéry), 1,
  284–285
Montagu, Mary Wortley,
  176–177
Morinis, Alan, 180–181
Morton, William, 64
Mosher, George Clark, 159
"Mourning and Melan-
  cholia" (Freud), 210
Musset, Alfred de, 4
Mystery: pain as, 23–26

Narcotics: hospital
  addition to, 22; under-
  medication with, 22,
  191, 281–282, 295n;
  heroin and cocaine, 191–
  192. *See also* Anesthesia
"Nature of Suffering and
  the Goals of Medicine"
  (Cassell), 244–245
Nazi Doctors (Lifton), 186
Neal, Helen, 145–146
Nietzsche, Friedrich, 45,
  79, 100, 195, 254, 284
Ninomiya, Eizo, 22
Numbness. *See also* Pain,
  insensitivity to

Oates, Joyce Carol, 256–
  263, 266, 283, 332n
"Ode on Melancholy"
  (Keats), 207–208
Odyssey (Homer), 221–222
Oedipus Tyrannus (Sopho-
  cles), 245, 247–248,
  259, 263, 265
O'Keeffe, Georgia, 196–
  197
On Boxing (Oates), 256–
  263, 266, 283
On Death and Dying
  (Kübler-Ross), 264
120 Days of Sodom, The
  (Sade), 230–231, 235
On Job (Gutierrez), 146,
  148–151
Original sin: as source of
  pain, 44
Other: pain and, 39–40;
  woman as, 122; death as,
  260–261; Levinas on,
  287
Oz, Frank, 79

Pain and Its Conquest
  (Gibson), 23
Pain Game, The (Shealy),
  193
Pain: anatomy and
  physiology of, 154–156,
  268–269; in Sade,
  231–232; in Descartes,
  269–271; "on"-cells,
  280–281
Pain: as punishment, 33–
  34, 90–93, 134, 138–141
Pain: behaviorist theories,
  142–144, 150, 246–
  247, 313n
Pain: chronic vs. acute. *See*
  Chronic pain
Pain: denial of. *See* Denial
Pain: insensitivity to, 12–
  14, 39–43, 92–93,
  101–102; numbness,
  115–120. *See also*
  Analgesia; Anesthesia;
  Apathy
Pain: learned, 72, 142–144,
  246–247
Pain: medical education

Designer: Seventeenth Street Studios
Compositor: Wilsted & Taylor
Text: 11/14 Granjon
Display: Granjon
Printer: Princeton University Press, Printing
Binder: Princeton University Press, Printing